LOVE AWAKENS THE HEART

Love Awakens the Heart

The Californians

Whatever Tomorrow Brings

As Time Goes By

Two Bestselling Novels Complete in One Volume

Lori Wick

Inspirational Press • New York

First Inspirational Press edition published in 1998.

Inspirational Press
A division of BBS Publishing Corporation
450 Raritan Center Parkway
Edison, NJ 08837

Inspirational Press is a registered trademark of BBS Publishing
Corporation.

Published by arrangement with Harvest House Publishers.

Distributed by World Publishing
Nashville, TN 37214
www.worldpublishing.com

Library of Congress Control Number: 97-77413

ISBN: 0-88486-344-1

Printed in the United States of America.

Contents

The Taylor and Donovan Families–1871

The Taylor Family

William Taylor
Wife—Mabel (May)
Children—Marshall Riggs (Rigg)
Jeffrey Taylor
Gilbert Taylor
Nathan Taylor

The Donovan Family

Patrick Sean Donovan II (Patrick)
Wife—Theresa
Children—Kaitlin Donovan
Patrick Sean Donovan III (Sean)
Marcail Donovan

Maureen Donovan Lawton Kent—sister to
Patrick Sean Donovan II
Percy Lawton—son to Maureen Kent

The Bradford Family

Jake Bradford
Wife—Maryanne
Children—
Roberta (Bobbie)
Troy

Book I

Whatever Tomorrow Brings

*This book is dedicated to
my parents, Harland and Pearl Hayes,
whose life together began in the
Hawaiian Islands. Thanks Dad and Mom
for the years of love and support,
in times of laughter and in times of tears.
I think the world of you both.*

One

Hawaii—January 1871

KAITLIN DONOVAN SMILED as the mid-morning sun hit her full in the face. She'd slipped from her shoes and stockings while hiking among the trees and now, as she moved toward that hot globe in the sky, her toes sank into the pure smooth sand of the beach. She walked until she was just short of the Pacific Ocean waves that lapped in easy rhythm at the shore.

The seemingly endless horizon stretched before her and the wonder of it, a wonder that never waned, made the breath catch in her chest. Kaitlin was content to stand and stare for a long minute before she walked a lazy path down the shore line.

Coming to the beach always brought her thoughts to God in a very special way. Today was no different. The vast expanse of water made her think of His overflowing love and the sand beneath her feet reminded her of a verse in Psalms that said God's thoughts of her were as numerous as those tiny grains.

Some 50 yards up the beach Kaitlin stopped her tour of the shore line and looked once again out to sea. The rest of the world felt so far away and, in actuality, it was. But it was more than just the miles, of this she was positive, even though her remembrance of a home before this one was vague.

Her parents sometimes spoke of their life before the mission but until recently none of what they said had been of much interest to Kaitlin. She couldn't imagine living anywhere else and she believed herself to be content, but there was a restlessness rising within her

5

that she'd never experienced before. It was both confusing and exciting, as if something special was about to happen. But she couldn't think of what that something might be so there was never any relief from those restless feelings when they occurred. She prayed and tried to place her restless heart into God's loving hands; and peace came, as she knew it would.

Much too soon the sun rose until nearly straight overhead and Kaitlin knew it was time to be home for lunch. She'd just laced her shoes when she caught sight of a couple walking along the shore. Kaitlin recognized them immediately as two of the village young people who attended her father's services. Normally she would have called out and waved but seeing their hands linked together made her hesitate.

What would it be like to have someone hold your hand? It wasn't the first time such a question had occurred to Kaitlin and, as always, she looked down at her own hands. But again, as in times past, she found no answer as she examined her long fingers.

When Kaitlin's attention was once again drawn to the shore, she saw that the couple had stopped to face each other. Sure that she was about to be an unwilling witness to an embrace, Kaitlin turned quickly into the trees and walked toward home. As she went she prayed about the restlessness that again reared its head after seeing that couple.

The sun's position told her she was late for lunch and she knew she'd have to apologize. But she also knew she would not be scolded—not today, that is. Today was much too special. This was her twentieth birthday!

Two

"I DON'T THINK IT'S fair." The little girl spoke to her mother from a stool in the corner of the kitchen.

"It's very fair, Marcail, and you know it. I warned you this morning at breakfast that if you were too far away to hear me calling, then you're far enough away to be punished."

"But I came as soon as Sean told me to."

"I shouldn't have had to send your brother at all. If you had stayed where you were supposed to, you would have heard me calling."

"I'll bet Katie's been to the beach. Will she be punished for making lunch late?"

The attempt to divert Theresa Donovan's attention to Kaitlin didn't work and she sent her eight-year-old daughter a look that told her she had heard enough. Marcail lowered her eyes and sat quietly for her punishment, wondering as she did if someone would remember to call her for lunch.

"I'm sorry I'm late, Mother." Kaitlin spoke as she entered the kitchen and bent to kiss her mother's cheek.

"That's all right dear, but be sure to thank Sean, he set the table for you."

"What did Marc do?" Kaitlin wanted to know, as she looked at her sister in the corner.

"She can tell you if she wants."

Kaitlin's brows rose in question and her look was kind. Marcail cocked her head to one side and admitted in a small voice, "I was down at Loni's."

Kaitlin nodded. Loni was Marcail's best friend but her hut was on the beach and Marcail was not allowed to go there alone. Loni's mother was dead and her father was rarely home during the day. The lack of adult supervision had forced Theresa to decide that if Marcail and Loni wanted to play, it would be at the Donovan home.

Theresa had watched the exchange between her daughters and smiled as she went back to work. Theresa's sweet spirit had given her very special relationships with her children. It wasn't any wonder that Marcail responded well to Katie, who was so much like Theresa.

Not that they were alike physically. In fact Katie's resemblance to her father was almost frightening. She was tall and full-figured with deep brown eyes that looked right to your soul with compassion and kindness. Her face, with its well-shaped nose and high cheekbones, would probably be considered beautiful were it not for her strong square jaw. It lent a look of stubbornness that her nature rarely exhibited.

Marcail's tiny frame on the other hand, was the physical image of her mother. But there the resemblance ended. Marcail's personality was very much like her father's. Theresa didn't have half the energy her husband possessed and never once would she have questioned someone in authority over her. Marcail had no such inhibitions and that, along with her questioning mind, was enough to wear Theresa to the bone.

Sean was already at the table when the food was carried in. At fourteen his appetite was voracious. He was already showing signs of having his father's large build. An inch taller than Kaitlin, people who didn't know them often mistook them for twins.

Theresa sat at the head of the table since she wasn't expecting her husband until evening, and looked at her children as they began to eat. As always she felt a little amazed at how, with their black hair and tanned complexions, they resembled the Hawaiian people to whom they ministered on the island.

"Mother, aren't you feeling well?" The question came from Kaitlin who had observed her mother's untouched plate.

"I'm fine dear. I'm just growing sentimental in my old age."

"You're not too old, Mother," Sean stated in his logical way.

"Thank you, Son." His mother's tone was dry.

"Will father be late tonight?" Marcail chimed in.

"The usual time, I think," Theresa answered, with a little sigh that made her children stare at her.

"Mother," Kaitlin's brow furrowed slightly, "have you lost weight?" Theresa became instantly alert.

"Am I looking poorly, Kate?" she evaded the question neatly.

"Oh, no, Mother, you always look lovely." Kaitlin smiled sincerely, even as she noticed her mother's face was flushed. Kaitlin was rewarded with her mother's beautiful smile.

ment, not an insult, even though she was not the least bit interested in him as a husband.

"Well, it's late," Scott's voice was hoarse, "I'll be on my way and let you retire. Good night."

"Good night, Scott."

The door closed and no one spoke. Kate's composure, held so neatly in place while in the presence of Scott, slowly crumbled until her face was buried in her hands and the sound of crying filled the room.

Her brother, who was sitting nearest to her, said quietly, "Maybe I should have warned you, Katie. I knew he was coming tonight, but I just didn't know how to tell you. Even though I think he would have been good for you, well, it's not your fault you don't love him."

"When did he talk to you, Sean?" Mother asked as she put her arms around her crying daughter.

"This afternoon. I'm sorry if I—"

"It's all right, Sean," Kate's voice was ragged. "You were sort of caught in the middle. But what really bothers me is that I think Scott's right—that we'll never see each other again—that we'll never come back to Hawaii."

Father came close at that point and waited until he had Sean and Kate's attention. "I want you to listen to what I'm going to say, not just listen but believe it with all your hearts. Our lives will be changing in the weeks to come and even though we are making plans to return I can't predict the future. But whatever tomorrow brings, God will be with us. Whether we're in California or Hawaii or some place we've never even thought of, God will go before us and keep us in His precious care."

Father hugged his family, then, and had a brief word of prayer. Reassuring Kaitlin about her feelings toward Scott, he told her, as her mother had, that love would come in its time. He then sent his children off to get their much-needed rest.

Five

THE *PACIFIC FLYER* was a beautiful ship that stood proudly in the water. And to the family of five she would bear eastward, indeed she was the most glorious ship on the sea.

The farewells on the beach had been tearful, but all were aboard now and cast-off was moments away. With the enthusiasm of first-time travelers, Sean and Marcail tried to take everything in at once. Kaitlin was no less excited but the openly flirtatious looks some of the crew were sending her way made her stay close to her parents by the railing. The wind snatched at some of the words, but Kaitlin was able to hear part of her parents' conversation.

"I'm worried about the promise you made to Pastor Graves."

"Why would you worry about that?"

"Because you never break your promises."

"And you think I'll have to break this one. You think we won't return."

The rest of the words were swept away on the breeze, leaving Kaitlin to wonder what was worrying her mother. Whatever the source of her concern, it was causing her mother to lose weight and sleep. She'd never seen her mother so thin and weary. Of course, getting ready for the trip was enough to tax anyone. Why, yesterday she'd been teaching the island children and today she was on a ship headed for the California coast!

"Katie, come and see this," Marcail called to her sister, affording no more time to speculate about her mother.

The next days of the trip proved enlightening as the Donovan females showed themselves to be natural seafarers. Kate and Marcail were rarely below deck and their faces reflected their contentment as the wind drove the trim vessel across the waves. The deck was often slick with sea spray, which added to the excitement of being aboard ship.

Kate's apprehensions did not ease concerning the overly interested sailors but there were a dozen other passengers aboard and she never really felt threatened.

The girls loved to watch and listen as the sails cracked in the wind and to feel the spray that hit their faces when the wind caught a high wave.

"Put your bonnet on, Marcail." Mother said as she approached her "Vikings."

"How are Father and Sean?" Kaitlin wanted to know. Her father and brother had not taken to the sea swells as the women in the family had. They lost most of their meals as the ship moved into deeper waters.

"Both sleeping," Theresa answered with a tired sigh. "I got a bit of broth into them and I'm praying they'll keep it down. I certainly wish they had your sea legs, Kate."

"I have sea legs, too."

"Yes, you do, Marcail and I'm glad. If you lost any weight you'd blow away."

"Mother, why do all the men on ship look at Katie?"

Theresa's head snapped up in surprise and after a startled look at Kate, her eyes scanned the deck. Father had tried to warn her, but he'd been feeling so sick she could barely understand him. "Keep an eye on Kate. She'll draw attention." His words became suddenly clear, and, with her spouse so sick, she felt anxious over not having been more aware. They had all been sheltered for so long.

"Has someone approached you, Kaitlin?"

"No, but the sailors, well, they stare." Kate shrugged rather helplessly and Theresa looked almost stern to cover her dismay.

"Kaitlin, I'm not accusing you of anything, but you need to be careful. You are a very attractive young lady and I'm afraid you cannot be friendly while on this trip. I realize it's not normal for you to ignore people, but a smile on this ship can be taken the wrong way."

The fact that Kate towered over her mother did nothing to diminish how young she looked at that moment. Being leered at was something she'd never before experienced and she didn't like it at all. Her hand went self-consciously to the severely high neckline on her dress

and she glanced down at her chest. For the first time in her life, the sight of her full breasts caused her to hunch her shoulders.

Theresa's heart turned over in her chest and she reached to touch her daughter's arm. "Kate, honey, I don't want to make you ashamed of your lovely face and figure, but ship life is unlike anything you've ever experienced. Maybe you should wear your cloak, even if it's warm."

"All right, Mother." Kate's voice was a mixture of sadness and confusion. Theresa felt like something precious and innocent had just been destroyed. The thought persisted even as Theresa watched Kaitlin go below decks to care for the others. But then she remembered the rough life around the docks of San Francisco and mentally compared them to the relative calm of the ship. *Please Lord,* she prayed silently, *please help Patrick to be on his feet before we land.*

"Are things well, Mrs. Donovan?"

Theresa turned to find the Captain addressing her. He was a tall, well-built man and might be considered handsome by some, with his wind-roughened cheeks and full head of steel-gray hair. His eyes were kind and Theresa responded to the kindness she saw there.

"The girls and I are faring better than my husband and son I'm afraid, but we'll be fine. Thank you for asking."

The Captain tipped his hat, smiled at Marcail, and moved on toward another family at the railing. Tempted to call him back and complain about the conduct of his men, Theresa was sure, on second thought, she'd be wasting her breath.

"How much longer, Mother, before we see Aunt Maureen?"

"I'm not exactly sure, dear. Much depends on the winds."

As it turned out, the winds were steady to the east and a week later the docks of Theresa's previous musings were before her eyes.

Father leaned heavily on the balustrade beside her. As they neared land, he began to adjust to the rolling of the ship and believed himself to be on the way to recovery though he had dropped over 20 pounds. Not so, Sean. He was very shaky, staying on his feet by willpower alone, or so it seemed.

The docks swarmed and buzzed with activity as the ship berthed. Passengers aboard the *Pacific Flyer* felt the excitement over the imminent disembarking and even Sean perked up a bit.

As the Donovans made their way down the gang plank, Sean leaned heavily on Kate. Marcail's hand was clenched in the material at the back of her sister's cloak in a hold that was not to be broken. They moved slowly and close together as Father scanned the docks for someone familiar. He was not disappointed when, before he could spot her, his sister Maureen called and rushed toward them.

in the mission, the children were never involved. She's never known hate or rejection.

But she has the Lord, and there's nothing more I would ask for her. Oh, Father in heaven, Theresa's thoughts turned to prayer, *please keep her close to You. I trust You to give only what she can take. Please help her believe that too. Her world will be changing so quickly over the next weeks, please help her to keep her hand in Yours.*

"It's Father!" Marcail bounced up a moment later, the first to hear his feet on the path. Patrick Sean Donovan II was greeted with the usual enthusiasm his family afforded him.

"Every man should come home to this kind of love." It was his customary statement but hearing it often never erased the smiles from the faces of his wife and children.

"Are you hungry, Father?" Kaitlin asked anxiously.

"Not really. I think I'll have my evening swim before we eat." Kate, so excited over her birthday, missed the twinkle in his eye. Her face fell with disappointment, but she didn't complain. Grumbling, and rightly so, was not allowed.

"Father is teasing you, Kate," her mother spoke softly to her daughter and then louder to her mate, "For shame, Father. If you could have seen this girl pace around in anticipation all afternoon you would not torment her."

"Anticipation of what?" Father asked with his eyes wide. Katie smiled, seeing that he was not done with her.

"I'm not sure myself," Katie teased back. "Since I see no packages at my place."

"Well, we'll have to see what we can do about that. Happy Birthday, Kaitlin." This time his smile held no teasing and the embrace he gave her warmed her to the depths of her soul. He released her to wash quickly for supper and in a few minutes they were seated around the table.

In the Donovan birthday fashion, gifts were opened before supper. Sean and Marcail were as excited as Kaitlin when father smiled at all of them and began to speak.

"We don't have anything for you to open, Kaitlin."

"What Father means, is that there was no way to wrap your gift. But we hope you'll be pleased," Theresa quickly added with a smile.

"Now, in the past," Father went on, "the gift would have been strictly your own and the choice to share it would have been yours. But this year we are asking you to share your gift with all of us." He stopped a moment, meeting the confused glances of his son and younger daughter before looking back at an equally confused birthday girl.

"I've booked passage on the *Pacific Flyer*. We all leave for San Francisco in a month!"

It took a full minute for this statement to sink in and then questions poured in a torrent from the three young Donovans.

"You mean California?"

"Will we see Aunt Maureen?"

"How big is the ship?"

"How long will we be gone?"

"How long does it take to get there?"

"Can I have a new dress?"

"What of the mission and school?"

"Can I invite Loni?"

Father's hands were in the air in an effort to gain some quiet. His voice was full of laughter as he spoke.

"Hold on, everyone, hold on. I'll explain everything to you as we eat."

Father thanked God for the food and the twenty years with Kaitlin. As dishes were passed he explained the plans for his family.

"As you know, Katie, you were only five years old when we came to the islands and we haven't been back to California since. Your mother and I both feel that it's time.

"I've written to Aunt Maureen and she's expecting us. I haven't chosen an actual date to return here to the islands, but I imagine we'll be at your Aunt's for six to eight weeks.

"Now, back to your questions. We'll see if we can't come up with new dresses for each of you girls and maybe a shirt for Sean." Father took a moment to inspect his son's hair and clothing. "On second thought, maybe you should just get something from my clothes. Theresa, when did he get so big?"

Sean smiled at the compliment from his father and then Kate asked, "What of the mission and the school?"

"Things are in good shape right now, Katie, and even if they weren't, it's time for us to have a break. Your brother and sister have never been off this island. I also think the other missionaries are overly dependent on us sometimes. We won't be gone for too long, and it will be good for them to see they can do very well in our absence.

"There are at least three men who can fill in for services. Things at the school are a little trickier because both you and your mother will be gone, but I've talked it over with everyone and I'm sure they'll work it out.

"You children were never aware of it, but this is not the first time we've made plans to leave Hawaii." Father saw that his words were a

shock. "But in the past God has always closed the door on our plans, and your mother and I have accepted that. This time I feel very certain that, even if something unexpected arises, God's leading is for us to sail to the states."

"Can Loni go with us?"

Father's eyes became very tender as he looked at his youngest daughter, so like his beloved Theresa in appearance. He slid his chair back and held his arms out to her. Marcail settled in his lap and then looked up at him. He kissed her brow.

"You wouldn't want us to leave you here when we sail, would you, Marcail?"

"No."

"Well, it's the same for Loni. We wouldn't want to take her away from her family. Think how lonely she would be for them." The little girl looked thoughtful and then asked if they could take Loni's whole family. Father smiled but answered with a definite no.

"Marcail, you need to finish your supper, dear," her mother reminded her. "Tomorrow are Sunday services and I want you in bed on time. Kaitlin, Sean, please try to eat. I know you're excited but we're not leaving for a month and . . ." Theresa stopped talking when she saw that her children were hundreds of miles away. Husband and wife exchanged a smile.

"And you thought she might be disappointed about not having something to open," Patrick whispered to Theresa, who gave him an exaggerated sigh and then chuckled.

"You were right, Patrick, as always, you were right."

Four

THERESA DONOVAN CALLED Kaitlin's name three times before she responded, and the children at the school found this highly amusing. Kate smiled good-naturedly at their laughter as she made her way to the rear, but inside she was scolding herself. The day before her father had asked her about something he'd said in his sermon. Not an unusual occurrence, but Kaitlin had been very embarrassed over having to admit that she hadn't been paying attention.

I've got to pull my mind out of the clouds, she told herself, as a child came toward her with a question. Even as she worked patiently with the little girl, she despaired of ever getting over her dreamy state. A trip to California and seeing Aunt Maureen! Who would have thought her twentieth birthday would be so wonderful?

"Miss Katie, is this right?" Kaitlin was surprised to see that the little girl she'd been helping had returned to her seat and Joseph, one of Kaitlin's favorites, was waiting for his work to be inspected.

"This is very good, Joseph, but you missed question 14." Kate looked into the little boy's eyes as she spoke and they told her his incomplete work had been deliberate.

"Joseph," she reproved gently, and watched his eyes fill with tears.

"Are you really going away, Miss Katie? Are you really leaving the island?"

"Yes, I am, but . . ." Kate stopped just short of telling Joseph she would be back. Something inside her wouldn't let the words come.

14

She searched for other words of comfort even as the thought persisted that she wouldn't be returning to Hawaii ever again.

"I'll miss you, Joseph, very much, but you're my little brother in Christ and I know that He'll care for you. And we can remember each other in our prayers." She reached out a gentle hand then, and brushed at the tear sliding down his cheek. Then her hand went to sweep back the thick, black hair on his forehead.

Marcail appeared in the next instant and Kate had no choice but to send Joseph back to his seat. She watched him for a moment and was relieved when their eyes met and he smiled.

"He has a crush on you."

"Do you think so?" the older sister whispered to the younger.

"Yes, I do. His sister told me that he talks about you every day after school, all the way home."

"Well, it's too bad he's not a little older—" Kaitlin let the remark hang.

"Scott Harper is older and I saw him holding your hand yesterday."

"It wasn't what you think, Marc," Kate said, as she remembered the scene with the son of one of the other missionaries.

"You're really going, Kaitlin?"

"Yes, Scott, we leave in a month," Kate answered the tall, painfully thin young man who had been in love with her for years.

"When will you be back?" The question had been asked, almost desperately, and Scott had touched Kate for the first time, grasping one of her hands in both of his own.

Kate had no desire to encourage him but neither did she want to hurt him. *"My father says we'll be in California for about two months."* Kate gently disengaged her hand as she spoke.

Scott's eyes, big and dark like her own, were looking at her in a way that always made her feel regretful. Here was a man her own age, who was in love with her, and she didn't feel anything. Oh, she cared for him and he didn't repulse her but she wasn't in love with him. With both their families involved in missionary work on the islands, it would have been very comfortable and practical if she had been in love with him.

But when she'd said as much to her mother, Theresa had told her in plain terms that love was neither practical nor comfortable.

"Did I upset you because I said something about Scott?" Marcail's soft question broke into Kate's memory.

"No, Marcail, I'm fine and we both better be about our business."

The rest of the day slipped by, and Kaitlin was thankful that she was too busy to think about California—or the pathetic look in Scott

Harper's eyes when she'd left him. In fact she didn't give another thought to him until late that night, when he knocked on the door.

"Well, Scott, come in," Father spoke kindly, as he answered the light tap. "What brings you out at this hour?"

"I know it's late, Mr. Donovan, but I have something important to ask you."

Marcail had been sent to bed but the rest of the Donovan family watched as Father led the nervous young man to a chair. Kate's heart grew heavy and she began to pray when she noticed that Scott did not look in her direction or acknowledge her in any way.

"What can I do for you, Scott?"

"I've come to ask you for Kaitlin's hand in marriage."

Patrick Donovan, a wise and loving parent, was careful not to look at his oldest daughter. When he spoke, his eyes looked directly into Scott's and his voice was gentle.

"Did Kaitlin know of your plans to come here this evening?"

"No sir, she didn't. And the truth is, I know Kaitlin doesn't love me. But sir, I know I've got enough love for both of us and I think in time she would learn to love me."

Sweat glistened on the young man's face and Patrick was deeply moved at the sincere look in his eyes.

Scott rushed on before he could speak. "I'm not trying to keep Kaitlin from making the trip to California. In fact, I was hoping you could marry us right away so I could go with you. I'm afraid if she leaves without me I'll never see her again." Scott's voice had dropped to a whisper, as he continued to look at the man he hoped would be his father-in-law, his heart in his eyes.

"My parents' marriage was arranged Scott," Father began quietly after a moment. "My mother was from a different part of Ireland and my father had never laid eyes on her until a week before the wedding. There was no love at first sight like the books tell about, but it was a good marriage, and I believe they did grow to love each other.

"It was different in my own life. The first time I saw Theresa my heart nearly jumped out of my chest, much the way I suspect your's did when you set eyes on Kaitlin four years ago.

"But Scott, lad, four years is enough time for Kaitlin to know her heart. I'll not force her into a lifelong union when I know she's not in love."

The young man's shoulders slumped but his face wasn't angry or disrespectful. For the first time, he let his eyes go to Kate's. He was thankful that he saw no pity, only the kindness he had come to expect from her. There would be no embarrassment when they were to-gether again, because Kaitlin would treat his proposal as a compli-

Three

THE AFTERNOON MOVED by quickly as friends came to visit and some baking was done. Kaitlin found herself wishing her father would come home a little early but it was not to be. By the time the supper hour neared, Kate was pacing like a caged animal.

"Katie, you're walking a hole in that floor mat."

"I know, Mother, but I thought Father would be here by now."

"He'll be here, Katie, he'll be here," Theresa said as she worked on her school lessons for next week. She and Kaitlin taught together in the mission school which was attended by both village and missionary children.

Kaitlin flopped onto a stuffed pallet on the floor and tried not to think about her birthday supper and the gifts that would be presented in the Donovan tradition. But it was no use. Her eyes went again and again to the table already set for the meal, especially the lack of gifts next to her place.

After a thorough scrutiny of the table, her eyes swung to Sean. He usually teased her senseless about knowing what her gift was. This year he hadn't said a word.

Marcail was the next person to come under Kaitlin's regard, but she was looking at a book and not at her anxious older sister. Had Katie cared to look at her mother she would have found herself being studied quite intently.

She's a young 20, Theresa thought to herself. *Not physically of course, but emotionally. Her world has been protected. Even when there was trouble*

10

"Patrick, oh Patrick," was all she could say for at least five minutes as she embraced her younger brother. Likewise, Sean held his sister close in his arms for long minutes. At 46, she was five years Patrick's senior. Her hair was a beautiful shade of gray, and her clothing was well-made and fit her plump figure perfectly. When her brother released her, Maureen wiped at her streaming face and moved to hug Theresa.

"Oh, Theresa. I've missed you so. How was the voyage? Oh this can't be Katie! Oh, my! And Sean, so tall for fourteen!" Her words tumbled over each other as she embraced everyone again and again until she realized she had missed one child.

"Marcail? Where is Marcail?" Maureen caught Kaitlin's smile over the question and smiled back in understanding.

"Marcail, come out now," Mother spoke gently. "Aunt Maureen is waiting to meet you."

The little girl obeyed with obvious reluctance, and Maureen watched as a miniature Theresa stepped from behind Kaitlin.

"Oh my," Maureen breathed, "she's a picture of Theresa." The tears that had ceased began again, and it was some minutes before Maureen could contain herself and tell everyone that her carriage was waiting to take them home.

Six

THE SIGHTS OF the docks were too much for the exhausted Donovan family to take in, so everyone's eyes were trained upon Maureen Kent's back as she broke a path through the fray.

They stepped around massive coils of rope and barrels stacked high. The air was cold and the sky threatened rain. Overhead, flocks of sea gulls made their presence known with the flap of wings and high-pitched cries.

They hadn't walked far and before anyone expected it, Maureen stopped beside a large coach, pulled by two perfectly matched bays. Fascinated, the children stared at the horses and rig, then at the coachman who alighted from his high seat to assist them with their bags. They believed in those few moments that their aunt was quite wealthy. It would be some time before they understood that Maureen's home, carriage and belongings, although ample, were not San Francisco's finest.

"Is everyone settled?" Maureen smiled in genuine delight at her family as the coach lurched into motion.

"We're fine," her brother assured her and smiled. Maureen smiled back and turned to speak with Theresa.

"Were you terribly seasick, Dear?"

"No, the girls and I weren't sick at all."

Theresa was mentally prepared for the startled look that came over her sister-in-law's face. She reached out and took Maureen's hand. "We'll talk tonight, when the children are in bed."

22

Maureen had to be satisfied with that, but she was shaken. Kaitlin, who had just looked over at her mother and aunt, glanced curiously between them. Theresa, having known that Maureen would see the physical changes in her, was able to smile at her daughter. Maureen was so shaken over what Theresa might tell her later, she could do no more than stare at her oldest niece and then her brother.

"See down this street? Mother and I had an apartment there when we were first married," Father said.

"Can we go see it?"

"Not today, Marcail. Let's get to Aunt Maureen's and settle in. We're going to be here for a while. I promise you, we'll see everything. Oh, Maureen, I forgot to ask you if Mitch is in town." It took Maureen a moment to answer the question about her husband, but she was glad for the diversion.

"No, he's been gone about three months. He did say that this would be a short trip and maybe he'd be back to meet you before you have to return."

"Father, did you know we would be going three months ago?" Kaitlin asked in surprise.

"Yep. Kept a good secret, didn't I?" He winked at his daughter. "Maureen, where is Percy? Still in Europe?"

"Yes. I doubt you'll see him, unless of course he runs out of money." These words were said with a tired sigh.

"Is this where you live, Aunt Maureen?" Sean asked in awe as the carriage pulled up before a large, two-story home. Maureen did not miss the looks of wonder the house was receiving.

"This is the place. You children may not be aware that my first husband, your Uncle Stan, was in real estate. He left me very comfortable." This was said so matter-of-factly, that Katie blinked. She didn't know her Aunt Maureen beyond letters over the years and had no idea what a survivor she was.

Her full legal name was Maureen Olivia Donovan Lawton Kent. She was a land owner in her own right and very much in love with her second husband, Mitchell. Mitch's job with a shipping line never had him in port for more than a few months at a time.

The two of them had no children together, but Maureen did have a son from her first marriage, Percy Lawton. He was much like his hardworking father when it came to spending money, but fell short in his lack of ambition for making the money he so wanted to squander.

Percy was Maureen's one weakness. Oh, she was aware of his spendthrift ways and his devil-may-care attitude toward life, but the truth was, she loved him to distraction. She honestly believed he would outgrow his immature ways and settle down some day with a lovely woman who would give her a handful of grandchildren to spoil. That Percy was 28 years old and showed no sign of ever changing his ways was where Maureen was utterly blind.

Life was always quieter when Percy was away, and, whenever both Mitch and Percy were home at the same time, well, it became nearly unbearable. Maureen was, at that moment, saying a prayer of thanks for the very fact that both her men were gone and she could devote all her time to her brother and his family.

"Sean, dear, you're looking so pale," she spoke to her nephew as he stepped carefully from the carriage. "We'll get you right into bed."

Sean wanted to argue. There was so much he wanted to see and explore. He'd never seen a house like this and here was an entire street lined with them. But they would all have to wait until he felt better. He prayed it would be soon.

Marcail had reached for her mother's hand after alighting from the carriage and held on tight. She wasn't sure she liked California. It was so big and noisy. The houses were huge and she hadn't seen very many children. Their trip was just starting and she already missed Loni so much she wanted to cry. Staring up at the house as they climbed the front steps, she wondered if it was going to eat them alive.

Kaitlin smiled warmly at the young groom who had come forward to hold the horses. He was nice looking with blond hair and blue eyes and his smile was respectful and sweet. Kate turned to pick up a small traveling case and before she could take a step he took it from her hand. She thanked him and felt herself blushing, an unusual occurrence. Kate smiled as she walked into the house behind her mother and sister. So far, she liked San Francisco very much.

The front entry to Maureen's home was enough to stop a person in his tracks and that's exactly what it did to Kaitlin. Across from the front door, a large archway covered the stairs going up. Kaitlin watched her mother and sister disappear up those stairs but couldn't bring herself to follow them.

The banister, stairs, and the walls of the foyer were a light, stained oak. A grandfather clock stood against one wall. The rug beneath her shoes was multicolored and plush. Kate finished her inspection with the high ceiling and its beautiful brass chandelier. She stared until her father bumped her with the bags he was carrying in.

"It's a little bigger than you're used to, isn't it, Kate?"

"Oh, Father, it's well, it's . . . big!"

Patrick laughed at his daughter, enjoying her look of wonder over the beautiful home. Maureen bustled back down the stairs in the next moment.

"I wanted to help Sean, but he seemed embarrassed by my being in his bedroom with him. Maybe you should go up, Patrick."

"Thanks for your help, Mo." He bent and kissed her cheek.

She positively glowed at the use of her family nickname. "Percy's room. You know the one."

Katie was still frozen in place near the front door when she turned to find her aunt watching her.

"Your home is lovely." Kaitlin spoke the words almost shyly.

Maureen smiled and her eyes misted. "I'm glad you like it." She stopped when her throat clogged with tears. Kaitlin looked at her in gently inquiry. "I'm just so glad you're here, I—" the words were stopped again as a tear slid down the older woman's cheek.

Kate went to her aunt and put her arms around her. They were alike in height and she loved the feel of her aunt's sturdy arms tight around her.

"Would you look at me? Standing here getting us both wet with you probably hungry and dead on your feet. I'll show you your room and see about dinner."

Dinner was quiet with just Maureen, Patrick, Theresa, and Kaitlin. Sean was having a tray in his room and Marcail had fallen into an exhausted slumber that would not be disturbed.

Patrick spent most of the meal answering his sister's questions. Maureen wanted full details on their trip over and it was quite late before she remembered how fatigued they must be.

Maureen would have understood if her brother and sister-in-law had headed right to bed, but, after they kissed their daughter good-night, they moved with Maureen into the parlor.

A fire blazed in the hearth and Theresa warmed her hands before taking a nearby chair. Patrick watched his wife. When Maureen could stand the silence no longer, she spoke.

"You haven't come for a visit, have you? I mean, it's not a vacation trip for you and the kids is it?"

Theresa shifted in her chair to face her sister-in-law. She was thin and pale and appeared much older than her 39 years.

"The children don't know of this, Maureen, but we've come back to San Francisco because there's something wrong with me and we don't know what it is."

$\mathcal{S}even$

"W$_{E'VE}$ NEEDED A BREAK for a long time, Maureen, you're aware of that. But every time we planned to come back to the states the plans were interrupted. With Theresa feeling the way she does, we knew it was time to come back. We need to see a doctor while we're here."

"Theresa," Maureen said gently, even as hope burgeoned within her that this was not as serious as it seemed, "did you think of your age? I mean, the changes a woman goes through? I hear it's a little different for everyone."

"I've heard the same thing, Maureen, but I've never heard of anyone developing sharp chest pains and a dry cough."

"You have a cough?" The words were almost whispered as the older woman's hopes faded quickly.

"A dry cough and every afternoon and on into the night I run a fever. It keeps me awake. I don't think the children suspect anything, although I feel more burdened every day to tell Kate and Sean."

They talked for another hour and Maureen went off to bed with a heavy heart. Her hopes had been dashed so quickly in the face of Theresa's cough and fevers. For the first time in many years, Maureen Kent was terrified.

Kaitlin woke up the next morning when Marcail climbed into bed with her.

"I'm freezing, Katie," the little girl's teeth chattered and Kate pulled her close. They lay in the quiet house and listened to the rain hitting the windowsill.

The previous afternoon they had come into a cloudy San Francisco and thought it chilly. They realized now that yesterday had been warm compared to this cold-to-your-bones feeling brought on by the rain.

"Katie?"

"Hmm?"

"Do you miss Hawaii?"

"Not yet, but I'm sure I will."

"I miss Loni."

"She probably misses you, too. You can write her, you know."

They fell silent and dozed off. They woke again when Sean lightly tapped on their door and came in. Seeing that Marcail's bed was vacant, he slid slowly beneath the covers, shivering all the while.

"It's freezing here," he said in a tired voice. "I thought California was sunny."

"Not in February," Kaitlin said. "How do you feel?"

"A little better. I'm weak, but that's probably because I'm starving."

"You're always starving." Marcail stated.

"That's true," Sean answered in his logical way. "This is a big room," he added.

"What's yours like?" his little sister wanted to know.

"It's big too, everything is black and gold." Sean looked around the green and white room that belonged to the girls with some envy. His own room was dark and gloomy. The room belonged to his cousin Percy, and he would never have complained. Actually, he was very thankful. The bed was the most comfortable one he'd ever slept in. A small shudder went through him as he remembered the nightmarish days aboard ship in that tiny bunk. The return voyage popped into his head and he stubbornly pushed it away.

Everyone took things slowly at first and by the third day all were well rested.

Maureen had come to some decisions on the first night and had already begun to act upon them. She was going to take care of this family. She was going to see Sean on his feet doing things with other boys his age, and she was going to get a playmate for Marcail. Kaitlin, with her looks, well, it would be no trouble finding a few young men to escort her around town. That would give her plenty of time to take care of Theresa.

Why, her brother and sister-in-law were a team, she couldn't let anything separate them! In fact with no cleaning and cooking to do, Maureen could already see that Theresa was feeling better. Maureen had sent for the doctor and he arrived shortly after breakfast. As she paced in the upstairs hallway outside of her brother's room all these thoughts ran through her mind. Both he and Theresa were in there with the doctor. Maureen wondered how long she would be able to stand the suspense.

"Did you notice anything, Sean? I mean, did you think mother was sick? I know she's had a cough, but I just thought it was that cold hanging on." Kaitlin looked stricken and Sean felt helpless as he shook his head.

That morning while Marcail was playing in the kitchen, Patrick and Theresa had sat their oldest children down and told them that a doctor was coming to see Theresa because she hadn't been well.

Kate and Sean had said little as their father spoke and now questions came to mind almost faster than they could handle. How sick was she? When did it start? Who is this doctor? Is this why we came to California?

The questions filled their minds again and again, even as they knew they would have to wait for their answers. And as they both tried to pray, Doctor Weston was asking his own set of questions.

"How old are you, Mrs. Donovan?"

"Thirty-nine."

"Have you normally enjoyed good health?"

Theresa looked up at Patrick who stood by her chair. It wasn't that it was a difficult question to answer, it was just something they'd never thought much about.

"We're hesitating, Dr. Weston, I think, because we have enjoyed such good health. Theresa was sick with the pregnancies but, I think as a whole, the five of us have all been very healthy and obviously taking it for granted."

"How many times have you been pregnant?"

"Three."

"But you were always up and about soon after?"

"Sean's was the most difficult, but even then I bounced right back."

Doctor Weston was very thorough. He asked about Theresa's family history, her grandparent's deaths, her parents' deaths and the deaths of any siblings. At times he only nodded and made notes; other times he wanted specifics.

Theresa explained to him that she'd caught a slight cold last fall and had not been able to shake it off. She told him of her recurring fever and how hot she was at night. When she told of her dry cough, his face went from concerned to grave. Patrick's heart began to pound in his chest as he prayed.

"Do you ever cough up anything?"

"Not until we were on the ship traveling here. I coughed up some blood." The words were whispered.

"Theresa!" Patrick's voice was pained.

"You were so sick, Patrick," tears came to Theresa's eyes as she spoke. "It was just a little blood and you had enough to worry about. I didn't want to do anything to spoil our trip."

Patrick's arms were around his wife and Dr. Weston walked over to the window to give them some privacy.

Paul Weston had known Maureen Kent for years. When she'd asked him to come and see her sister-in-law, he'd cut into his busy schedule and came without delay.

Fifteen years ago he'd have told Mrs. Donovan she had consumption. But they had a name for her ailment now, not that it did any good. Theresa Donovan had tuberculosis, and if she was coughing up blood there was probably little he could do for her. He turned away from the window to tell the Donovans his prognosis, wishing all the time that he'd been out of town when Maureen's note arrived.

$\mathscr{E}ight$

"YOU WOULD THINK I was already dead by the way you're all acting." Theresa Donovan's family looked at her in utter shock when she spoke these words from the doorway of the library.

"I've had to wait for a time when we were all gathered without Marcail to speak with you. I know I've shocked you but I'm still here and I don't want to see my family in mourning."

Theresa stopped to give them all a few moments to digest what she had said. Doctor Weston's news was over a week old and after lunch everyone had moved to the library, a room as elegant as the rest of the house, to stare at the fire as they'd done every day since the man left.

"We just want you to be comfortable, Theresa, and not overdo." Father cleared his throat when Theresa gave him a stern look.

"I'm not yet an invalid, Patrick, and I think I can gauge when I need to rest. Now, I've faced facts and the first fact is that I won't be returning to Hawaii with you. Secondly, Marcail is going to be nine years old in two weeks and not one plan has been made for her birthday. And finally, all of San Francisco is waiting to be explored and if you won't go sight-seeing with me, well, I'll go by myself!"

"But mother! We thought you were feeling sick and we—" Sean's voice was so young and confused that the anger drained completely out of his mother.

"Please, all of you listen to me." Theresa's eyes moved to each one, Patrick, Sean, Kaitlin and Maureen, holding their gaze for just a moment before going on softly. "I have times when I feel quite good and

30

all of you know that. Just sitting around and waiting for my fever to go up in the afternoon accomplishes nothing. Starting tomorrow I would like to begin going out. I want us to start with a tour of the city if it isn't raining. We shall take each day as it comes. Now, are you with me?"

"Of course we're with you, Love," Patrick spoke as his arms surrounded her slight frame. "Please forgive me for treating you too fragiley. Fragiley? Is that a word?"

Everyone laughed and they all talked about what they wanted to do in the days to come. As Theresa made her way out of the room to lay down for a rest, she gave them some words that would long live in their hearts.

"We need to thank God for this thing He has brought into our lives. It's a precious gift that He's given us by allowing us to know what's wrong with me. So many die without warning. This way we can have special times and you'll have memories to hold close in the days to come when things look black.

"My prayer is that you'll know how much I love you and that whatever tomorrow brings God will be your all when you need comfort."

Theresa left the room then with a pleading prayer in her heart for wisdom and words. It was time to talk to Marcail of the future.

"I started a letter to Loni."

"May I read it?"

Marcail handed the letter to her mother and awaited her approval. She was in her father's lap on the settee in the room she shared with Kaitlin, all snuggled into her nightie and robe. Theresa had told her husband of her plans to talk with Marcail at bedtime and he'd wanted to be with them. Now that the moment had come, Theresa was thankful for his presence.

"You did very well. Are you really cold all the time like you said in this letter?"

Marcail nodded almost apologetically and her mother leaned to kiss her cheek. "We'll have to get you some warmer clothing."

"But what will I do with the warm clothes when we go back to Hawaii?"

This question from an eight-year-old might have surprised some, but Patrick and Theresa both knew their daughter was very bright.

"Do you miss Hawaii so much?"

"Well, not really Hawaii, just Loni. There's no one here to play with."

"We'll find you some playmates as soon as we can, Marcail, but right now Mother and I have something to tell you." Patrick took a deep breath and asked God to give him the words.

"You know why we live in Hawaii, don't you Marcail?"

"Because you work there, preaching and baptizing and helping people in the village."

"Right. And I do that because I believe that God's Son died for everyone and I want the people there to know Jesus Christ." Marcail nodded in complete understanding.

"Marcail, do you remember last year when Loni's grandfather was very sick and I went and talked with him?"

"He died."

"Yes he did, but before he died he understood how much he needed a Savior."

"I remember. He asked Jesus into his heart." A smile lit the little girl's face.

"Yes he did, and we know where he is, don't we?"

"In heaven with Jesus."

"How do you know that, Honey?" her mother wanted to know.

"Because the Bible says if you believe in the Lord Jesus then when you die, you go to be with Him."

"And how do we know we can believe what the Bible says?" Theresa pressed her further.

"Because it's God's Word." This statement was made with such confidence that Patrick felt his throat clog. Clearing his throat, he asked his daughter another question.

"Can you tell me a verse that promises us a home in heaven?"

" 'I go to prepare a place for you.' Do you mean that one?"

"That's a good one from John 14. Verses one through six go like this: 'Let not your heart be troubled: ye believe in God, believe also in me. In my Father's house are many mansions: if it were not so, I would have told you. I go to prepare a place for you. And if I go and prepare a place for you, I will come again, and receive you unto myself; that where I am, there ye may be also. And whither I go ye know, and the way ye know. Thomas saith unto him, Lord, we know not whither thou goest; and how can we know the way? Jesus saith unto him, I am the way, the truth, and the life: no man cometh unto the Father, but by me.' "

"Those words are very special to me right now, Marcail." Theresa spoke gently when Patrick stopped. "You see, a doctor was here last week and I told him about how I've been coughing and not feeling well and he told me I have tuberculosis. He also told me that people with tuberculosis don't live very long. So the verses are special to me because I know when I die I'll be with the Lord."

It didn't take very long for the full import of Theresa's words to hit Marcail. Her parents watched as a single tear slid down their daughter's cheek. Marcail was the most heartbreaking person to watch cry because she made no sound.

Theresa reached for her and Marcail buried her face in her mother's neck. Theresa could feel tears against her skin along with the occasional shudder running through her daughter's small frame. Theresa thought her heart would break.

It was some time before Marcail could speak and when she did, there was a torrent of questions. Patrick and Theresa did their best to explain all that had transpired. For some reason, Marcail's young mind centered on Doctor Weston.

"I wish he'd never come here."

"Marcail, Doctor Weston's visit changed nothing. I'm thankful he was able to tell me what I have and how serious it is. That way my time with you can be extra special."

The little girl looked unconvinced and Theresa wondered if maybe she needed someone to blame. Marcail needed a little time right now to face all she'd been told. She was usually so grown up and had always been so intelligent that it was easy to forget she was still a little girl. Soon after, Theresa was tucking Marcail into bed and settling down to sit with her until she was deeply asleep.

Patrick let himself out of the bedroom to find Kate in the hall. The rest of the house was very quiet.

"How is she?"

"Pretty shook up. She blames the doctor. I suppose she needs someone to point a finger at and he's become the center of her blame. I'll talk to her in the morning."

They were quiet for a moment and Kate watched her father stare past the door that stood ajar to the bedroom. She knew he was watching his wife as she knelt by Marcail's bed. Kate's hands clenched at her sides and she turned away to keep from crying.

What would Father do without her? What would they all do without her? Oh God, her heart prayed, *You could do a miracle, You could heal her.* But even as the words came they were pushed away by others, *Your will, God. Your will, not mine.*

This is how Jesus felt at Gethsemane, only worse. With this thought Kate knew an aching desire to read those verses and she moved down the hall to her brother's door.

"Sean, it's me," she said as she opened the door. "Can I borrow your Bible?" Sean nodded toward the nightstand that was lit by an oil lamp. Kate lowered herself to the edge of Sean's bed where he lay looking at the shadows on the high ceiling.

He heard the rustle of pages for a few minutes and then silence. He broke it with words spoken in a whisper, "Read it to me, Katie."

"Luke 22:39–42: 'And he came out, and went, as he was wont, to the Mount of Olives; and his disciples also followed him. And when he was at the place, he said unto them, Pray that ye enter not into temptation. And he was withdrawn from them about a stone's cast, and kneeled down, and prayed, Saying, Father, if thou be willing, remove this cup from me: nevertheless not my will, but thine, be done.' "

Kate turned slightly on the bed to see her brother. His eyes were filled with tears.

"She's really going to die, isn't she Kate?"

Kate could only nod and hold the hand that her brother thrust toward her. They stayed together on the bed for a long time, neither one speaking, and both trying to understand their mother's illness and the thought of life without her.

Nine

THE DAY AFTER Theresa made her stern speech to the family and told Marcail of the illness, the entire clan set off to see San Francisco in Aunt Maureen's open buggy. The morning fog had burned off and, with the sun climbing into the sky, Maureen gave everyone a grand tour of the city.

They drove past mansions with balconies, widow's walks, columned porches, and towers. A few houses sported windows with beautiful stained glass. Every imaginable style of architecture could be found. The children gaped in awe at the sizes as well as the variations in color. It became very apparent as the day wore on that their aunt's home, grand as it was, was not the biggest nor the finest San Francisco had to offer.

They sat for a time at the shores of San Francisco Bay and looked across the water to Alcatraz Island. The prison on the island had been holding prisoners from the early 1860's, so Maureen informed everyone.

They finished their morning with Aunt Maureen treating them to lunch at one of the fine downtown hotels.

The coming weeks brought on a pattern of sorts. Most mornings the family would go on an outing and return home for lunch. Theresa spent the afternoons resting or writing letters. Even though she was taking it easy, she was growing worse. Almost daily now she would find blood on her handkerchief, and, try as she might to hide it, the whole family was aware of it.

But her spirits were buoyant and she was very pleased at how normal everyone was acting. Maureen, who was nearly convinced that the children were perfect, had her first glimpse of real family life one afternoon when she was visiting with Theresa in the bedroom.

"Marcail!" Kate, clearly furious, shouted her sister's name. Maureen's eyes grew round as laughter was heard from across the hall and then a furious tirade in a foreign tongue. Maureen, who had been staring at the open door to the hallway, turned to find Theresa's eyes filled with amusement.

"What is she saying?" Maureen almost gasped.

Theresa listened for a moment. "She's going to beat Marcail as soon as she catches her, and Sean had better stay hidden because when he comes out she's going to beat him too."

"But what language is she speaking?"

"Hawaiian. All the children are fluent. And Kate rarely speaks English when she's angry or flustered."

Things quieted down a moment later, and then Patrick let himself into the room. He closed the door and leaned against it, chuckling. The women waited for him to speak.

"Marcail was hiding in the wardrobe wearing a fake beard and a man's hat. Sean put her up to it and Kaitlin plans to get them both."

"I gave that beard and hat to Sean. I never dreamed—" Maureen let the sentence hang, obviously feeling like an accomplice.

"It's not your fault Maureen," her brother reassured her. "And even though Kaitlin is angry, believe me, the children have never had so much fun."

The older woman looked greatly relieved and by the time she saw the children, they were once again the best of friends.

Weeks later Father read aloud to the family a letter he'd received from Pastor Graves in Hawaii. The reply had come with remarkable speed after sending word of Theresa's condition. The letter reported that all was well but the Donovan family was sorely missed. Everyone sent their love and said they were praying for Theresa.

Patrick, his heart filled with regret, wrote back to say that Theresa's condition was deteriorating swiftly and that he had no idea when they would be returning. Taking his time, he walked slowly and deliberately to post the letter. His heart, although burdened with his wife's health, trusted God to do His perfect will in their lives.

"This is what Theresa was talking about on the boat." Patrick uttered the words aloud and came to an abrupt stop on the street. "I promised Pastor Graves I'd come back to Hawaii and I'll have to do just that after she's gone, even if only to explain my plans and pack the rest of our belongings."

He sat on a stone wall that landscaped a neighbor's yard for a long time, staring at nothing. The afternoon was quiet and no one disturbed him as he faced the promise he had made. He prayed long and hard and, when he knew what he would do, went straight home to talk with his sister and his children. The letter, at least for the moment, was forgotten in his pocket.

"But Father, you were so sick . . . I really think I should go."

"It's out of the question, Kaitlin, although I appreciate your offer."

Kaitlin and Sean looked grief stricken and Father was thankful that Marcail was not here. He knew it was very hard to talk as if their mother were already dead but it was better to know ahead of time what the situation would be. Patrick turned to his sister.

"You're sure, Maureen? I mean, I can make other arrangements."

"Don't be ridiculous, Patrick. Of course they can stay here."

"I'd be happy to go with you, Father."

Patrick's eyes filled with tears over the sincerely spoken words from his son. He knew very well how fresh his son's memory of the trip over was.

"I know that wasn't an easy offer for you to make, Son, and I thank you, but no, I want you to stay here.

"Now, I'm not going to make a promise to you that I'll be right back. I've prayed about this and right now I don't think I can go back as a pastor in Hawaii. I'm returning to settle things and gather our possessions. I'll return to San Francisco as quickly as I can. I want you to understand that I'll be back as swiftly as *God wills.* If something deters me, I trust God to care for you. As your aunt said earlier, this is your home for as long as you need it."

Everyone went their separate ways when Father was finished. He sat for a long time hurting, but sure in his heart that he'd done the right thing by warning the family of his plans.

Three days later his conviction was confirmed when Theresa Donovan, beloved wife and mother, slipped peacefully and with little pain, from her afternoon nap into the waiting arms of her heavenly Father.

Ten

THERE WERE FEW mourners at the funeral and Kaitlin was glad. Never in her life had she wanted privacy more. Not from the family, she was desperate to be near them. But the hardest thing she'd ever lived through was dealing with the undertaker—a stranger coming and taking her mother's frail body away to prepare for the burial. Every time she thought of it she felt ill.

Without warning, all the duties her mother had performed—the washing and cooking, the teaching and loving—rushed into her heart like a tidal wave. And just as suddenly, the weight of being the eldest daughter crowded in upon her.

I'm not ready to be a mother figure to Sean or Marcail, God. Her heart cried out to her heavenly Father and, even though she was looking into the grave, she was very conscious of Marcail's little hand seeking comfort within her own. Sean stood to the other side of her, so close that his shoulder brushed her own. Father had knelt down on the far side of Sean as though lessening the distance to his wife's body might comfort him in some small measure.

Kaitlin watched him rise a few moments later and, out of the corner of her eye, caught the movement of a man approaching.

"I'm sorry, Mr. Donovan," Dr. Weston spoke quietly as he stepped inside the small family circle.

"Thank you for coming." Father shook the doctor's hand and did nothing to hide his tears. Dr. Weston turned and spoke to Sean before moving on to Kate. Kaitlin was thankful for his kindness even as she became aware that Marcail was trying to hide behind her. Kaitlin held tightly to her hand and gave a little warning squeeze. Marcail did remember her manners and thanked the doctor politely when he expressed his sympathy to her but her eyes clearly spoke her distrust. Father had taken time for a long talk with Marcail, as he had planned, but Kate wondered when the nine-year-old would understand that Dr. Weston had nothing to do with their mother's death.

Dr. Weston spoke at length with Maureen, bringing her tears on afresh. The family watched him move toward his small carriage. It seemed the best time to follow suit. Within minutes the family was aboard their own transportation and headed back to the Kent home.

It was with great pain that the children bade good-bye to their father two weeks later. Kaitlin, already feeling as if something vital had been severed from her with her mother's death, was so overcome by Father's leaving that she could not stop crying.

Sean said little, wanting very much to be the man. But his eyes were almost angry, and Father held him tightly in his arms for a long time.

Marcail, having just a week before found out about her father's departure, was so upset she'd vomited twice. Father held her close and mopped her small face.

His heart toyed with the idea of gathering his children and returning to Hawaii for good, but even as the thought came he pushed it away. He didn't think he was in any shape to return and minister to the people there. They had only been in California a week before they'd been made aware of the seriousness of Theresa's illness, so this had not been a restful time as planned.

Father planned to leave very early in the morning so good-byes to his family were conducted at bedtime the night before. No one was asleep the next morning when he left, but everyone stayed in their rooms even as his steps were heard in the hall.

Maureen did her level best to occupy the children for two days before deciding that maybe they didn't need distraction so much as they needed to let themselves grieve. She planned to allow them a few days to themselves and was feeling very good about her decision when she heard heavy footsteps in the entry way. She was walking the length of the library when a tall figure appeared in the doorway. Maureen rushed forward with a joyous cry and threw her arms around her loved one. Percy was home.

Eleven

PERCIVAL LAWTON WAS immediately captivated with his cousin Kaitlin. In a foul mood he had left Europe on a ship he felt was beneath his station. He'd lost badly at the gaming tables in London. With his best friends still in Europe, Percy resigned himself to a life of boring social rounds with his mother until he could soften her into giving him some more cash. But to his infinite delight he arrived home to find the most beautiful creature he'd ever seen living directly under his roof.

Kaitlin, in her grief, was unaware of the heart-fluttering she was causing within the chest of her cousin. She had been spending many hours reading and talking with her siblings. This didn't leave much time for the other members of the household but Maureen understood, knowing they were going to survive this painful ordeal by those very actions.

Percy, on the other hand, was extremely frustrated over Kaitlin's lack of response to him. He knew he was good looking, and indeed he was, but it wouldn't have mattered if he were Prince Charming himself, Kaitlin was in no shape for a romantic attachment.

The thing that bothered Percy the most was the amount of reading Kaitlin did. He felt it a great insult that she could actually prefer a book to his engaging company.

It was not at all unusual to pass her bedroom on the way out of his own, and see her curled up in a chair reading her Bible. She also read in the library. Not books so much, but the newspapers. And not just the front-page stories, as he did, but every page and every word, he was sure.

What Percy failed to see was how starved these children were for current news after living on an island for so many years. Oh, there had been contact, but never this daily fare of words to be devoured at their leisure. And Percy was right, Kaitlin did read every word, even the want ads. Sean was just as bad, and even Marcail could spend an hour with whatever page she'd been allotted.

All of these seemingly simple pleasures, such as reading a newspaper and having time to themselves were working wonders in the hearts of the Donovan children. Daily they felt the pain of their loss and the separation from their father, but also daily, God was their comfort. And not having extra emotional burdens was more beneficial than even they realized, but Maureen saw it and knew she'd handled things the right way. There was a little something bothering her, nagging just at the back of her mind, but she couldn't quite put her finger on it. The children were fairly happy and eating well and she told herself she was worrying over nothing.

Unfortunately the secure world that Maureen had gone to such lengths to create for her nieces and nephew was about to be destroyed.

All four of the cousins were in the library reading one morning; Percy had joined them in an attempt to be near Kaitlin. He held the paper in such a way that he could watch her surreptitiously. He couldn't believe that black hair. It haunted him. And those eyes, deep brown and set in a face with perfect skin. Her skin was a bit darker than he was used to, but all the more beguiling because of that fact.

Even in an unbecoming black dress, Kaitlin had the best figure Percy had seen in a long time. A desire to hold her in his arms was clouding his already poor judgment. He was sure she'd never experienced passion of any kind and he was equally sure if he could just hold and kiss her she would awaken to a love for him that would have her falling at his feet.

Percy really believed on this day that he could wait it out, wait for her to put aside her paper and then invite her to go for a drive with him. But it was not to be. How they could all sit and read for hours was beyond him. When he could stand it no longer he came swiftly to his feet.

"Would anyone care to go for a walk?" His voice was curt but it was lost on the readers.

"Not just now, but thanks, Percy," Sean answered distractedly.

Percy was furious that Kaitlin had not even heard him. He tossed his head to show his irritation but Kate didn't look up until he slammed the door on his exit.

Kaitlin's surprised eyes met those of Sean's, who only shrugged in equal puzzlement. They were both headed back to their papers when Marcail said quietly, "He's in love with you, Katie."

"Who is?" Kate questioned in genuine ignorance.

"Cousin Percy."

Kaitlin waited a moment for Marcail to smile and tell her she was joking but it didn't happen. The little girl was serious. A frisson of alarm shot through Kate and she looked over at Sean to see that he was just as surprised.

"Why do you say that, Marc?" Kaitlin asked cautiously.

"He watches you all the time. Just like Scott used to."

"That doesn't mean he's in love with me." Kate's words didn't convince Marcail who just stared at her older sister and gnawed on her lower lip. In fact, Kate's words didn't convince herself.

There had been a few signs, she realized that now. But the whole idea had been inconceivable to her. They were cousins! When they'd first met she thought he was quiet, because all he did was stare silently at her. But she saw now that she'd taken him by surprise.

Kaitlin put her paper aside and went to her room. She prayed a long time about the situation. When she came down for lunch she was feeling some better and was almost relieved to find that Percy was absent.

Over the next few days Kate was very aware of Percy's actions toward her and knew that what Marcail had seen was true. Her cousin was infatuated with her.

Kate ended up in Sean's room one night talking to him about the way she felt. He'd taken his parents' room upon Percy's return.

"I just feel so bad. I feel like I've done something to encourage him."

"I don't think you have, Kate. I mean you're nice to people and he must have thought you liked him, well you know, in *that* way."

"But I don't and even if I did Sean, Percy and I are cousins!" The thought was so clearly distasteful to her that Sean laughed.

"Does it feel strange to be in this room?" Kaitlin asked when the laughter died down.

"A little. But in some ways I feel closer to Mother. Her clothes and things are still in here and I kind of like seeing them."

Kaitlin nodded in understanding and walked around the room. She reached out to touch a handkerchief that lay on the dresser. The small scrap of cloth still held their mother's fragrance. The scent brought tears to the young woman's eyes. She took a moment to gather her emotions and then told Sean she was headed to the library to get her book and then to bed. Sean lifted the handkerchief after she left and his own tears came as he held it tightly in his hand.

"If you would just talk to me. Maybe I can help."

"Just leave it, Mother. You know I don't like to be nagged."

"But Percy—"

Mother and son were in the library in a heated discussion as Kaitlin came down the stairs. That their voices were agitated did not register with her until she was close enough to hear every word.

"I mean it, Mother. Now just leave me alone."

"It's Kaitlin, isn't it?"

"I don't know what you're talking about." Percy's voice was strained, belying his words.

"Yes, you do. You're in love with her," Maureen accused.

Percy's chin jutted out on those accusatory words. "And what if I am?"

"Oh Percy, Percy, no. Don't I give you everything? Don't I let you have whatever you want? Kaitlin's your cousin. She's in mourning; please leave her alone."

"Honestly, Mother," the young man said with an offended sniff. "You'd think I was some ogre trying to throw myself at her."

"Percy, you're cousins!"

It was on those words that Kaitlin fled back up the stairs. Marcail was a very heavy sleeper so Kaitlin didn't attempt to wake her before scooping her up and heading across the hall to Sean's room. Sean was down to his pants in his preparation for bed and watched in surprise as his sister flew into the room and shut the door.

"Kate, what is the matter with you?"

"Sean," she panted as she lay Marcail on the bed. "Try to wake her while I find that newspaper you had earlier."

"Katie, what—"

"Just do it!" she commanded sharply, but Sean just stood gaping at her. Kate turned the lamp high and sat on the floor beside the bed. The rustle of papers was loud in the still room. "Here it is!" Kate finally said.

Santa Rosa—Schoolteacher
Wanted Immediately
For Remainder of School Year
Apply Burt Kemp Real Estate, Santa Rosa

Kaitlin looked over at Sean in triumph. Sean stared at her in complete confusion, which reminded Kate that he hadn't heard any of the conversation downstairs. She took a deep breath and told him the whole story.

"Kate, I think you could get that job but I don't think we need to move away. I mean Percy hasn't really done anything, and you told me you keep your distance."

"So you think I'm overreacting?"

"Yes, I guess I do."

Kate's shoulders slumped. "When I realized I'd caused an argument between Aunt Maureen and Percy I felt terrible and then when Percy practically said he loved me, I panicked."

"It's okay, Kate." They were silent for a moment and then Sean tried to encourage his older sister. "I guess it's kind of nice to know that you could get a job if you needed to. Santa Rosa is that nice town that Aunt Maureen told us about, isn't it?"

"She said she used to have friends there and she talked like it wasn't too far away."

Marcail had slept through the entire episode as well as Sean carrying her back to her bed. He spoke to Kaitlin before he took himself off to bed.

"I can see why it would upset you, Kate, but I think you'll be okay. If you want, I can sleep in here with you."

"No Sean, it's all right. I'm probably just too tired."

"Okay. Good night Kate."

"Good night Sean, and thanks."

It was some time before Kaitlin could sleep but as she prayed she became totally convinced that she had overreacted, which only made the incident that happened the next day even more upsetting.

Twelve

"I'VE BEEN WANTING to talk with you, Kaitlin."

"What about, Percy?" Kate smiled kindly and stood expectantly several feet in front of her cousin, in the library.

Percy was suddenly tongue-tied. Both of Kate's black dresses were being pressed and so she'd slipped into a light-weight spring fabric of green and yellow. Percy found her enchanting.

The warm expectant smile slowly died on Kaitlin's face as Percy's gaze grew intense. Kate's brain was telling her to get out of the room but she was so surprised she reacted too late. In the next instant Percy's arms were around her, attempting to pull her close. Kate's hands were on his chest pushing with all her strength.

"I've wanted to hold you from the moment I saw you," Percy whispered. "Please don't fight me, Kaitlin." Percy's head came forward and he tried to kiss her.

"No, Percy!" Kaitlin gasped as she twisted from side to side. She opened her mouth to call for help when a voice spoke in the doorway.

"Get your hands off my sister." The voice was deadly cold and Percy froze in surprise. It was enough. Kate took advantage of the loosening of his arms and twisted free. She had just arrived at Sean's side when Maureen and Marcail stepped through the door.

Maureen's gaze went from her white-faced disheveled niece and furious nephew to her stone-faced son. Something clutched around Maureen's heart and for the first time in her life she truly saw Percy

for the immature, selfish, and spoiled man that he was. Before she
could say anything, Sean made a quick decision and spoke.

"Aunt Maureen, we appreciate all you've done but we'll be moving to Santa Rosa. There's a possible teaching position there for Kate.
We'll be leaving in the morning."

Sean could see he'd shocked his aunt speechless. But he wasn't
finished. He turned to his cousin and spoke in a voice so like his
father's that both his sisters and aunt could only stare at him.

"If you ever touch my sister again, I'll thrash you to within an inch
of your life." Sean did not wait for an answer before he ushered his
sisters from the room.

He'd seen a flicker of fear in his cousin's eyes and knew he'd been
taken seriously. The truth was that he'd never hit anyone in his life,
but he also knew, with the way he was feeling right then, that he was
more than capable of carrying out his threat.

"Who will we live with?" Marcail wanted to know.

"We'll figure that out when we get to Santa Rosa," her brother
told her. The Donovan children had been talking for over an hour.
They had all three prayed and tried to think of what their father
would have done in the same circumstances.

"The problem is that this would never have happened if Father
had been here," Sean stated logically. "I am really sorry, Kate."

"Stop apologizing."

"But if I'd listened to you last night—"

"It's all right, Sean. We just underestimated the way Percy would
act. We're also causing problems between Aunt Maureen and Percy so
I think it's best this way."

"Is it my fault that he did that, Katie?" Marcail wanted to know.
"Because I said he loves you?"

"No Marc, it's not your fault. Percy is a grown man and he knew
better than to try and hug me when I didn't want to be hugged." Kate
was surprised at how normal her voice sounded. Every time she
thought of Percy a shiver ran through her. She folded her arms across
her chest and tried to push the whole episode out of her mind.

"Now, we need to take a vote. Do we leave for Santa Rosa in the
morning and pray that God gives me a job? Sean?"

"I vote we go."

"Marc?"

"I want to stay with you and Sean. But mostly I want Father to
come back."

Kate hugged her where they sat on the floor of the girls' bedroom.
A few minutes later there was a knock at the door. Sean answered it.

Aunt Maureen stood on the threshold looking pale with strain and worry. Sean held the door wide and she entered wordlessly.

"Is there anything I can say, Kaitlin?" The older woman came straight to the point.

"It's not your fault, Aunt Maureen."

If only that were true, the older woman thought, but said in a voice that shook with emotion, "Are you really going to leave?"

Kate went to her. "Aunt Maureen, I have to tell you something. When I came downstairs last night, I heard you and Percy talking. I panicked when I heard how he felt about me because I thought I'd done something to cause that."

"Oh no, my dear, please don't think that."

"Well, I'm feeling better about it but the thing I need to tell you is about the ad I saw for a teaching position. You said Santa Rosa wasn't too far from here."

"About a day's ride on the stagecoach."

"Well, yesterday morning I saw this ad and for some reason I couldn't get it out of my mind. At first I just thought it was because I knew I could apply. I think I was feeling prideful about being an experienced teacher but then after I eavesdropped and panicked, I told Sean I wanted to go and have a try for that job.

"Last night we figured I was overreacting but now we've talked and taken a vote. We'll check the fares and time schedule this afternoon and leave tomorrow morning."

"What will I say to your father?" Tears appeared in Maureen's eyes and Kate put her arms around her.

"I'll write Father. I'm not saying that he won't be furious with Percy but he also trusts Sean, Marc and me to do the right thing. When he gets back here and if I'm still teaching, he can come to Santa Rosa. If not we'll go wherever he wants."

"You sound very confident that you'll get the job," Maureen commented.

"Well, I guess I'm not *that* confident but I'm headed that way to find something and we'll have to wait to see what tomorrow brings. The thing I want you to remember, Aunt Maureen, is that we know God will take care of us."

Maureen nodded and went with them to check the stagecoach timetable. Feeling as though she were living a bad dream, she watched her brother's children pack their things that afternoon. The following morning Maureen drove them into town for the nine o'clock stage. She'd given them extra money for the trip and knew the line was a dependable one . . . but the papers were always filled with stories of robberies. It was tempting to call them back, but they were handling it all so well she knew she needed to leave well enough alone.

Percy made himself very scarce until after Maureen had returned to the house, whereupon he asked for more money to return to Europe. Maureen was more than happy to comply and Percy was surprised at how generous she was until he looked at his mother's face. It told him he would never get another penny from her.

Two hours later the Donovans were wondering about their decision. Nothing they had ever experienced had come close to preparing them for stagecoach travel. Their dark clothing was covered with dust, and it was so stuffy inside the coach that Marcail felt sick. The colorful language of their driver made their eyes open wide on more than one occasion. Well, they'd paid the fare to Santa Rosa, so Santa Rosa it was going to be.

Please God, Kate prayed as she looked at the strained face of her sister, *please let our money hold until I can get work. And Lord, if we've made a mistake, show us, so we can go back to Aunt Maureen's.*

She had much more she wanted to say to her heavenly Father but Sean was thrown almost on top of her when the coach dropped into a rut in the road. He came so hard against her she knew she'd have a bruise. Her last coherent thought before her mind refused to think any longer, was that she hoped Santa Rosa would be worth all of this.

Thirteen

Santa Rosa, California
March 1871

"HEY, RIGG, I THOUGHT you were headed to Burt's office."

"I am. At one, like we decided."

"It's quarter to two."

Marshall Riggs looked at the regulator on the wall and shook his head. "I tell you, Jeff, these accounts for the store are going to be the death of me."

Jeff laughed unsympathetically and the two men headed down the office stairs. Marshall, Rigg to nearly everyone, was the darker of the two with black hair and startling gray eyes that turned almost black if he was upset. Jeffrey Taylor, Rigg's half brother, stood just short of six feet, whereas Rigg was just over. Jeff's hair was a medium shade of brown and his eyes were light blue and usually smiling with mischief.

The stairway took the men down to the floor of one of Santa Rosa's mercantiles. It was a good business with every imaginable type of ware. There was even a row of chairs along one side for the men to sit in and chat when they brought their wives in to shop.

The brothers were passing those chairs now and, as always, Rigg felt a bit of envy. He wished his own wife was shopping somewhere in the store. But Rigg didn't have a wife. He believed that if he was to have a wife, God would provide one. But the fact that God was in control did not change his desires, the deepest of which was to have a family.

"I thought I told you to get rid of those hats Rigg," an elderly farmer spoke in a gruff, good-natured voice, causing Rigg and Jeff to smile. "They're costing me a fortune." As if on cue, the man's wife appeared with a hat on her head and one in each hand.

"I can't decide," she spoke before she saw the young men. "Oh, hello Jeff, hello Rigg."

"Hello, Mrs. Wallace," Rigg spoke. "I hope you're finding what you need."

"Well, I just can't choose between these hats. You always have such nice hats, Rigg."

"You could take all three," Rigg said with exaggerated innocence.

"Rigg!" sounded the gruff voice from the chair. Laughter was heard as the younger men chose to exit on that note.

The men were headed to Burt Kemp's office to check with him on the vacant teaching position. On the way, the teacher they'd just lost became the topic.

"Mom told me to look you over today and see if you're losing weight."

Rigg laughed. "I will admit to you that I miss Marty's cooking."

The last four schoolteachers had all been men, and Rigg's large home, situated two blocks from the school, had been the perfect place for the men to live. Rigg had gotten along very well with all of them, but he hadn't enjoyed anyone's company as much as the last one, Marty Wright.

Marty's hobby was cooking and Rigg hadn't eaten so well since he'd turned 23 and moved into his grandparents old home three years ago. But two weeks ago Marty had come down with a severe case of pneumonia. Rigg experienced the scare of his life at how quickly the younger man had gone down. School had been called off for a week, but it became clear even after it was no longer a life-and-death situation, that Marty was not going to be able to finish the school year. His parents, who lived in nearby Fulton, came and took him home to recover.

Thus, the ad was put into papers as far away as San Francisco. So far the response had been poor.

Burt Kemp was head of the school board and a kind man. He welcomed Rigg and Jeff into his cluttered office and told them no applications had come in.

"I really wish this had been settled. But I've talked with Greg Carson and he's agreed to take over for me when I leave. In fact he's coming over in a while to make sure he knows what to do."

"When do you go?" Rigg wanted to know.

"This afternoon, late." Burt said the words apologetically and shrugged.

"Don't be sorry, Burt. You need this time with your daughter. I'm sure Greg can handle it." Even as Jeff said the words, Greg's one fault came to mind. He was extremely tightfisted. It didn't often affect his position on the school board but it always made Jeff a little uncomfortable.

The men broke up later and Jeff made his way back to the shipping office that his parents, William and Mabel, May for short, ran. It was actually his father who was on the school board but he'd been tied up and asked Jeff to go with Rigg. He would fill him in after the next stagecoach was unloaded. It was due any time.

The stagecoach, with its weary travelers, slowed and came to a complete stop near the shipping office.

On the trip Marcail had fallen asleep and was now revived to full energy. Even Sean had dozed off and didn't look very tired. Kaitlin, on the other hand, was not sure her legs were going to hold her. Every muscle in her body ached and her mouth and throat were so dry they felt as if they had been stuffed with an old rag.

A young man who should be in school, Kaitlin thought vaguely, helped them with their bags and when Sean asked directions to Burt Kemp's office, he gave them politely.

"Who was that?" Jeff approached, as the Donovans walked away.

"I don't know," Nathan Taylor answered. Nate was Jeff's youngest brother. "They're headed to Burt's. I hope he's not a schoolteacher."

"I'll bet you do," Jeff laughed, knowing how much his 15-year-old brother was enjoying this time without a teacher. "Well, I wouldn't worry about it if I were you. He looked a little young to teach school."

"That's true," Nate said with relief.

The boys were joined then by the next brother, 18-year-old Gilbert, and all three of them went back to work.

"I can see I've surprised you, Mr. Kemp, and I know my appearance right now is rather a dusty mess, but I *am* qualified to teach your school."

Burt and Greg both stared in disbelief at the lovely young woman, dressed in widow's weeds. It took a few moments for Burt to recover.

"Please be seated, Mrs. Donovan. I'm sorry we—"

"It's Miss Donovan."

Burt blinked in surprise thinking that he'd misunderstood her when she'd introduced herself. He looked at her dress and Kaitlin knew she had to explain.

"My mother died recently." Her voice told of her grief. "I've never been married, although my brother and sister will be living with me."

The meeting, off to a poor start, came to a wonderful conclusion. The men had been hesitant to hire a woman but within a few minutes they were more than impressed with Kaitlin Donovan. The only cloud on the horizon was Kaitlin's lack of a teaching certificate. Greg was very bothered by this and came right out and said so.

"We can't very well give you a trial period since this is the end of March and school ends in two months but I do think we, as a school board, need to consider this. Maybe the best route to take would be a lower wage for the first month, you know, until you've proven yourself."

"That's fine, Mr. Carson." Kate assured him in her gentle way. Burt felt very guilty about such a move but the time was moving on. He didn't want this interview to make him late in leaving—he and his wife were going to see their eldest daughter, who was about to have a baby. He'd take up the matter with Greg, when he returned.

Sean and Marcail were ushered into the office and introduced. The next thing Kaitlin knew, they were being led down the street to a hotel for the night.

"Now, Mr. Carson will start first thing in the morning finding you a place to live." Burt was walking and talking so fast that Kaitlin was straining to catch his words.

"You should be comfortable here tonight." They were in the hotel now, going up the stairs at an amazing pace. "That will give you the weekend to get settled, and you'll be ready to start school Monday. Oh! The school records. Greg can bring you those. Oh, yes, my daughter . . . we're going on a trip but you'll have her when we return."

Mr. Kemp had seen them to their room and opened the door. He gave a quick look around before bidding them good-bye and nearly running from the room.

The door closed and the children stood still in the middle of the room. A moment went by, and then Kaitlin walked toward the only chair in the room and sank into it. She was nearly trembling with fatigue.

Marcail was fascinated with the idea of staying in a hotel and she did a thorough inspection of the room. There was only one bed, but there was a good-sized sofa, and Marcail declared it would be Sean's. Sean was too busy watching his older sister to pay much attention to Marcail.

"Are you going to cry, Katie?"

"I'm too tired to cry."

"Are you happy you got the job?"

"Yes, I'm just a little overwhelmed."

"Why don't I go get us some supper?"

"Would you, Sean?" Kate perked up at the very idea.

"Sure. Marcail and I will go find some food while you freshen up."

Kaitlin did cry then, because he was so thoughtful. Sean never knew what to do when his sisters or mother cried and then he remembered he didn't have a mother.

Please God, his young heart prayed as he moved close so Kate could cry onto the sleeve of his jacket, *please help me take care of my sisters. And please take care of me, too.*

Fourteen

THE NEXT MORNING Greg Carson walked with a jaunty step into the hotel dining area to find the new schoolteacher. She was easy to spot because the room was near to empty. If he'd thought her attractive yesterday, he didn't know what to think today. Kaitlin was well rested and in a clean dress.

"Good morning, Miss Donovan." Greg was irritated at the way his voice nearly stuttered, but to his relief none of the Donovan family seemed to notice.

"Good morning."

"I have good news for you." His stuttering was forgotten in his excitement. "I've found you a house. Now, I didn't rent it, because it's up to you if you want it. It needs a little cleaning up but the price is very good. . . ."

Mr. Carson went on to name an amount which caused Kaitlin to blink. This was the very man who had set her salary yesterday and then casually announced to her today that the rent for the house would be swallowing about 90 percent of her monthly income.

Moments before Mr. Carson had come in, Kate and Sean had been discussing the idea of Sean getting a Saturday job. Kate wasn't thrilled with the idea, but if the rents in town were high, they just might not have any choice.

After breakfast they walked to the house that Greg had found. The house turned out to be a one-room cottage. It was quaint, charming even, and painted white. Kaitlin was pleasantly surprised to see a stove and a table with two chairs. She became concerned, though when she saw only one bed.

"It's very nice."

"Then you like it?" Mr. Carson seemed so delighted that Kaitlin smiled.

"Yes, I do." She glanced around and then asked, "Is there any way we could have another bed?"

Mr. Carson looked a little surprised at the request and then looked at Sean as though seeing him for the first time. He'd been given no authorization from the school board to furnish the house and the thought went against his grain, even if he had.

"I forgot that there were three of you," he said almost absently and then a smile lit his face. "The male schoolteachers usually stay with Marshall Riggs. I'll bet he'd let Sean stay with him!"

Kaitlin felt her breath leave in a rush. Have Sean live somewhere else, with some man they hadn't even met yet? Kate didn't know what to do.

She asked cautiously, not wanting to complain, "Mr. Carson, when you were checking, did you see any places for rent that were a little bit bigger?"

"Not in this price range," he told her, not unkindly.

"Well—" Kaitlin began, but really couldn't think of anything to say. Greg took it as an agreement.

"Fine, fine. I can go over right now and explain the situation to Rigg and then I'll show you the schoolhouse. Can you find your way back to the hotel?"

"Yes, thank you." Kate's voice was strained but Greg didn't notice. With a quick wave he was gone.

"Are we going to go back to Aunt Maureen's?" Marcail wanted to know. "Katie, are we going to go back to Aunt Maureen's?" The little girl tugged on her sister's dress and Kaitlin finally looked at her.

"I don't know—"

"No, we're not," Sean interrupted in a strong voice. Kaitlin just looked at him. "We're staying here and giving this a try. I can go live with this Riggs fellow and you guys can stay here. You got the job, Katie, and I take that as an open door for staying here. I would rather that we were together but I still think we're going to be okay."

Kate stared at her brother and wondered when he had gotten older than 14.

"All right, Sean, we'll give it a try."

They made their way back to the hotel to pack and wait for Mr. Carson. He was knocking at their door soon after they'd closed their cases and once again all of the Donovans accompanied him, only this time to the schoolhouse.

For Kate, it was love at first sight. The school was painted white with flower boxes beneath the windows. Once inside, she smiled as her eyes caressed the dark wood on the rows of small desks and then the larger one up front for herself. A large flag hung on one of the side walls flanked by a picture of George Washington.

Whoever had come before her had been meticulous because everything was spotless. The blackboards covering the entire front wall were scrubbed clean. On the teacher's desk sat a globe of the world. Kaitlin moved it to a library table against the side wall. She continued to move around touching this and moving that in a way that reminded Sean and Marcail of their mother.

Mr. Carson was very solicitous and had all the school records with him. Kaitlin looked through them with great relish. That she loved to teach was written on her face and her every movement. She would have sat all day in that schoolroom planning for Monday, but Mr. Carson brought her quickly back to the present.

"I think Sean and I should go get your things at the hotel. We'll stop at your house first and then go to Rigg's, so Sean knows where it is."

Kate was quickly learning that when Mr. Carson had a plan, he executed it almost immediately. Before she could say yea or nay, he was gone with her brother in tow.

"Where will I sit, Katie?"

Kaitlin looked at her younger sister and thanked God for her. Marcail had a way of bringing Kate down to earth with her questions.

"Well, Marc, I don't know. We're going to have to wait and see." Kate watched her expressive face and smiled. Marcail was worried and trying not to show it. "What's bothering you?"

"I miss Loni and I wish I knew which desk was mine."

"Does it matter?"

"I don't know, I just wish I knew."

Kaitlin didn't try to sort through this. She just listened and went over to sit beside her sister on the long bench that stretched across the front of the schoolroom.

"Everything is so different here Katie, and I don't want to get a spanking."

"Why would you get a spanking?"

"Because we left Aunt Maureen's without asking Father."

Kate slipped an arm around the nine-year-old. "Marc, who is in charge when Father's not here?"

"You are."

"That's right. So if Father is angry about our move, and I don't think he will be, I'll be the one in trouble."

"Who will be in trouble?" A good-natured voice spoke from the doorway of the schoolhouse and two men came in with easy familiarity.

Kate had been startled to have someone speak so suddenly. Both she and Marcail had jumped up and spun around to see them approaching. That they were father and son was more than obvious as they came closer.

"I'm William Taylor and this is my son Jeff. I'm sorry if I startled you." He didn't look the least bit sorry and Kaitlin couldn't help but smile at the charming display of teeth he was giving her.

"It's nice to meet you both. I'm Kaitlin Donovan and this is my sister, Marcail. I was hired yesterday as the new schoolteacher."

The younger man, who Kaitlin had only glanced at when introduced, mumbled something about Nate being lucky, something Kaitlin didn't understand. But then Mr. Taylor was asking her a question and she didn't have time to pay any further attention to Jeff.

"We were staying with our aunt in San Francisco when I saw the ad for this job."

"How was the trip up?"

"Well, it was different," Kate tried to put it delicately. "You see, we'd never ridden in a stagecoach before and we were unprepared for the dust."

"Where are you from?" Jeff asked, as if Kaitlin had just sprouted wings. Kaitlin was not offended, in fact, she laughed and Marcail answered.

"We live in Hawaii."

"Hawaii? As in the middle of the ocean, that Hawaii?" Again Jeff was incredulous.

"One and the same," Kaitlin said with great amusement, even as she thought that Jeff Taylor was very nice looking.

Bill watched his son's face as he spoke to the new teacher. He doubted Jeff knew he was staring rudely, but then Bill was also compassionate. Kaitlin Donovan was a beauty, as was her little sister. May was going to love these girls.

"What I've come about is to ask if you would come with us to church Sunday morning and then join our family for dinner. And you can't tell me no, because my wife is already planning on you."

Kate was so pleased she took a moment answering. "We'd love to. Oh, my brother, that is, he's here, too, and—"

"The invitation includes all of you. Jeff will come by with the wagon Sunday morning about ten."

"That would be wonderful. My brother is living with—what was his name Marc?"

"I don't remember his name but I think he's the Marshall."

Bill and Jeff shouted with laughter over this, much to Kate and Marcail's confusion.

"I think you mean Marshall Riggs."

Marcail nodded.

"Marshall is his name and he happens to be my stepson. Rigg, as we all call him, lost his father before he was three. I married his mother the next year, the woman you'll meet Sunday. Actually I hadn't thought of it before, but if your brother is staying with Rigg then you can just all come to church with him. I'll ask him about it. Either way someone will be at your house that morning."

"I'm not sure how to tell you where our house is."

"We just saw Greg Carson," Bill assured her. "He told us where you're living."

"Oh, well, thank you, Mr. Taylor. We'll be looking forward to Sunday then."

"Anytime and if you need anything, I run the shipping office where the stage came in. Just come down and if I'm not there, someone will know where to find me."

Kate once again thanked him and then decided she'd best get to the house and get settled. She wondered, as she and Marcail walked to find Sean, if he was getting along.

Fifteen

"Two EVENINGS A WEEK and Saturdays."

"Thanks, Mr. Riggs!" Sean felt overwhelmed as he answered. He couldn't believe he was actually being offered a job, something he'd never had before, and by the man with whom he would be staying.

"I think, Sean, that if you're going to be living in my house, you should call me Rigg. Everyone does."

Sean nodded and took a bit of bread. He had a strange look on his face and Rigg noticed.

"Is anything wrong with the food?"

"No, it's fine. I just feel funny eating without Kaitlin and Marcail."

"I've got plenty here. When you're done, we'll take the rest over."

The young man thanked him in awe, finding it hard to believe how generous he was. Sean, quite frankly, had been terrified at the thought of going to live with this stranger, but he hadn't wanted Kate to know. She was a good teacher and even though things were going to be tight, Sean believed they could make it.

He'd come to this house with Mr. Carson expecting the worst, and before he knew what was happening, he was being shown a nice bedroom and given a plate of food.

And Marshall Riggs, well, Sean couldn't stop watching him. He was as tall as Father but Sean didn't think he'd ever seen such a powerful chest and upper arms on a man. Maybe he wasn't a very good judge, but Sean thought Rigg could break a man in two if he wanted.

But even as he thought of it he knew it would never happen. Marshall Riggs' powerful build was not from fighting, not with those beautiful white teeth that flashed at you when he smiled. And his eyes, they spoke of a deep kindness whenever he looked at you or when he offered a couple of strange girls the rest of his lunch. No, Rigg was not the fighting type.

When Rigg spent the next few minutes explaining to Sean what his duties would be, it wasn't hard to figure out how he'd built up his body.

"I get shipments of goods from all over, just about every day of the week. Anything that comes in on Sunday stays at the shipping office until Monday, but everything else I like unloaded right away. How much can you lift?"

"I'm not really sure." Sean was afraid he'd take the job away, but he had to be honest.

"Well, the important thing is that you don't overdo. Whoa, look at the time! I've got to get back to the store. Here, gather all of this up and take it to your family. I'll meet them some other time. Oh, and Sean, can you start this Saturday?"

"Sure!" Sean's expression showed all the enthusiasm he felt. Rigg put his hand out and Sean's smile nearly split his face as they shook.

Sean watched Rigg head out the door and move in a long-legged stride down the street. Watching until Rigg was out of sight, he bolted out the door to find his sisters, the bundle of food in his arms.

"You really got a job?" Kate asked around a mouthful of cheese. Sean laughed. It wasn't like his sister to be unladylike, but he knew how hungry she was.

"I start Saturday."

"That's wonderful. What's Mr. Riggs like?"

"He likes to be called Rigg."

"You don't call him Rigg, do you?"

"He told me to."

Kaitlin's brow furrowed with disapproval and Sean shrugged. Nothing more was said on the subject but it continued to bother Kate. She was a bit leery of such familiarity with strangers.

Of course, she told herself, *you agreed to have a meal at a home when you'd never before laid eyes on the man who'd asked you.* Kate took time right then to pray for God's protection and not to listen to fears that were groundless.

Some hours later the house was settled and clean but Kaitlin's battle with the stove had been a losing one. After an hour of trying she could not get it lit and Kaitlin looked like she'd been in a war. Her face was smudged with soot and her hair was coming out of its bun and hanging around her face. The front door stood open for air because she could only get one of the windows open. The family was sitting down to a cold supper.

Kate had found two cans of beans on the shelf which she'd opened and put into the one pot the house sported. There were no dishes or bowls. She'd discovered two spoons and a knife in a drawer. Sean had moved the table up to the bed to provide a third seat. Marcail sat on the bed and Sean and Kate took the chairs.

The pot was passed around and the girls shared one of the spoons. There had been a bit of bread left from lunch but that had been devoured earlier and now the pot was passed from person to person in an attempt to satisfy the appetites they'd built up cleaning the cabin.

This was the scene Rigg came upon. As the afternoon wore on, he realized he didn't know if Sean was coming back to the house for supper, so he'd gotten the address from Greg Carson to the schoolmarm's house. The picture before him was one he would not forget.

Rigg's frame, stealing all the light from the doorway, was the first indication to the Donovans that they were not alone. Sean immediately recognized their visitor and got up to welcome him.

"Hello, Rigg, come on in."

"Thanks, Sean. I don't want to take you from your supper." Rigg had spoken to Sean but he hadn't taken his eyes off Kaitlin. Kate was acutely aware of his scrutiny and equally aware of the way she must look. She came out of her chair in one graceful movement that belied what she was feeling inside, to meet their guest. Her hands fluttered around her face and hair before she forced them down to her sides.

For some reason she was overcome with uncharacteristic anger at being caught by this man in such disarray. Unfortunately, Rigg was to suffer the brunt of it. It didn't help that Sean was looking at his sister strangely as he made the introductions.

"Rigg, these are my sisters, Kaitlin and Marcail."

"Katie, this is Rigg."

"It's nice to meet you, Mr. Riggs. We certainly appreciate your letting Sean stay with you." She had to mentally stop herself from flying off into Hawaiian.

"It's my pleasure, and please call me Rigg."

"Thank you, Mr. Riggs, but I'm afraid I don't approve of such informality. Sean, Marcail, and I will call you Mr. Riggs." Kate knew she sounded like a terrible snob; even Marcail was staring at her.

Rigg was not the least bit offended, only fascinated by this beautiful, if disheveled, woman. That she wasn't normally so snippy was obvious in the looks her siblings were casting her. That she was exhausted and embarrassed would have been evident to a blind man. Rigg also knew that his staring at her didn't help in the least, but he was finding it hard to look away.

Rigg nodded in her direction and then turned to his housemate. "I just stopped Sean, to check on you. I'm headed home now and I'll see you when you get there." Rigg turned toward the door.

"Thanks, I'll see you later."

Rigg was not ten steps away from the house before he heard Sean's voice raised in anger. "Kaitlin, what is the matter with you?" It confirmed his suspicions about Kaitlin Donovan's actions of the last few minutes.

He had no desire to eavesdrop so he picked up his pace and was quickly out of earshot. Back at the house Kate was trying to make amends.

"I'm sorry, Sean."

"Why, Katie?" Sean's faced showed his keen disappointment. "I thought you would like him."

"I don't even know him." Kate began to feel defensive all over again as her mind pictured those beautiful gray eyes leveled so intently on her. "But you're right, my actions were inexcusable and I'm sorry."

Sean forgave her and helped her clean up the few dishes. He told his sisters he would see them in the morning and then took himself off to Rigg's.

$\mathscr{S}ixteen$

SEAN LET HIMSELF quietly into the house and when he would have gone straight into his room, Rigg hailed him from the kitchen. Sean came only as far as the doorway and leaned against it with his hands in his pockets.

"I'm sorry about the way my sister acted tonight. I don't know if it helps, but I've never seen her like that and I know she feels bad."

"Moving is hard work; I'm sure she's tired. How about some supper?" Rigg asked kindly and Sean was rather glad for the change in topics.

"I've eaten, thanks."

"I remember being hungry all the time at your age. Are you sure you wouldn't like something?" Rigg's mother had brought over a large kettle of stew and the aroma was floating from the stove straight in Sean's direction.

"Maybe I'll have a little."

Rigg turned away to hide his smile and filled two large bowls. There was fresh bread and butter on the table and a bowl of fruit. Rigg prayed for the food and the men ate without conversation for quite a spell.

"I normally stay out of my employees personal lives Sean, but would you mind if I asked you a question?"

"No, not at all." Sean seemed genuinely surprised and Rigg wondered at his first impression that all was not well for this new family in town.

"What brings you to Santa Rosa?"

"We saw the ad for the job and came, hoping that Kate would get it."

"Where are your folks?"

There was no mistaking the pain in those young eyes and Rigg waited in silence as Sean took a moment to answer.

"My mother just died and my father is in Hawaii."

Rigg didn't know what to say to this but he didn't have to speak because Sean was ready to talk. He came close to telling Rigg his entire life story—how he had been born and raised in Hawaii, when he'd made a decision for Christ, and right up to the trip to San Francisco, including his mother's death. He ended by explaining why his father left and that he was coming back soon.

"Did your aunt change her mind about your staying with her?"

Rigg considered the question a mild one in the light of all that Sean had shared but the change that came over the boy was startling. Tension radiated from Sean and again Rigg waited. He watched Sean move from the table to the window. He thought he might be calming down but when he turned from the window, his eyes showed deep anger and pain.

"I don't think it's right that a man forces a woman to do something against her will."

The hair stood straight up on the back of Rigg's neck over the image Sean's words created. One woman's face stood out in his mind, a woman he'd seen for so brief a time that it was unusual he would even remember her. But remember her he did, and he was surprised at the emotions flooding through him at the thought of someone hurting her. He worked at keeping his voice level.

"I certainly agree with you, Sean. Did you want to tell me about it?"

"I don't know. I don't want you to think badly of her. That is, I don't know why you would but it's just been so hard here. No one in Hawaii ever looked at my sister the way they look at her here. She told me that she even had to wear her cloak all the time on the ship because the sailors stared at her. And then our cousin grabbed her and . . ."

Sean could not go on, but then, he didn't need to. The picture was now quite clear to Rigg as to why they were no longer living with their aunt. He didn't think it had gone as far as rape but then it didn't need to, evidently, to leave lifelong scars.

Rigg chose his next words carefully. "Sean, is your sister all right?"

"I think so. She hasn't talked about it so maybe it didn't bother her as much as it bothered me."

Rigg didn't believe that for an instant, but kept the thought to himself.

"I'm glad I came into the library when I did or I don't like to think what would have happened." Rigg knew great relief with those words but also realized that even though the worst didn't happen, this was very serious.

"Sean," he finally spoke. "Are you afraid that your cousin will show up here?"

"I've thought of that but no, I think he's a coward. He won't come here."

"Then I'll tell you what you probably already know. You've got to forgive this man." Sean clearly did not want to hear those words and he sat back down in his chair with a dejected thud.

"Don't be discouraged by my words, Sean. God can help you to that end. I believe that with all of my heart."

"I believe it too," Sean admitted quietly.

Rigg could see that he'd said enough. Silently he decided to look up some verses on forgiveness in his Bible and share them with Sean when the time was right. The life of Joseph came to mind, as recorded in Genesis in the Bible. Joseph was a man persecuted by his family and yet, when he was given the chance, he forgave them.

The men cleaned up the kitchen and Rigg, checking on Sean less than 15 minutes after he'd gone to bed, found him sound asleep.

One street away Kate wished for sleep. She'd confessed her actions to the Lord and knew that in the morning she had to make it right with Mr. Riggs.

Outside of that, the only reason sleep wouldn't come was because she was freezing. After sundown the temperature had plummeted. Now in bed with only the lightest of blankets to cover them, the only warm spot on her was where Marcail was snuggled up against her.

She felt Marcail shiver and pulled her a little closer. She sighed in the darkness. It looked like it was going to be a long night.

Seventeen

THE NEXT MORNING Rigg awoke with a start. With everything Sean had told him, he'd completely forgotten to ask about the Donovans' financial state. It had been greatly on his mind when he left that small house where he'd seen two people sharing a spoon and all three of them eating from the same pot.

The next thing Rigg thought of made him sit up and reach for his pants. Santa Rosa's nights were very cold and he hadn't noticed any blankets.

Rigg was glad to see Sean up when he walked into the kitchen from his own room. He came right to the point.

"Good morning, Sean. I wanted to ask you something last night and it completely slipped my mind. Do you and your sisters have enough money?"

Sean felt uncomfortable about the question, as though answering would be hinting that he wanted a higher salary from the mercantile.

"Well, Kate and I really haven't started to work yet. We'll be fine as soon as payday comes."

Rigg began making coffee and thought how nicely he'd evaded the question. But Rigg was not to be put off.

"What about right now, Sean? Do you have enough money for right now?"

"We have a little."

"How much?" Rigg asked and was thinking, *When you break your rule about other people's business Rigg, you break it good.*

Sean could see that he wanted an answer but still he hesitated. Rigg's chest, just as tan as his face, became the focal point of Sean's unseeing stare as he tried to think of what to say. Rigg was silent for a full minute.

His hand moved over the hair on his chest and he smiled. "Sean, buddy, what are you staring at?" The amusement in Rigg's voice brought Sean's attention back and Rigg tried another tactic.

"Do you know how much money you have, or does Kaitlin keep track?"

"I know."

"Is it enough to get you through until one of you is paid?"

"No sir." The voice was quiet and resigned.

Rigg nodded. "What I'd like you to do, Sean, is run over and ask your sisters to come for breakfast. You don't need to rush them because I haven't even shaved. That way your sisters will have a meal and I'll have some time to think."

Rigg gave Sean no chance to question him as he put the coffee pot on the stove and returned to his bedroom.

Sean found Kate and Marcail still in bed. He let himself in quietly and called Katie's name.

"Oh, Sean, we must have overslept. It was cold in here last night."

It still is cold, Sean thought and knew they would have to do something to make this house a home.

"Hi, Sean," his little sister spoke up from her place beneath the covers.

"Hi, Marc. Listen you guys, Rigg sent me over to ask you to breakfast."

Kaitlin hesitated.

"He's got hot coffee."

The covers were whipped back and Kate jumped out of bed wearing both nightgowns and her robe. Sean stepped outside so they could dress.

Kate thought Rigg's house was beautiful. It was a rambling two-story painted a pale yellow. The front door put them directly in the living room, without an entry way or foyer. At the far end of the living room was an archway that showed a large dining table. Off the bottom of the stairs was a door and Sean led his family in to see his room. It was spacious with a full bed and dresser, a washstand and small table with a lamp.

Kate looked with some envy at the lamp. They didn't have one, so when the sun left the sky and darkness descended, Kate and Marcail were plunged into blackness. Kate had joked with her sister that they would have to wait for a full moon before they could move around without stubbing their toes.

When they again passed the stairway to exit Sean's room, he told them that the upstairs was closed because Rigg never used it. Back into the living room and through the dining area, Sean took them to the kitchen.

There were several doors leading off the kitchen, one was a pantry, one took you to the backyard and one led to Rigg's bedroom. But Kate didn't see any of these because her attention was centered on the man standing at the stove.

Rigg's pants were black and his shirt was snow white with a black string tie at the collar. His features were almost severe with his hawk-like gaze and aquiline nose. He would have been a little frightening if those beautiful gray eyes hadn't been so kind.

"Good morning," he greeted the newcomers. "Coffee?" He held the pot toward Kate.

"Please." Kaitlin wanted to say more but he had come very close to hand her a mug and after the way she'd acted the night before, she was embarrassed.

Rigg prayed for the meal and Kate knew in an instant that he was a believer. It took such a load off her mind about Sean staying in this house that she wanted to weep.

Rigg had made a large pot of cooked cereal and heated a half a loaf of bread in the oven. It wasn't fancy, but very filling. Sean put away enough cereal for three and even Marcail had seconds on cereal and toast. Kate's hard night was catching up to her and the only thing she wanted seconds on was coffee.

Rigg refilled their cups and let himself really look at Kate for the first time that morning. She was in the chair nearest his. Her black dresses must have been in the wash because she was in a dark blue skirt and white blouse that accented her dark hair and eyes to the extent that Rigg could not look away. Kaitlin's face began to warm under his regard and she knew she had to apologize now or she never would.

"Mr. Riggs, I'm very sorry about the way I acted last night when you were at our house. I hope you'll forgive me."

Rigg smiled in a way that made Kate's heart thunder. He wondered how long she'd rehearsed that in her mind before gaining the courage to voice it.

"It can't be easy moving and adjusting to a new job. I promise you, it's forgotten." Rigg reached out and touched Kate's hand where it lay on the table. It was a mistake. Kaitlin's face registered shock and Rigg pulled back swiftly, feeling almost as though his hand had been burned.

Rigg was a physical person, in the sense that he was not afraid to touch a person to help convey his feelings. He hugged his parents and brothers often and it wasn't at all unusual for him to touch the arm or shoulder of the person to whom he was speaking. Most people responded well to his warmth.

But, Rigg reminded himself as he began to clear the table, *it would be easy to give the wrong impression. And that is the last thing you want to do with Kaitlin Donovan.*

The first thing he wanted to do, and knew that he couldn't, was to touch her hand again to see if it was as soft and warm as he'd remembered.

Eighteen

NOT UNTIL THE dishes were ready to be washed did Rigg notice how quiet Marcail had been throughout the meal. His heart softened at the sight of her; she was so small and vulnerable. The family resemblance could be seen in all three of them but where Sean and Kaitlin had a very sturdy look about them, Marcail was almost frail in comparison. Rigg had a soft spot for children and set out to charm this little girl, whom he guessed to be maybe six or seven.

"Marcail," he asked her, "if I get you a chair would you dry these dishes for me?"

"Sure," was the congenial reply.

They worked for a time in silence as Sean and Kate continued to clear the table and straighten the chairs. Kate offered to wash but Rigg refused.

Sean disappeared and when Kaitlin had nothing else to do, she sat down at the table to read the newspaper. But it felt strange not to be working, and her eyes continued to move toward that broad back bent over the wash basin. Kate finally gave up on the paper and listened to the conversation between her sister and her host.

"Do you think you'll like having your sister for a teacher?" Rigg was unaware of how patronizing his voice sounded, thinking he was addressing a very young child.

"She was my teacher in Hawaii, too."

"How about Santa Rosa, do you think you'll like it here?"

"I think it's nice. I wish I had someone to play with. Do you have a little sister or brother?"

"I have three younger brothers but they're all a good deal older than you."

"We met your brother Jeff and your father. He stared at Katie an awful lot."

"My father?" Rigg's voice was surprised and Kate broke in from behind them in sharp Hawaiian.

"Marcail, you deliberately let him misunderstand you!" Whenever Marcail's siblings spoke to her in Hawaiian she always followed suit.

"Well, he thinks I'm just a baby because I'm small, and I'm not." Kate gave her a stern look but kept silent.

By now Rigg had turned from the countertop with dripping hands to stare at the females in his kitchen. Sean came in just then, and having heard the conversation, was smiling at the look on Rigg's face. He also took pity on the older man.

"You'll have to watch Katie, Rigg. She tends to forget that everyone here speaks English. And by the way, Marc is nine."

Rigg was still silent. Kate turned a disapproving eye on her brother for a moment and then glanced back at Rigg to find him studying her intently. He seemed to be waiting for something, so Kate apologized.

"No, don't be sorry. I'm just waiting for you to do that again."

Aunt Maureen had done this once so Katie was not totally taken aback. Of course, Kate was a good deal more comfortable with Aunt Maureen than she was with this man. She searched for something safe to say and after a moment spoke in soft Hawaiian.

"I'm not sure if I thanked you for breakfast and for letting Sean stay here, but please know that we're very grateful for both."

Rigg's eyes immediately swung to Sean who translated. A huge smile broke out on his face and he turned back to Kaitlin.

"You're welcome."

Kate answered with a smile of her own and Rigg went back to the dishes grinning like a fool. This woman captivated him, there was no getting around it. A plan had been forming in his mind and as soon as he was finished with the dishes, he was going to bring it up. As he worked he prayed for the right words and for the proper way to approach this young woman, this enigma, who'd landed so unexpectedly in his life and who was causing his heart to do the strangest things.

"So you see Miss Donovan, Sean is welcome here for as long as he needs, but for now I think you girls should go to my folks. We can make the announcement Sunday at church that you need blankets and dishes and things. I'm sure by next Sunday you'll have all you can use and more, and then you'll be able to move back to the little house."

"But Mr. Riggs, you haven't even checked with your mother. She's already having us for lunch on Sunday and we can't—"

"Yes you can. She would love to have you. What you can't do is go on freezing the nights away and sharing spoons. The other idea I have is that I'll move home until school is out and you can have this house." Kate stood up so fast she nearly fell.

"Put you out of your home? We couldn't possibly!"

Kaitlin moved away from the living room sofa where she'd been sitting with Rigg and began to pace the room. Putting some space between them helped her to think more clearly.

Didn't this man know he did crazy things to her insides? Kate was not what anyone would term petite, but while on the sofa next to him she'd felt like a little girl.

Rigg watched Kaitlin in silence, as did Sean and Marcail. When she stopped by Sean's chair and finally looked at Rigg, he spoke.

"You don't have to tell me right now what you want to do. But think about your options; there are advantages to both. Here you have everything you need but you'd have to relocate when school was out. The little house is more work because you're starting with nothing, but it might feel more like your own home and you won't have to move."

Kaitlin could only nod, understanding his logic but unable to fully concentrate with him in the room. She was silent for a long time.

"Have I upset you?" Rigg's voice was deep and soft, his gaze watchful.

"No," Kaitlin wished she didn't sound so breathless. "I'm just surprised and not sure what to do."

"I can understand that. You're more than welcome to stay here and discuss it." His look encompassed Sean and Marcail too. "I need to get to the store, it's nearly eight." He stood up and continued, "In fact, why don't you come down to the store today? It's the one you pass when you go from Burt Kemp's office to the schoolhouse. If I don't see you, well, just come up the stairs to my office."

Rigg left and Kaitlin felt like she'd been mowed down by a runaway stage. Marshall Riggs could be a bit high-handed, but he was also compassionate and kind. Kate couldn't believe he had actually suggested that they gather their things and land themselves at the door of the Taylor home.

Well, they had to do *something;* but what that something was to be, at the moment, she didn't have a clue.

Nineteen

KATE TOOK A TWO hour nap on Sean's bed and by ten-thirty she was refreshed and headed with her family to Riggs Mercantile. It was easy to find and one of the nicest stores she'd seen.

Large windows faced the street and the front doors were open wide. A variety of sights and smells assailed their senses, as they walked through those doors—leather goods, paint, bolts of new cloth and ready-to-wear clothing, the apple bin, a pickle barrel—Kaitlin tried to encompass everything.

Things were fairly quiet and Kaitlin took her time touring the aisles where high shelves were stocked with canned foods, sewing supplies, cooking utensils, pots, pans. And again it was almost too much to absorb.

Sean had gone off to find Rigg and Kate assumed Marcail was beside her as she looked at the wall full of beautiful bolts of cloth. Kaitlin was fingering a lovely blue gingham when a commotion started out front. She had no interest in the problem but it caused her to notice that Marcail was no longer at her side.

Looking calmly, then frantically down the aisles Kate then ran to the door. A crowd gathered and a woman's high voice, raised to almost an hysterical note, was accusing someone of stealing her handbag. Not until the woman shouted, "I tell you she stole it!" did Kate see Marcail being held by a man in uniform. Her heart leapt to her throat as she rushed on the scene.

"Where is it?"

Marcail's upper arm was being held by a short, square built man in a black law officer's uniform. The little girl's feet were nearly dangling due to the angle at which he was holding her. Every so often he gave her a shake.

"You'll tell us who you are right now. Where are you from? Who're your folks?" Each sentence was punctuated with a shake that was none too gentle and would have gone on all morning if Kaitlin's voice, so hurt and distressed, had not gained the attention of the officer.

"Please, you're hurting her."

The officer, who took his job very seriously, looked from this beautiful young woman addressing him to the child in his grip and slowly released her. Deep shame for his actions was bitter in his mouth as he realized that he'd let a screaming woman cloud his good judgment and that he had hurt a child. He had children of his own at home and he'd have challenged any man who dared to do what he'd just done.

When Marcail felt his hold loosen she ran into Kaitlin's embrace. Kate pulled her close and then watched in alarm as her little hand came up to cover her mouth. Rigg came on the scene just as Kate was holding Marcail at the edge of the boardwalk so she could vomit into the street.

There was some conversation behind Kate but the crowd had quieted. That a man had come forward, proclaiming Marcail's innocence and claiming to have witnessed the whole episode, Kate was not to know until later. She turned, seeing no one but the officer and spoke directly to him in a shaky voice.

"I'm sure there has been some mistake. My sister would never take something that didn't belong to her. I'm taking her home now."

His voice was a bit strained as he said, "That will be fine, miss."

Kate held her sister in her arms and was nearly to the house when Sean caught up to them. Once inside, she gave her sister a dipper of water and then held her as tears streamed silently down her face. She was so upset she vomited again.

"It's all right, Marc," Kate crooned softly, as she cleaned her up and tried not to be sick herself. "We know you didn't take anything. It was all a big misunderstanding."

Marcail sat trembling in Kate's lap when someone knocked at the door. Rigg and Jeff were standing there.

"Is she all right?" Rigg wanted to know straight away.

"I think so," Sean answered.

Jeff and Sean watched in silence as Rigg knelt down next to Kate's chair and spoke to Marcail. "You're kind of young to be in trouble with the law," he teased softly.

"I didn't take her purse," Marcail hiccuped.

"Of course you didn't. There was a man on the street who saw the whole thing, came forward and said it was some boy. Did you see a boy, Marcail?"

"No," she answered with some surprise.

"That's all right."

"Is that man going to come and take me away?" Her voice shook and Kate spoke with more confidence than she felt.

"I wouldn't let that happen, Marcail."

They talked a little longer and then Rigg took the frightened nine-year-old into his arms. Kate was a little surprised at how easily she went and watched her sister cling to the big man. He stood and spoke down to Kaitlin where she sat.

"I want you to collect your things now, Katie." Kaitlin was too surprised to notice his use of her name. "Sean can help you get everything, even your laundry. You and Marcail are going to my folks'."

"I really don't think it's your place, Mr. Riggs, to order us about." Kate had stood suddenly and was looking like an angry hen guarding her chicks. She opened her mouth to say more but Rigg, holding Marcail with one arm, reached with his free hand and cupped her chin.

"Marcail is so upset she's trembling in my arms." His eyes held hers with steely determination, his voice equally resolute. "And you're white as a sheet and look ready to collapse. Not to mention, there is absolutely nothing in this house to eat or to eat with. Now gather your things, Kaitlin, because you and Marcail *are* going to my folks'."

His hand slipped to her shoulder until the anger drained from her and she gave a small nod. Kaitlin still believed his actions were rude and overbearing but she was too tired to fight. Aside from all of that, Marcail was more upset than she'd ever been. And that was saying quite a bit in light of all they'd been through in the last several weeks.

Twenty

AT ANY OTHER time Kaitlin would have been thrilled with the farm on which the Taylors lived. The surrounding land was not owned by the family, but three of the acres, the house and barn were all theirs, including a small wooded area where the creek meandered through.

It was a wonderful place to grow up, as Rigg or any of the Taylor boys would have told her. There was always something to do as long as the sun was shining. Even on rainy days there was hide-and-seek in the barn, with its hayloft and numerous nooks and crannies.

Jeff had gone ahead to see his mother at the shipping office and explain to her all that had transpired at the mercantile. That he knew all that had occurred was by sheer accident. He'd simply come to give Rigg some papers at the time of the incident.

There had been no hesitation or irritation when Jeff told his mother that Rigg was bringing the schoolmarm and her sister to stay at her house. Normally she would have left it up to Rigg to settle this family, knowing she would meet them at supper, but when Jeff described what had happened with the woman's purse, she dropped what she was doing at the shipping office and had Jeff take her straight home.

Rigg plucked Marcail off the wagon seat as soon as he'd jumped down and then turned to reach for Kaitlin. Her cool fingertips in his palm made his heart race as he helped her from the wagon. Sean had taken his hat off when he saw a woman approaching and stood quietly, holding it in his hands.

All three of the children watched Rigg bend low to kiss his mother's cheek before he made the introductions.

"Mom, this is the Donovan family. Kaitlin is the new schoolteacher. Sean is going to work some evenings and Saturdays for me and this is Marcail. She's nine."

May Taylor beamed at the children before her. Her hair was liberally shot with gray and the corners of her eyes had many seams, as though smiling was something she did all the time. Her figure was full and the gray eyes, now smiling at everyone with warmth and welcome, were so much like Rigg's it was uncanny.

"It's so good to meet you, please come in." May was about to say more but she could see that Kate was hesitating.

"Mrs. Taylor, this is such short notice. Maybe we should come back another time."

May could see that Rigg was about to step in so she lightly touched his arm to stop him.

"I promise you, Kaitlin, it's wonderful to have you. God has blessed us with a large home and we've always opened it to anyone who might have a need."

Kate didn't know what to say to that and actually she didn't have time because Rigg was moving everyone toward the house. May watched her son with some surprise.

This was far from the first time Rigg had sent someone over to stay. In fact the last time a young woman needed a home there had been quite a misunderstanding. Rigg had spent a few uncomfortable hours explaining that his intentions had not been romantic. But this time, well, May was sure she'd never seen him so determined to see someone stay with his family.

They had gone in through the back door and Rigg was heading to the back stairway. You could also get upstairs from the living room but since they'd come in at the kitchen, it was the logical way to go.

Sean headed up first with Marcail behind him. May was given a chance to watch her son, as Kaitlin followed her brother and sister. She had given up believing that she would ever see that special look on Rigg's face. She wondered if he, as yet, could define what he was so obviously feeling. May's eyes swung to the spot that Kaitlin had just vacated on the stairs. Rigg was a wonderful man and May, not knowing her, couldn't help but wonder if Kaitlin Donovan was worthy of him.

Kate sank down into the bathtub with a heartfelt sigh. It didn't matter that it was Friday afternoon and not Saturday night; the water felt heavenly.

Kaitlin sat up and looked around the room. It was just off the kitchen and below the back stairway. By the size it had obviously been a storeroom, but someone had ingeniously converted it into a bathing chamber. The tub that Kate sat in was against one wall and from where she was facing she could see the stove on which the water had been heated. A huge pot was still in the middle of it, steam rising from the hot water within. There was a commode and even a bench to sit on. Kate relaxed a little deeper into the water and decided it was the most wonderful room she'd been in.

Coming downstairs from her bedroom, an hour later, Kaitlin was very self-conscious of her wet hair. But the only people in the kitchen were Sean, Marcail, May and a young man that Kate didn't remember seeing before, but thought he had to be Jeff's brother.

"Feeling better?" May wanted to know.

"Much. Thank you."

"Sit down here and have some lunch. Nathan, this is Miss Donovan, your new teacher."

"Hello."

"Hello, Nathan." Kaitlin smiled kindly and watched as Nate blushed to the roots of his hair. She took pity on him and turned her attention to the plate that May had set in front of her. Kate made short work of a slice of beef, potatoes, sliced carrots and a large helping of applesauce.

Marcail was sitting near her with a cookie in her hand and the other people in the room were talking about the farm. Kate, not wanting to embarrass her sister, spoke to her in soft Hawaiian.

"How are you doing?"

"I'm okay."

"If you want, I can fix you a bath. Believe me, it felt wonderful."

"That sounds nice." Tears came to the young girl's eyes. "Katie, I hate it when I get sick to my stomach."

"I know you do." Kate reached a hand over and stroked her sister's hair. "But I think your way might be easier, you know, just to get sick and get it over with. I hold things inside and then they bother me a lot longer."

Sean had heard part of the conversation and turned without thinking away from May and Nathan to ask his sister a question. The Taylors would have thought nothing of this at most times, but the Donovan children all continued to speak in a foreign tongue, completely forgetting they were not alone.

"Katie, did you have a chance to get writing materials to write to Father?"

"No. I've got to take care of that soon. Actually Sean, tomorrow is your first day at the mercantile, maybe you could just take our dollar and see what you could find. Maybe Mr. Riggs can show you what he's got. We could write tomorrow night and mail it before school Monday."

"Okay. How are you doing Marc?"

"I'm fine. I'm going to have a bath and change my dress."

"You don't smell very good," Sean teased her with a smile. Marcail had just made a face at him when they became aware of their audience.

"Mrs. Taylor," Kaitlin was red-faced and ashamed as she quickly changed to English. "You're going to think that we haven't any manners at all. Please forgive us."

"You've done nothing that needs forgiving. I only hope if something is wrong you'll let me help."

"I was just asking Marcail how she's doing and if she wanted to clean up."

"We also need to write letters," Sean added, sensing a genuine offer of help from this woman.

"No problem. Why don't you come with me, Marcail, and we'll see about your bath. And Nate can show you where you can write your letters."

May certainly had a gift for hospitality. She was so matter-of-fact about everything that no one was given a chance to feel like an intruder.

May disappeared with her littlest house guest and Nate showed Kate and Sean to a desk that sat in the huge living room. Kate took a seat and tried to gather her damp hair to lay it over one shoulder. She certainly hoped the rest of the young men in her class wouldn't stare at her as Nathan was doing.

But in a few moments she was oblivious to everything but the paper in front of her. She was rather glad she wasn't going to be there to see her father's face when he found out why they'd left San Francisco.

Twenty-One

MAY'S HEART, WHICH had begun to melt when she met Marcail Donovan, was now a puddle in her soul. She was the sweetest little girl she'd ever known. May guessed that her bone structure was very small by looking at her face, but when Marcail undressed, bone structure was the last thing on May's mind.

There was a bruise, gigantic and already black, nearly covering the little girl's upper arm and spreading across her shoulder. May saw that she was safely in the tub and then had to force herself to walk to find Kaitlin. She found her at the desk.

"Kaitlin?" Kate looked up from her letter in expectation.

"Marcail has a huge bruise on her arm. I've never seen one so bad. Maybe I should send for the doctor?"

Kate came to her feet. "I'll look at it, Mrs. Taylor, but I think you should know that Marc bruises easily and that man, well he had quite a hold on her."

May could only nod her head as she visualized Marcail being hurt. "Would you like me to stay here?" she asked when Kate rose from the desk.

"No, you can come. You could have talked with Marcail about it, she's had them before."

The women walked through the kitchen and Kate knocked gently before entering.

"Hi, Marc. How's it going?"

"Fine."

"You gave Mrs. Taylor a scare."

Marcail looked at the older woman in surprise.

"Your bruise," Katie informed her.

"Oh, it doesn't hurt unless I press on it."

May looked instantly relieved and said with a small laugh that she had been ready to get a doctor. The smile left Marcail's face and she nearly came out of the tub. Kate didn't miss her panic.

"It's all right, Marc. She was only kidding."

"I'm sorry, Honey," May said quickly. "I wouldn't do anything without asking Kaitlin first."

The little girl nodded and looked uncertainly at her sister. Kaitlin smiled. She figured something like this might happen remembering the hard time Marcail had with Dr. Weston in San Francisco.

Kate took her leave a minute later in order to finish her letter. Sean and Nate had been in the living room the entire time she was writing and Kate was pleased at how well they were getting along. Sean needed a friend.

"How's the letter coming, Katie?" her brother wanted to know as she came back into the room.

"Pretty good. Why don't you read what I've got?"

Brother and sister traded chairs and Kate found herself once again scrutinized. She tried to ignore it.

"How old are you, Nathan?"

"Fifteen."

"You're tall for 15. Do you like school?"

"Most of the time."

Kate grinned. "That was an honest answer."

Nathan grinned back, turning only a little bit red this time. Sean spoke from the desk. "I added a little to what you have Katie. Are you going to tell Father about what happened today?"

"I don't know. I don't want him to worry about us because I really do think Marc's going to be fine. What do you think?"

"I'd leave it out," Sean said and then thought, *Father is going to be upset enough when he finds out why we left San Francisco.*

The rest of the afternoon sailed by in a lazy fashion. Kate had gone to her bedroom for a while to read her Bible and then joined everyone else in the living room where they were poring over the newspapers. She was so intent on the article she was reading, that she nearly tore the page in two when Rigg startled her by sitting down on the sofa very close to her.

Twenty-Two

"YOU LOOK BETTER." Rigg's voice was soft and deep and his eyes were intent on her face from his close position beside her. Kate didn't want to know what he meant by better, so she lowered the paper only to find the room empty.

"Where did everyone go?" Once again Kate's voice was breathless and she wanted to pinch herself.

"They're all in the kitchen; supper's almost ready."

"Oh, my!" Kaitlin exclaimed, "I should be helping." Kate quickly folded the paper and hurried to rise but Rigg caught her arm and kept her in her seat.

"Do you always do the proper thing?" He sounded amused.

"I don't know what you're talking about."

"Don't you?" There was still a smile lurking behind his eyes.

"Mr. Riggs, if you have something to say to me, I'd appreciate you simply coming out with it."

"I do have a capacity for making you furious, don't I Katie?" He had changed the subject in midstream and Kate was having a hard time keeping up with him. She decided not to try.

"If you'll excuse me, Mr. Riggs, I think I'll go into the kitchen to see if your mother needs help."

"She doesn't," Rigg said as Kate tried to rise and found he'd sat on her skirt. That he was equally aware of his position became clear as soon as Kaitlin turned her head to look at him. His look was almost angelic.

They sat looking at one another for a long moment. Kate could see that Rigg was enjoying himself and even though she was frustrated with him, she had to admit that he was the best looking man she'd ever seen.

Very softly, so Rigg had to lean to hear her, Kaitlin said, "You, Mr. Riggs, are a flirt."

Kate was very satisfied with the look of shock that registered on his face. In the next instant she had tugged her skirt free and was headed toward the kitchen.

"And heavenly Father, we thank you for the family that has come into our midst. Please bless them and take care of them, and use all of us to Your good pleasure. In Christ's name I pray, Amen."

Mr. Taylor's prayer worked wonders at calming Kaitlin's nerves. It was a classical farm kitchen, the kind she'd only read about, with a very large table and plenty of chairs. Her place was between Jeff and Sean and unfortunately, across the table was Rigg. He was very solicitous to Marcail who was beside him, holding the bowls of food and anything else she needed to serve herself. But even though his attention was centered on the youngest Donovan, he was more than able to make Kate feel self-conscious with his intense glances and warm smile.

That Rigg was the only one staring at Kate, was thanks to Bill Taylor. He had arrived at the house with Jeff and Gil not too long before Rigg, only to find Nate staring at Kate as though he'd never seen a woman before. That his older boys followed suit the moment they arrived, had been a source of great disturbance to him. Kaitlin, intent upon her reading, did not see the father of these young men signal them out of the room to inform each of them that they knew better and to please not do anything to make their guest uncomfortable.

Sean had been an unwilling observer to the whole episode and every time he looked at Kaitlin he wanted to cry. His heart ached for Hawaii where Katie was just Katie and not the object of every man's attention, or where Marcail was not shaken and bruised by some man who never saw her steal a thing.

Maybe he was too young to understand all the ways between men and women but he told himself he was not ever going to stare at a woman as though she had two heads, or blush and stutter when spoken to, no matter how pretty she might be. After all, a person's true beauty was beneath their skin. He might be only 14 but Sean Donovan believed that with all of his heart.

Rigg watched the emotions scoot across Sean's face and wondered what was tormenting his housemate. Surprised at how paternal he felt toward this young man, he hoped they'd have a chance to talk on the way home.

Rigg would have been really surprised to know that he was the only person Sean didn't mind looking at his sister.

After supper Kaitlin volunteered to do the dishes and Jeff helped her. They worked quietly for a time and then began to talk like old friends.

"Is it normal to have your purse snatched here in Santa Rosa? I mean, it was right in front of all those people and well, I realize this is a big city, but I'm surprised."

"We certainly have our fair share of crime but please don't let today paint a black picture for you. Santa Rosa is really very nice. It's growing fast so there is a lot of opportunity here. There's also a good deal of community involvement if you're so inclined.

"Nearly everyone in my parents' generation is very concerned for the education of our generation and it shows in the schools they build and the teachers they hire."

"Was I just complimented, Jeff?" Kate smiled at him.

"No, I'm just trying to butter you up so you'll help me dry some of these dishes when you're done washing."

"Not a chance. If you remember, I gave you a choice."

"So much for chivalry. Next time I'll rope Rigg into doing this.

"Why did you do that?" Jeff said after a second.

"Do what?" Kate asked cautiously.

"Stiffen up at the sound of Rigg's name."

Kaitlin didn't answer and when she held out a dish to Jeff he just stood looking at her without reaching for it. Kate sighed and looked him in the eye.

"Jeff, I know you love your brother but the truth is, he's very high-handed and a flirt to boot."

"*Rigg!*" Jeff was astounded.

"I shouldn't have said that Jeffrey. Please forgive me. He's your brother, I had no right to speak ill of him."

"Kaitlin," Jeff's voice was serious now. "I don't know how to say this, but Rigg isn't what you think." He stopped when her look told him she was more than a little skeptical.

"I mean it, Kaitlin. Rigg is the nicest guy on earth and very much a man of God."

"I can see why you think that way, Jeff, but you did ask me and I thought I could be honest with you."

"You can be. I'm sorry I jumped on you." He dried a few more plates and then asked carefully, "Why do you think he's high-handed?"

"You were standing there, Jeff, when he ordered me to get my things and come here. Please don't get me wrong. I really appreciate your family, but your brother could have been a little more diplomatic.

"He also thinks I'm a rag doll. Telling me he'll put me in the wagon and nearly sitting on me when he thinks I'll move from the sofa.

"Whether or not you want to hear this Jeff, the fact of the matter is, your brother is very accustomed to getting his own way."

Jeff could think of nothing to say. All that Kate had mentioned was true. Also true, was the fact that Rigg wasn't normally like this. In fact Jeff had never seen him so forceful or intent on a person. Kaitlin would never believe it, but Rigg was a little shy around the women at church.

When Jeff said nothing Kate was overridden with guilt. "I don't know what came over me just now, Jeff. But I'm so sorry to talk to you that way. Rigg has been very kind to Sean and I know he wants to help us. I hope you won't hold this against me."

"It's all right, Kate, really." He gave her his most engaging grin and they finished the dishes over a discussion about the church the Taylors attended.

Twenty-Three

KAITLIN AND JEFF had been seated in the living room with Bill and May for just a few minutes when Rigg, right on down to Marcail, came in from outside where they'd been seeing the barn.

Marcail sat next to her sister on the sofa and Rigg took a place on Marcail's open side.

"You should see the barn Katie!" her sister told her with enthusiasm. "They have four horses but one is old and tired; they use him for burning hay."

Kaitlin laughed along with everyone else at Marcail's description. "I think what they meant was that he's too old to work so all he does is eat. That's a hay burner."

"I think Loni's brother must be a hay burner, but he's not that old."

The Taylors watched as Sean and Kaitlin exploded with laughter. The brother Marcail spoke of was 19 and very lazy. They had never heard it put that way before but it was very fitting.

When the laughter subsided, Gilbert asked a question of Marcail. "Who is Loni?"

"She's my best friend in Hawaii."

"And how old is her brother?"

Marcail looked at Kate.

"Nineteen I think," Kate supplied the expected answer.

"May tells me you sometimes talk to each other in—"

"Hawaiian." Sean supplied for Bill, who was speaking to Katie.

"Right, Hawaiian. Maybe you could give us a sample." His voice was coaxing and Kate could see he was fascinated, but before she could answer him, Sean spoke up.

"There's a sure way to get Katie to speak Hawaiian—just get her mad or upset." Kaitlin threw her brother a warning look but kept silent.

"I know some songs in Hawaiian," Marcail said.

"Please sing one for us, Marcail," May entreated from her chair near the fireplace.

In the next instant the room was filled with the sweet, high sound of Marcail's singing voice. Kaitlin and Sean joined her after a moment and the family with whom they were staying was transfixed at the beautiful words of the song and the perfect blend of the Donovan voices.

No one spoke after the song ended and when the silence continued, Kate told them in a soft voice what the words meant.

"Praise to our God who does save us, Praise to our God who is Lord. He is the Maker and Creator, we know Him better from His word. Praise Jehovah, Praise the Master, praise the Father and Holy Ghost, Praise with all your heart and being, here on earth and heavenly host."

May had tears in her eyes and Bill leaned forward in his chair. "Kaitlin, would you consider singing that for our church on Sunday?"

Kaitlin couldn't have been more surprised if he'd thrown something at her.

"Bill," May spoke softly. "Maybe you should give them a chance to get to know the people at the church. I mean, it doesn't have to be this Sunday, does it?"

The relieved look on Kaitlin's face told Bill his wife's insight had been correct.

"No, but you will do it sometime?"

Kate glanced at Sean who was looking as surprised as she was. "I think we could do that. If your church is very big though, I'm not sure our voices will carry."

"It's a small building." Rigg spoke for the first time. He realized how content he was just being in the same room with Kate. But something was on his mind and he thought that now might be the time to bring it up.

"Will you do me a favor, Marcail?"

"What is it?"

"Well," Rigg put an arm around her and brought her gently to his side. She snuggled against him and he continued. "If it wouldn't bother you, will you please tell me what happened in front of the store today?"

Rigg's peripheral vision told him Kaitlin had started at his request. He raised his arm from around Marcail and reached to touch Kate's shoulder. "You don't have to tell me if you don't want to, Marcail."

"No, I'll tell you. I can't remember everything, but Katie was taking a long time in the store and I heard a dog bark, so I went out front to see where it was. I don't remember seeing that lady or that man but then she started to yell and he grabbed me."

"You mean the officer?"

"Yes."

"And you didn't see anyone run away with the purse?"

"No."

"Okay, Marcail, go ahead."

"Well, he grabbed my arm and it hurt and the lady kept yelling and then he shook me and that hurt and then Katie was there and I got sick. That's all I remember."

Kaitlin bolted from the couch then, and Rigg, after giving Marcail a quick squeeze, went after her. May came over to sit with Marcail and Sean stood, gripped with indecision. He looked toward the kitchen where Kate had run and then back to Mr. Taylor, who smiled at Sean in understanding.

"Don't feel like you have to go out, Sean. I think Rigg will handle it." Sean looked relieved and sat back down. Jeff reached for the checkerboard and all in the living room were glad for something else to do besides wonder what was going on outside with Rigg and Kaitlin.

Kate had hit the backyard at a run and was almost to the barn before Rigg caught her. Running in front of her, he turned and gently brought her to a halt. Rigg watched as she buried her face in her hands and cried. He hesitated for a moment before tenderly pulling her into his embrace. Kate came without resistance and sobbed against him.

"I don't know how to be a mother to Marcail." Her voice was broken. "It's my fault she got hurt; I should have kept better track of her."

Rigg let her cry against him. He could tell that Marcail's story was hurting her and he'd honestly never given a single thought as to how *she* might react. His attention, when he asked the question, had been solely on Marcail. By the time he realized his mistake, he could only pray that his hand on Kaitlin's shoulder would be enough. But it hadn't been.

"We need our Father, doesn't God know that? I feel like we've been deserted." Her voice was growing calmer but Rigg still held her in the protective circle of his arms.

"Marcail doesn't blame you, Katie, and neither does anyone else. You're very good with Marcail and I can see she thinks the world of you. What happened today could have happened just as easily *with* your father here. Did you think about that? Marcail was in the wrong place at the wrong time. It's no one's fault."

Kate was still for a moment and then pushed free from Rigg's arms and stepped away from him as though she'd been burned. Rigg watched with some frustration as she smoothed her hair and looked up at him, once again the prim and proper schoolteacher.

"Thank you for coming out with me. I'm feeling better now."

"Are you really? Well, quite frankly I'm surprised since you seem afraid to face that this really happened. You seem hesitant to let yourself feel anything."

Kate had never been so hurt or surprised. He was angry with her and she didn't know why. Her voice told him how hurt she was.

"I've obviously done something to anger you, Mr. Riggs, and I'm sorry. You've been very kind and if I've offended you in some way, I'd be glad to apologize and make it right with you." Kate watched him rake an agitated hand through his hair. When he spoke, his voice was soft in the gathering darkness.

"I'm not angry Kate, but if you should find that you're still upset about what happened today, you can talk to me anytime."

"Thank you," Kaitlin said simply, and tried not to think of how nice his arms had felt and how solid his chest had been. *You've no business throwing yourself at the man that way, Kaitlin Donovan, you really should be ashamed of yourself,* Kate said to herself as Rigg walked her back to the house.

If Rigg could have read her mind he'd have been furious.

Marcail was waiting inside and the anxious look on her face made Kaitlin feel ashamed of the way she'd run from the room.

"Are you all right, Katie?"

"I'm fine Marc," Kate answered and hugged her.

The little girl held on to her sister for a long time, wanting to comfort as well as *be* comforted. When they finally crawled into bed that night, Kate's tears came on afresh when Marcail reached for her hand and whispered that everything was going to be fine.

Twenty-Four

"Is KATIE OKAY?"

"I think so," Rigg answered Sean as they rode home in his wagon. "She blames herself for today and I really wish she wouldn't."

"Did she tell you that?"

"Yes she did, and even though I told her it wasn't true, I don't think I convinced her."

"Maybe I'll talk to her." Sean's voice was thoughtful and Rigg was further convinced that he was a special young man who cared deeply for his family. Rigg didn't feel that the time was right to ask Sean if anything was bothering him, so he just prayed, asking God to show him the right time.

The next day Sean was awake at a very early hour, brimming with excitement. This was his first day at work. Rigg came into the kitchen to find his young housemate sitting quietly at the table waiting for him.

"How did you sleep?" Rigg's voice was still gravelly from sleep and Sean smiled.

"Fine. How about you?"

"Good. I thought a lot about your sister and I need to ask you something Sean." Rigg took a place at the table and leaned toward Sean, his face serious. "If I were to show interest in Kaitlin, I mean romantically, how would you feel about that?"

Sean answered without hesitation, "I'd think it was okay just as long as Katie did."

Rigg nodded. "She doesn't seem to like me too well, does she?"

Sean found this question embarrassing and didn't know how to answer.

"Don't feel bad, Sean. She's already told me she thinks I'm a flirt."

"Are you?" The words were so quiet that Rigg, who had moved to the stove to start the coffee, almost missed them. He turned to find Sean's heart in his eyes.

"No, Sean, I'm not. I'm not sure if I'm coming or going where your sister is concerned, but this is no game I'm playing." Rigg watched Sean's face to see if he understood and was satisfied with what he saw.

"Come on over here, Sean," he said after a moment. "I'll show you how to make coffee."

Rigg walked with Sean to the post office. After Sean posted his letter, Rigg sent him to the mercantile to ask for Joe Crawford, the man with whom he'd be working that day. As he watched Sean head eagerly down the street, Rigg grinned, remembering his first day at the mercantile. He then headed to the shipping office.

His father was in early as he expected. Heading into his office, Rigg shut the door behind him. He took the chair across the desk and looked at the man who'd been a father to him for most of his years.

"Did you see Kaitlin before you left the house today?"

"No, the only one up was your mother."

Rigg nodded and sat quietly.

"I've never believed in love-at-first-sight, Dad, but something is going on. I can't get that girl out of my mind."

Rigg spoke the words sincerely and Bill's heart ached for him. It had been over 23 years since he'd met May but he remembered very well how it felt to watch and wait and wonder. He also remembered befriending a little boy who, if he hadn't responded to him as well as he had, might have kept him from winning May's heart.

But the boy was not three any longer. He was a man, 26 years old—a godly man of faith, with his own business; a man with hopes and desires of his own.

"Do you remember the first time we met, Rigg?"

"My third birthday."

"Yep. I bought you a toy soldier."

"I still have it."

Bill didn't say anything else; he didn't need to. Rigg smiled at what he was thinking.

"Are you trying to tell me that you went through me to get to my mother?"

Bill grinned back at him. "Not exactly, but the fact that you liked me certainly helped my case."

"So you think I should go on as I am, being there for Sean and Marcail, but not pushing Katie?"

"Well, I certainly don't think you should propose—at least not until she relaxes around you."

"I have no one to blame for the way she treats me but myself."

Bill's brows rose in question but Rigg didn't elaborate.

"I guess I'd better get to work."

"All right. Are you coming to the house for supper?"

"I'm planning on it. Are you going to make that announcement about household items for Kaitlin to the congregation in the morning?"

"I'm planning on it."

Father and son grinned at one another and then Bill told Rigg he was praying for him.

"Thanks, Dad, thanks a lot."

Kate lay in the bed next to Marcail and knew she should get up. She'd had a very restful night that started almost as soon as her head hit the pillow. Heavy sleeper that she was, she'd been gone until morning.

She had wanted to pray and tell God everything she felt about Marshall Riggs, but her body had had other plans. Now this morning she couldn't think beyond getting ready for school on Monday.

Her mother had always planned for the following week on Saturday, and so that was what Katie planned to do today. She had brought the classification register that Mr. Carson had given her. She said a quick prayer of thanks for Sean's job, and asked protection for him as he worked, and then slipped out of bed. The thought of getting dressed made Kaitlin stop and pray again.

She pleaded with God about wisdom over wearing black for a year. It was easier for Sean, who simply put a black band around the sleeve of his jacket. But for her and Marcail, it was a major wardrobe change. Marcail had one black dress and Kaitlin had two. She also had a dark skirt but only a white blouse to go with it. The rest of her things, as well as Marcail's, were lightweight summer prints.

She stood for a moment, and then the decision was made. She would wear whatever was clean on any given day and sew the lace collars and cuffs back on her black dresses.

After having a huge breakfast and exploring the farm with Marcail, Kaitlin was back in the house to work on her lessons. A thrill shot through her as she opened the register and began to read, careful to pass over the percentages of the students. She didn't want any preconceived notions when she walked in that door Monday. Each student would have a fair chance to prove himself.

Kate's eyes skimmed over the names. There were eight students listed under "Upper Form," ranging from age 12 to 17. In the "Middle Form" there were nine children listed, their ages were 10 to 13. At the bottom of the page was the listing for "Primary Form," the ages being from 7 to 11 and totaling eight children. Adding Sean and Marcail to this list would give her 27 students.

Kaitlin went on to study the recitation program, taking note of who recited forenoon and afternoon. In an honest attempt to know as much as possible, she read every word of the teachers' reports. She wanted to ease the transition for this class.

Around mid-morning May came back from the shipping office where she and Marcail had gone with the boys. They didn't disturb Kate in the living room, but it wasn't very long before the unmistakable aroma of freshly-baked cookies floated in to assail her senses.

She worked a bit longer, taking notes on a pad May had given her, and then went to the kitchen.

"How's it going Kaitlin?" her hostess wanted to know.

"It's going well. I'm all set and really looking forward to meeting the class."

"They're normally a good group of kids. I think they'll like you." May smiled. "If they get out of line you can always speak to them in Hawaiian and shock them all speechless."

Kate and Marcail both laughed at the idea.

The remainder of the day was spent doing laundry and baking, and waiting for Sean to come and tell them about his first day at work.

Twenty-Five

JOE CRAWFORD, THE man Sean was to find and work with, turned out to be just a few years older than he was. Rigg had told Joe, who was moving out of town, that he'd found a replacement who would be starting Saturday. Joe was to train Sean and, from the look on the older boy's face, he was none too happy about it. Sean, sensing a hostility in Joe that frightened him a little, tried not to ask too many questions. He found himself wishing that Rigg had offered to show him the ropes.

"That doesn't go there." The words were surly and Sean stopped where he stood, holding a heavy crate. "I told you those go over there! Are you stupid or something?"

Sean said nothing, thinking that, indeed, maybe he was stupid. Never had he made so many mistakes. He couldn't seem to do anything to please his co-worker, but he stayed with it and tried to ignore the angry looks that came his way all morning.

"How is it going, boys?"

Sean watched Joe become a different person in the boss' presence.

"Just fine, Rigg. Sean's a great worker, real smart." That the words were sickeningly sweet, Rigg didn't seem to notice.

"Good. I knew you'd do fine, Sean. Why don't we break for lunch?"

Joe grabbed his lunch pail, went through the store and down the street. Sean stood in indecision—he didn't have any lunch. Rigg was checking the papers he held in his hand so Sean slipped quietly out the back door and walked up the street.

Not able to stop the flood of tears that began to flow, he sped up until he found himself on a quiet street. Ahead of him was the schoolhouse. He moved toward it and collapsed on the steps; his tears intensifying until he was nearly sobbing.

Rigg, who had not been far behind him when he left the store, had followed him when he hadn't gone straight home. From a distance he watched Sean bring his knees up and lay his face on top of them. His arms were over his head, as though trying to protect himself from a blow.

Rigg turned, cut across a few yards and dashed up the back steps of his house. In a matter of minutes he was out again, bearing a loaf of bread, three apples, half a pie and a jug of cider. He whistled as he approached the school steps, giving Sean a chance to know of his presence.

Sean wiped his face on his sleeve when he heard the sound and watched his employer approach.

"How about some lunch?"

"Thanks, but I'm not too hungry."

"Mind if I join you?"

"No."

Rigg sat down on the second step, bit into an apple, and watched Sean's profile. "How do you think you'll like the job?"

Sean continued to stare off in the distance as he answered. "It might take me a while to remember everything. I'll understand if you feel you need to get someone else."

Rigg had never known Joe to be sneaky or underhanded in any way, but Sean's words made him wonder what kind of morning Joe had given him. Joe was not very happy that his family was moving back East. Maybe it had been asking too much to have him train his successor.

"This pie is good, sure you won't have any?"

"I'm not a baby, Rigg. If you need to tell me that I'm fired, please just say it," Sean said with quiet dignity.

"You really have worked yourself into a mood, haven't you?" Sean looked at Rigg for the first time. "I think you're doing fine Sean, and if you're going to do a good job this afternoon, you need some lunch." Sean caught the apple Rigg tossed him and ate it in silence. He didn't refuse any more of the food that was passed his way and, miraculously, found that he did feel better.

Rigg hoped that Sean would share what was on his mind but he didn't. They returned to the mercantile. Sean prayed and took a deep breath before going into the back room. Joe was already there and his first words were a criticism.

"You're late."

Sean said nothing.

"Get that crate unloaded and out with the rest of the sugar—on the shelf where I showed you."

The next hour passed in a similar fashion. Sean said little and Joe reprimanded him nonstop. Sean stopped at one point and simply stared at Joe.

"I said, put that sack over there!"

For the first time he didn't move to do Joe's bidding.

"What's your problem, Donovan?"

"I was about to ask you the same thing."

"Don't give me any trouble Donovan, or I'll clean the floor with you."

"I don't think you will." Sean's voice had gone very soft and, unbeknownst to himself, his look menacing. "Now, I'm going to do my job here for the rest of the afternoon as best as I can. If you've got some problem with that, then you're welcome to go get Rigg. If he's not happy with the job I'm doing then he can fire me, but I want you off my back."

The older boy hesitated. He could see that he'd clearly pushed too far. Silently both boys went back to work. The atmosphere was no more friendly, but at least Sean was able to work in a semblance of peace.

"Okay, Sean, here's your pay."

"Already?"

"Every Saturday night at closing."

"Thanks," Sean breathed as he fingered the coins in his hand. Rigg watched him and suddenly felt choked up. To see the boy, you'd think it was a fortune. But this was his first job and Rigg remembered again how good it felt to be paid for a day of work.

Rigg found himself just as choked up when Sean went straight to his sister and turned the money over to her, once they'd reached the Taylor farm. Bill and the boys were not yet back from the shipping office so Kaitlin, Sean and Marcail had a chance to talk with only Rigg and May present.

"How did it go?" Kaitlin wanted to know.

"Fine. I made mistakes but I think I'm getting the idea."

"Good. I prayed for you."

"Yeah, Sean, we remembered you at lunch."

"Thanks Marc."

"Did you have enough to mail the letter?"

"Yes. I put the change with my wages."

"Good. I wrote to Aunt Maureen today. We can mail that letter Monday."

Kate's attention turned from her brother and, even though Rigg was talking to his mother, she had the feeling he'd been watching her.

He had invaded her thoughts at the most unusual times today. When she'd been working with May and Marcail she had actually wondered what type of cookies he liked. She had stopped just short of asking May and humiliating herself.

The Taylor men piled in shortly after that, and Kaitlin helped May put supper on the table. She decided that feeding this many men was a costly chore. After the prayer Kate watched a huge platter of fried chicken disappear, along with mashed potatoes, green beans, fried biscuits, turnip greens and two pitchers of milk. She had no room for the apple cake that was served with coffee after the meal.

May asked Gil, Nate and Sean to help with the dishes and everyone else moved to the living room. Rigg sat on the sofa and Kate took a chair across from him. She watched as he beckoned to Marcail with one finger. Marcail snuggled into the sofa next to him as if she'd been doing it all her life. Kate was amazed.

"I brought you something."

"You did?" The little girl's eyes grew wide as she watched Rigg draw a snow-white hair ribbon from his pocket.

"This is for me?" Marcail almost squealed, and Kate smiled.

"Yes ma'am," Rigg told her, and watched as she looked to Kaitlin for approval. Kate smiled at her and she hugged the thin strip to herself.

"Thank you, Mr. Riggs."

"You're welcome, Marcail," he answered and then turned a challenging eye on Kate. "I'd like it if you called me Rigg. What do you think about that?"

"That's fine with me, if it's fine with Katie. Is it fine with you Katie?"

Bill had to hold his paper a little higher to hide his smile. Rigg was digging himself into a hole, and fast.

Kate opened her mouth to say something but closed it. That Rigg was testing her was almost more than she could take. He had backed her into a corner and she came out fighting like a teacher. She ended up addressing Rigg as though he were a child.

"I am not used to having my authority questioned, Mr. Riggs. I feel I've already compromised my conviction by allowing Sean to call you by your nickname. As I told you before, Marcail and I will call you Mr.

Riggs, and if my sister continues to question me, I might have to punish her."

You asked for that Rigg and you know it, were the convicted man's thoughts. What he said out loud was, "I'm sorry Marcail. Your sister is right; I shouldn't have done that."

"That's all right. I still like my ribbon."

Marcail was off the sofa in the next instant and headed toward the kitchen to show her gift to May. Kate looked over to see Jeff taking it all in as though watching players on a stage. He grinned at her and Kaitlin couldn't take anymore. She mumbled something about needing air and went out the front door.

"Shame on you Rigg," Bill spoke softly when the door had latched. "Why do you bait the girl?"

"I wish I knew," was the tired reply. "I guess I'd better go apologize." Rigg stood up and Jeff couldn't keep from staring at him. He'd never seen his brother like this.

"Why don't you let me go?"

When Rigg's features washed with relief, Jeff followed Kaitlin to the front yard.

She had walked toward the copse of trees that stood tall and green on the south edge of the Taylors' land. Jeff caught up with her just as she reached the creek's edge. His feet broke a fallen branch and Kate started.

"Oh, Jeff, I didn't hear you approach."

Jeff could see that he'd frightened her.

"Sorry to scare you."

"I'm all right."

"It's pretty out here isn't it?"

"Yes, it is. Very nice," Kate agreed.

"It was a great place to grow up. We had such fun in this water. Not every kid lives on a creek. Most people don't know what they're missing."

"You're certainly right, growing up by the water is a little piece of heaven on earth." Her voice was so wistful that Jeff stared at her face and knew she was thinking of Hawaii. He glanced down at the stream of water at their feet and began to laugh.

"What's so funny?" Kate wanted to know.

"Oh, just me with my little creek, telling you how wonderful living by the water is, when you probably swim like a fish!"

Katie laughed with him then. "I do swim, that's true. And your creek is not the Pacific, but it's still beautiful. Actually, it isn't really Hawaii that I miss, but the people, and knowing that my father is there without my mother."

It didn't matter that Jeff had no words to say to that; he knew none were needed. After a moment, they talked of little things and then Jeff mentioned Rigg.

"He certainly enjoys seeing me upset," Kate said, feeling flustered all over again.

"He enjoys you period."

"Sure he does."

"I'm serious, Kate. You can't believe how many women have been interested in Rigg over the years—more than I can count. He's just never met anyone that he felt he could get serious about."

Kate was looking at Jeff with such amusement that he stopped. "What?"

"Don't you see, Jeff? I am evidently one of the few girls who hasn't thrown herself at his feet and he can't stand it. Somehow that makes me a challenge and it hasn't taken me more than a few meetings with Mr. Riggs to know that he loves a challenge."

"Oh, Kaitlin!" Jeff sounded truly distressed but all Kate did was chuckle. "That's utter nonsense. You can't really believe that?"

"And why shouldn't I? You were sitting in the living room tonight—enjoying everything that went on, I might add. You can see for yourself that I'm just a plaything to your brother." Kate's voice suddenly became very serious. "And if I can speak honestly with you, Jeff, it's the last thing I need. I have feelings and no one likes to be laughed at. My world has come apart at the seams in the last few months. I find myself playing mother to my brother and sister and falling way short of the mark.

"So your brother's actions are just insult on top of injury. You tell me he's a man of God. Well, you can understand why I have a hard time believing that. He brings my sister a present and then challenges my authority right in front of her. If he's such a man of God Jeff, can you tell me why he treats me like that?"

"Jeff can't tell you, but I can."

Kaitlin spun around so quickly that her dress flared. Rigg stood less than ten feet away and Kate knew the time for confrontation had come.

Twenty-Six

"I HEARD A LITTLE bit of what you said to Jeff, Kaitlin. Is there anything you want to add?"

Kate couldn't say anything. She wasn't really embarrassed, just wary of confrontations. She also knew that the thoughts she shared with Jeff should have been said directly to Rigg. Jeff tactfully left them alone, and the silence between them lengthened.

The sun was beginning to set; it was a little darker beneath the trees and the breeze had picked up, sending a cool draught against Kaitlin's bare arms. Crossing her arms in an effort to keep warm, she finally broke the silence.

"Even though it's hard for me to face you, I'm rather glad you came out when you did, or I would probably never have talked to you.

"I meant what I said to Jeff but I should have said it all to you. You couldn't be more kind to Sean and Marcail, but you treat me so strangely. One minute you're tender and the next you're ordering me about as though you owned me.

"I'm not a child, but neither do I have the wisdom of the ages, and I just don't know how to handle this underlying animosity between us. In another circumstance I would just keep my distance from you, but with Sean living with you and me staying temporarily with your folks, that's impossible.

"If I've done something or am doing something that is offensive to you, I'd be more than happy to clear the air. And I know I've said a lot but there's just one more thing. I hope that anything between us won't affect the way you treat Sean and Marcail. I know they like you and it's so hard to be here without our folks, I just hope that—"

"Kaitlin." Her name, softly spoken in his deep voice, brought her to a halt. He came close enough to touch her, but did not.

"I've been so wrong in the way I've treated you. Will you please forgive me?"

"Yes," she said immediately.

"I'll try not to be so bossy with you, but please understand that you and Marcail gave me quite a scare on Friday. In my mind, leaving you at that house would have been like leaving an infant in the snow. You had no money or food or even sufficient blankets for the bed. I was afraid you would refuse me so I ordered instead of asked.

"As for the other—the teasing—all I can say is that I'm not myself with you. We got off to such a bad start. I mean, right away you didn't like me, and I wanted you to like me. And not just because I let your brother live with me. Am I making any sense to you?"

Kate nodded. "Thank you for telling me. It clears up a lot. So much has happened to bruise my emotions, and my mind never goes more than an hour all day without wondering where my Father is and if he's all right.

"What I need right now is friendship. I hope you'll understand when I tell you I can't handle anything more than that."

"I do understand, and I hope you'll consider me a friend."

"Thank you." The words were whispered sweetly and Rigg watched as tears puddled in those huge brown eyes. Rigg mentally shook his head. He'd just offered to be her friend. *Husband* was much closer to what he had in mind.

Desperately wanting to be the man Kaitlin needed him to be, his heart cried out to God for help. He knew as he looked into those eyes that if it took forever, he was going to try to win this woman's heart. If he had to stuff his own emotions into a place deep within himself in order to do that, that was exactly what he would do.

"It's getting pretty cool out here. Why don't we go in?"

"Okay. Mr. Riggs, may I ask you something?"

"Anything." Rigg wondered how long he could endure being addressed as Mr. Riggs.

"Did Sean really do all right today? Were you pleased with the job he did, or did he get into some sort of trouble?"

"I think he did fine. Why do you ask?"

"He said something he's never said before, something about making mistakes and getting the hang of it. I've never known Sean to have a bit of trouble catching on to anything."

"The young man training him might have given him a hard time this morning. I checked on them several times this afternoon and even though they're not best friends, I think they both know where the other one stands."

Kate thanked him for explaining. She strongly suspected that Sean was putting pressure on himself to work and be the man in the family. She shared her belief with Rigg, feeling for the first time like she could really talk to him.

"And what bothers me the most is his schooling. Sean will be 15 in December. I don't want him getting it into his head to quit school and try to support us."

"I have noticed that he's very conscious of your welfare. I think he'll stay in school and it'll help that Nate is there. But I will keep my ears open and if he says anything to me about wanting more hours before summer, I'll discourage it."

"Thank you. I feel better knowing that you think he should stay in school. Some people think that once you're a teen, you've had all the school you need."

"Well, Santa Rosa certainly has some of those but I'm not one of them."

They were back at the house, Rigg walking with Kaitlin, his heart swelling with joy. She was talking to him like he was a friend. When he'd felt a very definite burden to join her and Jeff, he'd fought it. At the moment he couldn't have been more thrilled that he'd listened to his heart.

All the lamps were lit in the living room when Kate and Rigg stepped through the front door and Bill immediately told Kate they wanted to talk with her. Sean, Nate and Gil were taking their baths. Marcail was sharing Jeff's chair and they'd been reading a story until Kate came in. Kaitlin sat down on the sofa expectantly.

"I've been planning to make an announcement tomorrow morning to the congregation about your house needing supplies. I don't mind doing that, and I can promise you there will be a great response. But Kate, we'd really like you to stay here. That is, we want you to know that you're welcome here for as long as you'd like. We even have an extra wagon and Nate can drive all of you to school each day."

Smiling at the sincere faces of the people before her, Kate's voice told of her gratitude.

"You've been so kind to let us stay with you and I praise God for you. If I knew a little better when Father would be back, I might take you up on it. But I think Marcail and I should go back to the little house as soon as possible."

The Taylors respected Kate's wishes even though their disappointment was evident.

"I'll go ahead with the announcement as planned. May is ready to write down the things you need."

So Kate began, with Marcail and even Rigg adding to the list. Dishes, silverware, hollow-ware, pots, bedding, extra chairs; the list seemed endless.

"Now," Bill said when the list looked complete, "how are you set financially?"

"I got paid today." Sean had come down the stairs in time to hear the question.

"When will you be paid Kaitlin?" Rigg wanted to know.

"At the end of April. Since I don't start teaching until March twenty-seventh, that is, since the month is almost over, Mr. Carson figured he would just put those five days in March onto my April check."

"Has Mr. Carson been handling everything for you, Kaitlin?"

"Yes, he's been very nice."

Bill's face gave no hint of his thoughts, and even though Rigg and Jeff were exchanging a look, Kate didn't notice. None of them were exactly sure when Burt Kemp had left town. They were all hoping that Kate had worked with him, but it looked as if Greg Carson had been on the job.

"So Mr. Carson found the house for you?"

"Right."

"And how about your wages. Did Mr. Carson set that too?" Bill's voice was as smooth as honey, and Kate answered calmly with no signs of offense over such a personal question.

"Yes, he took care of that. You see, I don't have a teaching certificate and he felt it would be better to give me a little lower wage to compensate for that. The rent at the house takes a major part of my salary but we'll get by with Sean working." She smiled with genuine confidence at Sean.

"Kaitlin, would you think me intruding to ask how much your monthly salary is?"

"Oh no, I don't mind. Actually it's kind of nice to have someone to talk to because we've never lived on our own before." Kate went on to answer Bill's question and noticed that the adults in the room became very still. When Rigg spoke his voice was tender.

"Katie, your wages aren't a *little* lower than the usual teacher's pay, they're less than half of what they should be."

"Oh," was all she could say and she looked over at Marcail who had begun to gnaw on her lip, a sure sign of distress.

"Well," Kate said carefully—and maybe a little too cheerfully—her eyes on her sister, "you said the people at the church would be helping us with the things we need, so we just need to buy food."

"Did you have *any* money when you came into town?" Jeff asked kindly. No one had missed the focus of Kaitlin's gaze and all were sensitive to the feeling of security this little girl needed.

"Yes, our aunt gave us some. We used it to pay our rent," Sean supplied.

"And your rent is paid through April?" Bill probed.

"We had enough to pay for about three weeks, so half of April."

"And what had you planned to do then?"

"We've been praying about that."

Bill leaned forward in his chair to make sure he had Kate's attention. "Then will you consider me an answer to those prayers? I would like to give you some money and I would also like to speak with Greg. He needs to be made aware of your financial situation."

"Oh, I don't know. I mean, I don't want him to think I came running to you and complained."

"I can explain everything to him Monday morning, that is, if you agree."

Kate looked over at Sean who told her yes with the move of his head and the look on his face.

"All right Mr. Taylor. And thank you for everything."

"The pleasure is all ours Kaitlin, believe me." These were the first words May had spoken during this talk and Kaitlin would have run from the room if she could have read her hostess' mind. May had just thanked God for a Christian wife for Rigg.

Twenty-Seven

THE NEXT MORNING found the Donovans and Taylors in church together. A wonderful peace stole over Kaitlin as she entered the house of the Lord; she'd really missed being part of a formal service. Not all of the songs were familiar but they were still beautiful to her ears.

There was one embarrassing moment before the sermon, when Bill made his announcement and asked Kate, Sean and Marcail to stand and be introduced. He told everyone of their situation and that he'd start the list around. He concluded by saying that if anyone had anything to give, it could be brought to the shipping office.

When the sermon began Kate immediately liked Pastor Keller. His eyes were kind and his voice was filled with conviction as he preached from the Word. The morning's text was John 3:14 and 15. He began by reading the verses.

" 'And as Moses lifted up the serpent in the wilderness, even so must the Son of man be lifted up: that whosoever believeth in him should not perish, but have eternal life.'

"Let's pray. Our Father in heaven we believe You are the one true God who is able to teach us all things from Your Word. We ask now, Lord, that You open our hearts to Your truth and convicting spirit. In Christ's name I pray, Amen.

"If you remember back in the book of Numbers, God instructed Moses to make a bronze serpent and raise it high on a pole. The Word says that any and all who looked at the bronze snake would be healed from the poisonous bites of the snakes tormenting them.

"What I want you to think on this morning, is that those who had to look at the snake were condemned to physical death—they'd already been bitten by a poisonous snake. God proved His mercy toward the children of Israel, for when those bitten looked toward the serpent for healing, they were indeed healed.

"Each one of us has also been bitten and received a more dangerous poison: spiritual sin. That old serpent Satan bit all of mankind when he deceived Eve and Adam sinned. We must realize that we are now condemned to spiritual death, and each person must act for himself. In other words, it is *our* personal responsibility to look to Christ, who was lifted up on the cross, as our healing from the spiritual poison of sin, and to understand that without that salvation, we will know spiritual death.

"This is far from the first time I've spoken to you about eternity. Sometimes God burdens my heart so heavily that I know I can't go another Sunday without explaining this precious truth to you. Coming forward will not save you, believing there is a God will not save you. You must be born again by believing in the only begotten Son of God.

"Please, friends, if there is any doubt in your mind, come to me or any one of our elders. We want to see you know Christ in a most personal way."

Pastor Keller closed in prayer and then Kaitlin noticed a man go down front. Pastor Keller embraced him before they sat in the front pew and began to talk.

After the service many greeted the Donovans and told how they had prayed for a schoolteacher. It was a good beginning for everyone. After walking back to the wagon, Kate told Rigg how much she liked the church.

"What?" Rigg asked absently. He had the hardest time concentrating when she looked like she did today. Her dress was a pale pink with every imaginable color of flower swirled all over it. The white lace at her collar against the tanned skin of her face and dark hair was not merely distracting; it was hypnotizing.

"I was just saying that everyone was very nice. I even met some of my students."

"Good."

Kate finally picked up on his distracted attitude and became concerned. "Are you feeling well?"

"Rigg's just having a little heart trouble," Jeff answered as he approached and dropped an arm around Kaitlin's shoulders, as though he were a long lost brother. Kate could see he was having one on her.

"Honestly, Jeff, you'd think I was a hitching post the way you lean on me!" But she wasn't really upset.

Rigg, who had been sending warning glances to his smiling, unrepentant brother, reached up and tossed Jeff's arm away. Rigg's hands went to Kaitlin's waist and he swung her up onto the wagon seat. Jeff looked at the way Katie spread her skirts on half of the seat and then to Rigg who still stood by the wagon.

"I suppose this means I'll be riding in the back?"

"Maybe you can find something back there to lean on," Rigg replied dryly, and Kate laughed.

Jeff grumbled good-naturedly as he boarded and when the wagon pulled away he leaned against the seat back, his legs stretched out before him. He waved at friends and made a few observations as Rigg drove away.

"Hey, Katie, have you still got that black dress I first saw you in at the schoolhouse?"

"Yes."

"Maybe you should wear it to church."

"What is he talking about?" Kate inquired of Rigg.

"I think my brother, in his own klutzy way, is trying to tell you that you were turning heads as we left church today."

Kate turned in her seat to look back at the churchyard and then to Rigg to see if he'd been serious. He had.

"That's ridiculous," Kate said primly. "My skin is much too dark to be considered attractive and my jaw is too square." Kaitlin scowled as both men shouted with laughter.

"I don't know what's so funny about that. Honestly, if any of my class is witnessing this display I'll have my hands full in the morning." But even with her stern words they continued to laugh.

"I wish I'd ridden with your folks," she finally said, and Jeff and Rigg made an attempt to control themselves.

"Are you really mad?" Jeff coaxed from the back.

"Furious!" Kaitlin said, as she smiled and waved at Marcail in the wagon in front of them. Rigg glanced back at Jeff and the two men exchanged a smile.

"And don't you be grinning at each other as though you were actually pleased with yourselves. It's too bad you're too big for a trip to the woodshed. Oh, Mr. Riggs," Kate reached and touched his sleeve, all teasing gone. "Who is that little boy?"

"That's Joey Parker. You'll meet him tomorrow."

"How old is he?"

"I think about nine or ten."

"Why did you ask, Kate?" Jeff piped up.

"I noticed him outside the church but didn't see him come in. I'm glad I'll meet him tomorrow." Kaitlin watched as the boy walked across an open field. His clothes were filthy and his hair hung limply in his eyes. Kate wanted to hold him in her arms forever.

Both Rigg and Jeff refrained from telling Kate what a rough home life Joey hailed from. At the same time, they were both very happy for Joey that a new schoolteacher had been found and he could, at least for a few hours every day, be away from his father.

Twenty-Eight

"THANK YOU, MISTER . . . ?"

"Hodges."

"Thank you, Mr. Hodges."

"You're welcome, Miss Donovan. You don't know my wife, but when she gets a bee in her bonnet, well, let's just say there's no stopping her."

It was late afternoon on Sunday and one of the men from the church had just arrived at the Taylors' with a wagonload of household goods.

"I know this is quite a pile, so I thought if you'd come along with me and show me your house, I'd deliver it right to your door."

Kaitlin seemed to be in a state of shock so Rigg answered for her. "Why don't we both go with you?" He helped a silent Kaitlin into the wagon and they both listened as Mr. Hodges explained why his wife had sent so much.

"Both of our mothers are dead and you always want to hold on to some memories, but we've an attic full of things that haven't been touched in years. The wife couldn't see any point of them sitting there any longer. You might want to air the quilts, but I think you'll find them in good shape."

"I'm sure they'll all be wonderful." Kate's quiet reply caused Mr. Hodges to look over at her on the seat beside him, and then to Rigg. He spoke, after his attention was once again on the road, a smile in his voice.

"I don't suppose there'd be any point in writing to my unmarried son and reminding him that he hasn't visited in a spell."

"No point, Mr. Hodges, no point at all," Rigg answered without hesitation and didn't bother to look at Kate's face—he knew she was smiling. That knowledge made him the happiest he'd been since he met her.

Once at the house the three of them worked steadily to unload the wagon. Quilts, sheets, pillows, pots, a pack of needles and thread, a few dishes and bowls, two vases, a rug beater, cookie cutters and a cookie sheet—Kaitlin wondered when it would stop. When they were finished she flopped into a chair and stared at the pile on the bed and table.

"Mr. Hodges, please thank your wife for me and tell her I'll look forward to meeting her next Sunday. Thank you for bringing us to the house but you don't need to stay. I'll walk back to the Taylors'."

"I'll stay too," Rigg spoke up, and smiled at the twinkle that came into Mr. Hodges eyes. He walked him to the wagon where Hodges gave Rigg another box, and told him briefly who it was from.

Rigg left the front door open and set the box on a chair. He then went about forcing open the windows while Kate tried to sort through the piles. All the kitchen supplies went on the shelves near the stove, and then Kaitlin, who found everything fresh smelling, made the bed with the sheets and all three quilts.

While Kate organized, Rigg attacked the stove. He had it going in about 15 minutes, much to Kaitlin's delight. Rigg showed her a few tricks and then Kate noticed the box he'd brought in earlier.

"What's this?"

"Mr. Hodges said it was for Marcail. It's from his brother-in-law, who just happens to be the officer who was in front of the mercantile."

Kate looked surprised and then very pleased. Rigg watched as she lifted the lid. "Oh, my," she breathed as she brought forth a lovely doll dressed in an adorable sailor suit. It stood about 18 inches tall and the white suit, including the hat, was completely trimmed in plaid. The shoes and socks were removable and when Kate lay the doll back and brought it forward, the eyes opened and closed.

"Look at these." Rigg brought Kate's attention away from the doll to show her what he'd found in the top part of the box, wrapped in paper. He held up one of six tiny teacups and saucers. There was a matching teapot, sugar bowl and creamer. They were intricate in detail and all appeared to be hand painted.

"She's going to love these."

"I imagine she will. Are you ready to start back? Mom has probably started supper."

"Sure. Let me repack this doll and I'll leave it here for Marcail. She likes surprises."

They walked quietly for the first half of their journey. It was a comfortable silence, and Kate was newly impressed at how gentlemanly Rigg was. He had reached to take her arm several times when the path dipped and once, when a large dog came at them with teeth bared, Kate stepped instinctively close to Rigg, who slid his arm around her. He shooed the dog away with a shout and they were again on their way.

"I've been meaning to tell you, Katie, that I'm sorry about the loss of your mother."

"Thank you. I take it that Sean shared with you?"

"He was in a mood to talk our first night. I imagine it must be hard to have your father leave so soon afterward."

"In some ways his leaving is harder than Mother's death. I know where Mother is, but with Father I can only guess. On our trip over, both he and Sean were so seasick they could hardly stand up. Mother and I took turns tending them but this trip, with him being all alone—" she didn't finish and Rigg knew she was fighting tears.

"If everything went according to plan, is he in Hawaii now?" Kate saw the question for what it was, a chance to collect herself.

"Yes, he should be there. His plans when he left were to gather our belongings and return to San Francisco as soon as he could. If things really go smoothly, I'm not sure he'll get the letter. It could arrive after he's started back."

"You really miss it don't you?"

"Not Hawaii so much as the people."

"Is there someone special waiting for you in Hawaii?" Rigg didn't know where the question came from and wished he could take it back. "I'm sorry, Katie, that's none of my business."

"Don't be sorry, I don't mind." Kate hesitated and Rigg's heart sank. "There was a young man there, still is, who wanted to marry me, but I just never felt that strongly about him. He would make some girl a wonderful husband but I couldn't possibly marry because it was convenient. Could you? I mean, I'd have to be in love."

"I couldn't agree more. Even though it hurts the person whose feelings are stronger, it would be even worse to pretend you felt something that you didn't." Kate looked askance at Rigg as they talked.

"What did I say?"

"Nothing, you're just different than I first thought."

"I hope you mean it's an improvement."

"Now that would be telling." Kaitlin grinned impishly and side-stepped when he reached for her. The farm was in sight and she took off at a run. Rigg caught her in 20 strides and they walked toward the house.

"You didn't really think to outrun me did you?" he asked, with his hand on her arm. She laughed up at him and he desperately wanted to hold her, but must have kept his thoughts hidden because Kate was still smiling at him as if they were old friends.

"You'd have never caught Marcail. She's like lightning."

"I'll keep that in mind when she starts to follow in the sassy foot-steps of her sister."

"Sassy!" Kate was outraged and it was Rigg's turn to run. They charged in the back door to find May grinning at them and telling them to wash for supper.

Twenty-Nine

IF KATE LOOKED in the mirror once, she looked 15 times, to see if she'd picked the right outfit for the first day of school. She was downstairs an hour before it was time to leave, pacing and biting her nails. May watched her push her breakfast around and reached out and touched her arm.

"Is there anything I can do to help you relax?"

"Thank you, Mrs. Taylor. I guess I'm just excited. I've never taught without my mother. It feels strange."

"You'll do fine. And I'm sure if your mother knew, she would be very proud." Kaitlin's eyes grew moist and May bent over the table to give her a hug.

Nathan drove the wagon when they finally left the farm. Marcail sat in the back holding the lunch tin that May had packed for everyone. They stopped quickly at the post office to mail the letter to Aunt Maureen and then were, of course, the first to arrive at the schoolhouse. As soon as Kate saw the building her nervousness disappeared. Nate noticed the change in her and smiled. She was in her element now and everything was going to be fine.

"Katie, where will I sit?"

"I don't know. Maybe Nathan can help us with that." They were inside now, and Kaitlin opened the windows next to her desk for some fresh air. The morning was nippy but she didn't even consider lighting the potbellied stove; she had always loved crisp morning air.

"Nathan, will you give me a quick rundown of where everyone sat when Mr. Wright was here?"

"Sure. I sit back here with the older kids. The Middle Form kids are around in here and the little ones are in the front rows. Mr. Wright kept these two desks empty for any of the older kids who stepped out of line. He sometimes used the bench in front for the same thing." Nathan blushed suddenly as if he'd said too much, but Kate thanked him and gave him her warmest smile.

"Nate, were there any empty desks?"

Taking a moment to reflect, Nate thought he could remember three. He pointed them out. One was in the middle of the room.

"Well, Marc, it looks as if you might be right here. Why don't you sit down and if no one claims that desk it's all yours."

The little girl look thrilled and Nathan smiled at her. When he'd first heard that the schoolteacher and her sister were coming to live with them he nearly groaned. But Miss Donovan hadn't turned out to be anything like he thought she would be. She was really nice and sometimes even looked a little lost. He figured that was probably why Rigg was acting so funny. Rigg was a sucker for lost kittens and such.

Nate looked over at Marcail and smiled again. She was nice, too. Not at all a brat like he'd expected. It was like suddenly getting a sweet little sister.

A moment later Sean walked into the school. Kate asked him about his night and he said it was fine. She told him that she and Marcail were going to be moving back to the little house the next day. This was news to everyone, but she very logically explained that they had just about everything they needed, plus the money Mr. Taylor had given them for food, and that she felt it was time.

Kaitlin was at the door when the children began to arrive. Asking all of them their names, she introduced herself and then instructed them to sit in the desks they'd previously occupied.

No one was late and Kate noted with satisfaction that all but one of the children were smiling at her. Joey Parker was the exception. His hair was a mess and his clothes filthy. But for some reason, and Kate believed it was of the Lord, she was more drawn to him than any of the other children she'd just met.

The front rows were filled with little girls, mostly ages 7 and 8. Kaitlin looked with compassion at Drew Barsness who was 8 and the only boy in the Primary Form.

She'd checked her register that morning to find out Joey's age. He was 11 and was seated behind Marcail. Sean was a little further forward than he should have been. The desk at the front of his row was empty so Kate had Sean stand while everyone shifted down. His new seat put him where he was supposed to be.

"I've written my name on the blackboard for anyone who can't remember it. It's Miss Donovan. You have probably noticed that there are also two new students in school today. Their names are Sean and Marcail Donovan and I hope you'll make them feel welcome." There was no need to have them stand—it was obvious to all who they were.

"How many of you know where Hawaii is?" Kate surprised most of them with the sudden question.

Nate, Sean and Marcail's hand went up but Kate called on an older girl in the back row. She answered correctly and the class was given the chance to ask many questions concerning their teacher's background. It took most of the morning.

Kaitlin told them they could go to lunch a little early and then had to bite her lip to keep from laughing when one very snippy ten-year-old informed her that it was too early.

"Thank you for telling me, Leslie, but I'm hungry right now. If you're not, you could always eat your lunch during our afternoon break." She winked at the little girl and caught Sean grinning like a fool.

It was very clear to Kate that most of the students had never considered that a *teacher* would experience hunger. So no one would see her smile, she turned to the board to write the time she expected them back in their seats.

After lunch she again caught the students off guard when she called on them, one-by-one, to come forward and tell what they did during the four weeks without school. She had listened to six reports when Leslie raised her hand almost frantically.

"Yes Leslie?"

"You're writing something down. Are we being graded on this Miss Donovan?"

A few of the children snickered over this question and the class was given its first taste of disapproval from Miss Donovan. She stood up and scanned the room with a very stern look. No words were necessary, but a few of the older children looked to Sean, who was giving Kaitlin his complete attention. His look told them she would brook no disobedience.

"No, Leslie, you're not." She spoke when she was sure her point had been taken. "I'm just trying to get to know all of you a little bit better."

The little girl looked so relieved that Kate knew she had an overachiever on her hands. She smiled at her before calling the next name, which happened to be Joey Parker.

Joey, Kaitlin noted, refused to look at the class. His hands were stuffed in his pockets and his head was bowed. When, after a full minute he didn't speak, she coaxed him in a quiet voice.

"You don't need to give us a long speech, Joey, just share a few things that you did."

"I went to the creek and I hung around town." The boy beat a hasty retreat back to his desk and Kate thanked him as if he'd just shared great pearls of wisdom.

The remainder of the day flew by and Kate could hardly believe it when it was time to dismiss. Nathan and Sean went to get the wagon; Marcail tagged along. Katie was straightening her desk when Rigg walked in.

"How did it go?"

"Oh, it was wonderful. They're all so bright and respectful and fun. I mean we really had *fun.*"

Rigg had never heard her talk so fast and was sure she didn't know that she was switching back and forth between Hawaiian and English so fast that he could hardly keep up.

"I take it you had a good day?" Rigg smiled and asked when she came to a breathless halt. He noticed her eyes were sparkling with joy and knew it was a waste of time to hope that the intensity of his feelings for her would abate.

At that moment he found it hard to believe he'd only known her a few days. It just didn't seem possible that he wanted to marry this girl who was almost a stranger. But he did want to marry her and maybe, just maybe, Lord willing, someday he'd be able to tell her.

"Oh, I wanted to tell you," Kate spoke, as though she'd just thought of it, "Marcail and I are going to move back to the little house tomorrow. I'm ready, and if we have to do without a few things, well, I don't think we'll notice."

"You know there's no hurry. My folks meant it when they said you were welcome for as long as you like." Rigg said the words almost casually but he was feeling a little alarmed. Knowing that Kate was at his folks gave him tremendous security. Not that he expected something to happen, it was just nice to know.

"Oh, I know we could stay and it's comforting to know that they're there for us, but my mind's made up. And to tell you the truth," she whispered, "I'm a little excited about it. It's such a cute little place, and we'll be much closer to the school and to Sean."

Rigg's smile was very tender. She was flying high all right, and was probably going to be exhausted later. He didn't stay any longer but told her that he'd invited himself out to supper at the folks and that he'd see her then.

Thirty

Rigg's prediction had certainly been correct. Kaitlin fell sound asleep in the Taylors' living room after supper. Nathan and Marcail had already gone to bed and it was a few moments before anyone noticed that Kate was no longer with them.

She was in the rocking chair by the fire and Rigg moved toward her when her body began to slide forward. Surprised that she didn't wake up when he touched her, Rigg looked to his mother for help.

"Lift her gently Rigg, and I'll follow you upstairs."

Rigg did as he was told and expected Kate to wake at any moment, disoriented and upset over being carried to bed. But it didn't happen.

Marcail was already asleep and Rigg gently laid Kate on the bed. He exited quickly, and his mother shut the door behind him. He and Sean, who needed to get to bed himself, waited until May returned to the living room before getting ready to leave.

"Did she ever wake up?" Rigg asked.

"No." Sean supplied the answer before May could. "Once they're asleep, my sisters are like dead people. I've actually held Marcail upside down before and had her sleep through the whole thing." Everyone laughed at the idea. Sean and Rigg bid everyone good night and left a few minutes later.

Kate woke in the morning, refreshed and ready for the day. She didn't remember falling asleep in the living room so she made no inquiries about how she got to bed or why she'd slept in her shift and not her nightgown.

They left a little earlier for school that day so that Kate and Marcail could take their things back to the house. Nate helped them unload and then they were off to the schoolhouse.

The day flew by in a flurry of lessons and recitations. Kate promised a special treat the next day if the weather was nice. Right after school, Kate, Marcail and Sean, who was scheduled to work at the mercantile, made their way in that direction to buy supplies for their house.

Rigg was upstairs in his office which resembled a large indoor balcony at the back of the store. A railing allowed him to look out on the entire floor. When sitting at his desk, which was situated in such a way that he had a clear view of the front door, he could, if he were looking, see anyone who entered the mercantile.

To his great delight he saw Kaitlin enter. He was able to watch her for a time without leaving his desk. When she stepped out of his view, he moved to the railing. He noticed that Marcail stayed right at her side. Kate appeared to be a careful shopper and it was a few minutes before Marcail looked up and noticed him. She waved and Rigg signaled to her to come up.

He watched and listened as Marcail asked, and then as Kate looked up at him. She looked very surprised to see him standing above her, but she gave Marcail permission to go and Rigg watched her skip toward the stairs.

He was back at his desk when she arrived, so she took a chair near him and they talked like old friends.

"Did Kaitlin show you my doll?"

"Yes, she did. She's very pretty."

"I think so, too. Want to know what I named her?"

"Yes."

"Charity."

"That's very pretty."

"Aunt Maureen has dolls. Nice ones. She has a big house too, in San Francisco. We don't live with her anymore because cousin Percy tried to hug Katie." The nine-year-old's hand went to her mouth in surprise. "I'm not suppose to tell anyone that."

"It's all right Marcail, I won't tell anyone." Rigg was thankful that he already knew the details.

"What are you doing?" Marcail was looking at the books in front of Rigg now.

"These are the accounts for the store. I have to keep records of all the things I sell." His voice told her he didn't enjoy it.

"This line is wrong."

"What!" Marcail had been looking at the figures as he spoke and now Rigg spun the book around to check. He was flabbergasted when he rechecked the column to see that she was right.

"Katie's even better in math than me. You should ask her to do it."

"Ask me to do what?" Kate had come quietly up the stairs behind Rigg, carrying her supplies.

"Mr. Riggs doesn't like to do math and I told him you were good."

"Thank you, Marcail. Did you also tell him how well *you* do in math?"

"It's my best subject," Marcail told him. "Are we going now, Katie?"

"Yes. I have everything we need. We just need to pay."

"Where are the rest of your things?" Rigg finally said.

"This is everything."

Rigg didn't say anything but Kate could see his mind working.

"You don't think this will be enough?"

"I think the supplies will last you a while, but you're going to get a little tired of biscuits, beans and rice." Rigg noted that all of the items were the most inexpensive he carried.

He also noticed that Kate was looking very unsure of herself. He was torn between a desire to hold her and another to scold her for leaving the protective care of his parents. He opted for something in between.

"Come here, Katie, and sit down." She obeyed him without question. He watched her put her few selections on the edge of his desk. Reaching for paper and a pencil he asked Kate how much money she had. She drew her coin purse from her pocket and emptied it on the desk. Rigg did a quick count and then began to write.

4 packages Garland-brand yeast cakes	14¢
1 one-pound can Garland-brand baking powder	21¢
1 8-oz. bottle Iris-brand vanilla	30¢
1 five-pound box Thompson seedless raisins	44¢
1 five-pound sack Matoma-brand rice	33¢
2 cans red kidney beans	47¢
1 five-pound box Garland-brand soda crackers	35¢
4 bars Garland family soap	14¢
1 three-pound package Garland-brand washing powder	36¢

Kaitlin watched Rigg write swiftly and was surprised at how complete the list was when he handed it to her. He only gave her time to read through half of it. There was everything from yeast to soap. Of course this *was* his business.

"Okay, I think this will help. It's a list of items and what they cost. Head back down and pick up all of these. You have more than enough money and don't forget that Sean will be paid Saturday."

Kate searched for the right words to express her thanks but before she could open her mouth Rigg pushed a large woven basket into her hands and headed her down the stairs. When he sat down again at the desk, Marcail spoke.

"You like Katie, don't you?"

"I like all of you."

Marcail looked almost insulted and Rigg knew he'd underestimated her again.

"Does it bother you that I like Katie?"

"No, there's always someone who does, but I think I like you better than the others."

Rigg wondered how many more there had been besides the young man in Hawaii and cousin Percy. "How did you know, Marcail, that I liked Katie?"

"Sometimes you look at her the way Father used to look at Mother."

Rigg pushed his desk chair back and reached for Marcail's hand. He pulled her out of her chair and into his lap.

"You think I'm a baby, don't you?" The little girl was obviously disappointed.

"No, I don't. I just wanted to hold you."

Marcail let herself be snuggled against him then and Rigg kissed her brow. They were still cuddled together talking when Kate came back up with all the things on the list. Rigg walked them out of the store and they were even able to wave to Sean who was dusting shelves.

"I'll bring the basket right back to you, as soon as I unload it."

"Just keep it for now."

"If you insist, and thank you, Mr. Riggs."

He watched them until they were out of sight and then went in to see the clerk who had taken care of their sale.

"Do me a favor, would you, Cal? Before you leave, fill a sack with the same things the Donovans just purchased. Oh, and, put in a few special things too. Just leave it under the counter there and I'll get it later."

Cal exchanged a look with the other man who clerked for Rigg. It had taken a while, but it finally looked as though the boss had found someone special.

Thirty-One

"HOW IS IT?"

"I think I like poi better." Marcail phrased it as delicately as possible, by referring to one of the native Hawaiian dishes she'd grown up on. The result however, was the same—supper tasted awful.

The rice was no longer in tiny individual grains but had congealed into one slimy, tasteless mass. The potatoes were hard as rocks and ice cold. It actually hurt Marcail's teeth to bite into a biscuit. Kaitlin watched her nibble on the edge of one.

Kaitlin didn't know what was the matter with her. She cooked fairly well, although always with her mother. Maybe tonight she was just a bit panicked. Her mother had handled so much of the meal preparation, giving her and Marcail the job of preparing the fish, which they had practically lived on. Kaitlin could serve fish every night for a week and never fix it the same way twice.

"Oh, well," was all she said as she reached for her coffee, remembering as she did, that her mother had always prepared that too. She guessed she'd had worse.

That night both girls slept soundly in their warm bed. In fact, they were almost late for school in the morning.

"Is it almost ready Katie? We're going to be late."

"Almost." Kate was trying her hand at a big pot of cereal like the one Rigg had made them. She decided she must have added too much water because the stuff refused to thicken.

"What will we eat for lunch, Katie?"

"Oh, no!" Kate spun from the stove in dismay. "I completely forgot that I have to pack us a lunch. Look at the cans on the shelves Marcail. See if anything looks good."

Kate had not taken time to make bread and the cheese at Rigg's store had been too costly. If it had been a weekend, Kate would have tried for a regular meal.

She saw Marcail putting things into an old flour sack as she dished cereal into the bowls. The cereal had done a complete turnabout in the pot, going from watery to something so thick it would not come off the spoon.

Watching Marcail grimace over the taste, Kate spread some sugar on the cereal. After so little to eat last night, they couldn't possibly go until lunch with nothing in their stomachs.

"Do you have the lunch?" Kate asked, as she slipped into her sweater.

"All set."

They headed out the door and Kaitlin gave a prayer of thanks that Rigg was taking care of Sean. He'd surely waste away on her cooking.

"That was fine reading, Thomas. You may take your seat. We'll break for lunch now and afterward go for that walk I promised you."

As the students dispersed, Marcail came forward and sat on the front bench. Katie pulled their lunch sack out from under her desk and joined her. The first thing she pulled out was a package of yeast cakes.

"Marc, don't you know what these are?"

"Little cakes."

"Yeast cakes. They're used for baking."

"Oh. Sorry."

"That's all right we won't starve." Next came a can of molasses.

"I didn't know what that was either, but the man on the front looked so happy I figured it must taste pretty good." Kaitlin dissolved into helpless laughter while she tried to explain what was in the can. The last item in the bag was a huge package of raisins. Kate didn't even say grace before she began to tear it open.

Marcail's little hand shook as she raised a fistful to her mouth. They ate in silence until Kate laughed again about the molasses and choked on her raisins. Every so often she would go to the door or window and check on the children, but most were eating with no time for mischief.

Sean wandered in when he'd had his fill of what was in his lunch tin and asked the girls if either one of them wanted his last piece of fried chicken. Kate found herself grabbing for his tin like a woman starved, and then remembered that some of her class were eating at their desks.

"You eat it Marc." Kaitlin stood then and took a big drink from the dipper at the water bucket. When she sat on the bench again Marcail was waiting for her. She hadn't touched the chicken.

"We'll share this."

"Thanks Marc," Kate said gratefully, and had to stop herself from swallowing before chewing.

"Rigg told me you bought a lot of supplies. Why are you so hungry?" Sean had stayed close due to the strange behavior of his sisters.

"We do have food, I'm just not used to cooking and packing a lunch. We'll be fine." Kate laughed again when she thought of the molasses and Marcail had to explain. Sean did his own share of chuckling before reaching over to mess his sister's hair.

Offended by his rough treatment, Marcail would have started a wrestling match if Kaitlin hadn't stopped them.

The afternoon found the entire school on a walk. The older children had been put into specific charge over the younger and they ventured forth in small groups to find items that were on their spelling list.

When one was spotted, the find was reported to Miss Donovan and she marked it off the list. Nearly everyone found at least one item and the outing must have been a huge success since the children begged to make it a weekly trip. Kate, in her soft voice, restored order and said that she would consider it.

After school, the moment Kaitlin hit the door, she began supper preparations. She was a woman with a mission and in less time than she expected her efforts paid off. There was no butter for the biscuits or meat for the beans and rice but it was all pretty tasty and she and Marcail were able to eat their fill. Feeling proud of herself, she packaged up the leftovers for lunch the following day.

That night was prayer meeting and even though Kate did not feel up to the walk, she and Marcail started out in time to be there. Rigg, who told her she should have waited for a ride, brought her home. She told him in all honesty that it hadn't occurred to her and realized she hadn't thought of Sean all afternoon.

With her head so fuzzy, she figured the best place for her was bed. As usual she slept soundly. Breakfast was another fiasco and this time it did make them late to school.

"I'm sorry I'm late this morning, class. I'll certainly make an effort not to let it happen again. I want to thank you for all being in your seats. I'm proud of the way—" Kate stopped talking in mid-sentence because Joey Parker had come in late and put an apple on her desk, causing her to look at her desk for the first time that morning.

Her actions in front of a few of her students yesterday at lunch came sharply to mind as she stared at the array of food covering her desk top. Cans and boxes of food, baskets with napkins hiding treats within, two casserole dishes and a few fresh fruits. Tears filled her eyes at the tender hearts of her students. She took a moment to get herself under control.

"If I could choose any class, anywhere in the world to teach, I would pick this schoolhouse with you. Please accept my thanks and also pass it on to your parents for their generosity."

The faces of the children before her told Kaitlin she'd said the right thing. Smiling, her gaze encompassed the room.

"Good morning, class."

"Good morning, Miss Donovan."

Another school day had begun.

Thirty-Two

It WAS MID-MORNING and Rigg sat at his desk, fidgeting with the sack of dry goods he had not yet delivered to Kaitlin. He was concentrating on the conversation he'd had with Sean over breakfast.

"I sort of wish Kate and Marc had stayed at your folks'."

"Why?"

"I'm just afraid that they'll starve to death. I mean, Kate is a great teacher but she's never had to do everything before. Marc is trying to help, but when she packed the lunch yesterday, she took molasses, yeast cakes and raisins."

"So all your sisters had for lunch yesterday was raisins?"

"I had an extra piece of chicken that I shared with them." Rigg noted that Sean looked very guilty. Rigg tried to choose words to help ease that guilt.

"Kaitlin could ask for help."

"She probably never even considered it. She thinks of it as a challenge that she's never met before and thinks she should jump in and do it."

"Why don't you ask them to supper here tonight? I'm not a gourmet, but I can ask Kate if she needs me to show her anything." The conversation ended then as both men went their separate ways.

Now Rigg sat at his desk, his face almost brooding, praying about a way to help Kate without overstepping himself.

"I'm in love with a woman who can't cook." Rigg spoke softly even as a smile came over his face. He froze when he heard steps behind him.

"It's not like you to talk to yourself Rigg," Jeff said quietly. "Want me to leave?"

"No, come on in." Rigg watched as his brother folded his long frame into a chair. He dwelt briefly on the fact that the young ladies at church were very attracted to Jeffrey Taylor but he never responded in kind. It looked for a time as though Jeff might be headed for trouble where girls were concerned, but something had happened when Jeff was still a teen that seemingly changed him forever.

Rigg knew his younger brother to be as desirous of a wife as he was and wondered how Jeff was feeling about what he'd just overheard. He decided to ask him.

"I think the word infatuation fits a little better than love does, Rigg."

"You think it's too soon for me to be in love then?"

The younger man shifted uncomfortably over the vulnerable look on his brother's face. He, quite frankly, thought the world of his older brother and it was hard to see him unhappy. And then there was Kaitlin. It was not at all hard to see why Rigg believed himself to be in love.

"You started working in this store, Rigg, when you were only 14. And then Uncle Leo turned the whole thing over to you at 19. You haven't had any time to date girls or even spend much time with them and now Kaitlin Donovan comes into town and knocks you right off your feet. Naturally you assume it's love. Maybe it is, I don't know."

Jeff felt that he'd said enough and watched Rigg's face carefully to see if he'd upset him. When Rigg finally spoke, Jeff wished he had made him angry. Rigg was more upset than he was letting on and Jeff didn't want anything unresolved between them.

"Well, I doubt if you came by to discuss my love life. What did you need?"

"Rigg?" Jeff's voice was pained.

"No, Jeff it's all right. I *do* feel like I'm in love. But Kaitlin isn't ready for anything like that, and having to explore these feelings on my own is a hurting thing."

"And I just made it worse by saying you're not even in love."

"It's all right, Jeff." Rigg suddenly smiled. "I'll just make you eat those words at the wedding." Jeff laughed. This was the Rigg he knew; confident and purposeful.

"Rigg wants you to come for supper," Sean told his sisters.

"What about all this food?"

"I'll help you take everything home. By the way, Kate, I was telling Rigg that you can't cook so if you need help with anything, you can ask him tonight."

"Sean Donovan! How dare you say I can't cook!"

"Well, Kate!" The young man was equally indignant. "You told me yourself what a mess supper was. And don't forget I stood and watched you and Marc swallowing raisins yesterday without even stopping to chew."

The anger drained out of Kate and she began to giggle. Sean shook his head in mock despair. Neither one noticed that Marcail was very quiet.

"If you would catch some fish Sean," Kaitlin said between chuckles, "we could ask Mr. Riggs to our house instead of him always feeding us."

"He'd probably never believe that you weren't out to poison him."

Sean walked his sisters home and then went to see if they'd received any mail. He then headed to the mercantile to tell Rigg they would be there for supper at six.

"If there's some reason Marcail, that you'd rather not go to Mr. Riggs' for supper, you can tell me."

The girls were nearly at Rigg's and Kate, who'd finally noticed Marcail's behavior, had been trying for an hour to bring her out.

"It's fine if we eat here."

"Marc," Kate said gently, "what's wrong?"

They had come to a stop just short of the porch steps at Rigg's. He had seen them approaching and stood framed in the front door looking down at them.

Marcail looked down at the path beneath her feet and then glanced up at Rigg. When she looked back at Katie, a single tear slid down her cheek.

"I don't know if I can tell you." Her voice was soft but Rigg heard and stepped back as Kate led Marcail into the living room. The girls sat on the sofa and as soon as they were settled, Marcail turned her face into Kate's side and sat very still.

Kaitlin kept her arm close around her and stared up at Rigg and Sean who looked on helplessly.

"Marc," Kaitlin finally spoke softly, "please tell me what's wrong. Maybe I can fix it."

A few more moments went by and Marcail shifted until her cheek lay against Kate's side. Rigg, seeing the evidence of tears on her face, was surprised. He hadn't been aware that she was crying because she hadn't made a sound. His heart melted at the sight of those tears and he sat down beside her.

"Is there anything I can do, Marcail?"

"No."

"You might feel better if you talk about it Marc," Sean suggested from a nearby chair.

"Someone will get into trouble." Her young voice was almost depressed.

Kate cuddled her closer with new understanding. How many times had history repeated itself over this subject. One child had information over another child's sin and was in torment over whether or not the news should be shared.

"Marcail, I understand why you're upset but be sure to ask yourself if this person will end up in worse trouble if you *don't* tell."

Marcail was silent for a few minutes and the others in the room watched her chew her lip in indecision.

"Joey Parker told me today that he took that lady's purse. He said his father told him to." Marcail's face was once again buried against her sister's side. Rigg looked down and watched a shudder run over the child, the only indication that she was crying again. He looked up to see Kaitlin's face—it was white with strain.

"Would this man really do that?"

"I wouldn't be surprised." Rigg's voice was regretful.

The next hour was spent trying to calm Marcail down enough to eat supper. The food had gone cold but no one really seemed to notice.

Little by little, as they ate supper, Marcail elaborated. She said that Joey had approached her during afternoon recess and asked her if she'd told her sister who took the purse. Marcail hadn't known what he was talking about. When he realized his mistake, he'd become very angry and said it hadn't been his fault to begin with: He was just doing what his Pa had told him to do.

They all knew they were going to have to step lightly around this small boy in the very near future or he would surely know that Marcail had told.

Kate and Marcail didn't stay long after supper but before Rigg walked them home he asked everyone to gather in the living room for a brief time of prayer over what to do and how to reach out to Joey without causing him more hurt.

Thirty-Three

KAITLIN HAD TOLD herself on Friday night that she was going to sleep until noon on Saturday. She could tell by the angle of the sun that it wasn't that late but she awoke so rested she didn't care about the hour.

May had sent word through a blushing Nathan the afternoon before, that she and Marcail were invited to the Taylors' for supper on Saturday evening. They were to also plan to take their baths, stay the night and go with them to church in the morning.

Kate shuddered at the thought of tackling Marcail's hair. After visualizing herself washing that thick mass as well as her own in the dish-pan, she decided to accept May's offer. But right now the whole day stretched ahead of them and Kaitlin was going to start it with prayer.

As she remembered her family, her mind returned again and again to Joey Parker. Kate thought he was one of the most precious little boys she'd ever encountered.

She had surmised right away that he was not as well liked as the other children and even though they played with him, he was always on the outer fringes of their special talks. There were certainly other children who didn't really fit in either. But Joey was the only one who appeared to be from a very poor home. And after Marcail explained her tears the day before, well, Kate couldn't even think of the boy without her own tears starting.

Please Father, use me. Help me to help him. I want so much to go to him right now and hug him and ask him to church but it's too soon; I know that. And I also know that You love him and died for him. Please God, make the pathway to this little boy clear so I can tell him of Your love.

Kate prayed for many minutes in this vein, and not until she realized that Marcail was stirring beside her, did she begin to pray for her friends in Hawaii, Mr. Riggs, the Taylors and her other students.

"Good morning, Katie." Marcail's voice was heavy with sleep but she was always cheerful in the morning.

"Morning, Marc. How did you sleep?"

"Good. Are we staying at Taylors' tonight?"

"Yes, I think it's a good idea. It's hard enough to do your hair without you having to bend over for half an hour."

"Maybe we should cut it."

"What would Father say?"

"I don't know." She was silent for a moment. "He is coming back, isn't he Katie?"

"He said that he would and I know that he'll come as soon as he can."

The girls had a leisurely breakfast and then went to the post office. There was a letter from Aunt Maureen and they decided to wait until they returned home to open it. As they walked past the shipping office, Gil hailed them.

"Hi. What are you two up to?"

"We got a letter from Aunt Maureen," Marcail told him.

"Good for you." He smiled at Marcail and touched her shoulder.

Kaitlin thought he was one of the nicest men she'd ever met. Good-looking, too. Of course she believed that Gilbert and his brothers were all handsome, with their light blue eyes, medium brown hair and tall, lean physiques.

"I'm glad you came by. A few things were delivered yesterday from the church folks and I wanted to take them to your house. Are you headed home now?"

"We're going to the mercantile," Marcail informed him.

"But we can go right home if you want to meet us there."

"There's no hurry," he said with a smile. "Why don't you give me a time and I'll meet you then."

"Oh no, Gilbert, we don't want to put you to any trouble—" Kaitlin began but stopped when his eyes told her he was close to laughter.

"What time?" The question was asked again. Kate suggested ten-thirty before turning and moving down the street, a little bemused, wondering what Gilbert must have found so funny.

Gil watched them walk away, his eyes still smiling. *One of these days, Katie Donovan,* he thought to himself, *you're going to understand that the look in Rigg's eyes when he's near you, makes you and your family very special.*

Kate wondered how many times she would be able to walk into Riggs Mercantile and not feel a sense of wonder. It was all so delightful. She loved to look at the farm tools, the counter laden with jars of penny candy, paint supplies—from stove-pipe enamel to paint brushes of every conceivable size. There was a large selection of toys, with baby dolls and tea sets of fine china. You could find sports and fishing equipment and even a selection of ladies intimate apparel.

Kaitlin never stayed in that section for very long, but she was very curious and a little envious of women who wore muslin nightgowns trimmed with lace, or taffeta and silk underskirts with camisoles bordered in scarlet ribbon.

"This is pretty, isn't it Katie?" Kaitlin was brought out of her dreams when Marcail picked up an underskirt piped in pale blue ribbon.

"It sure is." The girls exchanged a smile of understanding. Even if their father were here and working steadily, he would not have allowed such an extravagant purchase.

Watching from his office, Rigg knew exactly what the girls were looking at even though he couldn't hear their words or see what they were holding. Sensing that he might be invading their privacy, he turned and sat at his desk.

Rigg believed it to be totally improper to give clothing to a woman who was not his wife, but the smile he'd seen on Kate's face led him to believe that such a gift would bring her great pleasure.

I need patience, Lord. I can't rush her and I want to do Your will but I can't get her out of my mind. Show me some peace Lord, show me how to be near Katie without scaring her off.

Rigg's prayers were cut short when the object of his every waking moment called from the stairway.

"Mr. Riggs, are you up there?"

"Come on up."

"We just wanted to say hello before we go home. Gilbert is bringing more stuff to us from the church," Marcail informed him. He stood until his visitors had found seats.

"Did you get everything you need?"

"Yes, we were just here for some little things," Kate answered, and noticed for the first time how heavy his beard was. He was clean-shaven, but the outline of whiskers was black against his tanned face.

He was very nice to look at and for the first time Kaitlin let her eyes have their fill.

She watched for a moment as Rigg talked with Marcail and then suddenly drew in a sharp breath. He was exactly like the man she visualized being married to one day! Kaitlin had grown up around well-built Polynesian men with black hair and dark skin and eyes. Rigg would never have been mistaken for one of the men from the island, but he did have the looks that Kate found most attractive.

Rigg's peripheral vision made him very aware of Kate's scrutiny but he kept talking with Marcail. He desperately wanted to know what was going through Kaitlin's mind but was afraid to ask.

When a few minutes later the girls said good-bye, Rigg wished he had questioned Kate. She had seemed uncomfortable when she left, almost as if she were afraid of him. For an instant he wondered if he reminded her of her cousin and then frowned at the thought.

After a few minutes he bent back over his account books, wishing as he did, that he had someone trustworthy to do them for him.

Thirty-Four

Dear Kaitlin, Sean and Marcail,

I've missed you so much and worry day and night over your safety. If you haven't written to me, please do so right away. I don't think I can bear another day without hearing from you.

I haven't heard from your father, but I did write him to explain. I suppose you did too.

There is one more thing I need to tell you—Percy is gone. He departed for Europe right after you left and I believe he's not coming back. Please consider returning to San Francisco. I promise I'll make everything wonderful for you. Please think about it.

Don't forget to write me.

Love to each of you,
Aunt M.

"Are you going to write today?" Marcail wanted to know.

"Probably after lunch."

"Katie, is Aunt Maureen saved?"

"I don't know Marc. Why do you ask?"

"Because she worries so much and she said something at mother's grave about her being gone forever. Mother's not gone forever, she's just gone from the earth."

Kate reached out and hugged Marcail. She, too, had heard her aunt's words and wondered at them.

"Father and I discussed it one night, Marc, and he's sure that his parents were born again. Maureen has always been a great support to Father but he's not sure where she stands.

"I think she believes in God and tries to do the right thing, but I don't know if she's ever confessed to God that she needs a Savior."

"Katie, I miss Sean. We never talk with him anymore."

"I miss him too," Kate answered, thinking how quickly a nine-year-old could change the subject.

"Are we going back to San Francisco?"

"No—at least not right away. I have to teach for two more months and I don't want to make another move until we hear from Father."

"Are you glad Percy is gone?"

"I'm glad for myself but not for Aunt Maureen."

Marcail nodded and then changed the subject once again. "What's for lunch?"

"Oh, I don't know," Kate said, this time relieved at the change in topic. "I thought we might have yeast cakes and molasses."

The remainder of the day flew by after Gil came with the wagon. The girls now had more blankets than they knew what to do with. Kate worked on some mending and her school lessons for the next week. Marcail didn't seem to notice how distracted Kate was. About an hour before supper they began walking toward the Taylors'.

"I knew you would do this," Jeff called to them as he brought his wagon to a halt in the road beside the Donovan girls.

"Do what?" Kate asked.

"Walk to my folks'."

Kate looked surprised and both Gil and Jeff grinned at her from the wagon seat.

"How else were we to get there?" Kate inquired after a moment.

"You were supposed to assume that we, being the fine gentlemen we are, would come for you."

Kaitlin laughed, but then surprised them by declining.

"I need the walk, but thanks anyway."

"What are we going to say to Rigg?" Gil let the cat out of the bag as to who had been the *real* gentleman and Kaitlin laughed again.

"Please thank Mr. Riggs for his offer, but I'm still going to walk. Marcail can go with you if she likes."

Marcail climbed into the wagon and Kate put their bag next to her. Jeff sat holding the reins in indecision.

"Will you be all right Katie?" Marcail asked as she leaned over the side.

"I'll be fine, thanks Marc." With those words Kate swung around and started down the road. Without Marcail, her long legs made quick work of the distance. Jeff, Gil and Marcail passed her and not too far from the farm Rigg and Sean came abreast of her. Kate stopped and watched as Rigg handed the reins to Sean and jumped down. Rigg was silent until Sean had pulled away.

"How was your day?"

"Okay," Kate answered quietly and when she stumbled a moment later, Rigg reached to steady her. He knew when she side-stepped his touch that he had to ask.

"Katie, have I done something to upset you?"

"No." Kaitlin answered honestly and with a little frustration. She had thought about Marshall Riggs all afternoon. She had come to the conclusion that she could fall in love with this man, but her life was so unsettled right now she didn't feel they had a chance. He hadn't even met her father. For that matter she didn't even know where her father was. A sudden image of his ship going down sprang to mind and Kaitlin felt a little sick.

"Then what is wrong?"

"What?" Kate's voice was distracted and breathless and Rigg brought her to a halt with a hand on her arm.

"Kaitlin, what is wrong?" His voice and face were a picture of determination and Kaitlin looked at him helplessly.

"I don't know exactly."

"Have I done something?"

"I don't think so." It was a vague reply but Kaitlin was suddenly feeling frightened. Rigg read all of those feelings in her eyes and one vast hand came up to tenderly cup her face. His voice was whisper soft when he spoke.

"Katie, whatever you're running from, run to me."

His eyes, having gone from gray to black, held hers captive and Kate stood mute for a long moment. She didn't know what to say or do. Running to him would be so easy. Being caught and held in those arms would be a haven of comfort like she'd never dreamed of.

But her mother had only been dead a few months and her father had not been in touch, plus the fact that Sean and Marcail needed her to be strong. She said something in soft Hawaiian and carefully pulled free of Rigg's hold.

He released her, longing as he did, to know what she had said. But it was obvious that this perplexed woman needed more time. It was a quiet couple that made their way to the farmhouse for supper.

Thirty-Five

WITH SEAN IN TOW, Rigg was at his parents' home bright and early the next morning, asking Kate to ride to church with them. He had been very watchful of her and considered the possibility that she was coming down with something or that she was just plain exhausted.

It never occurred to him that her feelings for him had changed and that that was part of the turmoil he was reading on her face. He assumed that her sudden unease around him was because of Percy. She was obviously remembering the way she'd been treated. In fact her memory had probably been spurred by something her aunt had written in the recent letter.

That Kate had not yet read the letter when her feelings changed, Rigg didn't know. She seemed rested, he noted, as they rode to church and she conversed easily with her brother. Once there, she greeted some of her students and met quite a few parents.

Rigg was turning to ask her a question when she suddenly darted away from him. He looked beyond her to see Joey Parker at the corner of the church. The little boy scooted out of sight when he saw his teacher bearing down on him, but Kaitlin pursued him and Rigg watched her disappear around the corner of the building.

"Joey," Kaitlin called, when he was once again in view. "Will you come here please?"

The little boy came with obvious reluctance. Kate accurately read the look of fear on his face. Fear that Marcail had snitched and he was in deep trouble. Kate ignored the look.

"How are you, Joey?"

"All right," the boy answered without taking his eyes off his dirty bare feet.

"I'm glad to hear that. Joey," Kate said gently, "would you like to come into church with me?"

The little boy's head snapped up, his eyes wide. She could see he was excited about the idea but then his shoulders slumped.

"I ain't dressed for it."

"I'm not dressed for it," the teacher in Kate automatically corrected him. "And I'm quite sure that God doesn't care how you look."

Joey considered this for a spell. "Maybe if I sat in the back."

"That's fine if you want to sit in the back. I'll sit with you. Oh! Here's Mr. Riggs. Mr. Riggs have you met Joey Parker?"

"No, I haven't. Hello, Joey." Rigg's huge hand came out and Joey stared at it a moment before offering his own grubby little hand.

"Joey and I just decided to sit together in the back."

"Great, may I sit with you?"

It took a moment for Joey to comprehend that the question was being directed at him. He couldn't believe this big man was actually waiting for his permission to sit with them in church. Joey muttered something and the next thing he knew he was being ushered into a rear pew.

The service had started and two songs had been sung, but Joey hadn't heard a thing. He was still working through the fact that Marcail obviously hadn't told on him. When they'd come in together and Miss Donovan had propelled him into the pew, he'd seen Marcail sitting with the Taylors. She looked back at him as though there was nothing the least bit unusual about his sitting with her sister.

Snatches of the sermon floated to Joey but for the most part he was too busy sneaking glances at Kaitlin. She looked real pretty, he thought, in her white dress. Sometimes at night Joey would lay awake and dream about what it would be like to have her for a mother. He would dream about her voice and the way she smiled at him. But then he would think about his house and knew that she would never even visit there, let alone come to live.

Thoughts of his house drew his attention to his father. He wondered how much trouble he'd be in if his Pa knew where he was sitting.

"In closing," the pastor was saying and Joey was finally listening. "Please take this thought home with you. God is our heavenly Father.

We need never be afraid to go to Him with any need because He loves us like a father does, only with such tenderness and compassion that we can't help but respond."

Up to that moment Joey believed that getting to know God might be a very good thing to do but he'd never before heard God referred to as a father. Suddenly he was not so sure he wanted to know Him.

"Joey, would you like to come back to my folks' place for some lunch?" Joey was brought abruptly back to the present when Rigg spoke to him.

"I gotta get home," he said with some reluctance.

Rigg and Kaitlin walked him outside and Kate told him she'd see him at school in the morning. They watched as he cut across a field in the direction of his house.

"What is his home like?"

Rigg hesitated and Kate pressed him.

"I want to know."

Rigg sighed and spoke. "It's pretty bad."

"Does he actually have a family?"

"A father."

"What's he like?"

"He doesn't work that I know of, and when he does get an odd job, he spends his pay on liquor."

"Maybe I should go for a visit."

"I don't know if that's a good idea, Katie. Parker is not exactly trustworthy." Rigg would never know how he managed to keep his voice so calm. What he wanted to do was grab Kate and tell her she was not to set one foot on the Parker property, not now, not ever.

"You keep calling him Parker. Doesn't he have a first name?"

"I've never heard it. Everyone calls him Parker. Of course you'll refer to him as Mr. Parker." Rigg's voice had taken on a patronizing tone.

"Now what did that mean?" Kaitlin demanded.

"Only that you're just a little too prim and proper at times for your own good." Rigg smiled at her outraged face, glad that he'd been able to change the subject as well as get a dig in about her calling him Mr. Riggs.

"There is nothing wrong with being proper and it's fine to be prim as long as you're not a snob."

"Is that a fact?" They were over by the wagon now and Rigg was close to laughter.

"Yes, it's a fact! Do you think I'm a snob?"

"No, I just wish you'd call me Rigg. Mr. Riggs makes me feel like an old man."

"I don't think I know you well enough to call you Rigg," Kate stated firmly with a tone she would have used on her students. In her mind the matter was closed; it wasn't in Rigg's.

"What do I need to do so you'll know me better, Kaitlin, kiss you?" Rigg watched as she blushed to the roots of her hair. He could also see that she was angry.

"If you did I'd slap you."

Rigg thought she might be serious but he was feeling reckless.

"Thanks for the warning. I'll be sure to hold both your hands when I do."

With those words he grabbed Kate's waist and lifted her aboard the wagon, effectively cutting off any reply she might be tempted to make. They made the drive to the Taylors' in silence; Kate wondering why her anger cooled so quickly and Rigg regretting that he hadn't kissed her right on the spot.

Thirty-Six

KAITLIN AND MARCAIL spent the afternoon at the Taylors' and Rigg took them home when he and Sean were ready to go. His words to her the evening before had told her that he'd noticed the abrupt change in her behavior.

So Kate had made a point of relaxing in Rigg's presence, and she was sure that she'd done a good job keeping her thoughts to herself. She blushed every time she remembered the words she'd said to him on the walk to his parents' house.

It didn't matter that he couldn't translate them—a young lady did not tell a man that she would love him if she could! What if he should ask Sean what she said? Oh! She couldn't bear to think about it.

Dealing with her topsy-turvy emotions all day left Kate very weary. She had thanked May again and again for sending them home with full stomachs and a tin for the following noon. Kaitlin suddenly smiled when she remembered Mr. Carson approaching her at church.

"Miss Donovan, how are things going?"

"Fine, Mr. Carson, thank you."

"I've heard wonderful things about your teaching and I know I told you it would be a month before your raise, but starting tomorrow you'll be paid full salary."

"Oh, Mr. Carson, thank you!" Kate's eyes had shone with gratitude and joy and she wondered over the strange look on the man's face.

What she didn't know was that Mr. Carson, at a hastily arranged meeting, had been told by Bill Taylor and the other men that he would adjust the teacher's salary, including back pay for the days she'd already worked plus a housing allowance. But the stingy monster rose up in Greg Carson and he decided on his own to start things on Monday.

Kate had no suspicions that anything was amiss. She wouldn't have caused trouble even if she had. The family was getting along fairly well now.

Of course, all of Sean's pants were too short, even though Kate had lengthened them as far as they would go. Marcail needed new shoes. In fact, if she wore the old ones much longer, Kate would have to slit the leather so Marcail's toes could move.

As for herself, she was badly in need of undergarments. It was not a matter she discussed with anyone but her Lord, confident that He would provide in His time.

As the days turned into weeks, Kaitlin reached out in a special way to Joey Parker. Whenever he was near she touched him or gave him a tender smile. He did not come to church again and with seeing him every day at school, Kate did not feel led to go to his home. She told herself though, that if on any given day he failed to show up for school, she would go immediately to his house to investigate.

Two more letters came from Aunt Maureen. Even though she hinted that the children should return, she seemed to accept that, at least for the time, they were staying where they were. Maureen had also mentioned coming to Santa Rosa for a visit, but Kaitlin wrote and assured her that they were doing well. Kate was happy to read in her last letter that their Uncle Mitch had come home. She knew that his presence would ease her aunt's loneliness, at least for a time.

One afternoon, when school had only four weeks to go, Kate and Marcail were in the mercantile. That very morning Kaitlin had had no choice but to cut Marcail's shoes. She knew Marcail was embarrassed but payday was not until the following week and she couldn't let her go on this way any longer.

Kaitlin needed some buttons and, even though it could have waited, she wanted to say hi to Sean, who was working that afternoon. It seemed they saw less and less of him all the time. He usually ate lunch with his friends at school and on days he worked, he left for the mercantile as soon as Kate dismissed.

When the Donovan girls entered the store and didn't see him, they made their way to the back of the store where they knew he would be. There was a platform area where the freight wagons from the shipping office could pull alongside to be unloaded. This is where they found Sean and today Rigg was working with him.

Both men were stripped to the waist and Kate saw in an instant why Rigg's shoulders and arms looked powerful enough to lift a draft horse.

Kaitlin watched as he hefted enormous crates without visible effort, sometimes swinging one onto his shoulders and carrying another under his arm. They were almost finished unloading when Rigg told Sean to put his shirt on, make a delivery uptown and then return the wagon to the shipping office.

Sean, Kate noticed absently, was damp with perspiration. Rigg, on the other hand, was not even breathing hard. Kate had not meant to stay as long as she did and was embarrassed when Rigg noticed her. He retrieved his shirt and vest, put them on and then motioned to Sean who was also covering himself.

The men approached and Kaitlin was glad she was standing in the shaded area because she could feel herself blushing.

"We just came by to say hello and to see how you were doing." Kate's voice sounded strained even to her own ears.

"I'm fine. I was going to come for supper tonight."

"Okay," Kaitlin said with a smile.

"I've got to get this wagon back. I'll see you tonight."

The girls bid their brother good-bye and Kaitlin noticed for the first time that Rigg was silently eyeing Marcail's feet. She couldn't tell exactly what he was thinking but when their eyes finally met she thought he might be angry.

"Did you come down today to buy shoes?" The words were said softly, deceptively so.

"No, but I get paid next week and we'll get them then." Kaitlin looked very pleased with herself.

"Marc, why don't you go in and look at the shoes? We'll come in later and you can show us the ones you like."

Marcail looked to her sister for approval and then went in the rear door.

"Kaitlin," he said as he tried to control his temper, "didn't Mr. Carson give you some extra money?"

"No. He told me about my raise though." Kate's smile faded when she saw how upset he was.

"My father told me that you were to get back pay for the money you should have been getting, a housing allowance *and* a raise."

"Well, maybe he's going to get it to me this week. Or next week when I get my pay."

"Either way, that is not what the board decided. You were to get the money immediately." Rigg ran a distracted hand through his hair and spoke as though he'd forgotten Kaitlin's presence. "Marcail's shoes aren't fit to wear and Sean's pants are inches above his ankles." An instant later he glanced sharply down at her feet.

"Let me see your shoes!"

"They're fine," Kate said quietly, but he was so upset that she lifted the front of her dress about an inch, thinking as she did that she would never tell him what was really needed in her own wardrobe.

His eyes were on her dress now and Kate's chin jutted out, daring him to question her further. Wisely he took the warning.

"All right Kate, I won't ask. But if you need something, I want you to go see my mom. Do you understand?"

Kate gave him a curt nod and went inside to find Marcail. Rigg was on her heels, thinking as he did, that he'd have to go to his father with this. He was too emotionally involved to go to Carson himself. He was certain to say or do something he knew would be displeasing to the Lord.

"Look at these Katie," Marcail called to them as they walked toward her. Marcail was holding out a small pair of black leather boots. They laced to the top and had low heels.

Rigg of course recognized them as his best pair of children's shoes so he carefully blocked Kaitlin's hand when she tried to reach for the price tag.

"You really should try these on, Marc. They look to be your size."

"Maybe we should wait until next week. I mean, it might be better—" Kate stopped because no one was listening to her.

"Oh Katie, aren't they pretty?"

Kate nodded lamely, having just checked the price on a pair still sitting on the shelf. How could she ever tell her that they cost too much?

"You know," Rigg was saying, "I don't think there's any reason why Marc can't have these now. Like you said, payday is next week." Rigg said this knowing that between now and then he'd figure out a way to keep her from paying.

Kaitlin was shaking her head and trying to signal him but Rigg continued to lace Marcail's shoe as though he had all the time in the world. In the next instant Marcail was on her feet moving around as if she'd just discovered walking.

"We can't," Kate was whispering furiously as she pulled on Rigg's arm, finally gaining his attention. "We can't afford those Rigg! She should never have put them on! Just look at her! She'll never want to take them off!"

Kate was so intent upon Marcail that she didn't notice Rigg grinning at her.

"Marc, I need to talk with you." Kate's voice was concerned but Marcail didn't notice.

"Oh Katie, can you believe how nice they are? And they don't hurt at all," Marcail said without ever taking her eyes off her new shoes.

"Your sister is so pleased she's speechless." Rigg's arm went briefly around Kate and he gave her a warning squeeze.

Rigg knew that she wanted to argue, but he silently tipped her chin so she had to look at him. With a small shake of his head he told her to be quiet and then went over to scoop Marcail up in his arms. She was so delighted with the shoes she threw her arms around his neck and hugged him with all her strength.

Rigg laughed in delight and turned to see Kate staring, as though seeing him for the first time.

"What's the matter Katie?" Marcail asked cheerfully, finally looking at her.

"Nothing." The answer was rather faint and she tried to smile. She looked at the man holding her sister and wondered if they needed to talk. He was being presumptuous again, but Kate's feelings were different this time and she recognized that fact.

Without really knowing how Rigg did it, Kate found herself out the door and on her way home, a few minutes later. He had assured Kaitlin he'd get rid of Marcail's old shoes. Kate had supper well under way before she remembered she hadn't bought any buttons.

Thirty-Seven

KAITLIN WOKE THE next morning with an awful premonition that Rigg was going to do something about her salary. She didn't want to get anyone in trouble *period*. Kate was convinced that Mr. Carson must have had a reason for his actions.

Knowing there would be no time to go and see Rigg before school, Kate planned on going to the mercantile immediately after. She was pleasantly surprised when he walked into the schoolhouse moments after she dismissed school for the day.

"Hello." His deep voice and pleased smile nearly made Kate forget what she was going to ask him. "How was your day?"

"It was great." Kaitlin felt herself blushing and wished she had better self-control.

"I came by because I wanted to ask you something." Rigg's eyes were watchful. He needed to gauge how she was doing to know how she would respond to his question.

"I'm glad you did because I wanted to tell you something too."

"All right. You go first." Rigg sat on the bench at the front, crossing his arms over his chest.

"Yesterday, well, I got to thinking that you might go to someone about my salary and I don't want you to do that. I know you were upset but I think Mr. Carson must have had a reason to do what he did and I don't want to file a complaint or anything like that."

"I'm sorry you feel that way, Kaitlin, because it's too late. I spoke with my dad this morning."

"Oh no," Kaitlin sighed and sank down into the chair behind her desk.

"Kate, it was bound to come out at some point and Greg Carson knew what he was supposed to do. I promise you that my dad will handle it gently. You'll get the money you've worked hard for and that will be the end of it." Rigg gave her a moment to ponder his words and realized he couldn't have asked for a better lead-in to his question.

"Actually, I'm glad you brought this up. I've been thinking about the fact that school is out in a month and you'll be out of work.

"Now, I think Sean will want to put in more hours and I can certainly use him. I can also use you and your gift for numbers. I would like to hire you to handle my book work."

Kate's mind was working furiously. Just last night Marcail had asked her what they were going to do for money when school was out. Kate had answered honestly and told her she didn't know.

"Would I work right at the mercantile?"

"Up in the office."

"What would I do with Marcail?"

"I don't want you to be upset with me but I've discussed that with my mother. She's been thinking for some time about cutting back on her hours at the shipping office. She told me if the only thing holding you back from accepting my offer is someone to be with Marcail, well, she said she'd be glad to watch her."

Kaitlin could only stare at him. "I've never done any bookkeeping before." It was the only thought that would come to mind.

"That's not a problem. I can show you my system and exactly what I would want you to do. For the first few weeks you'd probably be full time but then on most days, if you're as fast as I suspect you are, you'll probably be ready to go home by two."

How can I possibly spend all day working with this man? Kate asked herself. He had backed way off and had become her friend, just as she'd asked him to, but now her heart was changing just as his must have. Only she was falling for him and he obviously thought better of getting involved with her.

Oh, he was kind to her, really sweet actually, but the intensity he'd shown when they first met was gone. Maybe that was for the best.

"I've never noticed anyone working in your office."

"No, I've never hired an office clerk, but I've prayed a long time about someone to keep books for me, someone I could trust, and I just feel that the Lord sent you my way.

"If you're worried about us working alone in the office, well, it's very open. Anyone in the front-half of the store can look up and see all the way to the back wall. I'll have another desk brought in and, actually, if you're doing my book work, freeing me up for things on the floor, I shouldn't have to be underfoot very often."

In his next breath Rigg told her what he would pay, along with offering an employee discount on items in the store. Kate's mind reeled.

"What about my father?" His face suddenly sprang up in her mind. "I don't have any idea when he'll be back or where he'll want to live. I wouldn't want to leave you without help."

Rigg had already considered this and knew that he'd ask Kaitlin to marry him on the spot before he'd ever let her up and walk away.

"Well, I don't have any help with the books now, so however much time you can give me will surely help. Don't let that stop you from taking the job. We'll cross that bridge when we come to it."

"May I let you know?"

"Certainly." Rigg stood. "Take your time and just tell me when you've decided."

Kate thanked him and he left a few minutes later.

"You're going to tell him yes, aren't you?"

"Marcail Donovan! You were eavesdropping!"

"Yes, I guess I was," Marcail admitted from her place outside. She poked her head through the window that sat to the side of Kaitlin's desk. Rigg must have known she was there all along.

"What are you standing on?" Kate knew she wasn't that tall.

"A box."

"Well, get down before you fall and don't do that again." Kaitlin tried to sound stern but the truth was she was so pleased she couldn't scold anyone.

A job at the mercantile! It was something she'd never considered. A moment later Kate found herself almost wishing that her father wouldn't return right away and then instantly felt guilty for the thought.

She stopped then and there to pray for her father, wherever he was. As always it was a comfort to know that God knew his location and loved him more than she ever could.

Unfortunately, knowing God was in control did not lessen the pain of their separation. Kaitlin bit her lip even as she wondered if he was still alive. *My thoughts are not your thoughts, neither are your ways my ways,* the verse came softly to Kate and she closed her eyes against a sudden rush of tears.

Oh God, she prayed, *help me to go on without knowing. I wish he was here but I want to trust You.*

"What are you doing Kate?" The question came from her brother, who had entered quietly.

"I was praying and trying to find some peace about Father." Kate was not prepared for the angry look that came over Sean's face.

"Sean, what is it?"

"I just think he should be here! School lets out in a month and Rigg wants me for more hours but it isn't going to be enough to pay the rent on that house and—"

"Sean, he offered me a job at the mercantile," Kate cut into Sean's angry tirade. He gaped at her.

"Doing what?" the boy's voice was cautious.

"The book work, up in the office." Kaitlin watched her brother's shoulders sag and understood for the first time, the pressure he'd been putting himself under.

"Sean," Kate's voice was gentle. "We're going to be fine. God is going to take care of us. He always has."

The words failed to comfort him as they had in past times but he was careful not to show his sister. He nodded and smiled at her and then Marcail came in and they talked, each one agreeing that Kate should take the job. As Kate closed up the schoolhouse, she couldn't help but wonder what the next few months would bring.

Thirty-Eight

THE FINAL MONTH of school went by in a whirlwind of activities. Many of the families wanted to have the schoolteacher to dinner before summer break. Kaitlin, Sean and Marcail went to supper in ten different homes in two weeks. Exhausted, Kate was nevertheless bound and determined to put on an end-of-the-year program. The children were learning songs and poems and even writing pieces to share.

As the children's big night drew near, Kaitlin's nerves were fraying. Rigg was over at their house to finally give them the sack of groceries he'd had on his desk for so long, and Kate looked ready to come apart at the seams.

"What if no one comes?" Kate's voice was on the edge of panic.

"Everyone will come," he assured her calmly.

"You don't know that."

"Yes I do. The people in this district love their children and they'll be there. Kate, try to calm down."

"I am calm."

Rigg nearly laughed out loud. She was working very hard at being her prim and proper self while biting off every one of her nails.

"Why don't the three of us go for a walk right after supper?" Rigg asked the question with real enthusiasm but Marcail had just found some cookies in the bag of food and Kate was staring at the tabletop as though the secrets of life were written upon it.

"Katie, may I have some of these?"

"Sure," Kate answered without even looking at Marcail who was holding up the cookies. Rigg knew in that instant how really exhausted she was. Supper was on the stove and she'd just told Marcail she could have cookies.

"Why don't you wait until after supper, Marc?" Rigg asked softly, and the little girl nodded in agreement. Rigg then proceeded to put supper on.

"Kaitlin," he reached over and took her hand. "You need to eat." He watched as she gave her head a little shake as though trying to clear it. Marcail thanked God for the food and the evening went much better. Kate voiced many of her fears and Rigg did his best to reassure her. As supper continued, Kate relaxed. She even remembered to thank Rigg for the gift of food as he was leaving.

The schoolhouse was packed the night of the program, just as Rigg had told her it would be. But even in the crush Kate noticed that Joey Parker was absent. He didn't have a solo part, but Kate felt his absence in a very personal way and realized how much she'd come to love the boy.

The program went off without a hitch—well, almost without a hitch. Some lines were forgotten and there were occasional nervous giggles, but the children were respectful and the parents applauded after each recitation or song, as though seeing and hearing the greatest performers the country had to offer.

Parents and grandparents flocked around Kate to thank her for a job well done. When the formal program was concluded, the older students called Miss Donovan to the front and presented her with a gift. They insisted that she open it in on the spot and the room shook with laughter as Kate peeled back the paper to reveal a cookbook. Kaitlin hadn't realized how far afield the news of her cooking skills had traveled. But she laughed along with everyone else.

A few moments later she had to fight down tears when the younger students presented her with a lush bouquet of flowers. The evening closed with refreshments and everyone confirmed that it was a huge success.

The next day, a Friday, was the last day of school. The children were squirmy and Kate let them all go early. She was, she admitted to herself, a little squirmy too. Monday was to be her first day at the mercantile. She thought it might be rather nice to have a job that you didn't need to prepare for on Saturday. Of course the hours at the mercantile were different because so much of her schoolwork could be accomplished at home but Kate was looking forward to the challenge.

Rigg, Bill, May and all the Donovans sat down together to figure out a schedule for Marcail. It was agreed that on the days Sean didn't work, she would stay with him. The other days, May would stay home or run errands and Marcail would be with her.

Kate was very careful to check with her sister on all the plans, watching her face intently for signs of fear or feelings of being deserted. Kaitlin was relieved to see that Marcail found the whole idea a lot of fun.

With Kate's raise in pay from school and her final check, they were able to buy dress material. May planned to start sewing the very next week for her new little charge and Marcail couldn't stop talking about her new dress.

Kaitlin woke up Saturday morning with her new job on her mind. The day promised to be a relaxing one, with plans once again to go out to the Taylors' for supper and to stay the night. The girls had done so many little things as the day progressed that they didn't get to the post office until they were on their way out to Taylors'.

Rigg was driving them in his wagon and Sean and Marcail waited with him outside. When Kate exited the small building the smile she'd been wearing on the way in had been replaced by a look of worry and almost fear.

Two letters had arrived. One from Aunt Maureen, the other from Father.

Thirty-Nine

THE LETTER BEGAN "Dear Children." Kate read out loud from her place near the creek, where she, Sean and Marcail had gone for privacy.

"There is no way for me to express how helpless and angry I felt when you explained why you had to leave your aunt's. Please know that I'm glad you did. I was just about to write to you in San Francisco when your letter arrived from Santa Rosa. When I looked at the date you wrote, I know that God alone sped that letter to me.

"I wish I could tell you that all is fine here, but in truth we have suffered a major disaster. Two days after my ship landed, the islands were hit by a hurricane. No lives were lost, but the damage is extensive.

"If you write and tell me how badly you need me, I'll get on the next ship east, but I feel led to ask your permission to stay on here. I ask this in strong belief that you are doing well in your new surroundings. That isn't to say that we don't miss one another—and if you say the word, I'll leave immediately.

"I fear you'll think I'm telling you to be strong without me—I'm not. If you need me, I'll come straightaway. But if you are well then I'll probably stay on until fall or possibly longer. They need me here.

"Can it only be a few months since we were together? I miss you until I don't think I can stand it. To return here without you or your mother has given new meaning to the word lonely. If you're thinking of coming back to Hawaii, do not. I still believe we're to live there and I want you to wait for me.

"Kaitlin, make sure you are getting enough rest. What will you do for income when school is out? I love you, Katie. Sean, do not put pressure on yourself to take care of everyone. Work together and do not burden yourself overmuch. I love you, Sean. Marcail, be respectful of Kaitlin's teaching without mother. Obey your brother and sister and pray that they'll know the right courses of action. I love you, Marc.

"I'll anxiously await your letters. I've written to your aunt and she knows I'm encouraging you to stay where you are if all is well. But don't hesitate to go back to her. Percy is gone for good. Write me. I love all of you, Father."

Kate thought her head would burst in an effort to contain her tears. Marcail's tears streamed soundlessly down her cheeks and Sean kept his face buried against his upraised knees for a long time. The evening lengthened and even though Kaitlin knew that May would be keeping supper warm for them, she couldn't move to go inside.

It was almost dark when Rigg came out of the house to find them. His heart wrenched at the sight of them huddled together beneath a mammoth willow by the creek. He assumed that their father's letter told them his return would be delayed. He didn't try to talk to them but gently lifted Marcail into his arms. With his free hand he pulled Sean to his feet and then reached for Kate.

He carried Marcail all the way to the house and kept his arm around Kaitlin. He ushered them in the back door to his mother's tender care before he realized Sean had not come inside. Rigg stepped back outside just in time to see him retreating to the barn. With a prayerful heart he followed.

Sean walked into the barn, thinking as he did that it was darker inside of him than it was in the barn. He knew he needed to turn to God but he was so angry that his mother was dead and bitter that his father was gone.

He heard someone come in behind him. Not until a lamp was lit did he turn to see who it was, making no attempt to hide his tears.

Rigg's tall form stood next to the post where he'd hung the lamp. They regarded each other in silence for a moment, then Sean's voice betrayed to Rigg his pain and fury.

"I suppose you've come out here to tell me to be a man! To be strong for the girls!" The words were hurled as an accusation and Rigg stood quiet as a dry sob followed those embittered words.

Sean turned to lean on the door of a stall, his body now shaking with his cries. The older man moved toward him. There was no hesitation when Rigg's arms went around the young man. Sean turned and clung to him.

Rigg let him cry in silence, thinking as he did that 14 was not so very old. Sean was capable and responsible and looked like a man, but it didn't change the fact that at 14 you still need your father very much and Sean's only parent was many miles away.

Rigg thought back on his own life at 14 and how close he was to Bill, enabling him to ask questions about the changes in his body. Why everything felt so strange, as though he were living inside of someone else's skin. Rigg was quite certain that Sean would never be able to talk with Kate about how he felt. It wasn't that she was unapproachable, just a woman who probably didn't understand the transition from boy to man.

A few minutes later Sean pulled away from Rigg and wiped his face on his sleeves. "Are you ready to head home?" Sean's voice was quiet but not embarrassed, a fact for which Rigg was thankful.

"We can go if you want or you can have something to eat first. Mom kept things hot."

Realizing he was hungry, Sean nodded and started toward the door. It was on Rigg's mind to tell him they could talk later, but somehow, holding the boy as he cried was enough for now. It let him know that Rigg was there when he needed him.

Forty

KATE HAD A RESTFUL night but stayed home from church in the morning. She spent a long time reading her Bible, the book of James. She then took a leisurely bath, washed her hair and left it down to dry. May had set out some bread and eggs and after Kaitlin was satisfied, she started a letter to her father. As she began to write in the quiet house, she realized how long it had been since she'd been alone and how much she missed the solitude.

Dear Father,

We received your letter yesterday and even though we share your grief over this calamity, we're sorry you're not coming right home. Please stay in Hawaii where they need you so desperately. We are doing very well; please don't worry about us. We too wish we could be with you but understand your responsibility to the mission. Give our love to the people there and tell them we're praying.

School dismissed for the summer on Friday but I have a good-paying job at the mercantile where Sean works. I'll be doing the store's book work.

If you were here, Father, I would want you to meet the man who owns the mercantile, Marshall Riggs. He's the man with whom Sean lives. (Marc and I are settled in our small house. It's really very cozy.) I don't know how I feel about this man,

Father, but I feel something that I've never felt for anyone. He is a believer and when we first arrived, I thought he might be interested in me. I'm not sure now. It is, of course, his store in which I'll be starting work on Monday, June 5.

Please don't think he's been threatening in any way. I believe it's very safe to work for him. As I said before, the only thing not settled are my feelings. I know you'll pray for me and I feel better just having shared this with you.

Sean is working hard and Mr. Riggs is pleased with his effort. Marc will be with Sean on the days he's not working or with May Taylor, Mr. Riggs' mother. I am writing from the Taylors' right now. They have taken us under their wing and we usually stay with them on Saturday night and then ride with them to church. The family is William and May Taylor with sons, Marshall, May's son from a previous marriage, Jeffrey, Gilbert, and Nathan. Nate is one of my pupils.

I suspect you'll want to know about the church. The fellowship is good and the preaching straight from the Word. I miss your services though.

I'll encourage Sean and Marc to write this week. Please pray for me as I begin this new job and as I work closely with Mr. Riggs. I love you Father, and remember you're always in my prayers.

Katie

Kate felt drained when she finished the letter and went out to sit in the sun to dry her hair. Her mind strayed to Joey and the chance that he might have been at church that morning. With school out she wondered when she would see him.

The one time she'd mentioned going to his house, Rigg had discouraged her. He had tried to sound casual but Kate had been acutely aware of the tensing of his body so contrary to the nonchalant tone of his voice.

Well, she would have to do what she thought was right. Kate continued to dwell on Rigg and she thanked God for the way he'd gone to Sean the night before. Kate had been so drained, and she just wasn't as close to Sean as she once was. She wouldn't have known what to say even if she had gone to the barn with him.

She and Marcail had just been finishing their own supper when Sean had come in and polished off two large bowls of stew and Kaitlin didn't know how many biscuits. She hadn't seen him this morning before they left for church, but knew he'd be coming back for lunch.

Kate had talked to Marcail as they'd gone to bed and felt she was doing very well. Marcail was good about expressing her feelings. If something upset her, she usually talked about it or cried and then got on the road to getting over it or changing it. Kate envied her that trait.

Kate had a tendency to bury her hurts deep inside and when they tried to rear their ugly heads, she effectively pushed them right back down. Kate gave the appearance of handling upsets well, when in actuality she did not handle them at all.

It seemed there was much to pray about on this sunny morning and Kate's hair was completely dry by the time she left the porch. Once in her room, she scooped the blue-black mass into her usual chignon and went downstairs to peel potatoes for lunch. She had Sunday dinner well under way, much to May's delight, by the time the wagons pulled into the yard.

"Did you have a restful morning?"

"Yes, I really did. I haven't been alone in a long time and it felt good to sit and pray when it was so quiet. I also wrote a long letter to Father."

Rigg and Kaitlin were walking across the yard to the swing, where Marcail was sitting. Kaitlin had promised to come and talk with her after lunch. Rigg, not believing how much he missed having Kate with him in church, had followed her.

"It felt good to tell him how we're doing. I want to thank you again for giving me a job. I know it's a burden off his heart to know we're taking care of ourselves."

"You don't need to thank me, Katie. I didn't make the offer out of charity. I need you." Something in his voice, on those last words, caused Kate to turn and look at him. But she didn't see anything out of the ordinary and her heartbeat slowed down.

"Hi Katie," Marcail called to her from the swing.

"Hi Marc."

"Hi Mr. Riggs."

"Hello Marcail. You're holding on tight aren't you?"

"Sure." Marcail looked surprised and Kate chuckled.

"What's so funny?"

"I'm laughing because I still don't think you believe she's nine years old."

"She is small."

Their voices were low and Marcail wasn't paying much attention to them anyhow.

"She's the picture of our mother who was very petite. Sean and I resemble Father. We appear to be stronger and sturdier but in actuality it's Marc who has all the energy. In the morning she wakes up ready to go, and most nights I have to tell her to be quiet so I can go to sleep. Of course once she is asleep nothing could wake her. I'm the same way."

"Yes, I know."

"What?" Kate asked softly, looking at Rigg in open curiosity. Rigg wished he could hide somewhere. He had planned on telling her that he'd carried her to bed when they were celebrating their tenth anniversary and not before.

"How did you know?" Kaitlin pressed him, thinking that she would have to speak to Sean about sharing such private matters without her permission.

Rigg, seeing that she was waiting, took a deep breath and told Kaitlin he'd carried her to bed. He watched her eyes grow very round before she drew herself up in her teacher's stance, finger in the air, mouth open to speak. But Rigg cut her off.

"There you go. Getting all prim and proper on me again. We were getting along just fine and now you're the teacher again."

Kate was so surprised a slight breeze could have pushed her over. But she was quick to recover.

"Mr. Riggs—" she began, only to hear Rigg interrupt again.

"You start at the store tomorrow and I don't want to be addressed as Mr. Riggs." He watched Kate's chin go into the air but he was equally as determined. "You've called me Rigg once. I suppose when you forgot to be your prim and proper self, so I'll expect to be called Rigg from now on."

"I never—"

"Yes, you did."

They stood in stony silence for a moment before Kate saw that Marcail was no longer swinging but standing within earshot.

"Can we go see the barn?" her voice was tentative and Kate drummed up a smile to let her know everything was all right. Rigg joined them and Kate wondered if Marcail could feel the tension in the air. She watched as Marcail touched the velvety noses of the Taylors' horses and then climbed up into the buggy seat. When she moved to the ladder that led to the hayloft Kate called her back.

"It's very safe," Rigg assured them both and Kate gave her permission. She stared up anxiously while standing at the bottom of the ladder. Rigg watched her face as Marcail climbed.

"Now who's forgetting she's nine?" His voice was amused and Kate laughed at being found out. Marcail climbed with no problem and disappeared over the side.

"This really would have been a wonderful place to grow up, Mr. Riggs," Kate said as she looked around. "I almost envy you."

Rigg could see that she hadn't addressed him that way deliberately; it had become a habit. He moved around her and stepped up to the first rung of the ladder. He turned, holding on with his right hand and reaching for Kaitlin with his left. He spoke after he had her jaw in his palm.

"I'm going up to see Marc. And Kaitlin," he paused to make sure she was listening. "If you call me Mr. Riggs again, I'll kiss you." With a look that said he hoped she would, he turned back to the ladder.

Kate's mouth swung open and she stood like a statue as he climbed and disappeared into the loft. She doubted he would do as he threatened—but she couldn't be certain.

"And I have to go to work for him tomorrow." The words were said just above a whisper, as Kaitlin's heart thundered in her chest. Was it fear or something else entirely?

Forty-One

It DIDN'T TAKE Rigg more than a second to see that Kaitlin was terrified. He knew it was not what he'd said to her the day before because even though she'd been cautious, she had been fairly relaxed around him for the rest of the day.

No, this morning's nerves must have been the job and Rigg went out of his way to make her feel at ease.

"Here is your desk. And these are the books I want you to start with. Marcail took me by surprise when she found an error in my addition. I want you to check these books for mistakes—January through May of this year.

"This will also help you understand my system. I'm going to be working on an order so if you have questions, just ask."

Rigg went immediately and sat in his desk chair. Kate stood for a moment before doing the same. The extra desk was just a little smaller than Rigg's and he had pushed them so they faced each other. After sitting down, Kaitlin was painfully aware of Rigg directly across from her. She tried to look everywhere but at him and in doing so discovered what a wonderful view the office had of the store.

Kate opened the first book cautiously and began to read, pencil ready. Rigg's handwriting was a bold script, easy to read and a bit like her own in style. Kaitlin mentally congratulated the teacher who taught him the skill.

She worked for almost an hour, correcting some columns and putting a check by all she'd re-added, before she had a question. She loved numbers and once involved, it was an effort to drag her mind away. Rigg had been up and down and Kate, who would have said that no one could distract her, was finding out how wrong she was.

She tried not to stare at Rigg's dark hair and the way it curled slightly on his collar as she stood up with the January book and moved toward him. He looked up immediately, giving her his full attention.

"What do these letters mean?" Kate pointed to the side of the ledger next to the names of the brands.

"Those are my suppliers. H is Hicks, B is for Bates, Br is for Brenner and so on. They don't have any bearing on your work right now, but if at some point I show you the ordering, you'll have to know them. I'll write out a list of my suppliers for you over the next few weeks and give the letters for each one. Then if you need to refer to it you can." Kate thanked him and he smiled at her.

The remainder of the morning went by in similar fashion and Kaitlin was surprised when Rigg told her it was time for lunch.

"I was going to head down to the Binks, would you care to join me for lunch?"

Kaitlin was startled, not because his offer was such a surprise but because she'd once again forgotten to pack something for her noon meal. No wonder she and Marcail had both taken off weight. She kept forgetting to feed them!

"Yes, I would," Kate answered, and a moment later they were walking down the street to the Binks Hotel and Boarding House, the place where Kaitlin, Sean and Marcail had spent their first night in town.

The Binks was one of Santa Rosa's older lodging establishments and it was well managed. The food in the dining room was said to be the best in town. Rigg had gone to school with the present owner's son, Darrell Kolstad. Darrell ran the hotel with help from his wife, Jane. Darrell was on hand to greet Rigg and Kate when they came in and to see that they found a table.

Rigg asked Kate if he could order for them and she readily agreed. She wondered if he'd noticed her weight loss when he ordered the day's special. A mammoth plate of roast pork, mashed potatoes and gravy, brussels sprouts and green beans was placed before her. Kate stared at it and then at Rigg. He grinned at her.

"You don't really expect me to eat all of this, do you?"

"Not if you don't want to. I just thought you might be hungry. There's apple cobbler for dessert," he added, with another grin, and Kate shook her head at him and picked up her fork.

Their conversation was relaxed and when they were finished Kaitlin asked if she had time to go check on Sean and Marcail.

"Sure. Are you worried about them?"

"Not really. I just want to make sure that Sean gave her some lunch."

"I don't think you have anything to worry about—if Marcail is with Sean, she'll eat."

Kate agreed wholeheartedly. "You're certainly right about that. Sean's best friend is his stomach. But I'd like to see them just the same."

As they walked back to her cottage, she told him a little of what her father said in his letter. Rigg was a good listener as Kate shared some of her feelings about how suddenly she had become the main provider for the family.

"I really have been ignorant as to what it costs to house and feed a family. Sometimes I panic about what would happen to Sean and Marc if I got sick. Do you feel that way about the store?"

"I did when I was younger. My father opened the mercantile and he and his brother ran it. They were partners on a very unbalanced scale. Not that that ever bothered either of them, but my father owned around 90 percent of the business and Uncle Leo the other 10 percent.

"When my father died, Uncle Leo naturally stepped in and took his place. I started working there when I was Sean's age. Uncle Leo taught me everything, making it plain from day one that someday the business would be mine.

"It happened sooner than we all thought. I was just 19 when a rich Texas widow came into town for a visit. It was love at first sight for my uncle and the next thing I know he's handing the entire operation over to me. He's never been back, but we get a letter from him and Aunt Ruth at Christmastime each year.

"I told you all of that so you wouldn't be discouraged. In the early days, when I'd just taken over the store, I nearly lived down here for fear something would happen if I was away. Nothing had changed really. Uncle Leo had pretty much handed the reins over to me. I see now that it was the best thing he could have done.

"You're experiencing the same thing I did. The suddenness and the newness can be frightening, but you're doing great. If you're like me, you'll find yourself turning to God more and more about the doubts and fears. He's taking care of everything, just like you knew He would."

They were at the house now and Kaitlin turned before opening the door. "I need to give myself time, something I'm not very good at. Thank you for all you shared, Mmmrr—Marshall." She had come so close to saying Mr. Riggs that she had used the first name she could think of.

Rigg's brows were halfway to his hairline. The only person who ever called him Marshall was his mother and that was when she was getting after him over something. Kate hadn't used his name in an endearing way, but he rather liked the sound of it.

Kaitlin was watching to see how he would respond. She had made an effort all day not to call him anything lest she make the very mistake she dreaded, but it never occurred to her to call him Marshall until that moment and she wondered if he minded.

"Are you going to go in and see if they're here?" Rigg's question propelled Kate through the door and also told her he wasn't upset.

As it was, Sean and Marcail were not there but Kate wasn't really worried. As they walked back to the mercantile, she guessed they were at Marshall's.

The rest of the day went by very well until almost closing time, when Kate spotted Joey Parker passing by the window. She hadn't had time to think about him all day and now as she prepared to leave for the day, her heart ached for him.

That ache continued through the evening and Kaitlin opened her Bible and asked God for comfort. She had just finished reading through 1 Thessalonians. It was on her mind to go on to the next book but she stayed in 1 Thessalonians and reread the first two chapters.

A half hour later Kate closed her Bible. She was surprised at the words she'd missed the first time through. Kate hugged the Bible to her and asked God to give her wisdom in applying the truths she had read.

Forty-Two

"ARE YOU HEADED home Katie, or out to Taylors'?"

"I'm going to walk out to Joey Parker's and then to Taylors'. I'll see you when you get there."

It was the Saturday afternoon of Kaitlin's first week at the mercantile and she and Sean had both worked that day. Marcail was with May. Sean watched his sister head out of the store, his heart a little doubtful about what she was doing.

Sean had more work to do and he told himself, as he headed back to the loading platform, that Katie wouldn't do anything stupid.

Kaitlin's first view of Joey Parker's home made her wonder if it had been such a smart idea to come. It wasn't the house itself, but the location. Kate knew that the church was not too far away—but no one would be there on a Saturday night. There was a wooded area that bordered two sides of the house, giving it a feeling of being closed off from the world.

She had prayed very seriously about coming here and just how God would want her to handle her relationship with Joey, or if she was even to have a relationship with him.

The event that clinched the decision for her was remembering the way he had hung around the church. He hadn't been back since she took him in and sat with him but Kate was sure he was interested. This little boy needed Christ.

Her thoughts kept her feet moving toward the rundown building. Kate stepped carefully around the junk in the front yard and at one point caught her dress on some rusty barbed wire. Her hand returned again and again to her nose and she tried not to think about what might be causing the dreadful odor that hung in the air.

Her knock at the front door brought furious barking from within. If Kaitlin hadn't been frozen in terror she'd have bolted for her life. She thought she might faint when the door was thrown open and a dog the size of a small horse, stood in the doorway, barking as though he was going to devour her on the spot.

"Stop it Frank, be quiet," Joey maneuvered himself beside the huge animal and was shouting almost as loud as the dog barked. It took Kate a moment to realize they'd been joined by a third person.

"You must be Joey's father." Kaitlin had to shout to be heard. "I'm Miss Donovan, Joey's—"

"*Shut up!*" the man suddenly bellowed, and Kate, Joey and Frank all halted in their tracks. The dog lay down next to the stoop with his head on his paws, looking for all the world like an innocent pup.

Kaitlin's hand had gone to her throat and she was hoping Parker wouldn't ask her in because she didn't think she could move her legs. She was also conscious of Parker's eyes on her, so she tried to collect herself enough to speak.

"I hope I'm not coming at a bad time, but I really wanted to see Joey. I'm his teacher, Miss Donovan, and I've missed him since school let out. I came to see how he was doing." Kate made an instantaneous decision about returning to this place.

"Mr. Parker, would you have a problem with Joey coming to visit me in town?" There was no reply. In fact, Kate was beginning to wonder if he'd understood anything she said.

If Kaitlin thought the yard smelled bad, she didn't know what to think of Parker himself. His shirt had holes in it and was covered with grease and dirt. His boots hung open and Kate could see no socks on his dirty legs. His binders hung down around his knees and she was a little worried he was going to lose the filthy pants he wore.

Most of his teeth were missing and his hair and beard needed trimming. He wasn't that much taller than Kaitlin but looked a good deal heavier, with a stomach that protruded far over the waistline of his pants. His eyes were dark and watchful and they looked Kate in the eye with a keen intelligence she'd not been expecting.

When a full minute had passed and Parker had still not spoken Kate tried again, this time with Joey.

"How have you been Joey?"

"Fine." His voice was carefully neutral but his eyes revealed that he was glad to see her.

"Joey, would you like to come and visit me? I work during the day, but if you want to come any evening during the week, I'd welcome you. Do you know where I live?"

"Yes, Miss Donovan."

"Good! Then all we need to do is get your father's permission." Kate turned with a smile she didn't feel and looked inquiringly at the man. When he still did not give an answer, she managed to stretch her smile a little farther and say with false cheerfulness, "Well Joey, it seems your father has no objections so I'll expect to see you sometime next week." Kaitlin watched as the little boy looked to his father. He must have seen something affirmative because he looked back at Kate and gave a slight nod, his face lighting briefly with a look of yearning.

"I'll look forward to seeing you. It was nice to meet you, Mr. Parker. Bye now."

Kate forced herself not to look back until she was just about to step out of sight. When she did turn around, she saw that they were both as she'd left them—even the dog was still lying quietly. She gave a small wave that Joey returned. A few seconds later the trees hid her from view and her tears began to fall.

"You can't have him, Kaitlin. As much as you want to go back and steal that little boy and cherish him forever, you can't."

Kate cried and walked in the direction of the Taylors', praying as she went that Joey would come next week. She didn't think she could ever go back to that place. But then Joey's dirty little face and yearning eyes swam before her. She told the Lord that she had to reach that boy, that she'd do whatever He asked of her if it would give her a chance to tell him of Christ's love.

"Did Kate head home to get her things?" Rigg asked. He and Sean were closing up for the night.

"No, she sent everything out with your dad this morning when he picked up Marc. She went to see Joey Parker."

"Is that what she said?"

"Yeah. She plans to walk to your folks' after." Sean felt uncertain and then fearful at the look on Rigg's face. What was this Parker guy like? Sean didn't ask the question aloud, but followed Rigg as he made a beeline for the wagon.

Kate had her tears under control by the time Rigg's wagon rolled into view. The horses were approaching so fast that Kaitlin thought something might be wrong. Rigg jumped down almost before the wagon stopped and ran toward her through a cloud of dust.

"Are you all right?" He grasped her upper arms and waited for her to answer.

"Yes. What's happened?"

Rigg didn't answer. His relief was so great that he pulled Kate into his arms and held her almost fiercely. She was too surprised to be upset and looked at him with wide eyes when he once again held her away from him.

"Was Parker home?"

"Yes, he was there."

Rigg's hold tightened and Kaitlin flinched.

"I don't want you to go there again." Rigg's eyes had gone black and he strove desperately to control his voice. "It's not safe for a woman alone and I want your promise that you won't go back."

"I can't do that. I mean, I invited Joey to come and see me but if he doesn't, I just might have to come back out here. So I can't make you that promise, Marshall."

It was more than clear to Kate that Rigg was not satisfied with her response. She watched as he pulled in a deep breath and relaxed his hold on her arms.

"Will you make me this promise—that you won't come out here again without telling me?"

"Yes." Kate was able to answer him right away. The pain and worry in his eyes were very real.

"Please tell me why it's so dangerous," Kate said softly.

Rigg hesitated and then glanced at Sean who had come to stand with the horses.

"A woman was raped in these woods a few years back. There was no proof as to who did it, but the description the woman gave and everything she said pointed to Parker. He was even arrested but the woman was afraid to come in and identify him. Without some evidence they had to let him go."

Kate's hand had come to her mouth and Rigg pulled her into his arms one more time. This time, when he released her, his hand came up and the backs of his fingers stroked feather-light down her left cheek, his eyes once again telling her how frightened he'd been.

They were all a little drained as the wagon moved toward the Taylors' and Rigg found himself touching Kate as they talked.

"Did I hurt your arms?"

"No," she assured him softly.

He leaned forward slightly to see her face better and for a long
moment their eyes met. It was Kate's turn to touch Rigg when she
saw the caring in his gaze. And he briefly covered the hand she put on
his arm with his own, thanking God as he did for this woman and also
asking Him to keep her safe.

Forty-Three

SUNDAY PASSED IN a relaxed fashion. The next day both Kate and Sean had to work so Marcail stayed with the Taylors. After work on Monday, Rigg asked Kate to join him and Sean for supper. They planned to collect Marcail a little later in the evening.

Kate told Sean that she was going home to clean up and that she'd see them at the house. She was totally unprepared, but thrilled, to find Joey Parker on her front step.

"Hello Joey." Kate's smile was genuine.

"Hi," was all the boy said, but his eyes told Kaitlin he was glad to see her.

"How are you today?"

"O.K."

"Would you like to go somewhere with me, Joey?"

"Sure." He looked confused but agreed—anything to be near his beloved Miss Donovan.

"If you'll just wait right there, I'll go inside for a minute and then we'll go to Mr. Riggs' for supper. How does that sound?"

"Fine." Kate watched his small face carefully lest he be intimidated about going to Rigg's and leave when she was inside. But she need not have worried; he was waiting patiently for her. Within minutes they were standing on Rigg's front porch.

"I brought a guest with me," Kate said to Sean when he opened the door.

"Hi, Joey," Sean greeted the boy and opened the door wide. Rigg was in the kitchen and everyone headed that way. Kate silently thanked Rigg for the way he handled Joey, treating him as though his coming to supper was an everyday occurrence.

"Okay Joey," Rigg instructed him, "wash your hands and you can help Sean set the table."

The adults in the room were quiet and tried not to stare as Joey solemnly assisted Sean. Kaitlin could see that he took his task very seriously and she kept her face averted so he couldn't see the way she was struggling with her emotions.

Rigg and Kaitlin made a nice team as they efficiently put supper together. Two whole chickens were fried—a job Kate tackled. Rigg mixed biscuits for the oven and Kate also made gravy and then sliced fruit for a salad.

"You're a better cook than Sean led me to believe," Rigg commented at one point, when Sean and Joey had gone into the other room.

Kaitlin chuckled. "It's been slow in coming. The only thing I cook well is fish. One of these weekends I'm going to send Sean to the creek and then I'll be able to cook for you and your family for a change."

"Gil and Nate love to fish. I think they'd probably bring back enough for an army."

"I'll have to mention it to your mother when we go for Marc. I can pick up the things I'll need this week."

Rigg didn't answer; he couldn't right then. It felt so right having Katie here, working beside him. He didn't want to get his hopes up but he was sure she was looking at him these days with different eyes. At first her eyes had been almost hostile and then had gone to guarded. And now they were changing from friendly to tender.

At least that's what Rigg thought. But that was the problem, the difference between *thinking* and *knowing*. He knew he still needed to bide his time or take the chance of destroying everything they had built between them.

Sean and Joey came back in just as supper preparations were complete. As they began to eat, it became apparent that Joey did not use utensils. Kaitlin felt deep compassion watching him dip his fingers in the gravy when his biscuit was gone.

When he picked up his plate, intent on licking it, Kate paid close attention to her own food, as did Sean. Rigg leaned close to Joey to instruct him in a few table manners. Spoons and forks were clearly a new concept to him, but in his eagerness to please, he gave them a try.

When Sean found out there was nothing for dessert at Rigg's, he suggested they go get Marcail and raid Mrs. Taylor's baked goods. Joey was again treated as one of the family and was not even asked if he wanted to go. The little boy stood in obvious indecision next to the wagon. Kate ignored his look.

"Climb in, Joey. Mrs. Taylor is the best baker I know. You don't want to miss out on her cookies."

Rigg swung Kate onto the seat and was pulling himself aboard when Joey jumped in the back with Sean.

Marcail was thrilled to see her sister and talked nonstop for the first ten minutes. It seemed that she and May had done a great many things that day and Marcail had had so much fun that she was determined to tell her oldest sibling about it in one breath.

Joey was introduced to the Taylor family and then followed Sean's signal to help himself to the cookies. Sean and Nathan were used to walking away with as many as they could carry. Joey was more circumspect.

"You may have more than one Joey." May smiled and held another cookie out to the little boy. He was cautious as he reached for it; he captured May's heart in that moment. His hair was hanging in his eyes and his clothes were torn and filthy.

"Gilbert and Nathan were pretty hard on clothes when they were your size, Joey," May began, and Joey looked at her strangely. "But they had occasional growth spurts where they outgrew the clothes before they could ruin them. I have a pair of pants and a shirt just about your size, if you'd like to have them."

As Joey had been doing the entire evening, he looked to Miss Donovan for approval. She smiled and nodded at Joey as though she'd never heard a better idea. May asked Joey to go upstairs with her. When they came down Joey was aglow in his *new* clothes, his old tucked under his arm. His face flushed when Kate made over him and his eyes were shining under her approval.

"Now Joey, I think I'd better get you home. While we're there I can check with your father to make sure it's all right for you to keep the new clothes."

It was quite plain that Kate's plan to take Joey home was news to Rigg. He looked thunderstruck, but Kate was telling Marcail to gather her doll and tea set and get to the wagon. She grasped Joey's hand, thanked May and sailed out the back door.

Nearly everyone followed their progress to the barn, Rigg with his eyes on Kate alone. Joey and Marcail were close to Bill as he hitched up the horses and Rigg was able to get Kaitlin alone. Putting his arm around her waist, he led her just outside the barn door. When they stopped he stood face-to-face in front of her with his hands behind his back, his whole body bent to speak directly into her upturned, attentive face.

"You made a promise."

"I'm not breaking my promise," she told him. Her own hands were clasped behind her back and she cocked her head a bit to stare up into his gray eyes with honest candor. "I said I wouldn't go out there alone and I'm not. You're going with me."

"And if I refuse?"

"I'll ask Jeff." Her chin came up just a bit and Rigg brought one hand out to grasp that chin between his thumb and forefinger.

"I knew the first time I saw this chin, that you would be stubborn."

"I am not stubborn!" Kate denied, but made no move to step away from his touch. "And further more, Mr. Riggs, I feel very strongly that we need to be involved in this little boy's life and not just once in a while. And that is going to involve our going to his house once in a while—"

Rigg had a very strange look on his face and Kate stopped.

"Are you finished?" he wanted to know.

"Yes," Kate answered tentatively.

"You can't say I didn't warn you."

Kaitlin watched as Rigg's head lowered and his mouth brushed across her own. She was too stunned to move.

He smiled tenderly into her eyes when he raised his head. "I've changed my mind Katie," his voice was deep and soft. "You can call me Mr. Riggs anytime you want."

The entire family spilled out of the barn then, with the wagon ready to go. Rigg, Kate, Sean, Joey and Marcail were halfway to Joey's house before Kate realized she was no longer standing outside the Taylors' barn.

Forty-Four

PARKER'S DOG FRANK, bearing down on the wagon, was the needed element to bring Kate back to earth.

"Shut up, Frank!" a voice bellowed and everyone, including Parker standing by the house, stared at the young schoolteacher. The dog dropped to the ground as if by magic and looked up at Kaitlin with soulful eyes.

Kate climbed down from the seat, unassisted, patted the dog and moved toward the house. Knowing Rigg did not want her here, she took matters firmly into her own hands. Not unexpectedly, Rigg's feet had hit the ground as soon as Kate's did. All he could do, however, was watch her.

"Good evening, Mr. Parker. We were out at the Taylors'. I hope we didn't keep Joey out too long." Forging right ahead, Kate continued, "Mrs. Taylor gave Joey some old clothes that her boys have outgrown and I wanted to make sure you didn't have any objections."

Kate had walked closer as she talked and even though Rigg and Sean held their places by the wagon, they were watchful.

Kate stood about five feet from Parker now and waited. She noticed he looked a little better than he had before and wondered at the reason. When her statement went unanswered, she asked straight out.

"Mr. Parker, may Joey keep the clothes?"

The man's eyes moved over his son who stood next to Kate and then back to the men by the wagon. He looked at Kate a moment before speaking in a voice that sounded like it wasn't used much.

"How much did she want?"

"She wanted to *give* them to Joey because her boys can't wear them."

He shrugged after a moment and then spoke again.

"Sure." The answer, although brief, was enough. A smile broke across Joey's face.

"I need to get home now, Joey. I'll see you later. Good evening, Mr. Parker." Kate had all she could take for the moment. This family needed so much and right now she was feeling too emotionally drained to deal with any more of it.

Kaitlin and Marcail waved from their seats in the wagon and Kaitlin was surprised when Sean and Rigg did too. Her heart felt like a heavy weight within her as she left Joey in that run-down home with no warmth or caring. And then the Lord reminded her that Parker had let him keep the clothes.

Kate praised God for this and thanked Him for May's tenderness and generosity. She then began to pray for Parker. Kaitlin was so intent on her thoughts that it took a moment for her to realize when the wagon had stopped in front of her little house.

It was growing late. Both Sean and Rigg got down to help the girls. Sean took Marcail inside and Rigg stood next to the wagon with Kate in front of him.

"You were a thousand miles away just then."

"Not a thousand, only about two."

"Joey," Rigg guessed correctly.

"And Mr. Parker," Kate said softly. Her gaze centered on nothing in particular in the gathering darkness.

Rigg's brows rose but he didn't question her. With Kate's mind on Joey he wondered if she'd even remembered his kiss. He couldn't get it out of his thoughts.

"Do you suppose that Joey has ever told his father that he loves him?"

"I don't suppose he's given the boy much to love," Rigg answered honestly. "He's too young to understand that the drinking his father does is not his fault, and yet, in a manner of speaking, he is the one who gets blamed when Parker is drunk and abusive."

"Are you sure that Mr. Parker is abusive? I mean, I've been to their house and I can see that they're poor. I could tell that just by his appearance at school and how little lunch he would bring. But I'm not sure I believe he's been abused. Neglected, possibly. Abused—I'm not too sure. Do you have firsthand knowledge that Mr. Parker abuses Joey?"

Rigg had never been asked that question before and he had to think a moment. He was a little ashamed to admit to Kate that he wasn't sure if what he'd heard was fact or town gossip.

"I feel rather ashamed."

"Oh, don't feel ashamed!" Kate said, her face wreathed in a smile. "I'm *glad* you don't know if it's true because it changes the way I feel about Joey and his father." Rigg looked confused by her logic and Kaitlin went on.

"I'll admit to you that I have a hard time with Mr. Parker when I think he might have hurt that woman or harmed Joey. But Rigg," both of Kate's hands came up to grasp Rigg's shirt front. "What *I* feel doesn't matter in the least. No matter what kind of a man Mr. Parker is, Christ died for him!" Kate pulled on his shirt a little more, her face and movements telling Rigg how badly she wanted to be understood.

"Please go home and read 1 Thessalonians chapters one and two. Please do that, Rigg, and tell me if we've reached out to him in the nurturing way those verses instruct. Does our love go out as God's does—unconditionally—or are we the type of people who only want to minister to the lovely, to the people who are easy to be near?"

The tears that flooded Kate's eyes were now flowing down her cheeks. "I want," she whispered tearfully, her voice breaking, "for Joey to come to Christ. But I also want Mr. Parker to know that someone loved him enough to die for him."

Kaitlin was utterly spent. Rigg watched her whole body sag before enfolding her in his arms and laying his cheek on the top of her head. He held her that way for a brief moment and then with a promise that he would read the chapters, called Sean to the wagon.

Forty-Five

THE CHAPTERS RIGG read that night before going to sleep were familiar to him. But never before had he read them with a person's face so clear in his mind. Parker.

It would be very easy to answer Kate's question after reading 1 Thessalonians 2:7—"But we were gentle among you, even as a nurse cherisheth her children." No, we haven't reached out as we're admonished to—"as a nurse cherisheth her children."

Rigg knew these chapters were describing Paul with Silas and Timothy, and the way they ministered to the people at Thessalonica. Paul stated in 1 Thessalonians 2:2 that a previous experience in Philippi did not keep them away, even though they were treated shamefully. But still they went to Thessalonica because God was leading them to the people there.

Rigg couldn't help but wonder how they'd been treated when they first arrived at Thessalonica. In 1 Thessalonians 1:5 Paul states that it wasn't just lip service on their part, but that they lived among them, in an effort to lead them to Christ, and lead them to Christ they did.

1 Thessalonians 1:6,7—"And ye became followers of us, and of the Lord, having received the word in much affliction, with joy of the Holy Ghost: So that ye were ensamples to all that believe in Macedonia and Achaia."

Rigg went on, going to 1 Thessalonians 2:8, "So being affectionately desirous of you, we were willing to have imparted unto you, not the gospel of God only, but also our own souls, because ye were dear

176

unto us." If Rigg had any doubts about whether or not he was as burdened as Kate was for the Parkers, this verse cleared them immediately. At some point in Kaitlin's dealings with Joey, her heart had become very burdened for his soul. Now her heart was just as burdened for Parker.

Rigg read the chapters through one final time and fell asleep praying about how he could be involved in the Parkers' lives.

The remainder of the week was busy giving Kaitlin and Rigg little opportunity to discuss the Parkers. But when they did talk about it, they decided that the weekend would be the best time.

In the days leading up to the weekend, Joey came to Kate's house three times. She ministered to his physical needs—his elbow when he cut it, his stomach when it was empty, water for his thirst and shelter from the sun that shone down fiercely in the middle of the summer.

And unbeknownst to Joey, his emotional needs were being met as well. In a hundred little ways Kate made him feel special. Her hand on his shoulder, the way she smiled when he talked to her and the most special times of all, when she took Joey's chin in her hand, raised his head to look at her and told him he was so special to her and that she loved him very much.

During these visits Kate had done the majority of the talking. This trend changed on Saturday morning when Joey came to the house just as Kate was finishing with Sean's hair.

"I'm going to be late for work, Kate. Are you nearly through?"

"Yes, I am. Although Marshall will say your tardiness was worth it, now that you no longer look like a gypsy."

Marcail found this highly amusing and Sean made a smart remark to her in Hawaiian. Standing in the doorway unnoticed for a time, Joey listened to the heated discussion in a foreign tongue.

"Hi, Joey," Marcail said in a loud, surprised voice and all conversation stopped.

Kate could see that the little boy was ready to leave and spoke quickly, "Come in, Joey. I just cut Sean's hair. Would you like me to cut your hair?"

Joey's eyes went to Sean's head and Kate had a hard time holding her laughter. Sean let himself be inspected before flipping his cap onto his head. The cap was a brimless number with a visored front. Sean wore it rain or shine, giving him a jaunty look. It had been a gift from a Scottish missionary who'd been visiting Hawaii and Sean cherished it. He looked at Joey for a moment longer before winking at the younger boy, thanked his sister and headed out the door.

It took a little coaxing, but Kate persuaded Joey to sit down. She covered his clothing with a sheet and began to trim. Marcail was busy with her doll and for the first time Joey initiated a conversation.

"My Pa told me to thank you for the bread." Kate had ended up with an extra loaf of bread the day before and had sent it home with Joey.

"You're welcome Joey," she said simply and continued to snip.

"I haven't been to the church lately."

"No, I guess you haven't." Kate tried to keep her voice neutral, even through the surprise she felt that he was talking at all, let alone mentioning the church.

"Is God really like a father?"

"Yes Joey, He is. The Bible describes Him that way many times, but you need to remember that there is a difference between an earthly father and a heavenly Father. We love our fathers here on earth but they're not perfect. God is."

Joey was quiet for a time, as was Kaitlin. She wondered if, in the past, she had done too much talking or if it was because he was faced away from her as they spoke.

"Do you really think God hears when you pray?"

"Yes, I do. The Bible says God hears us and I know He's answered my prayers all my life."

"You always get what you ask for?"

"No I don't. Sometimes God's answer is no."

Again the little boy dwelt on this in silence. Kate was praying with all her heart and knew that she had to ask this child about eternity before he left her.

"I know all about Christmas," Joey shared softly. "I know that Jesus was born. But a little baby shouldn't die for a person's sins so I don't understand what Jesus it was that did that."

Kate was again surprised, this time at his knowledge. "Were you always the size you are now, Joey, or were you once a baby?"

"I was a baby."

"But you didn't stay a baby and neither did Jesus. He grew to be a man and it was that man who died on the cross to save the world. The baby and the man are the same Person, God's only Son."

"Does it say that in the Bible?"

"Yes, it does. Would you like me to show you?"

He nodded and Kate made a few more cuts with her scissors, removed the sheet, brushed him off and retrieved her Bible. She opened to the book of Luke and began to explain.

"In Luke 2, Joey, Christ's birth is told. Do you remember the story?"

"With the angels."

"That's right. In verse 11 it says, 'For unto you is born this day in the city of David a Saviour, which is Christ the Lord.' And if you keep reading it says that the shepherds came to see Him."

Joey nodded and Kate went on. "Well, if you read even farther down to verse 41 and 42, it says that when Jesus was 12 He went into Jerusalem with His mother Mary and her husband Joseph. So you see right there He's already 12 years old.

"And there's more. The last verse in chapter 2 says 'Jesus increased in wisdom and stature, and in favour with God and man.' Increased in stature means His body grew. The next chapters in Luke tell all about Jesus as a man, the miracles He performed and so much more. Then, if you turn all the way to chapter 23, it tells of Jesus Christ's death. How they nailed His hands and feet on the cross and how He died there for our sins. But Joey, He didn't stay dead. When the people who loved Him went back to His grave it was empty. He even appeared to some of them at their homes and on the road. Jesus is alive, Joey, and He's still alive today, saving all who believe in Him."

Joey's eyes had never left Kaitlin's face—even when she'd pointed at her Bible or read. He took a deep breath and stood. Kate's heart sank as he moved to the door and she exchanged a confused glance with Marcail.

But Joey stopped on the threshold. "Thank you for cutting my hair and thank you for explaining about Jesus. It's not what I thought it was. I gotta go."

Kate was left with those cryptic words and an anguished heart. *How silly you are, Kaitlin,* she said to herself. *To think that the moment he heard the gospel he'd be jumping out of his seat to know Christ. It doesn't always happen that way and you know it.*

Kate prayed and tried to reason with herself but it wasn't working. Tears were just beneath the surface and when Rigg showed up at the door, they overflowed.

He stood for a moment and watched the woman he loved sob into her hands and then he glanced at Marcail. She answered his unasked question.

"Joey was here and Katie witnessed to him and then he just walked out. He seemed so interested and then he thanked her for telling him and left."

Rigg went over and hunkered down beside Kate's chair. "It's all right Katie. You're forgetting the verses in 1 Corinthians 3, where it says that some plant the seeds and some water, but God gives the increase. You remember those."

"I know but I just thought—" Kate was choked up all over again and then felt terrible. "I have no business crying," she sobbed. "It's just my pride. I wanted to see it happen today. He's only been coming here for a week." Even as Kate reasoned with herself, she continued to cry. Rigg reached for her hand and looked to Marcail for help.

"Katie cries easier when she's tired."

"I do not," Kate denied, having heard the softly spoken words.

"She says that too," Marcail stated logically and Rigg's hand came up to rub at his upper lip. Kate, whose tears were abating, saw the movement and scowled at him. The fierce look was spoiled when she sniffed. Rigg grinned at her.

"I came down to see if you'd trim my hair. Sean didn't mention that I'd need an ark." Kate pulled her hand from his. With an indignant toss of her head she wiped her face on the handkerchief he offered her.

"Thank you," she said after a moment, and began to look truly embarrassed. Rigg was immediately sensitive.

"We'll keep praying, Kaitlin," he assured her softly and she thanked him with grateful eyes.

"Did you really want your hair trimmed?"

"If you would."

Kate nodded and Marcail came around to sit in front of Rigg so they could talk. Kate was quiet, her mind on Joey. She continued to pray as she cut Rigg's hair and an idea came to mind. She decided to keep it to herself for the moment; tonight they were headed out to the Taylors'—that might be the time to mention her idea.

Forty-Six

THAT SATURDAY AFTERNOON Kate and Marcail made their way to the mercantile. Kate hadn't worked that day and even though she enjoyed her day off, it felt a little strange to go into the store where she earned her living.

Kaitlin bought the needed spices for the fish dinner she would prepare at Taylors' Sunday evening. Then she and Marcail waited for Rigg and Sean to close the store so they could all go out together.

May's first comment when she saw the riders in the wagon was praise that both Rigg and Sean had been to the barber.

"Katie cut it," Rigg informed her and May looked at her in surprise.

"I don't suppose you'd care to cut three more heads tonight?"

"Sure," Kate answered with a smile. "But only if they're willing."

"Oh, I can see to it that they're very willing," May joked. "I'll tell them that they won't get fed unless they agree to line up in front of your scissors right after supper."

The first to sit quietly for her hair-cutting skills was Nate. She could see that he was not against the idea, but neither was he jumping for joy.

Once May and Bill had taken care of the dishes, they joined the family on the front porch. When Nate headed in for his bath, Gil took his place. His hair was very thick and lay nicely when cut. He told Kate he liked his a little longer in the front and she was careful to do as he asked.

Kaitlin felt like she was cutting the same head of hair twice when Jeff sat in the chair; it was so like Gil's. Thick and medium brown in color, it had just enough wave to make it a dream to cut and shape.

"Have you always cut Sean's hair, Katie?" May wanted to know.

"No," she answered softly as she finished with Jeff. "Mother usually cut Sean's and Father's hair. She showed me what to do but I can't say as I've had much experience."

"You've had some practice though," Sean commented from his place on the edge of the porch. Kate laughed and Sean explained.

"Mother first showed Katie when she was 17. She was pretty proud of her new skill and decided to practice on Marc and me. Well, my hair had been cut just a few weeks before but she badgered me into sitting for her. I looked like a skinned rabbit when she was done." Everyone laughed, including Kaitlin who was sweeping the porch.

"What happened to Marc?" Rigg asked. All three of the Donovans laughed and then Kate answered.

"I didn't have to coax Marcail—she wanted her hair cut. I thought it would be so simple to just brush it out and cut straight across the bottom—only I didn't cut so straight. I kept getting one side shorter and then I'd have to cut the other side to make it even. We figured that I'd cut about a foot before I knew I had to stop."

"A foot?" Rigg was incredulous and reached over to touch Marcail's hair. He turned her until her back was to Kaitlin. "So it was up to here?" Rigg's hand was almost to Marcail's neck.

"Marc's hair wasn't as long as it is right now. I had her hair above her shoulders."

"What did your parents say?"

"Mother was very understanding but Father wanted to punish me. Mother talked with him; she felt I had tried my best and that I'd probably learned my lesson."

"Mother was always understanding," Sean said quietly. "Remember my boat?" Kate and Marcail both nodded.

"When I was nine my dream was to have a boat. I was going to paddle around the island with a friend and prove to my parents I could take care of myself.

"My friend and I worked hard on that boat, all in secret. The day before we were to set off, two younger boys found our hiding place and took the boat quite a ways offshore. They nearly drowned when the boat capsized in the rough surf.

"I was punished but not as severely as Father wanted. Again, Mother said I'd learned my lesson. She was right."

"I never learned my lesson," Marcail admitted, and her siblings laughed at her.

"What Marcail is trying to say is that she was punished regularly. I'm afraid Loni was not always a good influence on Marc," Kate smiled at her sister before she went on, "along with the fact that Loni's mother is dead, so there was very little adult supervision at their house. But I think even Marc would admit that Mother was always fair."

"She was," Marcail said in a small voice as a tear slid down her cheek. Kate beckoned and Marcail moved away from Rigg and into her arms. Kate talked as she held her sister close.

"I remember when Sean was born. Mother had been so sure it was another girl and they hadn't settled on any boys' names. 'You're kidding me!' Father said when he found out. He actually went and checked under the blanket before he believed that they'd actually had a boy." Kate chuckled and went on.

"And then the name! Father was sure that Mother wanted to name the baby after her father and Mother was sure that Father wanted to name Sean after him and his father. It was a mess. But Mother was adamant and so Sean is Patrick Sean the third.

"Father only agreed, if Mother would name the next little boy after her father. And lo and behold it was a girl! So Marcail is named after her maternal grandmother."

"Remember the surprise party for Father's thirty-fifth birthday?" Sean said with a laugh. "It was a fiasco. Everything that could go wrong, did!"

"You see," Kaitlin picked up the story, "Mother's and Father's birthdays are only two days apart. That year Father's was on Friday and Mother's on Sunday. The logical day to celebrate was Saturday and our parents decided to have surprise parties for each other on the same day. We knew about all the plans but we couldn't say a word. The other family that was helping us plan stayed quiet and made it a dual celebration.

"I remember when we all walked down to the beach to the big luau. Everyone yelled *surprise* and Mother turned to Father and said, 'You don't look surprised.' And he said, 'Why should I be, I planned all of this.' I've never seen my parents laugh so hard."

The last word was said on a sob and Kate buried her face against Marcail's hair. Her body shook and Sean went to join his sisters. They sat huddled together crying and talking in soft Hawaiian. The Taylors stayed on the porch, not intruding, but showing concern with their presence.

Rigg thanked God for their emotional display. He knew from talking to Sean that with their busy schedules and uncertain future, this family hadn't taken time to discuss their mother's death—at least not since arriving in town.

"I can't believe she's really gone. I mean, I know that we'll see her again but I want to see her *now.*" The words were Sean's and Kaitlin felt Marcail shudder against her. She didn't want to stifle their grief but it did no good to concentrate solely on their mother's absence.

"At least we know we will see her." Kate's voice was choked as she tried to stop crying. "And she's not suffering anymore like she did with the tuberculosis. I read that it could have gone on for years. God was merciful to take her so quickly."

Kate's words, after a time, had the desired effect and the children's conversation turned to their father—how he was and when they would see him again. The tears eventually stopped and Kate prayed aloud for their father. She asked God to deliver their letters to him safely and to let them hear soon how he was doing.

The evening was growing long and Kate sent Marcail to have her bath. Rigg and Sean were getting ready to leave when Kate turned to May and Bill with a question.

"I really appreciate the way you let us come every weekend and how at home you make us feel. But this is still your house so don't be afraid to say no to the question I want to ask you."

Bill and May looked at one another and then back at Kaitlin.

"May I invite Mr. Parker and Joey to our fish dinner tomorrow night?"

Forty-Seven

THE ONLY SOUND was the evening breeze rustling the leaves. Nate, Gil and Jeff were all finished with their baths, so the only person not staring at Kate was Marcail, who was still in the bathtub.

Kaitlin's face began to heat and she was about to apologize for her question but instead her chin came out with steel determination.

"Like I've said, you've always made us feel so comfortable and I don't want to take advantage of that. I've prayed about inviting Mr. Parker to my little house in town . . ." Kate halted when Rigg came abruptly to his feet.

"*But,*" she went on, looking straight at him, "I know that would be improper and not a good testimony. I feel so strongly that we're—I should say *I'm*—to have some type of outreach to this family. Right now I can't think of any other way to get close to them." Kate went on and briefly explained what had transpired that morning with Joey and how badly she wanted to keep the door open for further witnessing.

The group fell silent once again. When the silence became too heavy, Kate excused herself to check on her sister, fighting the tears that threatened.

Marcail needed help rinsing her hair and Kate was thankful for the diversion. She decided not to go back to the porch and, after she settled Marcail into bed, she prepared her own bath. The steam rising around her did wonders toward relaxation and this time she didn't try to stop the tears.

"Oh, Lord," she prayed, "I really believed they would share this burden with me. I know they don't like Mr. Parker but You love him and You've given me a love for his soul and Joey's. I can't do this by myself. Please Lord," she sobbed, "show me what You would have me do."

Kate would have put her head beneath the water if she knew that Bill was lingering outside the door, allowing him to hear her prayer. He'd come to tell her that she could invite whomever she wanted, anytime. But he was doing so with a reluctant heart.

He leaned against the wall a moment and then went back to tell his family that they needed to support Kate with their whole hearts. He prayed for a miracle in his own heart; a miracle that needed to take place between now and supper-time the following night, when he would face Parker.

"Do you mean it? They said I could ask them over?"

"That's what they decided. I know they felt bad when you didn't come back last night. That's why I'm up here this morning." Sean spoke from his place on Marcail and Kate's bed where he'd thrown himself upon entering the room.

He and Rigg had arrived early, as they usually did, and Bill told them that Kate hadn't come back out, even after they'd left. Sean volunteered to go up and talk to Kate.

"That's wonderful," Kate said softly, silently thanking God for His provision. It took a moment for her to realize that her legs were falling asleep from the knee down.

"Sean, you're putting my legs to sleep."

Sean shifted and they talked for a bit longer before Kate shooed him away so she and Marcail could get ready for church.

As soon as she sat down to breakfast Rigg asked her how she planned to invite Parker and Joey.

"If Joey's at church this morning, I'll ask him then. If not I'll walk over when the boys go fishing."

Rigg's eyes held hers for a moment and Kate remembered his words outside the barn when he'd threatened not to take Joey home. Kate was the first to lower her eyes and defeat washed over her. She didn't want to fight everyone over this; she wanted to think that someone was behind her, otherwise she would doubt her wisdom of getting involved at all.

Kate decided not to ask anyone to accompany her. There were enough men at the table to overhear Rigg's question and if someone wanted to go with her they could just offer. Otherwise, she'd made a promise not to go alone—

The incomplete thought hung in Kate's head and she found herself praying that Joey would be at church so she could ask him and simplify the whole matter. But Joey was nowhere to be seen.

Rigg didn't miss the way Kate reluctantly walked to his wagon for a ride to church. Or, after arriving and taking a seat, the way she looked toward the door time and again, for a glimpse of Joey Parker.

Rigg was learning about relationships. It was obvious to him, in a way it hadn't been before, that even if he and Kate were married, she would still have a mind of her own.

It had seemed to him as he was growing up, that his parents never quarreled about anything. But as he got older, he observed expressions and eye movements which spoke volumes. His parents didn't disagree in front of him or his brothers, but he would never have gone so far as to say it didn't happen behind their closed bedroom door.

And now this thing with Joey Parker. Rigg had no right to tell Kate no, nor was he sure he wanted to. He didn't own her and wouldn't own her even if they were married. But at least if they were married he'd have free rein to go to her the night before and talk about the question with which she'd surprised them. As it was, his father had gone and that was as it should have been. But that didn't stop his frustration, knowing Kate left with things so unsettled and him not able to change that in any way.

Gil, Nate and Sean went fishing as scheduled, just after lunch. Marcail wanted to play in the barn and Kate went with her. Marcail had just disappeared up the ladder to the hayloft when Rigg entered.

Kate was trying very hard to hide her disappointment and believed she was succeeding nicely. Rigg didn't let on that he could read her like a book.

"Have you ever been in a hayloft?"

"No, I guess I haven't."

"Go on up."

"No, I'm fine right here."

"Too prim and proper?" It was clearly a challenge; one that Kaitlin couldn't resist as Rigg stepped lightly up the ladder and then stood above looking at her. He watched as she grasped the ladder with both hands and began to climb. Rigg immediately dropped to his stomach to reach for her and in a few seconds Kate gasped when she found herself standing in hay up to her knees. Rigg still had hold of her arms and walked her away from the edge.

"Hi Katie, isn't this fun?" Marcail was rolling and hopping around, basically having the time of her life and all Kaitlin could do was stare.

She watched birds fly back and forth to their nests in the rafters and felt the temperature contrast from below. The aroma was wonderful and Kate breathed deeply and took a step. A second later she was flat on her face and could hear Rigg's laughter as he stood above her.

Kate rolled and threw a handful of hay at him but it only blew back in her own face, causing Rigg to laugh all the harder.

"Are you going to help me up or laugh all day?" Kate's voice was indignant. Rigg came down on his knees beside her and helped her to a sitting position.

His voice was soft as he pulled bits of straw from her hair. "Still upset with me?" Kate believed the question related to that morning and not the present. She was right.

"Not upset, just disappointed."

"Why didn't you ask me to take you to the Parkers'?"

"I wanted you to offer. I wanted to feel like someone cared as much as I do."

Rigg was quiet a moment and then sat down facing her. He leaned one hand across her and rested it in the hay so he could bring his face very close.

"I believe the caring is coming but it will never equal the way I care about you. You're so innocent and you talk about going over to the Parkers' as if you're going to see your grandmother. It's not the same. I fear for your safety because you don't. Do you understand what I'm saying to you, Kaitlin?"

Kate nodded. "I won't go if you don't want me to."

Rigg knew what it cost her to say that and his eyes became so tender and loving Kate feared she might be kissed again. She wasn't sure she was ready for that. Rigg's hand came up and with one finger he touched her chin.

"Such a stubborn chin." His voice was loving and Kate watched as his head lowered.

"Katie!" Marcail called and Rigg stopped, his eyes on Kate's.

"I forgot she was up here," he said with a half smile, his voice soft.

"I'm kind of glad she is," Kate answered and grinned at him.

Marcail plopped down in the hay next to Rigg and Kate a moment later. "Look at this." She held the fragile half of an eggshell within her cupped hands, holding it carefully for their inspection.

"What kind is it?"

"Barn swallow," Rigg answered promptly. "We found them all the time as kids."

"Katie!" Marcail said suddenly. "You've got hay all over you!" Clearly the nine-year-old had never seen her sister in such a state.

"Is Katie always so prim and proper then?" Rigg couldn't resist his standing joke.

"Tell him no, Marcail," Kate ordered, but the little girl just smiled.
"Let's go down now so I can show Mrs. Taylor my egg."

"All right but first I want Kate to do something that would *not* be considered prim and proper."

Kate could feel her temper rise. "That's ridiculous. I am not too prim and proper."

Kate rose ungracefully and started toward the ladder but Rigg was faster. He climbed down and stood on the ladder with the upper part of his body showing up in the loft. Marcail was trying to keep from laughing and Kate faced him, arms akimbo.

"I need to get down," she stated.

"Just as soon as you prove to me that you can throw off your 'schoolteacher cloak.' "

"That's ridiculous."

"What shall we have her do, Marc, sing off-key?" Marcail found this highly amusing and couldn't hold her laughter even when Kate's eyes narrowed in her direction.

"Sing us a song Katie," Rigg directed.

"No!" Kate was beginning to see the humor in this and a smile was breaking across her face as she came toward the ladder but Rigg could not be bluffed. She plopped down before the ladder and tried to muster up a glare.

"I'm a man with infinite patience, Kate-love. Sing us a song and you can have the ladder."

Marcail laughed again and Kate could see Rigg wasn't going to budge. She threw back her head and crowed out the silliest song she could think of. Her voice screeched and cracked, causing Marcail to howl with laughter and Rigg to beg her to stop.

"Are you satisfied now?" Kaitlin demanded.

All Rigg could do was laugh.

"Hello."

May's voice came to the three in the loft and Kate and Marcail both leaned slightly over the edge to see her.

"Is everything all right?" Her tentative question started the laughter all over again as they made their way to the ground.

"Your son thinks I'm too stuffy for my own good and I was proving to him otherwise. Oh! Marc, did you bring your egg?"

Marcail displayed her prize once again and then May surprised them all with a question to Kate.

"I was wondering, Kate, if you'd like me to walk with you to the Parkers', so we can ask them to supper tonight?"

Forty-Eight

RIGG STARED AT his mother, completely nonplussed. He almost asked if Dad knew what she was planning, something he'd never even thought of saying to her before.

"I can see you're surprised and I don't want you to think I'm going behind your father's back. If Katie says yes, then I'll ask Bill to take us in the wagon. If Katie declines, I'll tell Jeff he's to escort her." May looked almost sternly at her son.

"You've bullied her about this Rigg, and I don't like it. I can understand your anxiety but you need to talk with her, not stomp on her hopes with your disapproving looks."

Kate found herself wishing she'd stayed in the haymow. She told herself she'd made a terrible mistake which had caused May and Rigg to have words. Marcail was equally as uncomfortable and tried to stand as unobtrusively as possible behind Kate. Kaitlin, with Marcail behind her, inched carefully toward the door, not wanting to disturb the conversation between mother and son. But just when she thought the way was clear, Rigg reached for her.

"Is that the way you feel?" His hand was on her upper arm and she could see there was no escape.

"Come along Marcail," Kate heard May saying and glanced over to see them exiting the barn.

"Do you Katie? Do you feel I stomp on your dreams?" Rigg's gaze was as intense as his voice.

Kate sighed. How could she explain all the emotions that were swirling around inside of her? She wasn't sure, but she needed to try.

"Rigg, how would you feel if you brought a girl home to your family and told them you wanted to marry her and they were not the least bit comfortable with her? I mean, they didn't warm up to her at all. Wouldn't you wonder if you'd made the right choice? Wouldn't you begin to question your heart—no matter how right things might have seemed at one time?

"Well, that's the way it is with Joey and his dad. I really believe that I'm supposed to reach out to them, but if none of you feel the same way, then I need to rethink my stand. If I was a man or my father were here, it would be different.

"But I'm not a man and I don't have a husband or a father to make going there all right. So if all of you, my closest friends in Santa Rosa, are against this, then for now at least, I have to assume the door is closed. But that doesn't change my heart or my prayers that Joey and his father will come to Christ.

"And now this, today. I've caused you to have words with your mother and that can't possibly be of the Lord. So I think I'd better drop the whole thing before I cause any more problems." Rigg watched Kate's shoulders sag and was overcome with guilt.

"Thank you for telling me how you feel. I owe you an apology, Kate. You didn't cause Mom and me to quarrel; I needed to hear what she had to say. The caring is coming but I'm more concerned for you. Where Parker is concerned I probably overreact. I mean, he'd be coming here to eat and you couldn't be more safe."

"Then you'll take me?" Kate was truly surprised.

"Right now, if you're ready."

"What brought on the change?"

"It's not as sudden as it seems but we've had no time to talk. Those verses in 1 Thessalonians really spoke to me. I've read them over and over and I can't say I've been faithful in the way I reach out to the unsaved in Santa Rosa. And when I have reached out, it was to someone easy, not someone of whom I was suspicious.

"Paul says the people he worked with were 'dear to him' and that's what I've been asking God for in my own heart. A deep compassion that would make Parker and Joey dear to me. As I've said, it's coming."

Kate was so relieved she felt tears sting her eyes. Why hadn't they talked like this a week ago?

"Thanks Rigg," was all she said and he smiled at her before turning to hitch up the wagon.

Joey was the first to spot the wagon and Frank, having recognized Kate, didn't bother to bark.

"Hi Joey!" Kate called, and the little boy came close to the wagon to talk with her.

"My pa liked my haircut." He smiled and Kaitlin was amazed at how he'd blossomed in the week he'd been coming to see her. Their conversation of the morning before came to mind and Kate prayed for an opportunity to question Joey.

"Is your dad here, Joey?"

"Not right now." Joey's look became uncertain and Kate hurried to explain.

"Tonight?" Joey asked. "For supper? Both of us?"

"Right. We're having a fish dinner and you should be at the Taylors' about six. Don't forget to tell your dad."

When the wagon pulled away, Kate looked back to see Joey waving furiously. She returned the wave feeling absolutely buoyant.

The guys had returned from their fishing spot up the creek with their creels overflowing. Marcail was an old hand at the procedure and she and Kate enlisted the help of Rigg and Jeff. Kaitlin wanted to do this for May so she sent Bill and May on a walk.

The men stood back and watched the girls attack the fish on the back porch. The fish were cleaned in record time and then cut in perfect strips. Neither one was the least bit squeamish and the job was done neatly and efficiently.

The men, sure they were being pressed into service to clean the fish, were fascinated. Once the fillets were ready, Rigg and Kate worked together over a bowl of what Kaitlin said held secret ingredients. When the fish had been dipped, Jeff was put to work frying.

"What is that for?" The question came from Rigg who was watching Kate prepare May's large roaster to go into the oven.

"This recipe is best when the fish can bake after they've been fried. It also gives us time to finish the rest of the meal."

"Us?" Rigg and Jeff chorused.

"Of course," Kate stated with absolute calm. "Rigg, you can start the rice and when you're done at the stove Jeff, you can shred that lettuce. Marc and I will fix this sauce and cut up the rest of the vegetables."

"Marc," Rigg asked, wanting to know, "has she always been this bossy?"

"Don't you answer that Marcail Donovan!" her sister warned. "It could get you into a lot of trouble."

Rigg gave Marcail a conspiratorial wink and a giggle escaped before she could stop it.

The table was set with two extra places and Kate fluttered around in a nervous dither as six o'clock drew near. The smell of fish wafted its way through the house and if Nate said he was hungry once, he said it a half-dozen times.

Kaitlin had been pacing the living room when she glanced out the window and froze. Tears filled her eyes as she watched Joey walking beside his father toward the house. Bill came out of his chair and gave Kate's cheek a kiss before going to greet their guests. May smiled and followed her husband.

"Use this Kate," Rigg held his handkerchief out to Kaitlin. She quickly wiped her face.

"How do I look?"

"Beautiful," Rigg answered sincerely.

"No, really, do I look all right?"

"You look fine." Rigg shook his head at how satisfied she was with the word fine but Kate didn't notice. She was headed to the kitchen to check on supper.

"Katie fixed supper tonight. Come on in and find a seat." It was Bill's voice coming from the living room as he led Parker to the kitchen where Kate stood by the table.

"Hello Mr. Parker."

His head bobbed in her direction and before too many minutes passed the whole family was seated and Bill was returning thanks for the food. The meal passed in mild pandemonium with everyone talking at once, or so it seemed.

Kate's cooking was a great success and she was complimented many times over. She acknowledged those compliments absently because she couldn't take her eyes off Parker. His manners were impeccable. He'd brushed his hair away from his face and buttoned his shirt to the neck. Kate had fully expected him to eat as Joey had the first night, but other than his hands shaking occasionally, his manners were flawless.

And he was talking! He sat to Bill's right and the two men conversed like old friends. Parker declined dessert and he and Joey didn't linger long after dinner.

Kate wanted to hug May when she extended an invitation to join them again for the following Friday night. Parker accepted graciously and then he and Joey took their leave.

Kate felt emotionally and physically drained. She was drying the dishes that Gilbert washed but she kept coming to a stop in the middle of the kitchen and staring at the dish in her hand without really seeing it.

"Are you all right?"

"What?" Kate had finally heard Gil's question.

"If you're tired Katie, I can do this," he offered kindly.

"No, I can help you." Kaitlin wasn't aware of how her every movement and even her voice, spoke of how exhausted she was.

"You must be glad that the Parkers came." Gil watched in helpless surprise as tears filled Kate's eyes.

"I am glad Gilbert. I can't think why I would need to cry about it."

"I think I understand." Gil looked with desperation at his mother who entered the kitchen just then.

"Why don't I help?" May said cheerfully.

"You don't need to." Kate's voice caught as she continued to dry the dish she'd had in her hand for five minutes. May didn't answer, recognizing her fatigue and praying that Rigg would come in and rescue her.

He did just that a few minutes later. Marcail was staying the night because Sean had to work in the morning and Rigg, as gently as he could, shepherded Kate to the wagon.

Kate didn't know when anything had felt as wonderful as crawling into her bed. She fell asleep before she could thank God for the tender hearts of the Taylors and that He was still holding the door to Joey Parker wide open.

Forty-Nine

THE CLOCK IN Rigg's office on Monday morning read eight forty-five and Rigg debated what to do; Kaitlin was late. He'd half expected her to be late because of her weary state the night before, but there was the remote chance she was not well and for that reason, Rigg couldn't rest. He stood up, having decided to go check with Sean when he saw her rush through the front doors.

She was flustered and apologetic when she arrived in the office but she also looked well rested. Rigg told her that her rest was important and that he wasn't at all upset. Kate didn't believe him and continued to apologize and berate herself.

"All right," he said quietly. "You're docked a day's pay."

Kate halted and stared at him. He was dead serious and she told herself she'd asked for it.

"Do you feel better now?" Rigg asked quietly and Kate felt like an utter fool.

"Katie," his voice was gentle and without rebuke. "I tease you at times but I think you'll agree that I've never played games with you. I also know you well enough to know that you take your job seriously. I *really* don't mind your being late."

"Thank you." Kaitlin's cheeks were still heated. Thankfully Rigg had work to do downstairs and Kate was given a chance to calm herself.

Her pride had been involved this morning and it had made a fool of her. She'd been horrified to awaken and see how late the hour was and rather then come in and apologize, she'd carried on until she forced Rigg to threaten her. She didn't think he would dock her but she had no business backing him into a corner that way.

Kaitlin prayed and was able to put the incident behind her. She could feel that she and Rigg were getting closer to one another every day but that didn't change the fact that he was her boss and he had a business to run. She told herself that starting immediately she was going to show new respect to him.

Kate was making fast work of the account books for the year and Rigg was pleased with her progress. The morning flew by and Bill came over to say he'd treat at the hotel. Kate popped into the post office and found a letter from Scott Harper in Hawaii. She tucked it away to read after work.

Sean surprised Rigg and Kate by offering to fix supper that night, so as soon as he was finished with his work he left for home. Rigg had some last minute things to do, so Kaitlin passed the time by reading her letter. She sat on a bench by the back door, knowing Rigg would want to go home that way.

Dear Kaitlin,

Hawaii has not been the same since you left. I told myself that I would not carry on in this letter about the way I miss you. At the same time, I want you to know that it took a while for me to accept that you're not coming back. I still think of you every day.

The work here prospers and we're thankful to have your father with us, even temporarily. So much damage occurred during the hurricane that I believe God must have known we would need him. In spite of the losses there is a bright side, and I'm talking about the hearts of the people. History repeats itself and it's exciting to see the revival that has begun in the wake of this disaster. Please continue to pray for us.

When I asked for your address I was surprised that you're no longer in San Francisco. Why aren't you? I thought you were living with your aunt.

I hope you'll write to me but I'll understand if you don't. I'm praying this finds you well. My folks send their love and please tell Sean and Marcail I said hello.

As ever,
Scott

Kate had effectively put Percy out of her mind for weeks. There was no one here like him and that certainly helped. But the guilt she felt, that she had somehow been the cause for the way he'd treated her, continued to plague her. And now, a simple question in Scott's letter brought the whole ugly episode back to mind as though it were happening all over again.

A shiver ran over Kaitlin when she remembered the way Percy had pulled her toward him. Her hand went to her throat when she pictured the way his head had bent toward her before Sean's words had stopped him.

"Katie?" Rigg's voice caused Kate to start violently and then pull away from the hand Rigg had placed tenderly on her arm. She looked up into his confused face and thought she could never explain. He wouldn't want anything to do with her if he knew.

"Katie," Rigg questioned her perceptively, "what is in that letter you just read? Is your father hurt?"

"No."

"Your aunt?"

"No. No one, I'm just—" *Just what?* Kate asked herself, knowing that Rigg was waiting for an answer to his question.

Rigg watched the emotions run over Kate's face. He was glad they were still inside the store because he had the strong impression she was about to run from him. After a short period of silence Rigg spoke softly.

"Who is the letter from?"

"Scott."

"Who lives in Hawaii?"

Kate didn't even hear his question.

"He wanted to know why we aren't living in San Francisco." Kate hadn't meant to say that out loud.

If Rigg had been unaware of the reason she'd left San Francisco he'd have had no idea why Scott's question was so upsetting. As it was, he believed he knew exactly what was going through Kate's mind.

"Katie, there's something I want you to know. Sean told me why you left your aunt's." Rigg's words, though gently spoken, had a traumatic effect on Kaitlin. Most of the color drained from her face and her eyes dilated with hurt and betrayal.

"He had no right." The words were choked out.

"He needed to talk. He was very upset about your cousin's actions and didn't think it had bothered you very much. He didn't feel he could come to you."

"He didn't think it bothered me?" Kate was astounded.

"That's what he said."

"I guess Sean's never done anything he's ashamed of or he would know why I never brought it up."

"Kaitlin." Rigg's voice was tenderness itself. "You have *nothing* to be ashamed of."

"I must have encouraged him." Tears filled her eyes and Rigg felt something akin to violence for this faceless cousin who haunted the woman he loved.

"Katie, that's simply not true. You're a beautiful woman but that gives no man the right to touch you against your will."

Kate continued to fight her tears even as a single question haunted her.

"How long have you known?"

"Since the first night Sean stayed with me," he admitted quietly.

Humiliation washed over her anew to think that Rigg had known all along about Percy. And then another question came to mind and Rigg watched a look of horror cover Kate's face.

"Who have you told?"

"No one." Rigg uttered the words softly, almost to himself, and Kate shook her head as though to clear it.

"I didn't mean that. I'm sorry."

"Let's go to the house. You and Sean need to talk and I think I would like to be there if no one has any objections."

Kate wondered how she got through the meal Sean fixed. The food looked wonderful but everything tasted like sawdust in her mouth. Sean noticed how quiet his sister and Rigg were and wondered, as they all worked on the dishes, if they'd quarreled.

Sean didn't know what to do with Kaitlin anymore. Didn't she know Rigg was in love with her? Didn't she see what a nice guy he was? He told himself that when he found the right girl, he was just going to tell her outright that they had to get married, then and there. None of this unsureness for him; none of this tiptoeing around in order not to scare her away.

Sean had worked himself into a tumult of emotions when Rigg spoke and brought him abruptly back to earth.

"Kate and I were talking before we left the store, Sean, and I think she needs to share with you what we talked about."

It was an awkward beginning but Rigg felt all of this should have been said long ago. Awkward or not, it was time to get their feelings out in the open.

"I got a letter from Scott today, Sean."

"Is Father all right?" Sean came completely out of his chair and Kate was quick to reassure him.

"Yes, I'm sorry I scared you." Kate waited until Sean was reseated and then went on. "The letter wasn't about Father and Scott didn't say anything upsetting, but he did ask me why we weren't in San Francisco.

"It made me start thinking and—" Kate couldn't go on so Rigg spoke up.

"When I came down and found Katie so upset I asked her about the letter. I then told her that I knew why you had left your aunt's. She told me she thinks the whole thing is her fault."

"Oh Katie, no! It's *my* fault." A look of near desperation crossed Sean's face and tears came to his eyes. The agony he felt on that day began to crowd in on him all over again.

"Sean, that's not true," Kate told him urgently. "I've never blamed you. And I didn't know until Rigg said something that you were that upset by what happened." Kate's voice faded on these last words. Brother and sister stared at each other. After a time Sean moved next to Kaitlin who sat on the sofa. Kate put her head against Sean's arm and sobbed. Through her tears she shared every awful thing she'd been feeling. From feeling badly about leaving Aunt Maureen to wishing she had no figure at all to be attracted to.

Rigg entered into the conversation when he felt a need and even though both Donovans were completely spent in the process, an hour later all was out in the open.

There was no longer any guilt between them or even anger toward their selfish cousin. The three of them would probably have talked all night if Kate hadn't noticed the time.

"We've got to get Marc."

"I can go get her," Rigg offered. Sean thanked him and said he would stay home, but Kate said she was in need of some air and went with him in the wagon. Rigg knew that she'd had a painful evening but there was one thing he needed to know. As the wagon moved toward his folks the setting sun bathed them in an orange glow. He couldn't think of a better time or place to ask her.

Fifty

"I WANT TO THANK you Rigg, for giving Sean and me the push we needed to start talking. I don't know if we ever would have and, well, just thanks."

"You're welcome. I'm sorry it was so hard for you. I'll be praying that God continues to heal the hurt for you Katie, and if you ever want to talk, just find me.

"I need to ask you something Kate." Rigg went on. "Would you rather I didn't question you tonight?"

"No, I don't mind."

"It's a couple of things actually. Do I remind you of your cousin Percy?"

"No!" Kate said so vehemently that Rigg couldn't hold his laughter, some of which was relief.

"Why did you ask that?" Kate inquired.

"Because I'm hoping we'll grow closer than we are now and if I remind you of Percy then I'm going to repulse you. I don't want to do that."

There, Rigg thought, *it's out in the open. You'll certainly know in the next few seconds if the door is still open with this woman or not.*

"You don't repulse me." The words were said so softly that Rigg almost missed them. But hear them he did and they gave him courage to ask his next question. He did so without looking at Kaitlin.

"I've also been wondering if I upset you when I kissed you. I didn't ask your permission to do such a thing and I want to apologize if I need to."

"And it almost happened a second time." Kate's softly spoken words caused Rigg to finally look at her. She didn't return his gaze, giving Rigg a wonderful view of her profile. Rigg also didn't bother to correct her about how many times he'd *almost* kissed her, times when she'd been completely unaware of his intentions. Like when she brought the account books over for his inspection and he thought he would drown in the fresh smell of her hair. Or when they shared little moments, like doing the dishes together or how her face would flush with laughter over something he'd teased her about. But for right now it was best to leave those times unmentioned.

"I'm not upset with you about the kiss but I don't think I want you to do it again unless you give me a chance to tell you no." The words were said sweetly and without rebuke. Rigg felt as though a great burden had been lifted from his heart.

"I can appreciate that and I'll certainly honor your wishes."

My wishes, Kate thought, and almost laughed.

How many times had she wished Rigg would kiss her again or hold her in his arms? For a time she doubted that Rigg cared for her in a romantic way, but now she understood that he was taking his cue from her.

Maybe she *was* too stuffy for her own good because she just didn't know how to subtly let a man know she was interested in him. Once again Kate wished Mother or Father were here to talk with.

She thought of confiding in Aunt Maureen but didn't see how that was possible either. There was May—they had grown closer each weekend they stayed there. *But how did a woman ask the mother of the man she was interested in, how to show him—*

Kate couldn't even finish that thought. She realized that even if she had someone to ask, she wouldn't know the questions.

Marcail was picked up without fuss and Rigg was as sweet as ever when he delivered them home. Marcail had to fall asleep with the lantern burning because Kate was writing to Father.

Dear Father,

I wish you were here more than I can say. I've always been able to tell you how I feel and I won't hesitate now. I think I'm in love.

I say think, because I have no idea what it feels like to be in love. I was never one of those girls who spent much time daydreaming about the type of man I'd marry. I mean, I thought of it certainly, but just in passing. And then, wham, right out of the blue, I'm looking at Rigg in a whole new light.

At one time he made me furious every time we were together. But now I'm disappointed when he leaves and ecstatic when I know I'll see him again. He's so tender with me; and not just me but Sean and Marc too.

Now you're probably wondering how he feels about me and I can't honestly say that I know. He told me tonight that he hopes we'll become closer. Well, he can't mean physically because we work in the same office every day, sit together in church and I spend all my weekends at his folks', so I assume he means closer emotionally.

Was that the kind of thing you said to Mother, when you fell in love with her? I'm so confused. What if he does tell me he loves me before you return? I don't even know where you want to live when you come back, and what would I say to him?

Kate continued on in a frenzy of thoughts and nearly unintelligible print. She went on to tell her father that she believed Rigg to be a man of God and that her heart did funny things when he was near, even though sometimes she wanted to strangle him.

Kate ended the letter with news on Joey and pleas for prayer. She also asked her father to write back immediately and to come home soon, wherever home was.

When she finally went to bed, she fell asleep swiftly—but not before she asked God to speed her letter across the sea and thanked Him for sending her to Santa Rosa and to a man named Marshall Riggs.

Fifty-One

THE MIDDLE WEEKS of summer sped by and Kate waited anxiously for news from her father. Aunt Maureen had been in touch several times and reported that Uncle Mitch was back out to sea. Once again she was lonely. Kate had long ago replied to Scott's letter, carefully giving him no hope of a future relationship with her.

Mr. Parker and Joey came to supper at the Taylors' nearly every week and Joey also continued his visits with Kate from time to time. Kaitlin was to learn new meaning for the word patience, as no opportunity afforded itself to talk with the little boy about his need to trust in Christ for salvation.

Mr. Parker blossomed slowly under the tender ministrations of this family and they soon found that no one had ever made a move to help this man. In bits and pieces it came out that he was an orphan, abandoned when he was five. He lived with a number of different families until he was ten and the father of one household beat him until he couldn't stand up. The next day he took every dime of money he could find on the place and left. He'd been on his own ever since.

Parker never outright admitted it, but the Taylors were able to gather that he hadn't been married to Joey's mother. He also didn't know if she was dead or alive. They hadn't laid eyes on each other since Joey was nine months old.

But of all the things that Parker shared, Joey's words to Kaitlin one night were the most revealing.

"One morning," the little boy said, "the marshall came and took my Pa. Said he'd hurt a woman. But he didn't do that, Miss Donovan. I know because he'd been drinking and Pa can't hardly stand when he's been drinking, let alone go off in the woods and hurt somebody.

"He didn't leave home all day, I told them that. But they wouldn't listen and when he was in jail I was the most scared I'd ever been in my life. I hated staying by myself. Even if Pa's passed-out drunk, I want him there. When they kept him a second night I snuck into town and slept outside his jail window."

Kate had no words for the sober confession from this child. She put her arms around him and held him close. Joey clung to her and Kaitlin begged God with a renewed burden to use her in the life of the boy.

While Kate's relationship with Joey became stronger, the closeness she'd always shared with Sean began to wane. It was heartbreaking for her but she knew the steps from boyhood to manhood were awkward and confusing. Some things you couldn't share with your sister.

Kate and Marcail were as close as ever, but Kate found herself dealing with an unexpected well of emotions over Marcail's closeness to May. Kate's heart asked God if nine was young enough to forget your real mother. It seemed that every week Marcail was with May she became more her daughter and less Theresa Donovan's. What would Father say?

It wasn't that Kate didn't love May—quite the opposite—she thought the world of her. But she was also having to realize that a 20-year-old's need for a mother were quite different from a 9-year-old's.

And very recently, as with most things in Kaitlin's world, she had talked to Rigg about it. They had grown closer just as Rigg had hoped and there weren't many things they hadn't discussed. Sometimes in calm logic, other times at the tops of their voices.

The subject of Marcail was the most recent to come on the table and Rigg would never know how close Kate came to throwing her arms around him for his sensitivity.

It was Wednesday night. Rigg, Kate, Sean and Marcail were all walking home from mid-week service; Rigg's wagon was undergoing repairs at the livery. When they'd arrived at the church Marcail had gone immediately to May and wrapped her arms around the older woman's waist. To watch them you'd think they hadn't seen each other for days.

On the way home Rigg seemed almost pensive as he walked at Kate's side, Sean and Marcail far in front of them, kicking a can as they went.

"You're quiet," Kate commented.

"Just thinking."

"About?" Rigg was usually very open, giving Kate the freedom to ask without feeling an intruder.

"I was thinking about Marc and my mother and feeling rather thankful that your father can't see how little she seems to miss your mother."

Kate stopped Rigg with a hand on his arm. "Oh Rigg," she whispered, "I've agonized over this. Please don't get me wrong. I adore May. But I can't believe Marc has forgotten Mother. I tell myself that Mother isn't here and May is but it doesn't make it any easier and I don't dare say anything to Marc."

"Kaitlin, I wish you'd have come to me. I just noticed it this evening."

"I've been seeing it for a few weeks. And just this week when Sean and I both had to work, I told Marc to write to Father because May always has ink and paper handy. But when I picked her up she said she'd been too busy cleaning house with your mom.

"I'm trying to remember how young she is but—" Kate shrugged helplessly and Rigg reached for her hand. They walked that way for a time and Kate reveled in the comfort she found in the simple act of having her hand swallowed up in Rigg's. They were both disappointed when Sean and Marcail stood still and waited for them to catch up, causing them to let go of each other's hands.

Once at the house Sean didn't wait around but headed straight for Rigg's. Marcail went in to ready for bed and Rigg lingered outside, as always, reluctant to leave Kaitlin.

"You haven't heard from your father lately, have you?"

"No. I'm expecting a letter soon though. I always pray when I send mine that God will speed it to him but I'm afraid service to the island usually takes a while. Why do you ask?"

"I guess I was just wondering if you'd ever mentioned me to your father and if you did, what he had to say?"

"I've written about you, yes," Kate replied carefully, remembering how in her last letter she'd told Father that she thought she loved this man. "But like I said, I'm waiting to hear from him now."

"Has your father ever mentioned where he wants to live once he returns?" The question was a study in casualness but Kate wasn't fooled.

"As a matter of fact, I brought that subject up in my last letter. Like I said I'm—"

"Waiting to hear," Rigg finished for her, his eyes on hers, serious and intent. "I hope you understand Kaitlin, I can't just let you walk away."

Kate understood very well but could find nothing to say in response. She watched Rigg step close and let him take her hand once again. They stood for a moment, enjoying one another without words. Finally Rigg gave her hand a small squeeze and spoke.

"Good night, Kate-love. I'll see you in the morning."

Kate was sure she could still feel his hand holding hers long after he'd disappeared into the dark.

Fifty-Two

"DID WE REALLY agree to do this?" Kaitlin asked Marcail as they readied for church the next Sunday.

"Yes, we agreed," Marcail informed her. "Katie, what are you so upset about? You've sung in church a million times."

"This is different."

"Why is it different?"

Because Rigg will be there, Kate thought, but didn't bother to voice that sentiment to her sister. Kate was certain she was going to go in front of that church and make a total fool of herself. Why, she'd never be able to face Rigg again!

Kate knew the minute she saw Sean that he was just as nervous as she. They exchanged an agonized glance and did little more than play with their breakfast.

It would have helped to be called to the front immediately after the service began, but there were announcements to be made and then the congregation sang a few songs. When the time finally came, Bill was not satisfied by just allowing Pastor Keller to call them forward. He went into the pulpit and introduced them as though they were a traveling band.

"I know all of you have had the privilege of meeting Kaitlin, Sean and Marcail Donovan, and probably most of you know that they grew up as missionary children in Hawaii. But I don't think many of you know that all three of them are fluent in Hawaiian. And this morning they've agreed to sing for us in that beautiful language."

On those words Kate, with her heart pounding and wishing they'd had some sort of accompaniment, led the way to the front. None of the Donovans realized how beautiful they sounded a cappella.

The song they shared was the same one they had sung for the Taylors many weeks ago and since it was short, they sang it through twice. Both Kate and Sean were nearly giddy with relief that it was over, when Pastor Keller jumped from his seat and asked them for more.

For a moment the two older Donovans stood frozen, their minds blank and then Marcail saved the day by suggesting another hymn. This happened two more times making a total of four songs and at one point, Kate remembered they were singing to the Lord. As she committed the lyrics to God along with her voice, all self-consciousness disappeared.

When they moved from the front back to their seats, Kate sat down next to Rigg. She didn't look at him but could feel his eyes on her. When he reached over and gave her hand a squeeze her whole being melted with relief. Kate smiled at Rigg with her heart in her eyes.

Pastor Keller began his sermon just after that. Kaitlin had been too uncomfortable up front to look beyond the second row or she would have seen Joey Parker sitting in the last church pew.

She did catch sight of him as they exited, disappearing around the corner of the church toward home. She nearly ran to intercept him and he stopped reluctantly. He looked at her with shy embarrassment.

"Hi Joey. Did you hear me sing?"

"Yeah. It was nice." He smiled at her and as always, Kate's heart turned over.

"I could teach you a song in Hawaiian sometime. Would you like that?"

"Yeah." Joey's face came alive with the idea but when Kate asked him if he wanted to come for lunch he stepped away from her, declining as he went.

Kaitlin watched him walk away, her heart heavy. He was so young to be fighting God but Kate was convinced this was exactly what he was doing. Pastor Keller had challenged everyone in the room that morning to settle their eternity before leaving. Kate was certain that if Joey had trusted in the Lord that morning, he'd have told her.

"You're quiet," Rigg commented as they drove toward his folks.

"I was thinking of Joey. I know God is speaking to that boy but he's fighting Him and making himself miserable in the process."

Rigg agreed with her and then told her he liked the songs she sang.

"Were we really all right?" Kate's hand went to Rigg's arm and he was suddenly conscious of his brothers in the back.

"You were great. Your voices harmonize beautifully. I almost hope for Sean's sake that his voice never changes. He's a great tenor."

"Poor Sean," Kate commented. "He thinks he sounds like a girl. He hates it."

"There's nothing feminine about the way Sean sings," Jeff commented from the back. "He has nothing to worry about."

"Unless it's the number of teenage girls who nearly fall out of their seats when he passes by," Gil commented almost absently, but Kaitlin's head whipped around in surprise. She never thought about girls finding her brother attractive. Sean was cute, or at least she'd always thought so, and now she was seeing for the first time that she wasn't alone in that belief.

"I can see Gil surprised you." Rigg was watching her and Kate felt her face heat up.

"It's hard to see your own brother in, well, that way," she admitted.

"We know what you mean, Katie," Jeff called forward. "We don't see how you can stand to spend so much time with Rigg."

"She must feel sorry for him because he's so homely," Gilbert added in a stage whisper.

"You can both be replaced you know," Rigg informed them. A giggle escaped Kaitlin but when Rigg turned to look at her she gave him the most innocent look she could muster.

"Are you going to tell me I can be replaced too?"

"No. I don't like to tell lies."

"Now would you listen to this!" Jeff said with disgust. "What do we have to do to get a little appreciation around here?"

"For one thing, it would help if you smelled better."

Everyone laughed at Jeff's expense but he took it well. They were still chuckling when they got home and found Burt Kemp waiting for Miss Donovan.

"I know I shouldn't be doing business on Sunday but I missed you at church. And truth is, I just heard that they need a schoolteacher over on the west-side of town and I didn't want them to steal you away from us."

All of these words had been directed at Kate as he'd helped her from the wagon. She now stood staring at Burt in confusion.

"Mr. Kemp, you'll have to forgive me, but I'm not sure what you're talking about."

"Why teaching in the fall of course." He smiled at Kate as though he'd just offered her a lifetime contract. That such a thing never occurred to Kate was clear by the look on her face.

"Is there some reason you don't want to come back and teach at our school?" Some of Burt's enthusiasm drained away and he rushed on to sell Kaitlin on the idea.

"Oh, I know there was that whole mess with your salary, but Greg is sorry about that and you would be hired full-time at full pay. And if you don't like the dates we've picked for school to begin and end, we could certainly discuss that."

Rigg could see that Burt was prepared to go on all day. May and Bill were now on the scene and Rigg was thankful when his father interrupted.

"It looks like Kate needs to think on this, Burt. I don't think you need to worry about her going across town though."

Kate agreed with a smile, even as her mind raced. What if Father came back in the fall and wanted to move away? What if Rigg pressed his suit?

"Thanks Mr. Kemp, for checking with me but I'll need to pray about this and talk with Sean and Marcail."

"Oh certainly, Miss Donovan. I'm sorry if I was out of line in any way."

"Not at all. And I consider it a great compliment that you want me back." Kate was using her gift for making people feel at ease, something for which everyone was thankful.

Burt took his leave then and Kate went inside with May to fix lunch. The older woman noticed her houseguest's solemn look and commented on it.

"I know Burt didn't mean to upset you."

"I'm sure you're right May. But the truth is, I'm not sure what my father would want or if Rigg wants me to continue on the books through the fall."

"Or if he possibly had another job in mind for you, one a little more personal?" May said the words softly and Kate felt her lungs empty of air. She stared at her hostess for an instant and then busied her hands with potatoes. She tried to ignore the words she'd just heard, knowing as she did, that it was a mistake.

"How would you feel about that, May?" Kate asked the question quickly before she could talk herself out of it.

"Oh, I'd probably rant and rave at him," May came close to Kate and smiled into her eyes, "and ask him why he took so long."

Kaitlin's jaw dropped in a most unfeminine way and May laughed. In the next instant the two women were hugging each other and laughing hard.

"Can I get one of those hugs?" Bill asked from the doorway and Kate watched in surprise, as May moved so that the table separated her and her husband. Bill's brows rose, telling her he'd accept her challenge if he had to.

"No hugging in front of the children," May stated as primly as she could and Bill laughed. She allowed him to close the distance then and Kate watched unashamedly as they embraced. When she did go back to working on lunch, she did so thanking God for the special family He'd sent her way.

Fifty-Three

KAITLIN AND MARCAIL lay on their stomachs in the haymow looking out the loft door to the yard below. Lunch was over and the girls were feeling lazy. They heard movement behind them and a moment later Sean flopped down on Kaitlin's open side.

"Did Burt Kemp really ask you to teach again?" Sean wasted no time in asking the question that had been on his mind through lunch.

"Full salary."

"He did?" Marcail asked, wondering where she had been all the time this was going on.

"What will you do?" Sean wanted to know.

"You can't teach here in Santa Rosa, Katie. Father will probably want us to live with Aunt Maureen."

This was something she'd already thought of but hadn't bothered to mention to her sister.

"It would be easier to leave the mercantile than it would the school if Father came back," Sean stated logically. "But if you plan to make Santa Rosa your permanent home then you need to be discussing with Rigg where you should work."

Two in one day, Kate thought.

She wondered if Rigg had been telling people something that he should have discussed with her first.

You know better, Kaitlin, she immediately said to herself. *The way he feels about you is written on his face, for all the world to see.*

"I want us to be together," Marcail said after a moment.

Sean and Kaitlin would have been surprised if Marcail *hadn't* understood the gist of their conversation, so they made no pretense in front of her as they continued to talk.

"Marc," Sean began, "do you understand what's happening between Katie and Rigg?"

"They love each other."

"Right. And that's how it should be. We don't know when Father is coming back but we do know that until then, we'll be together. If Kate marries Rigg, and Father is still gone, then we'll still be here in Santa Rosa. She's not going to ship us off to San Francisco by ourselves. Isn't that right, Katie?"

"Right." Kate was relieved that that was all she had to say; it was all she *could* say.

"And you never know, Marc," Sean went on. "Maybe Father will like Santa Rosa enough to want to stay."

Marcail looked very satisfied and Kate put her face against Sean's shoulder to cover her tears. She couldn't stand the thought that Marcail would be hurt by her relationship with Rigg. The thought of being separated from her siblings, even if it meant a lifetime with Rigg, was more than she could deal with at the moment.

"Are you all right Katie?" Marcail asked softly.

"Yes."

"Katie, where would we live if you married Rigg?"

Kate's tears came harder and Sean kept still as she wet his shirt sleeve.

"You know," he said finally, "maybe we're jumping the gun here. He hasn't asked her—or has he, Kate?"

"No." Kate sniffed and then complained, "I don't know what's the matter with me these days. All I do is cry."

"That's okay," Sean said. "Rigg calls it a late reaction. As least that's what he said when I told him I hadn't cried much about Mother. He said sometimes we don't need to cry and then we find ourselves crying nonstop."

Sean was so sweet with Kate that she only felt worse and suddenly very tired. A few minutes later Rigg climbed up to join them and Sean eased away from his sister. Her head fell against her outstretched arm and for the first time Sean saw she was asleep.

Sean stood and looked down at her and then at Rigg. Whispering, he asked Marcail if she wanted to come, but she shook her head no. Rigg and Marcail watched him leave and then Rigg motioned for Marcail to join him where he sat against the barn wall.

"Was Katie crying?" Rigg immediately asked, still speaking in hushed tones.

"Yes she was. It almost made me cry too."

"That would have been okay," Rigg assured her.

"I don't like to cry, it makes my head hurt and sometimes I throw up." Her admission was so honest, her face so creased by her frown that Rigg couldn't help smiling. He adored this little girl.

"Tears aren't ever fun but they're sometimes very needed. Were Katie's needed?"

"I think so. Rigg, are you going to marry Katie?"

Rigg's eyes went to Kaitlin's sleeping form. He couldn't see her face but knew she was out cold. "I don't think it would be right to talk to anyone about that before I've talked with Katie. Do you know what I mean?"

"Yes." They fell silent again and then Marcail had another question. "Does the man always ask?"

"The girl to marry him, you mean?"

"Right. Can the girl ask the boy?"

"I guess so. It's tradition for the man to ask and from everything I've heard, most people like it that way."

"Do you?"

Rigg could see Kate stirring so he answered Marcail's question very softly. "I think when two people love each other, it doesn't matter who asks, just as long as they can be together." Marcail seemed content with that answer. She had more questions but Kate was stirring. They watched as she came slowly to a sitting position. Kaitlin blinked at Rigg and Marcail as if she were dreaming them.

"Hi Katie. How did you sleep?"

Kate didn't answer her sister; things were still too fuzzy. She continued to frown at them until Marcail giggled.

"Would you like to get down?" Rigg asked. "I can help you on the ladder." But again Kate didn't answer. She pulled her knees up and wrapped her skirt around herself. Once she had curled herself into a ball, she stared out the door at the trees.

"I dreamed that Father was back," Kate said softly. "He'd grown a beard and we didn't recognize him at first. I think I miss him more than ever." Marcail moved over to Kate and she drew her close.

Rigg's eyes met Kaitlin's over the top of Marcail's head and his look told Kate he was very aware of her pain. Quietly Kate began to talk, not reminiscing as they'd done on the front porch earlier, but about her fears. At first she held back, not wanting to upset Marcail, but Marcail shared a few of her own fears, surprising Kate with the intensity of her feelings.

Rigg listened attentively and spoke with tenderness, telling the girls how normal their fears were and how much he believed God was going to take care of their every need.

They talked until the heat of the loft drove them down the ladder. Once outside the barn they walked toward the house, seeking the cool interior and something to drink. They were almost at the back door when Joey Parker came shooting into the yard.

"My Pa's been hurt!" he cried in panic. "There's blood everywhere and he won't wake up."

The entire family heard his screams and within seconds everyone was gathered in the yard, trying to understand his hysterical chatter. When they could see that he was not going to calm down, Bill, Rigg, and Jeff jumped in the wagon, grabbed Joey, and headed for the Parker house. Kaitlin wanted to go along to comfort Joey, but Bill stepped in and forbade her.

"I have no idea what we'll find and I'm not about to take you into that situation."

Kate stood with the rest of the family until the dust had settled on the road, covering Parker and the loved ones in the wagon with their prayers.

Fifty-Four

THE ODOR INSIDE the Parker house was overpowering. It was also dark and therefore took a moment for the men's eyes to adjust and find Joey's father.

There was indeed blood everywhere but he was breathing. He had evidently passed out from drink and hit his head. Commenting that head wounds were typically gushers, Bill told Joey to try and calm Frank down. He was barking in a near frenzy over being shut outside. No one believed he would attack, but the noise he made was very annoying.

"Let's get Parker outside," Bill commented. "I need air and I think he must too."

Joey was sent to fetch water and using an old shirt, they attempted to clean Parker's head. Coming around some when the gash at his temple was touched, he tried to shove the ministering hands away from him.

"Should I go for the Doc?" Jeff wanted to know.

"I want your mother to see him first. She's always good with head wounds. If she thinks we need to go for the doctor, then we will."

They learned quickly that the easiest method for moving Parker was simply to let Rigg lift him in his arms. No small task, the muscles corded in Rigg's neck as he strained under the load. They were, however, on their way in no time with Joey and a half-conscious Parker in the back.

May examined Parker while he was still in the wagon and decided she could patch the cut herself.

"But first, I think he should have a bath. Are you up to it?" May asked her sons and husband and they agreed without hesitation. As it was, Parker awoke as soon as the water touched his skin and Bill stayed in the bathing room to assist him.

Joey would not believe that his father was going to be all right, so Rigg took him in for a brief visit. He then tried to get him to eat.

"This bread was made yesterday Joey, it's real fresh." Rigg put together a chicken sandwich for both of them while Kate poured lemonade. May cut apples into slices. All the adults watched the little boy's eyes move repeatedly in the direction of the room his father was in.

"What are you afraid of Joey?" May asked softly, thinking it was time someone addressed the fear usually masking this child's face.

"I'm afraid my Pa will die," he admitted. His face was so vulnerable that Kaitlin wondered if she might need to leave the room. "And I'll be left all alone."

"May I tell you a story Joey?" May waited for him to nod before she began. "When I was just a young woman I married a man and we had a baby—a son. I was the happiest woman on earth. But then, when my son was only two years old, my husband died.

"I didn't think I could go on. I loved him so much and he was a wonderful father to our son. I don't know when I've ever felt so alone . . . but then a wonderful thing happened. I remembered a Bible verse that said God would never leave me nor forsake me. I remembered that my husband was with the Lord and that the Lord still loved Rigg and me.

"But Joey, I want you to listen to me very carefully. I wouldn't have known that about the Lord if I hadn't made a decision to trust Him for my salvation when I was young. When I was about your age, I understood that I needed a Savior. Without my believing that Jesus Christ died on the cross for my sins, I would go to hell. I didn't want to go to hell, Joey, I wanted to live forever with God.

"I was sick with grief right after my husband died but God reminded me of His love and that changed everything inside of me. I was no longer afraid or believed I'd been deserted. I knew that God loved me and died for me and that meant there was nothing more to fear. Not being alone, not dying, nothing.

"Joey, do you have that peace, that special quiet inside of you because you know God is your Savior? Have you faced God and confessed your need for a Savior?"

There were tears puddling in Joey's eyes as he shook his head no. She went on to ask him if he wanted to pray right at the table. He then voiced his second fear.

"But what if Pa never believes in Jesus?"

"Oh, honey, I can't promise you that he will. But I do know that you are not responsible for your father. When you stand before God, He's not going to say to you, 'Joey, why didn't you save your father?' Only God can take care of that and right now the best thing you can do for your father is to trust God yourself.

"God died for your father too, and he might see the change in you and want that change for himself. But even if that doesn't happen—"

"I'd still be God's child," Joey broke in and May nodded, her own eyes beginning to fill.

The people in the room watched in awe as Joey looked up at the ceiling with his eyes wide open. His voice was clear and without hesitation as he spoke to God.

"I know You're up there. I've known it for a long time. I'm ready now to be Yours, if You still want me. I'm ready for You to take away my sins and live in my heart."

The look on Joey's face was indescribable. The peace of God had descended upon this small child and there was almost a visible difference. He didn't say anything for a few minutes and all in attendance found themselves afraid to breathe. Rigg, May, and Kate were in the kitchen with him. Just out of sight in the living room, sat Sean, Marcail, Jeff, Nate and Gil.

"Can I tell Marcail?" Joey finally asked. "And Sean too?"

"That's a wonderful idea Joey," May said. "They're in the living room; go right in. Then maybe you'll want to go in and tell your father what's happened." Joey nodded and left the kitchen.

Upon Joey's departure, Kate surrendered to the battle with her tears. She and May embraced for a long time and when they broke apart, Rigg hugged his mother.

"Thanks for stepping in Mom."

May's smile was still watery but her face was radiant as she made her way to the back stairway. As soon as she left, Kate and Rigg began to pray for the man to whom Bill was ministering. They both had a premonition that there would be a long road ahead for all of them when it came to Parker and his attempts to bury the past and present in drink.

Fifty-Five

PARKER WAS SITTING at the table eating when Rigg and Kaitlin left the farm. Joey was beside him and, as Kate thought back, she wondered if she would ever forget the poignant scene of Joey telling his father he'd trusted in Christ.

Parker had stared at his son for a long time before nodding and going back to his plate. Parker, with his forehead bandaged and wearing clean clothes, looked like a new man. Kate found herself praying that he would soon understand that he needed to be clean on the inside, too.

Sean did not have to work the next day but May did. So, thinking Sean might like the change of pace, May asked Sean to stay at the farm the next day so he and Nate could care for Marcail.

Rigg thoroughly enjoyed having Kate to himself for a few minutes and told her so.

"I like it too," she admitted softly.

"How are you feeling about Burt Kemp's offer?"

Kaitlin immediately remembered Sean's words about discussing that subject with Rigg if she was going to make Santa Rosa her *permanent* home. The thought made her blush, turning her face a fiery red, so red that Rigg noticed in the gathering dusk.

"You're blushing." He stated the obvious as he lifted her down from the wagon. He dipped his head to look her in the eye since she wouldn't raise her gaze to his. "What did I say?"

Kaitlin didn't answer him.

"Let me see." Rigg spoke quietly and continued to watch her. "My last words were about Burt's offer—oh! There she goes again."

Kate hated her lack of self-control as her face began to heat all over again. She wished it had been darker when they arrived back at the house.

"Please don't tease me Rigg." The words were spoken softly and Rigg took both her hands in his own as they faced each other.

"I'm sorry. You don't have to tell me."

Kate was silent for a moment. She could feel Rigg's eyes on her but kept her face averted. Finally, "May I ask you a question?"

"Sure."

"What would you do in my place?"

"I can't tell you what to do Katie."

"No, I guess you can't but you must have some feelings about it. I'm just asking you to share those with me."

"All right. Answer some questions for me. What do you *want* to do, teach or work at the store?"

"I love teaching but I think I might like working in your office just a little more, but then I feel guilty because I know they need a teacher. I also have guilt because you hired me and I can't just walk out on that job. And if Father returns I'll probably have to quit, no matter what position I take."

"But you need work now. And don't feel guilty on my behalf. Do what you feel the Lord would have you do. I'll be praying that you'll know His will and follow it."

"Thanks Rigg."

They stood for a moment longer and then Rigg bent and placed a soft kiss on Kaitlin's forehead. Her heart nearly burst at his tenderness. But she wasn't prepared for his next words.

"Kaitlin, I'm in love with you." The words, spoken in Rigg's soft, deep voice, were humble and sincere.

"Oh, Rigg." Kate breathed, wanting to tell him of her love also but being so unsure of her future, she held back. "If only I knew—"

"Shhh." Rigg's voice was gentle as he stopped her. "You don't need to say anything. But I wanted you to know how I felt and I also want you to be secure in my love, not intimidated by it."

Once again Rigg kissed her brow and then placed his arms around her. Kate held tightly to him, thinking that nothing had ever felt so wonderful.

We need to be together, she told the Lord as Rigg pulled away from her and climbed into the wagon. *He loves me and I love him. I've prayed so long to know Your will. Show us Lord, show us Your path for our lives. Give us Your blessing heavenly Father, to build a marriage in You.*

As though he could read Kate's mind, Rigg prayed as he drove home. He too longed to be with her and felt it was God's will. He also knew what a weighty thing it was for Kate not to hear from her father. Rigg sternly told himself that he needed to bide his time in pursuing her. In the light of his belief that it was God's will they be together, he needed to wait for God's timing.

"I'm completely caught up on the past books, Rigg. Would you like me to start on this month?" It was Friday afternoon, and Kate and Rigg were in the office.

The week had sped by. Burt Kemp had checked with Kaitlin one more time but again she had put him off. It was as though her life hung in the balance until she heard from her father.

Rigg told Kate she could go home for the day and plan to start the next journal on Saturday. As she'd done every day that week, she headed to the post office. Today was different; today there was a letter from Father.

Kate noticed that, for the first time, it was addressed to her alone. She clutched it to her chest and hurried home. Kate prayed as she sat alone at her small kitchen table and asked God for help in dealing with the contents of the letter.

My darling Kate,

I write to you today with a bittersweet feeling in my heart. Bitter, because I'm so far from you at this wonderful time when you've fallen in love, and sweet, because I know—I remember so well how you are feeling.

Katie, I can't urge you strongly enough to follow God and your heart. If this young man desires you for a wife and you know that to be God's will, *do not hesitate.*

My words may surprise you, but your mother and I talked about the possibility of you meeting someone on our furlough and not returning to Hawaii with us. We both wondered how we would ever survive the separation but a child is not meant to live with her parents forever. Your desire to want a husband and a home of your own is completely normal. We would never have stood in your way.

Now, I'll admit to you that I always assumed I would know the young man, but you've introduced him in your letters, as have Sean and Marcail. And I will make this request: If he does want to marry you, that he write and ask me. I don't expect you to hold your plans until I reply. In fact, Marshall can tell me the date in his letter, but I would like this small courtesy if he's sincere about marrying my precious Katie.

If things have not progressed this far in your relationship, let me know. But I think now is a good time to warn you that I'll not be coming in the fall, as I'd hoped. It will be some time after Christmas.

Kate had to stop reading at this point. Her eyes had flooded with tears until she couldn't see the print.

She had been ready to deal with Father telling her not to get involved, something he hadn't done. But she wasn't ready to deal with his continued absence, even though he had warned them that it might be fall or later until he returned. Kate had not really believed him. She had not *wanted* to believe him. She needed him here.

There was no more doubt in Kaitlin's mind as to whether or not Rigg was going to ask her to marry him; it was just a matter of time. But this was August! How could she ever tell him they had to wait until after Christmas to be married? And then there was still no guarantee that Father would be home. The letter said *sometime* after Christmas.

It also said "do not hesitate." Kate pulled herself together and finished reading.

It hurts me to write this to you, but my reasons are joyful. There is tremendous revival going on here and the need for spiritual leadership is greater than ever.

When we left Hawaii I felt it would be good for the mission to be without me, and then in San Francisco I was not certain I could return as a ministering pastor. There are no words to describe my loneliness for you, but God is using me and I feel I must stay on.

Maureen has been in touch, she hopes we'll all be in San Francisco for the holidays. She will be keenly disappointed when I write her. Maybe you can see her? If not for Christmas, then possibly Thanksgiving. But do as you think best.

Having to communicate like this, with miles separating us, is difficult at best. I am praying for you as you knew I would be, and trusting God to guide your heart.

Give my love to Sean and Marcail.

Love,
Father

Kaitlin read the letter over a second time, knowing when she was finished, what her next course of action would be. This was what she'd been praying for. The uncertainty was gone; she now knew what direction to take.

With the letter tucked safely into the pocket of her skirt, Kaitlin went to find her brother.

Fifty-Six

KATE FOUND SEAN on the loading dock at the back of the mercantile, preparing to leave for the night.

"Sean." Kate's voice was urgent. "I need to talk with you."

"What's the matter?"

"I want you to help me talk with Rigg."

Sean eyed her with a curious look. "You don't have any problem talking with Rigg. What's up?"

"This." Kate thrust the letter at him and waited as he read. She watched the emotions play across his face as he came to the part about their father's delayed return.

"I'm sorry, Sean. I know you're disappointed and I know my timing is bad but I need a favor. I want to tell Rigg that I love him but I know I won't be able to get it all out in English and I want you to translate."

They had begun walking toward Rigg's house and Sean turned his head to look at his sister as though she were crazy.

"Kaitlin, are you serious?" He sounded so incredulous that she felt ashamed.

"It's all right Sean. That was a terrible thing for me to ask you. Just forget it, okay?"

Sean didn't say anything to that. He knew she was embarrassed about having to ask him in the first place and then he had made it worse by ridiculing her. They walked on to Rigg's and Kaitlin asked Sean if she could wait for Rigg. Her question made him feel terrible and he nearly stuttered as he told her to make herself comfortable in the living room. Rigg looked very pleased to see her when he came in an hour later.

"I stopped by your place; we must have missed each other," he said with a smile.

There was no sign of Sean and Rigg noticed for the first time that Kate was looking rather agitated.

"I need to talk with you, Rigg."

"All right." Rigg answered, thinking that Kate had made up her mind about teaching in the fall. He sat next to her on the couch. When Kate sprang up away from him and stood in the middle of the room, wringing her hands, a frown covered his face and he doubted his own thoughts.

"I just haven't known how to approach you about this or really when to approach you. I mean I've prayed and—"

Rigg listened and watched without interrupting as Kate went from tears to anger and back to tears again, speaking all the time in Hawaiian. Near the end Rigg caught on that she was talking about them. But by now an intense look of regret had come over Kaitlin's face and Rigg felt his heart sink.

"I'm not able to say it," Kate finally said, and Rigg felt that she was apologizing, not for her foreign words, but for something far more personal.

"Maybe if you give me a little time."

"Sure." Rigg wondered what he had just agreed to and watched, his heart feeling as if it were caught in a vise, as Kate moved toward the door.

"Katie," Rigg called softly as she started to leave.

But Kate only looked at him with tears once again filling her eyes. "I'm sorry." With those words she was gone, leaving Rigg in painful confusion.

Sean, who had been listening from the kitchen, came into the living room and cleared his throat uncomfortably.

"I'm sorry, Rigg."

The older man stared at him, misunderstanding his apology.

"She was talking about us, wasn't she? Kate was explaining how she feels about me?"

"Yes and I'm sorry. I had no business being here but after she asked me to help and I told her I wouldn't, I got to thinking about how much she cares for you and how—"

"Sean," Rigg cut in, "did you hear what she said?"

"Yes."

"I want you to come in and tell me everything."

Rigg was more baffled than ever. He thought Kate was telling him
that she couldn't love him and now Sean had blurted out how much
she cared. Sean was obviously ill at ease and Rigg reassured him.

"Just tell me what you can. First of all, what did Kate ask you to
help with?"

"Kate told me that she needed someone to talk with, you know,
about you and her, so she wrote to Father. She's been waiting to hear
how Father felt about her getting involved with someone. And today a
letter came."

"And that's what she said to me?"

"Some of what she said." Sean was looking uncomfortable again.

"You still haven't told me why she wanted your help."

"She wanted me to translate for her. You know how frustrated she
gets and she knew she'd never be able to get it all out in English."

"Get all what out?" Rigg was feeling a little frustrated himself.

"That she loves you. But she's never flirted before and she probably *is* too stuffy for her own good because she just didn't know how to
tell you or show you how she feels." Sean felt out of breath, but he
guessed Rigg understood because he was grinning like a fool.

The bigger man came toward Sean and pulled him out of his chair
and into his arms. He gave Sean a mighty hug, thanked him and
headed for the front door.

Kaitlin sat bent over the kitchen table. She was on her third piece
of paper. She had cried all the way home over making a complete fool
of herself and then, with a determined glint in her eye, she sat down
to write a letter to Rigg to tell him how she felt.

The door opened without a knock and Kate looked up to see Rigg
leaning against the jamb. His hands were stuffed into his pants pockets
and his totally nonchalant stance belied the rush of emotions inside
him. Kate felt herself blushing as he simply stood and looked at her.

"Do you know how many years I've prayed for you?"

Kate shook her head, unsure of how she was supposed to reply.

"I don't think there is ever a time, Kaitlin, that I walk by those
chairs in my store, you know the ones where the men sit while their
wives are shopping, without wishing my wife was shopping somewhere in my store.

"And the times I've ordered dresses and undergarments, wishing
as I did, that my wife could be with me when I unpacked them, so she
could have first pick. Or when the boxes of children's shoes come in,
wanting to have children of my own to put those little black shoes
on."

Rigg pushed away from the door then and came to the table. He placed his hands on the top and leaned down, his nose almost touching Kate's.

"Do you understand what I'm trying to say Kaitlin?"

"Yes." Kate felt out of breath and she couldn't take her eyes from the man across from her.

"Then tell me, Katie, will you be that wife? Will you marry me?"

Kate couldn't speak. Her heart thundered with joy and wonderment that he had come to her. She finally managed to nod, searching Rigg's face as she did, to see if he understood.

"I have one more question for you, Kate-love. And it's the last time I'll ask. Hereafter, I'll take my welcome for granted. May I kiss you?"

"Oh, yes." Kaitlin had no trouble with those words at all. Rigg kept his hands on the table and leaned until their lips met. The kiss was brief and gentle. Kate was unsure as to whether or not she'd pleased Rigg and voiced her thoughts as soon as she could speak.

"I've never done this before."

"I haven't either." Rigg's voice was equally as soft as Kaitlin's had been and once again their lips met. No longer satisfied to remain so far from the woman he loved, Rigg moved around the table to take her into his arms.

When Kate could think once again, she found that Rigg had taken her chair and pulled her into his lap.

"I can't sit in your lap!" Kate was appalled and moved away from him. "We're not married."

"But we will be, very soon, Miss Prim and Proper." Rigg followed her right out of the chair and silenced her protestations with another kiss as they stood in the center of the room.

"You did say that your father was coming in the fall, right?" Rigg did nothing to conceal his enthusiasm—Kaitlin was finally going to be his wife!

Kate pulled the letter from her pocket and handed it to Rigg. As he read, she watched his face as she had with Sean. It occurred to her in the silence that she didn't know why Rigg had come after her and proposed. She was about to ask him when he sat at the table and took yet another fresh sheet of paper. He was a study in concentration as he began to write. A few minutes later he handed the paper to Kaitlin.

Dear Mr. Donovan,

It would give me great pleasure to be speaking with you in person but your delay doesn't make that possible. I would like your permission to wed Kaitlin. I just now asked her. She said yes, and showed me your letter. Thank you for the blessing to proceed in your absence. We have not discussed a date but my hope is that it will be this fall.

I have prayed long for a wife such as Katie and I thank you sincerely for the wonderful person that she is. I know the love that she bears for you will cause her grief at the time of our wedding but if you are agreeable, I would like you to marry us again at the time you return.

My prayers are with you and I look forward to the time we can speak face to face.

Sincerely,
Marshall Riggs

Kate read the letter and smiled through her tears. "Thanks Rigg. He'll be so pleased."

"It's my pleasure. I meant every word." He hugged Kate for a moment before taking her hand. Heading out the door, Rigg had one cryptic comment.

"That's one down, and two to go."

Fifty-Seven

JUST AS HE'D hoped, Rigg found Sean at the house. He was eating supper and, with a mouthful of chicken, he stared at his sister and his employer. Sean noticed a marked difference about both.

Rigg's eyes, although always kind, held a certain tenderness that Sean had never seen before. And Kaitlin. She looked as if she needed a piece of string to keep her on the ground.

"I have a question to ask you Sean," Rigg stated quietly. "I just wrote to your father and asked if I could marry Katie. Now I want to ask you and then Marc. Do you mind if I marry Kaitlin?"

Sean wiped his mouth and hands on a napkin and then looked up at the two with an expression that was older than he was.

"I just have one thing to say to you Rigg," Sean paused and smiled slightly. "It's about time."

Kate laughed and moved to hug her brother. The two shared a long embrace before Rigg came to claim him. He held Sean by the upper arms and looked him in the eye.

"I love you Sean," Rigg told him honestly. "And I want to thank you for what you did to bring Kate and me together. I know you're disappointed about your father and I'm praying that he'll come home soon.

"But I want you to understand that you still have a home. I think Marcail will probably want to be downstairs here or have you upstairs with her. Whatever you both want. If you'd like to be upstairs, go up and pick out a room. Or better yet, do that later and come to my folks with us now, so I can ask Marcail.''

Sean's eyes were shining with happiness and when Rigg finally hugged him, he held on tight. Being offered a home and a choice on a bedroom might have seemed a small thing to someone else but to a boy whose life had been so unsettled of late, it was a lifeline in a stormy sea.

As it was they all went upstairs together, a first for Kate and Sean. There were three bedrooms and Sean, surprisingly enough, chose the smallest. It had a large bed, dresser and a standing full length mirror.

''It's cozy,'' he told them. ''And I like the view.''

Sean planned to move his gear in the morning so they headed back to Kaitlin's so she could get a sweater and then on to the farm. Rigg was careful to hide his disappointment once they arrived and found both Jeff and Gil gone. A friend of Jeff's, who'd been away from the area had returned so he was at her house for supper. Gil, May informed Rigg, was coming back anytime. He'd just had some errands to run.

Rigg knew that his parents were suspicious with the way he and Kate asked Marcail to go for a walk but they stayed quiet even though they were more than a little curious.

''How was your day, Marcail?'' Kate asked as Rigg sat quietly and watched them. The three had climbed into the loft in the barn.

''It was okay. I wrote a letter to Loni and one to Father. I think you need to read the one to Father though, Katie, because I told him I want him to come home. I don't want to send it if you think it will hurt his feelings.''

''I can read it for you, Marc, but I got a letter today and Father said he wouldn't be coming until sometime after Christmas.''

''But Katie, Father said he was coming in the fall.'' The little girl's face showed her disappointment and Kate didn't know what to say. Too much more of this and Marcail would begin to doubt her father's honesty. As Kate searched for the right words to reassure her, Rigg stepped in and saved the moment.

''I've only known you for a few months, Marcail. But even though it's only been since March, I really like being with you and talking with you. I can only imagine how much your father likes to be with you because he's known you your entire life.

''You can believe, honey, that if he can't be here, it's not because he doesn't want to be.''

Marcail nodded and both adults could see she was relieved.

"You know Katie," Marcail stated a moment later in a logical tone, "you should marry Rigg, he's very nice." Marcail's hand flew to her mouth as she stared in horror at her sister.

"I'm sorry Katie, I'm so sorry."

Rigg rolled from his sitting position to lay in the straw, until he was nearly nose to nose with Marcail.

"I'm glad you brought that up Marc," Rigg told her. "Because today I wrote to your Father and asked if I could marry Kaitlin. Now I want to know if it's all right with you?"

"What did Katie say?" Marcail asked cautiously, not wanting to make another mistake.

"She said yes."

"Did you ask Sean?"

"He said yes."

Kate had been doing fine up to that point, letting Rigg handle everything. But Marcail's next words were her undoing.

"I knew this would happen Katie, I just knew. Rigg looks at you just like Father looked at Mother."

Kate reached for her sister then and held her tight. She couldn't stop the tears that fell and Rigg gathered them both in his arms as Kate sobbed. Finally he pressed his handkerchief into her hand and she made an attempt at containing herself.

"I told you she does this a lot," Marcail informed Rigg seriously.

Rigg thanked his young, future sister-in-law for the reminder giving her a conspiratorial wink.

"We were at my house when I asked Sean, and I told him he would be living with us, as will you. He decided to take another bedroom upstairs so you can have his old room on the first floor or pick one of the other ones upstairs.

"Sean's new room has a bed and so does one of the other bedrooms. If you want the room that doesn't, then we'll just move furniture around."

"Thanks, Rigg." Marcail smiled at him. "Katie, are you going to teach school or work with Rigg?"

"Oh!" Kate said in surprise.

"We haven't talked about that yet," Rigg informed the little girl. "But we'll let you know what we decide. How about we go down now and tell everyone else?"

"How come you asked Sean first?" Marcail suddenly asked, frowning at her sister as though she'd been betrayed.

Rigg scooped Marcail up and planted a kiss on her cheek, effectively wiping the scowl from her face. He also stole a kiss from Kaitlin as they were climbing down the ladder. Before Kate was even back on the ground, Marcail was running for the house and shouting at the top of her voice that Rigg and Kate were going to be married.

Fifty-Eight

GIL HAD RETURNED while the three were in the barn and he was as excited as everyone else to hear the news. May was ecstatic and couldn't stop hugging Rigg and Kate. She brought out her good dishes for the cake she'd just baked and coffee.

"What date have you picked?" This question came from a beaming Bill and Rigg told him they hadn't talked about it. May had more questions and everyone did a lot of laughing over how many times Rigg was forced to answer, "We haven't talked about it."

Gil asked how the whole thing had come about, and Kaitlin learned for the first time how Sean had been in the kitchen and emerged to translate what she'd said. She thanked him from across the room with a grateful look.

As the evening grew long, Kate began to wilt. She wondered if it was normal to tell people so soon. Everyone had very logical questions for them and they had no answers. Kate hoped they would leave a little early so they could talk. She hadn't even had a chance to tell Rigg that she loved him.

Feeling teary all over again, Kate mentally scolded herself. *He'll change his mind Kate, if you don't pull yourself together.* Kate never took into account that she was tired for several good reasons. It was the end of the week, the emotional upheaval of hearing her father was being delayed again and going to Rigg to tell him how she felt only to make a mess of the whole thing.

She told herself that Rigg's proposal and her acceptance just might have a bearing on her physical and emotional state as well. And if all that wasn't enough, she had completely forgotten to eat supper!

Bill noticed that Kate hadn't touched her cake or coffee and his voice came softly to her from his place next to her on the couch.

"Katie, are you all right?"

"I don't think I am, but I don't know why." She felt tears at the back of her eyes, but she was too tired to let them fall.

Rigg had heard his father's question and Kate's answer. He was feeling rather drained himself and, even though he knew his family would be disappointed, he said it was time to go.

Sean had to work in the morning but said he wanted to stay at the farm with Nate. Marcail wanted to stay, too, and Rigg was quietly thankful to get his intended alone.

"We didn't eat supper," Rigg commented when they were almost to the house.

"No, I guess we didn't."

Kate was silent as Rigg stopped the wagon and helped her down. She wondered why she wasn't out of her head with excitement. They were leaning against the side of the wagon and Rigg had his arm around Kate. She let her head fall against him.

"I don't know what's wrong with me."

"We're both tired. There are a million things to talk about, but I think they'll wait until morning."

"I think so, too." Kate moved from his embrace and stopped just out of reach. "You're probably too tired to kiss me, so I'll see you in the morning. Good night Rigg."

Kate's hand was on the doorknob when Rigg's hand covered her own, stopping her retreat into the house. She tipped her head back to look at him and he could see she was smiling.

"I said I was tired, Kate-love, not dead."

Kaitlin laughed and said softly, "I love you Marshall Riggs."

"And I love you Kaitlin Donovan." He smiled and kissed her in such a way that Kate didn't doubt his words at all.

Kate woke up feeling rested and refreshed. She turned to some of her favorite Bible verses in the book of Lamentations. Chapter 3:22–26 said, "It is of the Lord's mercies that we are not consumed, because his compassions fail not. They are new every morning: great is thy faithfulness. The Lord is my portion, saith my soul; therefore will I hope in him. The Lord is good unto them that wait for him, to the soul that seeketh him. It is good that a man should both hope and quietly wait for the salvation of the Lord."

Kate prayed after she read these verses, taking time to thank God for His saving love and say that she had accepted that gift.

Spending such a long time praying for her loved ones, Kate was late for work. She hurried along the boardwalk rehearsing her apology only to find Rigg waiting out front for her.

"Good morning."

"I'm late," Kate stated, her planned apology melting away the minute she set eyes on Rigg. August was hot so Rigg was in simple dark slacks and a crisp white shirt, already rolled at the wrists with no vest or coat.

"Did I forget to tell you last night *not* to eat breakfast?"

"Yes, you did forget to tell me."

"So you've eaten?"

"Yes."

"I'm sorry. Maybe you'd like a cup of coffee while I eat?" Rigg took Kate's arm and led her up the street. She naturally wanted to know where they were going.

"To the hotel. I've told my clerks that I'll be out for a while. You and I need to discuss a few things and since there's nothing pressing today, I think this is a good time."

Saturday mornings were busy in the hotel dining room but Rigg found a secluded table for two and led Kaitlin to it. He'd been carrying something under his arm and as soon as they were seated he pulled it out: It was a calendar.

"I think the first thing we need to do is pick a wedding date."

"I already have. I checked my calendar this morning, just before I left the house."

"Great," Rigg grinned. "What's the date?"

"December second. It's a Saturday."

"October seventh is a Saturday, too," Rigg stated, having also checked the calendar. Kaitlin blinked at him.

"October? I don't think that's enough time."

"For what?" Rigg asked in all honesty and Kate looked a little frustrated. "You *are* marrying me, aren't you, Katie? I mean, you don't need more time to decide, do you?"

"I am definitely marrying you, but doesn't it take a while to plan a wedding?" Kate had never participated in one before but when they had been in San Francisco, Aunt Maureen had helped with one and the way she carried on you would have thought the Queen was coming. She was also hesitant to tell Rigg that she needed time to save for what was sure to be a major expense.

Rigg watched Kate's face and spoke honestly. "Katie, I wish we were already married, so October sounds good to me. But if you want to wait until December, I'll go along with your plans."

A harried young woman appeared at their table and splashed some coffee into their cups. Rigg told her what he wanted before she moved off in the direction of the kitchen.

Kate studied her coffee cup a moment. She didn't really know what she wanted, except that she wanted it to be special. Other than that, and thinking a white dress might be nice, she didn't have any other desires. But she knew from weddings she'd attended in Hawaii that there was always plenty of food. Sean didn't have a decent suit and Marcail would certainly want a new dress; although the one May had made her was very pretty.

"Tell me what you're thinking."

"I'm thinking that it's different in Hawaii. I don't know as many people here as I did there. In Hawaii, dozens of people would have come forward to offer their help, their food, their homes, or whatever was needed.

"Along with the fact that I have almost no trousseau and I've never done this before—"

"Money!" Rigg broke in, suddenly understanding. "You're worried about the money."

Kaitlin wouldn't answer him.

"I don't know if talking here was such a good idea," Rigg said after they'd been interrupted by the arrival of food. Kate was looking so uncertain that Rigg wanted to hold her.

"How would you feel if we found my mom as soon as I'm done eating, and talked some of this over with her?"

Kate nodded and tried to drink her coffee.

May was at home with Marcail. Rigg sat in the living room with Kate at his side, his hand engulfing hers. When May had given Marcail a job in the kitchen, she joined them. Rigg's explanation was brief and May listened silently until he was through.

"Tell me, Katie, when do you *want* to be married?"

"I wish we already were."

"So, your wanting a December date is not because you're unsure about marrying Rigg?"

"No, I'm not at all unsure about that. But this is August nineteenth, and I can't imagine having everything ready for a wedding by the seventh of October."

May spent the next hour reassuring Kate about her wedding. Kate learned that the church had a special group of ladies, of whom May was one, to handle wedding arrangements. May also told her daughter-in-law-to-be, that she would love to make her a wedding gown. Kate was feeling like the sun had broken through on a cloudy day. She was actually going to be married seven weeks from today.

"Are you ever a hard guy to track down!" Jeff stood at the entrance to the room and spoke to Rigg, "I understand congratulations are in order." Rigg stood up and Kate watched the two men embrace.

"I can't think what you've done to deserve her," Jeff commented as he leaned to kiss Kate's cheek.

"You've got some nerve, insulting me and then kissing my woman," Rigg laughed.

Kaitlin and May fled on that note, both thinking that the two of them were hopeless. They joined Marcail in the kitchen and filled her in on the news.

Kate and Rigg did end up going to the mercantile just after lunch, but Kate was in a fog. She couldn't have told anyone what she'd done that day if her life depended on it.

Fifty-Nine

KATE FOUND IT delightful to be greeted with a morning kiss. It was Sunday. She had stayed with the Taylors and when Rigg had come to take her to church, he'd kissed her as he helped her into the wagon.

They talked as they rode, and Kaitlin brought up a subject they'd completely forgotten to discuss the day before.

"Burt Kemp is going to want an answer from me today and, in all fairness Rigg, I need to give him one. Do you mind if I teach again this year?"

"I have only one problem with your teaching and that is the chance that you'll be pregnant before the year is out." Kate thought her face would flame it was so hot.

"I wonder how many years we'll be married before you stop blushing in front of me," Rigg remarked softly.

"You took me by surprise," Kate explained without looking at him. She took a deep breath and continued.

"You've got a valid point, though. Mother taught when she was carrying Sean and Marcail. In fact Marc's delivery was so easy that Mother's labor began about an hour before school was to let out, but she didn't tell anyone. And then she sent for Father after she dismissed. We were only home about two hours before Marcail was born.

"There is, of course, no guarantee that things will be the same for me but I don't think the possibility of my having a child should keep me from teaching."

They were not yet within sight of the church and Rigg pulled the team to a stop in the middle of the deserted road. He put his arms around Kate and she looked up into his face, so near her own.

"We've never talked about children. You do want some, don't you Katie?" His words, said sweetly, almost hesitantly, made Kaitlin wonder if he was feeling a little insecure about something.

"I wouldn't mind if we waited a little while, but I would like some—no less than five, to be exact." That statement earned her a beaming smile and another kiss.

As Rigg drove the remaining distance to church, Kaitlin told him of her conversation with Joey. "You should have seen his face, Rigg, it was heartbreaking.

" 'Miss Donovan,' he said, 'you are going to teach school this year, aren't you?' He nearly burst into tears when I said I hadn't decided."

"Maybe he'll be there this morning," Rigg commented, "and you can tell him the good news."

Rigg and Kate's wedding plans spread like wildfire and many members of the congregation offered felicitations, before and after the service.

Kate had been correct about Burt Kemp. He tracked them down within seconds of the benediction and then nearly hugged Kaitlin for saying yes. Kate and Rigg both felt comfortable with the decision and Burt made an appointment with Kate later that week to go over anything she might need.

When they finally made it to the wagon they found Jeff waiting for them. For the first time Kate could remember, he wasn't alone.

"Kaitlin," he said by way of greeting, "I want you to meet Sylvia Weber. Sylvia, this is Rigg's fiancée, Kaitlin Donovan."

"It's nice to meet you Sylvia," Kate greeted the other woman and tried to keep the awe out of her voice. Sylvia was beautiful, strikingly so. Her dress was a deep rose velvet which accented every curve of her perfect figure. The feather on her matching hat was so high it brushed Jeff's forehead when Sylvia stepped close to him.

"Congratulations." Sylvia's voice was smooth and cultured. "I'm sure you and Rigg will be very happy." Kate couldn't help but respond to the genuine sincerity in her eyes and the four of them talked for a while.

It seemed that Sylvia and Jeff had finished school the same year. Sylvia's family, all except her married sister, had then moved east shortly afterward. Sylvia was here staying with her sister for an indefinite period of time.

"Are you coming to the house for lunch?" Rigg asked.

"No, Sandra and Carl are expecting us," Jeff supplied.

"Sandra is my sister," Sylvia told Kate. "And her husband is Carl, Carl Boggs."

The couples went their separate ways a moment later and Kate turned in her seat to watch Jeff and Sylvia climb into a snappy little buggy pulled by a dapple gray mare.

"She's beautiful."

"That she is. I've always liked dapple grays."

Kate's head whipped around to see if he was teasing her but saw in an instant that he was dead serious.

"I meant Sylvia."

"Oh."

"Rigg, are you really trying to tell me you didn't notice that mass of blonde hair and those huge blue eyes?" Kaitlin's voice told him she wouldn't believe him no matter what he said.

"Sylvia is very pretty," Rigg said, his voice full of logic. "But my tastes run to Irish girls, black hair, eyes as soft and brown as pansies and stubborn chins."

Another wagon was coming toward them or Kate would have thrown her arms around Rigg. He had meant every word.

"I love you Rigg." Kate was feeling so emotional that the words were not in English.

"Are you going to translate that for me?"

Kate shook her head. "Just trust that I meant it." Those words weren't in English either, but Rigg could tell by the look in her eyes and the sound of her voice that he was loved.

"Now if you will come into the living room," May said with barely contained excitement, "your father and I have something to tell you."

Rigg and Kate exchanged a glance and seated themselves on the sofa.

"We've been discussing a wedding gift for you. I think we've just the right thing. We want to fix up Rigg's house—the cost will be on us! We'll paint, wallpaper and make new curtains. We also want to replace any of the rugs that are worn, such as the one in the living room.

"I figured we would need to do most of it after the wedding but we'll start in the bedroom and see how far we can get. What do you think?"

Rigg leaned forward on the sofa to see Kaitlin's face. She looked worried.

"Katie?" When Rigg spoke her name she looked at him.

"Rigg, have I said something to make you think your home isn't suitable?"

"Oh no, Katie," having heard the question, Bill broke in. "We know you would live there without a single complaint but things are showing their age and it's nice to start out with a few new things."

"Is it all right with you?" Kate asked Rigg. "I mean, it's your house and if you'd rather things were left alone—"

"It's *our* house and I like the idea. I probably won't be much help in the color selection but whatever you and Mom come up with will be fine."

"Well, it's all settled," May beamed. "Come in the kitchen Kate and I'll show you some fabric I picked up yesterday."

Rigg looked at his father after the women left. Gil was sprawled in a chair with the newspaper but Rigg knew he was the soul of discretion.

"How long did it take for Mom to start thinking of your things as hers? And money . . . how long did it take for Mom to get comfortable enough to say she needed some money?"

Bill looked at his son with compassion. "It'll come, Rigg, just give her time. Tradition states that the bride's family pays for everything and Kate has been somewhat worried, since the day she arrived, that she was a burden to us. Keep reassuring her that you're going to take care of her.

"And unless I totally miss my guess about everything I've heard about Aunt Maureen, I think Kate will have a wedding the likes of which she's never dreamed."

Sixty

RIGG HAD MAILED his letter to Patrick Donovan in Hawaii first thing Saturday morning. On Monday, Kate sat down and wrote to her father, as well as to her aunt. Aunt Maureen was in Santa Rosa a week later, on the first of four such trips she would make before the wedding.

Maureen Kent was a welcome surprise to the Taylors. She genuinely desired to help yet did not take over. And she wanted to pay for everything!

After two days, Kate stopped arguing with her because Aunt Maureen's response was always the same: "This is the way your father would want it."

On Aunt Maureen's third trip to Santa Rosa, three weeks before the wedding, she brought her niece a sizable box of nighties and feminine apparel. Maureen watched as Kate took the clothing from the box and exclaimed in delight over each one.

"Thank you Aunt Maureen," Kate breathed when the box was empty. "They're all so lovely and I've never had anything like these before."

"The pleasure is all mine, Katie," the older woman assured her warmly. "Katie," Maureen spoke again and something in her voice immediately snagged Kate's attention.

"I can't help but think that you must miss your mother *more* at a time like this. Am I right?"

"Yes," Kate replied softly.

"I know you and Theresa were very close and I'm assuming she has talked to you about the intimate side of marriage."

"When I was fifteen."

"I'm glad to hear that, honey, but your mother isn't here now and I want you to come to me if anything is bothering you. But I want to tell you something, Kate, that not many women practice. After you're married, the best person you can talk to is your husband.

"Rigg adores you; I can see that every time he looks at you. If anything is bothering you be sure you go to him. He might suggest you see May or contact me and that's fine, but I'm in my second happy marriage and I've found that men want their wives to enjoy every aspect of married life. And they'll go to any length to see that we're happy and cared for. I'm quite certain Rigg is no different."

The words were spoken so tenderly that Kaitlin felt for the first time that she'd missed something precious and dear by not being able to be closer to this woman.

Kate thanked her aunt with a hug and they talked for a while longer.

"Kaitlin," Aunt Maureen spoke almost hesitantly. "Have you ever forgiven my son?"

"Oh, Aunt Maureen," Kaitlin said with deep feeling, sensing that her aunt had agonized over this issue. "I can't tell you that it didn't bother me, but I'm all right. Sean and I have talked about it and so have Rigg and I. Percy has been forgiven and blame is not being cast on anyone, including myself, as I once did."

"You don't know how happy that makes me, Katie," her aunt spoke tearfully. The women embraced again and, because it was Saturday, Kaitlin had to excuse herself soon after to work on her school lessons.

School had gotten off to a good start for everyone but Sean. Kate had worried when they'd arrived in Santa Rosa that Sean would want to quit school and work full time. Kaitlin's suspicions had been correct, but it happened in the fall.

Rigg promised him as many hours as he could handle, but Kate could see he was still unhappy. He did his schoolwork, but with no extra effort. Two other boys who sat near him were able to distract Sean with barely a word or glance, and Kate was just sick each time she had to reprimand him in front of the class. She finally told him one day after school that he should write to Father.

"You're angry because he hasn't come and I think I understand. What I don't understand is why you're taking it out on the rest of us. If you've got some anger to vent toward Father, then do so. But when you're in my school, you'll show proper respect to me and the other students.''

Sean had slumped low in his seat and looked at the empty desks around him. It took Kate a moment to realize he wasn't going to say anything. Her sigh was almost one of defeat.

''Just think about it, please, Sean.'' The surly 14-year-old finally nodded, acknowledging this time that he'd at least heard her.

The problem with Sean was not the only ripple on the surface for Kaitlin. She had cried for a solid hour after she and Rigg met with Pastor Keller to discuss the ceremony.

''My father should be here, Rigg. I feel like I'm betraying him. He should be here to marry us.''

Rigg had been tender with his distraught fiancée but also adamant that they were making the right move. He reminded her that her father had encouraged them to go ahead with their plans.

''Katie, we don't know when he's coming, you said so yourself. If I thought it would be soon after Christmas, I'd say let's wait. But it could be months and I don't think I'm being selfish in wanting us to start our life together now.

''Like I said, we could set a date sometime in January and let your father know. But that only pressures him to come here even if the time is all wrong. I believe he was sincere when he said don't hesitate and follow your heart.''

Kate was comforted by Rigg's words and admitted to him that she hadn't really wanted to delay the wedding. She also told him he was going to have to be patient when she missed her father so much that all she could do was cry.

The ever present handkerchief appeared from Rigg's pocket and he informed Kate that she could cry on him anytime she wanted.

May had the wedding dress done in record time and Kate couldn't believe how beautiful it was, especially considering it was made of cotton.

''You'll thank me Katie,'' May had told her when they'd decided on a pattern and fabric. ''We always have Indian summer in October and your wedding day is sure to be a scorcher.''

Kate stared in awe at her reflection in the mirror. The dress was snow white with a high neck and three-quarter sleeves, the cuffs of which were trimmed with valenciennes lace. The skirt fell straight to the knees and then flared to the floor with a deep flounce.

Kate fingered the intricate embroidery on the bodice and wondered in amazement how May had accomplished such a feat in so short a time.

''Oh May,'' Kaitlin whispered.

"Don't hug me, Katie," May said with a smile, "you'll wrinkle."

"But where did you get this lace and how could you have embroidered this so quickly?"

May was grinning at her with an impish light in her eyes, when someone knocked on the door.

"Come in, unless you're Rigg and then you'd better not open that door!" May called in a loud voice.

Jeff's head appeared through the crack and the rest of him emerged when he spotted Kate. He whistled appreciatively at the sight of her.

"It's not too late to change your mind and marry me," Jeff teased as he plopped in a chair.

"What would Sylvia say?" Kate asked, her brows raised in censor.

"Did you need something Jeffrey?" his mother wanted to know. She was somewhat immune to his charm.

Jeff hemmed and hawed a bit and Kate had the distinct feeling that he didn't want her to know what he'd come to say. She excused herself without giving anymore thought to Jeff's actions and headed to "her" bedroom at the Taylors'.

After the wedding dress was hung on the wardrobe door and Kate was once again dressed in her calico skirt and simple blouse, she stood and stared at the dress.

Can you see my dress, Mother? Has God let you peek down and see how happy I am and what a wonderful husband Rigg will be? Can you feel how much I miss you Mother, or would that make you sad? Kate was not even aware of the tears that streaked her cheeks.

There wasn't a day that passed when she didn't think of her mother and had to face the fact all over again that she really was gone. Today was no different. The fact that Aunt Maureen was coming and had been so valuable in the past weeks was a balm to Kaitlin's pained heart.

Kate's mood lifted when she remembered that Aunt Maureen was scheduled to arrive on October second. When that happened, Kate had only five days to wait until she became Mrs. Marshall Riggs.

Sixty-One

SANTA ROSA WAS blanketed in fog the morning of the wedding. The CLOSED sign that Rigg had hung on the doors of the mercantile the night before was still in place long after the store should have been open.

Uncle Leo had surprised everyone by showing up on Thursday evening with his wife Ruth. It was his first visit since he'd moved to Texas. He announced that he'd come to run the store while Rigg was on his honeymoon.

This news came as more of a relief to Jeff than Rigg, since Jeff had agreed to take care of things while the bride and groom were in San Francisco. But even though Leo Riggs was on the scene, Rigg opted to keep the store closed on Saturday. That way everyone could enjoy the wedding.

Rigg had not banked on being so nervous that he couldn't eat. Jeff had stayed the night at the house with Rigg and Sean and was able to observe his older brother in as close to a state of panic as he'd ever seen.

"Why don't you eat some breakfast Rigg?" Jeff suggested.

"I'll get something on my shirt."

"You're not wearing a shirt," Jeff pointed out, but Rigg only stared right through him.

The wedding was set for one o'clock and, when Rigg disappeared to get dressed, he spent so much time in his bedroom that Jeff finally pounded on the door to tell him it was twelve-thirty.

246

Rigg hurried out, struggling into his coat and asked Jeff how he looked—something he'd never done before.

"You look good. In fact, Kate is so in love she'll even forgive you for not shaving."

Rigg's hand flew to the heavy stubble on his jaw before he began tearing his jacket off with enough force to rip the seams.

"You don't have time Rigg," Jeff pleaded, but found himself ignored. Sean told Jeff he should have stayed quiet.

While this scene of bedlam was being played out at Rigg's residence, a most serene bride was being helped from the wagon at the back of the church.

"Thank you, Gilbert." Kate adjusted her skirts. "Do you suppose they're here yet?"

"I don't think so. Let's get inside out of the heat."

May had insisted that Kate go in Gilbert's wagon and that they use the back door of the building in an effort to avoid most of the dust.

Tables had been set up under the huge trees that lined the churchyard. Arriving guests delivered every type of food, from hot dishes to fruit salads, to be shared at the reception following.

At three minutes to one, Gil joined Kaitlin in the small room in which she was waiting and told her that all the guests had been seated.

"Are they here, Gil?"

"No," Gil answered and watched Kate in amazement. She didn't seem to be the least bit upset that her intended was nearly late for his own wedding.

"What do you suppose happened? You don't think Jeff is up to something, do you?"

"No, I don't," Gil said with conviction and then muttered, "he might do something after the fact but not before."

"Should I be getting worried?" Kate asked but just then Bill came in with good news.

"Here's Sean. We're all set."

Brother and sister were left alone to wait for the music that was to be their cue to come down the center aisle of the church.

"You're beautiful, Kate."

"You look quite handsome yourself." Sean grinned over the compliment and straightened the neckline of his shirt.

"What happened to you guys?"

"We were all ready to go and then Jeff reminded Rigg that he hadn't shaved."

Kate giggled. "Did Rigg really forget to shave?"

"You can laugh, Katie, but I swear the man nearly panicked!" Kate was still chuckling when the music sounded and they moved into position at the back of the church. Kaitlin caught sight of Rigg and then lost him again when the congregation stood.

At the front of the church Sean handed Kate over to the waiting groom. She felt Rigg's hand tremble within her own.

"Second thoughts?" she teased in a soft whisper.

"Absolutely not," he assured her, his eyes dark with emotion.

The ceremony was perfect, not overly long but with everything they'd wanted. Kate thought her heart would burst when she was finally able to turn and look out over the sea of friendly faces as Mrs. Marshall Riggs. They came down the aisle, her hand in his, their smiles nearly stretching off their faces.

The reception was a delightful affair of laughter, best wishes, good food and precious fellowship.

Rigg no longer looked ready to flee and Kate teased him about being late.

"The best things come to those who wait," Rigg teased her back and stole a pickle off her plate.

At different times throughout the afternoon, people had pressed in on the newlyweds and they'd been separated. They thought nothing of this, secure in the knowledge that eventually they'd be alone.

Kate was talking with Joey when Jeff approached and announced that he needed her inside the church. Kate figured he was taking her to Rigg who was going to tell her it was time to leave. She unsuspectingly accompanied her brother-in-law.

"Now Katie," Jeff began to speak the moment they were indoors, "you just need to stay quiet and go along with my little plan. I promise Rigg won't be the least bit upset with *you*."

"Jeffrey," Kate said, "what are you up to?"

"Oh, it's just an old custom called 'stealing the bride.'"

"No!" Kate spoke adamantly and turned to leave but Jeff grasped her hand and began to hurry her toward the front of the church. He was making jokes as they went, and Kate became weak with laughter. She also didn't believe he would really go through with this.

Kate tried to reason with Jeff but he was talking as fast as he could and she couldn't do anything to make him release her hand. Jeff stopped at the front of the church and opened a small door.

"In you go."

"Not on your life," she refused. Kate glanced into a small room, little more than a cubicle really, and gasped in surprise. Jeff had set a chair and small table in place on which sat a cup filled with something and a plate full of food.

"How long have you been planning this?"

"Since I found out Rigg was in love with you and if you don't get in there right now, you're going to ruin all my work."

Kate looked at him indulgently. "Jeff," she said with the patience of Job. "There is nothing to keep me in there, just as soon as you walk away, I'll let myself out."

"That's a risk I'll have to take," Jeff told her sagely.

Kate shook her head, but being the good sport she was, she walked in and sat down. Jeff grinned, winked at her and shut the door.

"I hope you'll forgive me Kate!" Jeff said softly as he flipped the small lock shut—a lock that Kaitlin hadn't noticed. "Now that I think about it," Jeff said, still speaking out loud, "I hope Rigg forgives me."

"Where in the world is Katie?" May asked her newly married son.

"I don't know. I haven't seen her for about fifteen minutes. But she was talking with Joey just before I saw Jeff come and claim her."

"Well, if you see her, please ask her to find me. I want her to meet the Crawfords." May sailed off at that point to check on the food.

Rigg was stopped by a few more people but he answered them a bit distractedly. Where was his wife? Rigg checked with his father, Sean, Marcail, and then Nate. He'd decided to run Jeff and Gil down and question them when he spotted them in deep conversation at the edge of the reception. The closer he got to them, the more convinced he was that Kaitlin had not disappeared on her own.

"All right, where is she?"

"Who?" Jeff's face was angelic.

"You know who!" Rigg said with a smile.

"You're not having trouble keeping track of your wife already are you Rigg?" Jeff was appalled. "Now, let me see, why it's only four-thirty! Married just these few hours and already apart. That's not good, Rigg my boy, not good at all."

Rigg was trying very hard not to laugh. Gil, on the other hand, had succumbed until tears came to his eyes. Jeff opened his mouth to start again when suddenly the shoe was on the other foot.

"Hello Rigg. Hello Jeff and Gilbert." Kate's voice was saccharine sweet. "I'm sorry I was gone so long, but a certain gentleman detained me. He insisted that I sit down in *private,* and have a bite to eat."

Jeff's eyes were sparkling with laughter and he gave Kate a mock bow. "You, madam," he stated with great finesse, "are a worthy opponent."

"Thank you."

"Just what did he do with you?" Rigg finally asked.

"I'll tell you later, after we're on our way. Hopefully by the time we return, you won't want to strangle him." Gil began to laugh again and Jeff joined him. Rigg broke into their glee.

"Speaking of being on our way—" the bridegroom let the sentence hang.

"I'll get my things." Kate said good-bye to her brothers-in-law, her eyes telling Jeff he was forgiven.

"How did you get out of there?" Jeff whispered when he hugged her.

"Joey followed us and witnessed the whole thing." Kate's smile was so audacious that Jeff roared.

They took some time to say their good-byes to the family and remaining friends. Their plans for a honeymoon trip began in town with supper at the hotel and then back to their own home for the night. They would board the mid-morning stage the next day and start in the direction of San Francisco.

When they arrived in the city they'd stay at Aunt Maureen's for a few days before taking the stage home again. A substitute teacher had come for the following week and Rigg left without a qualm, knowing Uncle Leo was in charge.

The days in San Francisco were idyllic as they toured the city by day and spent most of their evenings in the privacy of their lavish bedroom, having supper and falling even deeper in love with every minute they spent together.

"We start home tomorrow," Rigg said almost sadly; it was their last night at Aunt Maureen's.

"I'm looking forward to getting back."

"You are?"

"Mmm hmm. My class will call me *Mrs. Riggs*. Doesn't that sound wonderful?"

"Indeed it does. But I know something that sounds even better."

"What's that?"

"I love you Kaitlin, and praise God for our marriage."

Kate gaped at him. He'd said the words in perfect Hawaiian. "How did—"

"Sean's been working with me ever since I proposed."

"Say it again."

Rigg obliged. Kate, laughing in delight, threw her arms around her husband.

"The language isn't important you know," Rigg said as he kissed her softly. "No matter how I say it Katie, I'm head over heels in love with you."

Épilogue

"STAY DRY!" JEFF called to Sylvia as she dashed from the shipping office to her carriage in the pouring rain. "And I'll see you tonight."

It was December twenty-third and Sylvia Weber was hosting an informal Christmas party at her sister's house. She'd invited nearly all the young people from church.

Bill, who was watching from his office doorway, struggled with his feelings. He had no right to ask Jeff to change his plans but Rigg, Kaitlin, Sean and Marcail were coming to trim the tree and stay the night. This would be the first tree party where one of the boys would not be with them. It was also their first Christmas with Kate, Sean and Marcail.

"Dad," Jeff turned when Sylvia's carriage was out of sight, "what were you saying?"

"Come in and sit down." The two men made themselves comfortable around the desk and then Bill looked his son in the eye.

"I was saying that your mother has been praying about her work here at the shipping office for many months. She doesn't want to quit outright but she's ready for a break.

"And now that Katie is expecting, she told me she'd like to take a little time for herself before she becomes a grandmother."

"Well, we can certainly fill in, Dad, for as long as we're needed. In fact, she doesn't ever need to come back. We'll get by."

"That's what I've told her and that was going to be our plan until yesterday when Jake Bradford was in." Bill watched his son closely and continued.

"Bobbie is coming back to town. She's going to be married and wants to come home for a while before she makes that step. Jake tells me she's been working at the shipping office in Jenner for over three years. She's not going to be here permanently but it sounds like it will be enough time for your mom and me to make a decision on her working with us.

"I haven't discussed this with anyone but your mother. If you say the word, I'll drop the whole idea and no one need know we were considering Bobbie. We would all be working in this office together and if that's going to be too uncomfortable for you, I'll understand, and we'll figure out something else."

Jeff was thoughtful. It certainly wasn't the first time he'd thought of Roberta Bradford. In fact, he wished she'd come home years ago. But never did he picture himself working with her six days a week. And how would *she* feel about it?

A few minutes of silence elapsed and then Jeff spoke with quiet conviction. "I hope we've all done a good deal of growing up in the last five years. I can't say as I ever imagined myself working side by side with Bobbie, but I would like to see her. I don't really have a problem with her working here, but she might."

"That's true. But if it doesn't bother you, then I'll ask Jake for her address."

"I think that's fine. She's obviously an answer to prayer, and I mean it when I say it will be good to see her again."

Kaitlin sat down in the living room to reread her father's letter. It was a letter of joy. There was tremendous revival going on in the islands and, understandably, that was almost all her father could talk about.

He explained that his return would be delayed for an indefinite period of time and although Kate was disappointed, she was also accepting of the fact that he needed to stay in Hawaii. She shifted on the sofa to a more comfortable position and kept reading.

"Did the baby move?"

"Oh Rigg," Kate laughed. "Your mother tells me I won't feel that for a long time."

"I guess not," Rigg admitted softly and Kate smiled at him before going back to her father's letter which, unfortunately, told them he would be delayed again.

"Did the baby move, Kate?" Marcail had heard the question from the kitchen and Kaitlin's reading was interrupted once again.

"No," Rigg answered. "And if we don't leave her alone, we're going to drive Kate out of the house."

Rigg's statement wasn't too far from the truth. Rigg had been thrilled with the news that they were expecting and whenever he and Kate were in the same room, he could be found measuring his wife's waist with the span of his fingertips.

Marcail had been a different sort of problem. For a solid week after hearing the news, she had stared at Kaitlin's stomach. The question Kate had been awaiting came a week later. Kate remembered so clearly when her mother had explained the mysteries of conception and birth to her.

But Marcail had more questions at nine than Kate had had at 14. After an hour-and-a-half of intense conversation, there wasn't much that Marcail didn't know. Kate had recounted their conversation to Rigg and he'd been very practical about the whole thing; telling her that Marcail had obviously been ready and that explaining the facts to her was the best possible move.

Sean's reaction had been much briefer.

"Good grief, Kate! Already?"

Kate had blushed to the roots of her hair but that only caused Sean to grin mischievously at his sister and brother-in-law. Rigg remembered very clearly what it was like to be 14 and gave his young brother-in-law a stern look.

Now it was December twenty-third and the four of them were putting on wraps to leave for the Taylors'.

"I won't have any trouble being thankful this year."

"About what?" Kate responded to her husband's cryptic remark.

"Mom has us share every year what we're thankful for."

"And what will you say?" Kate asked and slipped her arms around her husband's large frame.

"Well, that we've had plenty of rain for the crops, of course."

"Of course," Kate agreed, and smiled into his eyes.

"Ah, Kate-love," Rigg sighed, "you're awfully nice to have around."

"And I'll stay around too, just as long as you keep calling me that." Kaitlin sealed her words with a kiss.

"The rain has stopped, what's holding them up?" Sean called to Marcail from the porch.

"The usual, Sean," Marcail stated in calm logic. "Just the usual."

Book II

As Time Goes By

I wish to dedicate this book to my sons,

Timothy and Matthew.

Thank you for sledding, ball tag, cartoons in bed,
and times of quiet play, so I'm free to write.
You fill my life with love and joy,
and I praise God that you are mine.

Prologue

Santa Rosa, California
December 1871

JEFFREY TAYLOR TIPTOED up the back stairway of his house in stocking feet. His parents and brothers were all asleep and he stepped carefully along the upstairs hallway to avoid the reliable creaks and groans of the hardwood floor.

Once in his bedroom he lit the lantern and undressed for bed. The sights and sounds from the Christmas party he had just attended came back to him. Jeff knew everyone there, had grown up with most of them. They had laughed, sang, played games, and eaten for hours. And then the hostess' face, Sylvia Weber, swam before his eyes.

"What's the matter with you tonight, Jeff? You haven't been very attentive this evening." Her voice was irritated and Jeff was quick to apologize.

"I'm sorry, I must be a little tired."

"I'll forgive you," Sylvia said with a teasing light in her eyes, "if you come over right now and have one of these desserts I made."

Jeff had gone, telling himself to perk up, but Sylvia was right; he had been distracted the whole evening. It was almost a relief to leave.

He lay in bed now, stretched out flat—almost six feet of him— hands pillowing his head. His body was ready for sleep, but his mind, full of the day's activities and conversations, was moving like a runaway stage. Earlier that day Jeff's father, Bill Taylor, had talked with him. Bill informed Jeff that Jake Bradford had been in to mention that his daughter Roberta was coming back to town and looking for a job.

Roberta Bradford, "Bobbie" to most, was the answer to his parents' prayers because she was an experienced shipping clerk and only needed the position temporarily until she got married.

Jeff had known they were going to be needing someone at the shipping office, owned and operated by the Taylor family, because his mother, May, was taking some time off.

Bill's consultation with Jeff about hiring Roberta was far more than just professional courtesy over the fact that they would all be working together. Bill told Jeff outright that if he didn't want Bobbie to work there, they would drop the whole idea. The reason for such words from father to son dated back five years.

Finally allowing the years in his mind to fall away, Jeff let his thoughts slip back to the summer of 1866, the summer when Jeffrey Taylor's thoughtless actions hurt Bobbie Bradford enough to drive her from her family and home for over five years.

One

SEVENTEEN-YEAR-OLD Jeff Taylor was not hearing one word of Pastor Keller's sermon. While keeping his head totally still, he could shift his eyes until he had a perfect view of Sylvia Weber's profile. Unfortunately he could also see Richard Black.

How dare Sylvia sit with Richard in church when only last night she had let Jeff hold her hand! The sight of them made Jeff fume, but his anger didn't last. Sylvia smiled at him as soon as church was over, causing his irritation to immediately dissipate.

"We're leaving, Jeff."

The words, spoken by his mother, came much too soon for Jeff's tastes. Why, he had only had a few minutes to talk with his friends and *no* time to speak with Sylvia. She looked wonderful in a pale blue dress shot with flowers of dark blue, the perfect foil for her blonde hair and striking blue eyes.

Jeff wore a brooding look as he climbed into his folks' wagon. He usually rode with Rigg, his 21-year-old brother, but today Rigg had stayed home with a summer cold.

Actually Rigg was his half-brother—Marshall Riggs. Rigg had been a toddler when his father died and his mother married Bill Taylor. Bill and May had three more boys as the years went on: Jeffrey, Gilbert, who was 13, and Nathan, the youngest at ten.

A huge lunch of fried chicken and dumplings was enough to take Jeff's mind from Sylvia for a few minutes—that and the job his mother had given him of taking some soup up to Rigg. Rigg wasn't really sick enough to stay in bed, but May had wanted him to and he had done so to please her.

"Ready for something to eat?"

"Sure." Rigg put aside his Bible and pushed up in bed. "Smells good."

"Chicken soup."

"How was church?"

"All right."

"You wouldn't know it by your voice."

"Sylvia sat with Richard."

"So it's Sylvia this month." Rigg's voice was dry.

"What's that supposed to mean?"

"Calm down, Jeff." The older man's voice was gentle. "I've just noticed that you don't stay interested in any one girl for very long."

"It's different with Sylvia." Jeff spoke adamantly, a little too adamantly.

Rigg nodded sagely, wisely holding his peace. His food saved him from replying for a few minutes, and then he told Jeff that he needed to get some sleep so he could be at the store in the morning.

Jeff nearly accused Rigg of being married to the store that bore his name—Riggs Mercantile. But the one time he had hinted at such a thing, Rigg gave him quite a tongue-lashing. He told Jeff flat-out that he wouldn't know a day of hard work if it bit him in the seat of the pants.

Jeff had silently agreed with him but replied that these were his fun years. He would have to work the rest of his life, so why start now? Rigg, who had been working at the store since he was 14 and was in complete charge since he was 19, had only shaken his head and walked away.

Jeff consoled himself with the fact that he helped out at the shipping office from time to time. The fact that his ten-year-old and 13-year-old brothers did more work than he did was conveniently ignored as Jeff once again told himself that he would be working the rest of his life. At 17 you were supposed to enjoy life to its fullest.

Jeff was just leaving Rigg's room when his mother called him from the kitchen.

"You have a visitor, Jeffrey."

Certain that Sylvia had come to apologize, Jeff flew down the stairs, only to find Pastor Keller waiting in the living room and talking with his father.

"Hello, Jeff," the pastor greeted him. "Sorry to intrude on your Sunday afternoon, but I have something I'd like to discuss with you."

"Sure." Jeff took a chair and gave the pastor his full attention.

"We're planning an outing for the church. I think everyone will enjoy it. We're going boating at the lagoon."

"Hey, that sounds great!"

"I was hoping you'd say that. We're planning a little something special for the young people, though, and here's where you come in. Right now there are 12 young people from 15 to 17, six boys and six girls. What I'd like to see you do is ask the six boys to invite the girls on this outing. We'll have a picnic and some games before the boating, which isn't scheduled until four in the afternoon. The date is three weeks from today."

Pastor Keller held out a piece of paper to Jeff, who took it and read in silence.

Jeffrey Taylor	Angie Stallsworth
Tom Freemont	Sylvia Weber
Richard Black	Roberta Bradford
Deacon Briggs	Kimberly Miller
Dan Walton	Dorothy Nelson
Jeremy Reeve	Lydia Caminiti

"You're one of the older boys, Jeff, and I think a leader. I was hoping you could talk to the other fellows and ask them if they'd be willing to invite a girl from the list."

Pleased at being referred to as a leader, Jeff nodded and continued to listen.

"If you think this is going to make anyone uncomfortable, we'll just drop the asking part and invite the young people as a whole."

"No, this is great," Jeff answered from a purely selfish standpoint, thinking how much fun it would be to attend an event and have Sylvia all to himself. "I'll talk to the others right away and let you know."

"Thanks, Jeff. I knew I could count on you." Pastor Keller took his leave shortly after that and Jeff asked to borrow the wagon. Within two hours all six boys from the list were in the Taylors' yard demolishing a platter of cookies that May had delivered to them.

"So that's the story," Jeff explained. "These are the girls, and Pastor wants us to do the asking."

"Who asks who?" Richard wanted to know.

"That's what we have to decide," Jeff told him without much friendliness in his voice.

"I'll ask Lydia," Jeremy offered, and the other boys, save Jeff and Richard, began to speak up. Within minutes it became apparent that two boys wanted to ask Sylvia and no one wanted to ask Roberta.

"You told Pastor this was a great idea, Jeff; *you* ask four-eyes."

"Hey, Richard, don't talk about Bobbie that way. She's really nice."

"Then you ask her, Deacon," was Richard's surly reply. But Deacon wanted to ask Angie, and being one of the younger boys, he fell silent rather than stand up to Richard, who was almost as old as Jeff.

"It looks like we tell Pastor Keller that it's not going to work out." Jeff voiced his solution even as he told himself that he would just ask Sylvia on his own.

"We could draw straws to see who asks Bobbie Bradford." This was Richard's suggestion, his voice betraying to everyone that he was sure it would never be him. The group fell silent for a moment, and each boy felt weighted down with guilt over the way they were talking about Bobbie.

Deacon was right—Bobbie was a very nice girl but she wasn't at all attractive. She was the youngest girl on the list, not yet 15, and it appeared to anyone who cared to observe that Bobbie was never going to develop any female curves.

She was about as straight up and down as a young girl could be, and even with her short height she appeared to be all arms and legs. Her eyesight was the next thing that weighed on everyone's mind, as each young man pictured the wire-rimmed spectacles she wore on the bridge of her turned-up nose. They made her eyes look like those of an insect, or so the boys thought.

And if those reasons weren't bad enough, Bobbie had the ugliest hair in town. A dirty blonde color, it refused to curl or lay straight, but fluffed out from around Bobbie's head and shoulders like the wool on a sheep.

The Bradford family was not what anyone could call affluent, but Mrs. Bradford was a whiz with a needle and thread, and most people never dreamed that Bobbie wore her mother's made-over dresses. Bobbie had a brother who was 13 and an older married sister, who was expecting her first baby.

The family was well-liked at church and known for their hardworking, generous attitudes. Mr. Bradford did odd jobs around town and was the gravedigger for the church cemetery—not a glamorous position, but appreciated by most. Mrs. Bradford cleaned house for two of Santa Rosa's wealthier families, and had a small business of sewing and mending clothes in her home.

But even though Bobbie's family were hard workers and she was a nice girl, none of the boys in the Taylor yard had the desire to ask her to the outing at the lagoon. The six talked a while longer, and though most of them were overwhelmed with shame, they agreed to draw straws. The fact that this went on in the barn, out of sight from Bill and May Taylor, said much.

Jeff's brother Gilbert wandered into the barn, but he observed from a distance and was not one to talk about anything he had seen or heard.

The youngest boy of the group, Tom Freemont, was elected to hold the straws. Within seconds Jeff stood with the long straw in this hand, trying to control the fury massing inside him.

"Well, that was easy enough." Richard smiled with cruel contentment. "Since we both wanted to ask the same girl, this makes it quite simple."

Jeff forced a smile onto his face. "That settles it all right."

The group dispersed a few minutes later, most of the boys thinking what a good sport Jeff was. Jeff stayed in the barn for a long time trying to calm down. Gil, who had seen the others off and gotten three more cookies, came back into the barn. He flopped into a mound of hay and spoke.

"You should have told Richard to shut up."

"I don't need *you* to tell me what I should have said!"

"You better hope Dad never finds out about those straws."

"Well, he's not going to find out from *me!*" The full import of that statement made Gil come straight up out of the straw. "I never snitch, Jeff!" Gilbert's eyes flashed angry fire and Jeff looked down at his shoes. He knew he should apologize. He wanted to, but Gil stormed out and Jeff was left alone.

Two

"DID ALL THE boys leave?" May asked Jeff as soon as he walked in the kitchen.

"They're gone."

"Did they like the idea?"

"Yeah."

May was bent over a pot on the stove and missed the stormcloud on her son's face.

"How did you work it out? Are you asking Sylvia?"

"No, Richard is asking Sylvia. I'm asking Bobbie Bradford." This announcement was enough to spin May around to face her son.

"Why, Jeffrey!" May exclaimed in delight. "That's wonderful! Bobbie is the sweetest girl on earth." May went back to her cooking with a huge smile on her face.

'Maybe Jeff is growing up after all,' she thought to herself. 'Seventeen is such a *self*-absorbed age. It's nice to see him thinking of someone besides himself for a change.'

May was oblivious to the turmoil going on within her young son. Jeff sat a moment longer deciding what to do. If he went up to his room on a hot Sunday afternoon, his mother would think he was ill. He couldn't go see Rigg because Rigg could read him like a book and would know instantly that something was wrong. If he went to find Gil, and Gil was still mad at him, his parents would want to know what they were quarreling about. Finally, with a small disgruntled sigh, Jeff went into the living room to hide behind a book.

266

"I can never beat you in checkers, Bobbie," Angie Stallsworth complained as Bobbie jumped Angie's last two checkers and still had four more of her own on the board.

"That's all right, Angie, you can beat me in spelling any day of the week."

Best friends, the girls were sitting at the Bradford kitchen table on Monday afternoon. School had only been out a month and they were already restless for something to do. Angie had come over wanting Bobbie to go for a walk along the creek, but Bobbie's mother was working and she had strict orders to stay home with her younger brother Troy.

"What'll we do now?" Angie asked.

"Wel-l-l-l," Bobbie drew out the word as she rose silently from the table. "We could head in to town and rob the bank. Gottcha!" Bobbie flung the half-closed door wide open to capture her brother, who was crouched there listening to the girls' conversation.

"Troy Bradford, what were you doing back there?" Bobbie had her brother by the collar and stood looking down at him like an enraged warrior. She let go when she saw how red his face was. He scowled at her for embarrassing him. They apologized to each other and Bobbie spoke quietly.

"Why don't you get a cookie from the tin?"

"Thanks." Troy retrieved his cookie and glanced at Angie before going outside. Bobbie felt sorry for him. She knew he had a crush on Angie. 'But then who wouldn't?' Bobbie thought with a twinge of envy.

Angie was adorable with her dark curly hair and big dark eyes. She had a round little chin and a bright smile. *And* she was developing a figure—something Roberta Jean Bradford was sure would never happen in her own body.

Her mother kept reminding her that she was not yet 15, but Bobbie knew girls who were younger and who had more of a figure than she did. So the words were no comfort.

"Want to bake cookies?" Bobbie suggested.

"It's too hot."

"I guess it is."

"I never thought I'd ever say this, but I miss school."

"Me too." Bobbie agreed. "I miss seeing all the other kids."

"*All* the other kids?" Angie questioned her. "Or just one in particular?"

"Did you see that he was sitting with Sylvia on Sunday?"

"Yeah," Angie said with disgust. "Some guys. I mean, so what if she does have a great face and figure and gets good marks in school? What else has she got?"

Bobbie dissolved into giggles at the comical look on Angie's face. But both girls sobered a moment later; they knew what the other girl didn't have: Sylvia Weber was not a nice person. On more than one occasion Angie or Bobbie had been at the receiving end of her vicious tongue.

"I thought Jeff liked Sylvia," Bobbie commented suddenly.

"I thought so too. At least Jeff and Sylvia deserve each other. He's sorta stuck on himself."

"I've noticed." Bobbie agreed quietly. She didn't like to criticize people, and in fact she went out of her way to say nice things about even the hardest to redeem. "But Jeff is one of the best-looking guys in school."

"That's true. But never forget Bob—all men are fickle."

The girls dissolved once again into shrieks of laughter because Angie herself was in love with a new boy every week.

The afternoon went by in a lazy fashion and the girls ended up playing a game with Troy and having a great time. They parted company just before supper and made plans to meet downtown the next day to browse in the store windows. But Angie was back at the Bradfords' an hour or so before bedtime.

"Hello, Mr. Bradford," Angie said breathlessly when Bobbie's father opened the door. "I need to see Bobbie; can she come out for a minute?"

Bobbie appeared at her father's elbow and Angie nearly dragged her from the house.

"What is the matter with you, Ang?" Bobbie laughed as she was pulled along. Angie stopped under the tree in the yard.

"The church is having an outing at the lagoon and Deacon Briggs just asked me!"

The girls stared at each other for a full five seconds before they screamed in unison and threw their arms around each other.

"I think he's liked you for a long time."

"You do?" Angie's face flushed with pleasure.

"Tell me everything," Bobbie pleaded, and her friend was more than willing to comply.

"We were just finishing supper when he knocked on the door and asked for me. My father made him sit for a few minutes in the parlor and I *know* he was embarrassed. But anyway, we sat on our front porch and he asked if I'd heard there was going to be a boat outing for the whole church."

"The whole church?" Bobbie cut in.

"Yeah, a week from Sunday. But the young people are going early to have a picnic and then boating when everyone arrives."

"Oh, Angie," Bobbie said. "I'm so happy for you. Deacon is one of the nicest boys at church."

"I think so too. He's not stuck on himself, either."

The girls chattered until it was nearly dark and Angie had to go or face trouble at home. Bobbie went back into the house in a dreamy state. Angie's first date. . . . The next best thing to having it happen to *you* was having it happen to your best friend . . . and with Deacon, too, who was so tall and quiet.

Bobbie took great delight in telling her brother about the boat outing, since he usually knew things ahead of her. But when she climbed into bed a short while later her mood wasn't quite so buoyant.

She carefully repeated her nighttime ritual of placing her glasses on the corner of her nightstand. That way she knew where they were even if she was half-asleep. When Bobbie was ten she had once left them on the plant stand in the hall. The glasses afforded her depth perception which she had sorely missed that morning, and she ended up falling all the way down the stairs.

Bobbie rubbed her nose where the spectacles had sat. It was a relief to remove them, since they had a tendency to pinch.

'I wonder if someone will ask me on a date when I'm 15,' Bobbie wondered as sleep began to crowd in upon her. She fell into slumber visualizing the clothes in Angie's closet so she could tell her tomorrow what she should wear on her date.

Three

THE BOAT OUTING was only four days away when Jeff rode into the Bradfords' yard. They had an old house that they had painted and kept up. The swing that hung from the tree in the yard was just a piece of wood with a rope knotted in the middle.

Troy moved lazily on that swing, pushing himself in circles with one bare toe. As though embarrassed at being caught on the swing at his age, he jumped down the moment he saw Jeff.

"Hi, Troy. Is Bobbie around?"

"In the kitchen."

Jeff tied the horse's reins to a tree limb and moved toward the house in his long-legged stride. His knock on the door went unanswered, and for an instant he entertained the idea of leaving without seeing Bobbie.

"Just go in," Troy called from where he had sat down under the tree. Jeff glanced at the younger boy, hesitated, and opened the door. He found himself in the living room.

"Bobbie." His voice was hesitant and soft.

"*Bobbie.*" Louder this time. Jeff heard someone move in the next room, and then Bobbie came out drying her hands on a towel.

"Well, hello, Jeff, how are you?" Bobbie greeted him with natural ease, smiling the smile that came so easily for her.

"I'm fine, thank you." Jeff sounded too formal, even to his own ears.

"My folks aren't here right now, but I can give them a message if you'd like." It never once occurred to Bobbie that Jeff was there to see *her*. She also knew that Troy was in the yard, and that if Jeff had wanted him he would never have come in the house. Her parents were the only ones left.

"I'm not here to see your folks."

"Oh." Bobbie took a moment to absorb this. "Why don't you come in to the kitchen? I've got cookies ready to come out of the oven." Bobbie turned and walked away, taking for granted that Jeff would follow.

Jeff took a chair at the kitchen table and glanced around the Bradfords' kitchen. It was spacious and sparkling clean, but Jeff didn't really notice amid his reluctance to be there. A moment later Bobbie set a hot pan of cookies on the table.

"Help yourself, Jeff. I'll get you something to drink."

Jeff thought the cookies might take his mind off the inevitable, so he picked one up and bit into it. It was delicious.

"I hope you like cider," Bobbie said as she set a cup before her guest and took a seat.

A moment passed before Jeff saw that Bobbie was waiting peacefully for him to state his business. He said the first thing that came to mind.

"These cookies are good." He sounded so surprised that Bobbie smiled.

"Thank you. Have as many as you like."

"Thanks." Jeff ate a few more.

Bobbie continued to wait quietly, but began to feel distinctly uncomfortable. She didn't really know Jeff Taylor and couldn't think for the life of her why he would come to see her. He suddenly cleared his throat and spoke.

"I suppose you've heard about the outing at the lagoon."

"Yes, I heard."

"Well, I came by today to ask you if you'd like to go with me."

Jeff watched the eyes behind those glasses blink at him even as he prayed she'd say no. It wasn't that he found her repulsive, because Deacon was right, she was very nice. But he was sure that if Sylvia saw him with Bobbie he would never hear the end of it—not to mention the fact that he didn't want to do anything to ruin the fragile thread upon which their relationship hung.

"I'd like that, Jeff. Thank you for asking me."

"Sure."

"Is there anything I can bring?" Jeff, becoming more relaxed by the second, bit into another cookie before he answered.

"No, I don't think so. Oh, I'll be picking you up early. You see, we're going to have a picnic and some games, then everyone else will come at 4:00 and we'll all go boating."

"That sounds fine. If you find out I need to bring something, just let me know."

"Okay." Jeff stood on that word and reached for another cookie. "These are really very good."

"I'm glad you think so. I was a little worried because you only ate seven of them."

Jeff's head whipped back as he was walking away from her. She was actually teasing him! Her eyes sparkled with mirth and a small smile played around the corners of her mouth.

If Jeff had taken the time to really look, he would have noticed the beautiful green color of Bobbie's eyes and how given her pretty mouth was to smiling.

Jeff's own mouth raised in a small smile and he thanked Bobbie for the cider and cookies.

"I'll see you Sunday," Bobbie called to him as he rode out of the yard. Jeff waved and Bobbie walked back into the kitchen and plopped into a chair.

"Jeffrey Taylor just invited me out." Bobbie hoped it would seem more real to her if she heard the words aloud, but it didn't. She continued to sit almost in a daze. Troy came in and finished eating the pan of cookies Jeff started, but she didn't notice.

Bobbie was thinking back two years in time, to the fall and the first day of school. They had not attended the same church as the Taylors in those days, and so Bobbie had not seen Jeff over the summer.

She couldn't believe how tall he had grown over the summer months, and neither could most of the other girls. He became the object of so much attention in the first few weeks that he began to change. He had never been mean or vicious, but suddenly he went from open and friendly to aloof and unapproachable.

The *old* Jeff had shown kindness to Bobbie on more than one occasion, even defending her when she was teased about her eyesight. Now he stayed quiet if the older kids made unkind remarks, or he just behaved as though she didn't exist. Any little infatuations Bobbie had for Jeff had been slowly crushed beneath the heels of his indifference.

And now he had just come over and asked her to the boat outing. Bobbie was thrilled. Her open, honest approach to life made her somewhat naive to the underhanded ways and thought processes of some people. It never even occurred to her that Jeff had asked her for any other reason than the fact he wanted to spend the day with her.

"Roberta!" Maryanne Bradford's outraged voice broke through Bobbie's dream world. "You're burning the cookies!"

"Oh no, I'm sorry, Mom." The women reached simultaneously for the oven pad to rescue the burning pan but Maryanne ended up doing the work.

"Honestly, Bobbie, it wasn't as if you weren't sitting right here," her mother said in some exasperation.

"I know and I'm sorry, but Mom, the most wonderful thing just happened. Jeff Taylor came by and asked me to the boat outing on Sunday!"

"He did?" Maryanne said with a smile.

"I can go, can't I? I know I'm not 15 yet, but Daddy will say yes, won't he?" Maryanne looked into her daughter's eyes, so full of hopeful entreaty, and smiled.

"Jeff is a nice young man. Of course he'll say yes."

"Oh thanks, Mom, thanks!" Bobbie threw her arms around her mother and squeezed her tight. Then she broke away suddenly, her face showing her horror.

"Mother! What will I wear?" Maryanne watched her daughter flap her hands in a state of panic and then charge for the stairs. She was back down before she had gone five steps.

"Angie! I've got to tell Angie!" This time she watched Bobbie fly out the front door running as fast as she could.

"What's her problem?" Troy asked his mother, who was standing at the door still watching her daughter run.

"Bobbie needs to tell Angie something. No problem really."

"Well, whatever it was, it made her burn the cookies. I can smell 'em out here." Troy made no effort to masquerade his disgust.

"Well, I wouldn't worry about it, dear, since you've never let singed edges stop you before."

"No, I guess I haven't." Troy slipped past his mother and into the house. Maryanne followed a few minutes later, joining Troy in the kitchen. She emptied the contents of her purse onto the table and began to count, praying as she did that she would have enough for a surprise for her daughter.

Four

MARYANNE BRADFORD WENT a little out of her way as she walked home the next day after work. She had left that morning feeling regretful over not having enough money to buy fabric for a new dress for Bobbie. She wished they had had more notice; then she could have put a little aside over a few weeks.

But then Mrs. Walcott, the lady for whom she cleaned two mornings a week, had asked her to do a few additional things, and Maryanne had been paid extra. It was still going to make things a little tight until next week, but they would get by; they always did.

Maryanne walked into Riggs Mercantile and headed straight to the fabric counter. She had priced and fingered several bolts when someone spoke behind her.

"Hello, Maryanne."

"Hi, May, I didn't even see you."

"I was upstairs talking with Rigg. Are you looking for fabric?"

"Yes, I'm sure you know that Jeff asked our Bobbie to the lagoon outing, and I want to surprise her with a new dress."

May smiled. "I almost asked how you could have it done in time, and then I remembered I was talking with Maryanne Bradford."

Maryanne beamed over the compliment and asked May what she thought of a certain piece of cotton. The background was a jade green with a pattern of tiny white flowers.

"Bobbie's eyes are green, aren't they?"

"Yes."

"Oh, this will be perfect."

"I emptied my purse last night to see if we could afford this, and then had to ask the Lord to help me accept the fact that we couldn't. Then today I got paid a little extra. If we're careful until next week, Bobbie should have her dress. I usually cut my own dresses down for her and she never complains, but I can't wait to see her face when she finds out she'll have a dress from *new* cloth."

"There's something inside us, isn't there, Maryanne, that yearns for our children to have all they need and a little more?"

"Isn't that the truth! Don't get me wrong, May, I'm not hearing wedding bells or anything, but you wouldn't have believed the look on Bobbie's face when she told me Jeff asked her. It was a mixture of excitement and fear all rolled into one."

"I know they'll have a good time." May touched Maryanne's arm and then said she had to be on her way. Maryanne took the fabric to the front and started home again in a few moments.

Bobbie had started supper and was up to her elbows in a flour mixture for fried chicken. Maryanne made her wash her hands and sit at the table.

"But, Mom, I'll just get them all messy again when I pick up the chicken."

"I know, but for the moment you need clean hands. Now close your eyes." Bobbie's brows lowered for a moment, but then she did as she was told.

Maryanne popped into the living room to retrieve a small parcel wrapped in plain brown paper. Her husband, Jake, came in the front door at that instant and Maryanne signaled him over.

"All right, now you can open your eyes and the package." Mother and Father stood silently by as their daughter tore the paper back to reveal the most beautiful fabric she said she had ever seen.

"It's for you—for a new dress to wear on Sunday afternoon."

"Oh Mom, Dad!" Bobbie breathed as she smoothed the wonderful material with her hands. She missed the meaningful glance exchanged between the adults.

"I'll explain later," Maryanne whispered softly as Jake put his arm around his wife. They had discussed it the night before and Jake had been as regretful as Maryanne over Bobbie not having a new dress.

The women went to work right after supper and Bobbie was so excited she could barely hold still. The dress was finished by lunch the next day and all she could do was stand in front of the mirror in her parents' room and look at herself.

Bobbie thought her mother had to be the most clever seamstress in all the world. The dress bloused out at the waist, which gave hint to a fuller chest than there actually was. The sleeves were short and puffed and the neckline was high. The fullness at the waist also made Bobbie's hips more attractive for a change and not just skinny.

"I take it you're pleased."

"Oh Daddy, didn't she do a wonderful job?"

"She always does."

"Do you think Jeff will like it?"

"How could he not?" Her father said with a smile, and Bobbie turned back to the mirror with her eyes shining.

'How could he not?' She repeated to herself. 'How could he not?'

Jeff and his date were the last to arrive at the lagoon. Bobbie noticed the change in Jeff from the wagon ride over, where he had been fairly talkative, to when they joined the other young people and he had grown very quiet. She didn't understand it or question him, though she wanted to.

"Hi, Jeff; hi, Bobbie." Pastor Keller's wife greeted them as they came toward the blankets spread with a picnic lunch. The day was beautiful, with a slight breeze, and there was plenty of shade under the huge willow trees.

Bobbie and Jeff ended up next to Angie and Deacon on the edge of the blanket. The girls immediately began to visit, and within seconds Deacon joined them. It didn't immediately register with any of them that Jeff was playing with a blade of grass, not looking or talking to anyone.

He perked up a bit when they ate, but the fact that Richard and Sylvia were right across from him was almost more than he could take. He told himself not to look at Sylvia, but he did, again and again. Each time her eyes challenged him in a way that should have made him angry but instead just made him want to be with her all the more. Jeff also found it very satisfying that Richard himself noticed how often Sylvia looked across the blanket.

After lunch they played a few games. The Kellers had more planned but nearly everyone said they wanted to sit and talk. Couples sat together at a distance or small groups visited and laughed in the sun.

Jeff and Bobbie ended up back by the picnic lunch, where Bobbie watched Jeff watching Sylvia. She was more confused than hurt. If Jeff had wanted to ask Sylvia, why didn't he? Bobbie didn't believe that he had asked and been turned down, not with the way she had been looking back all afternoon.

"Would you rather we joined one of the other couples, Jeff?" Bobbie asked solicitously. Everyone else was in sight and Bobbie so much wanted to enjoy the day. But if Jeff kept this up it was going to be miserable.

"No, I like it here under the trees." Jeff had finally looked at Bobbie when she spoke to him, and for the first time he caught a very vulnerable look on her face. He told himself he was being unfair to her, so he turned his whole body to face her, also making it impossible to see Richard and Sylvia.

"I like it under the trees too."

"Is this a new dress?" Jeff was hoping it was, since he had never paid any attention to what Bobbie was wearing before. He wouldn't have known if she had worn it once or a hundred times.

"Yes. My mother made it for me."

"It's nice."

"Thanks. Do you want a carrot stick?" The basket was lying near and Bobbie offered it to Jeff after taking a stick for herself.

"No, thanks." Jeff's mind was wandering again. He wasn't looking at Sylvia but he wasn't talking to Bobbie either.

"I'm glad Troy isn't here."

"Why's that?" Jeff asked, thinking he really didn't care.

"He always puts carrot sticks up his nose."

"Well, kids will do that," Jeff answered noncommittally without even looking at Bobbie.

"Of course it isn't any wonder. My mother does it all the time."

Jeff looked sharply at the small girl beside him to see she was barely containing her laughter. His mouth dropped open when she spoke next because her voice was dripping with sarcasm.

"Very good, Jeffrey. You were actually listening." Bobbie grinned at him and Jeff found himself laughing hard.

"You," he said as he shook a finger at Bobbie, "are incredibly sassy."

"So I've been told," Bobbie admitted without apology. "But at least I don't put carrots in my nose."

"You know," Jeff said thoughtfully, feeling fully relaxed for the first time, "it might be kind of fun." He raised a carrot stick toward his face and Bobbie laughingly snatched it away from him.

"You have very nice teeth, did you know that?" Jeff asked Bobbie suddenly, and she looked surprised and then very serious.

"Is it really so important, Jeff, to be with someone good-looking? I mean, do good looks mean that much to you that you need to find something about me that's attractive?" Bobbie could see that she had shocked him, but she kept her eyes on his and could tell he was thinking.

"I think you're right. I do put too much stock on good looks. If I hurt you just then, I'm sorry."

"Oh, don't apologize Jeff, or feel bad." Bobbie's voice grew dry, but her eyes were sparkling. "You're just a teenage boy and they usually don't know any better."

Jeff looked shocked again, and then let his head fall back against the tree and laughed—a deep-down laugh that came from the pit of his stomach and nearly made it ache.

They talked undisturbed for the next half-hour. Jeff couldn't believe what a good time he was having. Roberta Bradford was a lot of fun. He had even managed to forget Sylvia, until he looked up to see her and Richard headed their way.

"My, but there's a lot of laughter going on over here." Sylvia's mouth was smiling but her eyes weren't.

"Yeah, Jeff, how's the long straw?"

Jeff leveled Richard with a look that was almost dangerous. The other boy knew he had overstepped his bounds and immediately shut his mouth. Sylvia wasn't so tactful.

"Oh, come now, Jeff. Don't get so mad. I'm sure Bobbie understands that you wouldn't have brought her if you'd had a choice."

Once again Jeff's furious eyes were directed at Richard, now knowing that he had told Sylvia what they had done in the barn. Jeff then looked to the young woman with whom he believed himself to be in love. She had never had Jeff angry with her before, and it was almost frightening. When Richard pulled on her hand she left the other couple willingly. No one noticed that Bobbie's face had lost all color.

"What did Richard mean, Jeff?" Bobbie asked softly.

"It's nothing, Bobbie. Forget it."

"That's not true, Jeff, or you'd be looking me in the eye."

Jeff didn't answer, and Bobbie heard Richard's words again in her mind: "The long straw."

"You drew straws to see who would ask me, didn't you, Jeff?" Two other couples were close now, and when Jeff still wouldn't look at her, Bobbie's eyes traveled to the others.

'They all know,' she realized in an instant as their eyes regarded her with embarrassment and pity.

"I'm not feeling very well, Jeff. I'd really like it if you'd take me home."

"We haven't gone boating yet," Jeff said almost desperately, seeing how quickly the afternoon was about to be ruined. "See, all the boats are stacked over there waiting. All the families will be arriving in about a half-hour."

"You're welcome to come back and go boating, Jeff, but the truth is, I'm not feeling so well. I want to go home."

When Jeff made no move to comply, Bobbie turned and walked away from him. It took a moment before he could see she was going to walk home. He ran and stopped her with a hand on her arm.

"Bobbie, do you really want to leave?"

"Did you really draw straws or am I jumping to conclusions?"

"We drew straws." The words were fraught with shame.

"For all the girls or just me?"

Jeff swallowed convulsively. "Just you."

"Please take me home."

Jeff nodded. "Wait here while I hitch the horses."

Bobbie stood stock-still as Jeff went to get the wagon and to tell Pastor they were leaving. She didn't even acknowledge Angie when she called to her. She climbed into the wagon as soon as Jeff stopped beside her, even before he could help her.

On the ride home the silence became oppressive. Jeff didn't know what to say. Sorry wasn't enough. He found himself begging God to turn back the hands of time and let him live the last three weeks over; he promised he would do better.

There was no one home at the Bradfords. Bobbie told Jeff goodbye and went inside. Jeff sat in the wagon for a time, not sure whether to head home or to the lagoon. He finally opted for home. He knew he was going to be in more trouble than he had ever been in his life. But even if he was waiting to kill him, Jeff Taylor had to see his father.

Five

"JEFF, HOW COULD you?" The question came from his mother and her faced mirrored the torment within. "Maryanne Bradford bought dress material with money she didn't have to make this day special! I don't even know why I said that, Jeff; no one should receive the treatment that you gave Bobbie!"

Jeff didn't respond. He stood by the fireplace and let his mother's angry voice rain down on him.

It hadn't taken very long for the story to circulate among the group at the lagoon, which didn't say much for the congregation's ability to refrain from gossip. Understandably, neither the Taylors nor the Bradfords stayed for the boating.

Jeff had not waited long for his family to arrive back at the house. Gilbert and Nathan had discreetly disappeared and Jeff faced his parents alone. Bill said nothing as May berated her son.

"Your actions of the past weeks make perfect sense now—your waiting until the last minute to ask Bobbie and then doing so as though you were going to your own hanging." May continued to point out Jeff's faults, ending with the fact that he had deceived everyone, not just Bobbie. A moment later a look of silent communication passed between husband and wife and May exited the room.

"Sit down, Jeff," Bill said, once his wife was gone. Jeff sat on the sofa but could not get comfortable. He shifted several times even as his father pulled the rocker close in front of him.

"I want you to tell me everything."

Jeff did just that, beginning with the boys' conversation in the yard and the drawing of straws in the barn, to the moment he dropped Bobbie at her house and came directly home himself.

"You mean to tell me that Richard and Sylvia came right up to you and Bobbie and called her the 'long straw'?" Bill's voice reflected his amazement.

Jeff's eyes filled with tears and his shoulders began to shake. "You should have seen her face, Dad; she was crushed. And it's all my fault. I wanted to have Sylvia all to myself and I was willing to do any-thing—" Jeff's voice broke and he began to sob in earnest.

Bill joined him on the couch, and with his arm around his errant son, he listened as Jeff shared everything he was feeling and cried himself into near-exhaustion.

They talked for the better part of two hours and then prayed to-gether. Jeff confessed his selfish, deceitful actions and then listened in surprise as Bill confessed his lack of attention to his oldest biological son. Bill went on to pray for wisdom for Jeff when he apologized to Bobbie and her family as well as wisdom for himself when he went to see Richard and then Sylvia. Father and son were more than a little drained at the end of the prayer.

"Do you think I should go tonight?"

"No, son, I think you need to get some rest. You can see Bobbie in the morning."

"Thanks, Dad."

"I love you, Jeff." The men embraced and then Jeff took himself off to bed. He was up early, but not being sure when the Bradfords would be up and about, he waited until 8:30 to go over. When he arrived, a sober Mr. Bradford informed him that Bobbie had left on the morning stage. She planned to visit her aunt and uncle for the remainder of the summer.

Six

Jenner, California
January 2, 1872

"Have you got everything?"

"Yes, Aunt Joanne, I've got everything." Roberta Bradford uttered the words indulgently; it was the fifth time she had been asked.

"Oh honey," the older woman cried softly, and hugged Bobbie to herself. "What are we going to do without you?"

"You'll be fine."

"Is it wrong for me to pray that Cleve convinces you?"

Bobbie opened her mouth to say something but closed it again; she wasn't sure she wanted to touch that one. Thankful that Cleveland Ramsey had not come to see her off, Bobbie turned away from her aunt to face her Uncle Jasper. He was a replica of her father both in looks and personality, a quiet rock of support. But today he had tears in his eyes. Seeing them, Bobbie's own tears came very close to the surface.

"What can I say?" Bobbie said softly. Her uncle shook his head and enfolded her in his arms.

The stage pulled in a few minutes later and Bobbie's bags were thrown into the back. She gave her beloved aunt and uncle one last hug and this time the tears could not be stemmed. She waved from the stage window, her eyes still streaming as the stage pulled away.

Bobbie was thankful she had the interior to herself. She allowed herself a good cry and then let her head fall back against the seat, her thoughts drifting to the past and then jumping to the future in rapid succession.

Five years. She had actually been away from home for over five years. It didn't feel that long, not while it was passing, and not even now that it was over.

There had been talk over those years of her returning to Santa Rosa, but the plans were always delayed. At one point when she had been away three years, her parents had decided it was time she come home, but Uncle Jasper had fallen ill, making her presence at the shipping office crucial. No matter how many times she asked herself how the years had slipped by, no answer came. She really loved living in Jenner and she had been so young when she left Santa Rosa—a little girl in so many ways.

But she wasn't a little girl now. She was a woman, headed back to take a job at the Taylors' office—a job she could walk into with confidence because of her experience. Bobbie knew her aunt and uncle's shipping office was nowhere near as busy as the Taylors' in Santa Rosa, but she knew the routine, how to handle packages and treat the customers as well.

And she would be working with the Taylors. Mr. Taylor had given a full explanation as to why they needed her. Business had picked up to the point that May needed a rest. Bobbie was to take her place and her fellow employees would be Jeff, Gilbert, and sometimes Nate.

Jeff. A myriad of emotions flooded through Bobbie at the thought of Jeffrey Taylor, but none were anger or bitterness. They'd had no contact over the years except one note; Bobbie still had it. She had received it in the fall after that awful summer when he had obviously understood that she was not coming back for the next school year. It had been very brief, four short words, but they had meant the world to her: "I'm sorry, Bobbie. Jeff."

She hadn't replied and it hadn't changed the hurt, but it helped to know that he regretted the way he had treated her. At the time she received it, she hoped he was suffering too. But the next summer all of that changed when, for the first time, Bobbie truly listened to the man who was preaching at the front of the church she was in and Bobbie understood that she was a sinner.

When she was very young the man in the pulpit had never taught anything but God's love. And then the Bradford family started attending Pastor Keller's church and he had the courage to tell people that they must be born again, that without the saving blood of Jesus Christ they would not live forever with God. But Bobbie hadn't believed Pastor Keller.

She agreed with her first pastor, a man whose name she couldn't even remember, that God was a God of love. She didn't believe He would ever send anyone good to hell. And then it became very clear to Bobbie as she studied the Bible that God didn't send anyone to hell. It was man's choice, *her choice—Roberta Bradford's*—as to where she spent her eternity.

With Bobbie's belief in Jesus Christ came a new outlook on everything, especially the way she had been treated at the lagoon. The weight of bitterness was lifted from Bobbie as she studied the Word of God with her aunt and uncle. As she did, she learned that there was no room for unforgiveness in the heart of a Christian who desired to serve God with her whole heart.

Bobbie's drifting thoughts were interrupted again and again as the stage stopped and other passengers boarded or disembarked. It was well into the evening when a very tired young woman finally arrived in Santa Rosa. It felt wonderful to stretch her legs. As Bobbie set out on the walk home, she was also thankful that the skies were clear. Her fatigue fell away as she passed well-known sights—the post office, Riggs Mercantile, the barber shop—each one familiar and beloved even in the rapidly descending darkness.

Spotting her house, Bobbie began to run. Her parents were not expecting her for two more days, but they wouldn't be sorry to see her now. Bobbie stopped just short of throwing open the door. Drawing in a deep breath, she put her bags down. She rapped hard and stood still, telling herself to breathe as she waited.

Maryanne, never dreaming her daughter would arrive early, wished she had brought a lantern with her to the door so she could see who was on her front step.

"Who is it, Mary?" Jake called from somewhere in the living room.

"Tell him it's Bobbie," Bobbie said softly before her mother could make a sound, and then Bobbie watched her mother dissolve into tears. She didn't move to touch her daughter or try to speak to her; she couldn't. She cried uncontrollably in a way that she hadn't for over five years.

Jake came on the scene to find his daughter's arms around his wife, attempting to comfort her and stop her tears. Jake added his own tears as his arms went around both of his girls, and the three of them stood still, no one noticing the cold air coming in from the open door.

"Mom, try to stop," Bobbie pleaded.

"Come and sit down, Mary." Jake led his wife to the sofa and sat on one side of her. Bobbie quickly retrieved her bags from the porch and closed the front door. Not noticing that the house looked wonderful, her attention was centered wholly on her distraught mother.

"I'm sorry, Mom, I shouldn't have surprised you," Bobbie said as she sat on the sofa next to her mother. The words were like cold water in the face of the distressed woman.

"Oh Bobbie, no," she choked out. "I'm just so glad to see you and it's been so long." She cried some more but was finally gaining some control. Bobbie glanced over to see her father grinning at her. She smiled back.

"Welcome home."

"Thanks." Bobbie's smile nearly stretched off her face.

"Stand up and let me look at you." Bobbie complied and stood quietly for his inspection.

"Have I changed?" Bobbie asked the question with exaggerated innocence and her father chuckled.

"You're not much taller but there's definitely more to you." Jake Bradford's eyes sparkled and it was Bobbie's turn to chuckle.

"Well, I got my wish and finally developed in the front but the Lord was overly generous in the back." Bobbie's voice was dry.

Jake laughed in earnest then. The Bradford women were notorious for having smaller bustlines and larger posteriors.

"Don't you fret, Bobbie. You've got a nice figure, just like your mother's, and she's got a great—"

"Jacob!" Maryanne spoke sharply, and both husband and daughter laughed. Maryanne patted the sofa and Bobbie sat on the edge, turning to face her mother, who lay back against the cushions.

"Look at you," she breathed as she gazed into her daughter's face. "Why didn't we ever think to cut your hair? Just look at those dark blonde curls," Maryanne said with a small shake of her head. Bobbie only shrugged and smiled.

In truth her hair was darling, cut short all around her head and so curly. It was a natural curl that simply hadn't had a chance against the weight of Bobbie's previous longer style. The frames on Bobbie's glasses were a little different now, but other than the hair and glasses, she was very much the same. Her mouth still smiled just as easily and her eyes were still a beautiful deep green.

"Where's Troy?" Bobbie asked quickly when it looked as though her mother would cry again.

"On a date."

Bobbie's parents took great delight over the way their daughter's mouth dropped open.

"A date?"

"That's right. He'll be home pretty soon."

"Why didn't anyone mention this in their letters?"

"It just happened," Jake informed her with a smile.

Bobbie had a thousand questions then, and before her parents could answer them all, Troy walked in. He was a good six inches taller than she was and even had a mustache. Bobbie could only stare at her 18-year-old brother. Troy stared back.

"Hi, Bobbie," the young man finally said, his voice as deep as Jake's.

"Hi, brat," Bobbie said fondly. Another moment passed and then Troy grabbed her and squeezed her tight. They laughed and talked nonstop for the next hour before Bobbie told her family she was going to be too tired to walk the stairs if she didn't go to bed.

"Have you told her about our plans for the weekend?" Troy said softly as his sister started out of the room.

"No," Jake said when he was sure she couldn't hear. "I thought I'd surprise her over breakfast."

The three remaining in the living room shared a conspiratorial grin and then sat in silence and listened to the floor creak above them as Bobbie readied for bed. Maryanne couldn't remember when anything sounded so sweet.

$\mathcal{S}even$

"IT'S ABOUT TIME you got up." Bobbie was greeted by her brother's voice and she smiled sleepily at him.

"I'd forgotten how soft that bed was," Bobbie commented as she poured herself a cup of coffee and joined him at the kitchen table. "Where is everyone?"

"Dad's working and Mom ran uptown. She thought you might want to go but decided to let you sleep."

Bobbie moved from the table and began to fix herself some breakfast. She had eggs in the pan when she asked Troy a question that had been on her mind since last night.

"So tell me, Troy, how long have you been seeing Carla Johnson?"

"Yesterday was the third time."

"Where do you and Carla usually go?"

"Last night her folks asked me to supper and then we played a game. The times before that we just went for a walk."

Bobbie grinned and they continued to talk. There wasn't really much catching up to do, since they had all kept as close as the mail would allow.

"Did Cleve see you off?" Troy asked.

"No, just Uncle Jasper and Aunt Joanne. I'm kind of glad he didn't."

"You're not sure, are you? I mean, nothing is definite?"

"No, it's not. Cleveland is a wonderful man and we care for each other, but marriage is such a big step. I hate the idea of living away from Santa Rosa the rest of my life. Now tell me something, Troy—if I desperately wanted to marry Cleve, would it matter to me where I lived?"

Troy's brows rose. "I see your point."

As they discussed the matter Bobbie suddenly noticed a pair of her brother's jeans lying on the table next to the newspaper.

"I take it these need mending."

"They might after you put them on."

"What is that supposed to mean?" Bobbie's voice was indignant.

"Only that you probably won't fit as easily into my jeans as you once did for our camping trips."

"We're going camping?" Bobbie whispered, her voice and face radiating excitement.

"That's the plan." Troy answered her calmly, but inside he was as excited as his sister.

"When do we leave?"

"Since you don't have to be to work until Monday, we'll head out Friday afternoon and come back sometime Sunday."

Bobbie wanted to jump around the kitchen like a kid out of school. How she had missed the camping trips with her dad and brother! They continued to discuss the camping trip and then Troy said he had to leave for work.

Enjoying the feel of home once again, Bobbie stayed at the kitchen table for a long time. Her thoughts wandered and then centered on her family, primarily her sister Alice.

Alice had been pregnant when Bobbie left for Jenner and surprised everyone with twins. The twins had just turned five and Bobbie had never seen them, something she planned on changing that very afternoon.

Maryanne came in a short time later, and mother and daughter sat over coffee and talked like old friends.

"How is your Aunt Joanne?"

"When I left she was crying but she's doing well. I know she hopes I'll be back before the summer is out, as Mrs. Cleveland Ramsey."

"And what do you hope?" Maryanne inquired of her daughter.

"That Cleve will suddenly want to move to Santa Rosa."

"That would make him the perfect husband?"

"Not perfect, I guess, but certainly more appealing. And like I said to Troy, if I was wild to marry Cleve, would it matter where we lived?"

"You might find that you feel differently in a few months, honey; you might find you don't really want to stay in Santa Rosa after all."

Bobbie stared at her mother in surprise.

"Don't get me wrong, Bobbie," she explained. "I wish we could live out the rest of our lives living only a few blocks from each other, but I must face facts. Santa Rosa has changed in five years, and so have you. And you might miss Cleve so much that the miles between us won't seem near so important. As hard as it would be to see you go, I would understand. I feel God has been preparing me for something just like this for a long time."

"Oh Mom," Bobbie spoke as she hugged her. "I missed you so much."

Maryanne couldn't stop the tears as her own arms surrounded her daughter. They were probably closer through letters than they might have been if Bobbie had lived at home during her transitional teenage years, but it didn't stop the ache. It didn't ease the longing of wanting to touch and hug each other for all those years and not be able. Who would have thought five years would pass?

"Look at us," Bobbie said as she wiped her streaming face. "We really have got to stop getting each other wet. Now," Bobbie continued with determination, "I want to go see Alice and the kids. Do you want to come?"

"Sure. I just have a few things to do and then we can start. Do you need to stop at the shipping office?"

"No. When I wrote back to Mr. Taylor and accepted the job, he said that unless he heard otherwise he'd plan on my starting work the morning of the eighth."

"Good enough." Maryanne moved from the table to do a few things, and a half-hour later the women were headed to the other side of town. They had a mile walk ahead of them to the Townsend residence.

Alice Bradford had married Stuart Townsend the summer after she finished school. He was four years older and she had met him when attending a party on the far side of Santa Rosa. For Stuart, seeing Alice was love at first sight.

Alice was very shy, even where her family was concerned, and had been slightly overwhelmed by the attention of this stranger. She was not yet done with school, and she knew Stuart to be a man with his own room in one of the boarding houses *and* a steady job at the bank. Stuart was relentless, however, and by the time Alice completed her final year he had won her heart.

Stuart adored his wife and was crazy about his children. In fact he was so tender that he had insisted that Alice go to visit Bobbie when she had been gone for over two years. Maryanne had wanted to go in the worst way, but both of the ladies she cleaned for had planned parties and would not have been prepared to let her off for several weeks.

Maryanne and Bobbie walked the distance in companionable conversation. They were both dressed warmly, since January in Santa Rosa is usually rainy and quite cool, enough to chill a person to the bone if not dressed appropriately.

Alice's home was a welcome sight at the end of their journey, and the sisters embraced for long moments. Alice was much the same, and even though she was not talkative, her expression told her sister how glad she was to have her back.

They settled in the kitchen and Alice set mugs of coffee in front of her sister and mother. A moment later Paige and Wesley entered the room. They stood shyly near their mother at the stove as they greeted their grandmother, and then, seeing their Aunt Bobbie for the first time, they stared in wide-eyed silence.

"Hello," Bobbie said softly, and told herself she was not going to cry. Paige and Wesley Townsend were adorable. They were both blonde and freckled and their eyes were the exact shade of green as her own. Alice had dressed them warmly and in matching outfits. Wesley's pants were the same material as Paige's jumper, a heavy brown corduroy, and their shirts, a brown-and-red plaid, also matched.

Alice had been dressing them alike since the day they were born. Once, when the twins were four, she had mentioned buying fabrics that were different. The twins reacted with such vehement protests to this suggestion that Alice had dropped the whole idea.

Bobbie knew how easy it would be to overreact and throw her arms around these dear children, to whom she was an absolute stranger. They, on the other hand, were as familiar to her as they could be. Everyone, Troy included, had something to say about them in every letter—not to mention Alice's letters, in which she talked about little else.

The five-year-olds watched Bobbie reach for her bag. She brought forth a pair of blue mittens and a pair of red. Next she drew out an orange stick of candy which joined the blue mittens and a red stick to go with the other pair. And finally a red ribbon joined the pile of red items, all intended for Paige. A whistle carved from wood was set next to the blue mittens and orange candy, which were to go to Wesley.

"These are for you, Paige," Bobbie said as she pushed the red pile a little closer to the edge of the table. "And these," Bobbie said as she repeated the movement with the other things, "are for you, Wes."

"What do you say to your Aunt Bobbie?" Alice asked softly.

"Thank you, Aunt Bobbie," the children chorused in voices equally as soft. Bobbie's eyes filled with tears and she busied herself with her coffee to hide the fact.

The children came forward and stood next to their gifts. Bobbie, so wanting to get off to a good start with these little ones, did not immediately look at them. When she did, she found them both grinning at her. Bobbie smiled back with such delight that they both began to talk at once.

Within ten minutes Paige was in her lap and Wesley was sitting with his grandmother. It never once occurred to Bobbie that her family would talk to these children about her. Why, they knew everything!

"What do you look like without your glasses?" Wes wanted to know. Bobbie removed her spectacles and awaited their inspection.

"She looks the same," Paige stated calmly—"real pretty."

Bobbie hugged the little girl to herself and was surprised a moment later when Alice asked what they wanted for lunch. She couldn't believe how the morning had flown.

When Maryanne and Bobbie finally left, Bobbie was buoyant. She couldn't stop talking about her wonderful niece and nephew.

"Oh Mom, I've just had a terrific idea. Do you suppose Dad would let Paige and Wes go camping with us?"

"Oh Bobbie, I don't know."

"Well, I could at least ask. I mean, it's three adults and only two children; we outnumber them and I can tell what good kids they are."

"Oh Bob, I don't know," Maryanne repeated, and her daughter laughed.

"You're such a worrier, Mom. I'm sure Dad will say yes, not to mention Troy. He'll love the idea."

Maryanne didn't look the least bit convinced, but kept silent. This was one she was more than willing to let Jake handle.

Eight

"I KNOW ALICE WILL say yes if you talk to her, Dad. Tell her they can sleep with me. You know how warm we'll all be."

Jake Bradford regarded his daughter and tried not to laugh. She was 14 all over again as they discussed the camping trip. She had nearly leaped on him and Troy when they came in the front door for supper with her idea of taking Paige and Wesley with them.

Troy and Jake had exchanged a quick look; they had honestly never considered it. They also thought it was a great idea, but they weren't about to let Bobbie know that, at least not yet.

"They're pretty young, Bobbie," Troy said skeptically, his eyes just beginning to sparkle.

"We were younger the first time Dad took us," Bobbie pointed out logically, and for the first time noticed that her family was enjoying this.

"Well, maybe you're right," Bobbie went on with a show of disappointment that could have convinced an audience at any theater. "They *are* young and I've heard that neither one of you has the least bit of control where Wes and Paige are concerned. So I guess it's for the best."

"What's that supposed to mean?" Troy demanded.

"Only that you take a toy every time you go see them and are spoiling them rotten. And I've heard that Dad can't bring himself to say no, so they get away with everything when they're with him."

Bobbie might have gotten away with her bald-faced lies if she hadn't dropped in a chair just then and begun filing her nails with far more deliberation than necessary. She was a study in concentration until Troy sailed a sofa pillow across the room and hit her in the head. Bobbie whipped it back at lightning speed, catching her brother totally off-guard.

Smiling with satisfaction, Bobbie growled in her gruffest voice, "Now, do my niece and nephew go with us or do I have to get rough with you?"

"They can come, they can come!" Troy cried in mock terror.

"You still have to ask Alice," Jake reminded Bobbie.

"I thought you might ask her. She's always been putty in your hands."

Jake smiled at the description. It was true. He had always been close to his oldest daughter, even though she was painfully shy. She was more open with him than she was with Maryanne or her siblings, and Jake had always nurtured their relationship. The only thing to ever come between them was Jake's decision for Christ. Alice had been very hurt when her father had explained how he had come to see his need for salvation.

"But what have you been up until now, Dad, if you haven't been a Christian?" Alice had asked.

"I've been someone who thought I could get to heaven if I did my best and watched my step. I was leaving Jesus Christ completely out of the picture."

"So what you're saying is, if a person is good, it still won't be enough?"

"That's right, honey, the Bible says we get to heaven God's way, and that's through the death of His Son, Jesus Christ, who died to take away our sins."

"That's barbaric! I can't believe God would spurn our efforts just because we didn't choose to believe something so awful as Christ's death on the cross! I've read the Bible's account of the crucifixion, and, Dad, you can't tell me that God would honor such a horrendous act against His own Son!"

Jake had gone on to explain the best he could but Alice would have none of it. They had parted on good terms, but Jake's heart had been heavy. He found himself wishing they had attended Pastor Keller's church years before, when Alice had been younger and possibly more receptive to the gospel.

Today father and daughter were as close as ever, but Jake knew he had to tread lightly when the conversation turned to church attendance and salvation. Alice had made it quite clear that she thought her parents attended a church full of snobs who had the ridiculous notion that they knew the only way to heaven.

And as always, when Jake visited Stuart and Alice, their beliefs and the church they attended weighed on his heart. But he knew he did a good job of hiding this fact, since she and her husband always welcomed him with open arms.

"What brings you out on this cold January night?" Alice asked her father when he had settled himself on the sofa.

"Your sister. We're going camping this weekend, and Bobbie wants Paige and Wes to go with us." Jake would never have spoken so plainly if the children had been present, but he knew it was at least an hour past their bedtime.

Stuart and Alice looked at each other for a long time. They, like Jake and Troy, had never considered the idea. Suddenly Alice chuckled.

"Leave it to Bobbie to come up with something like that."

"She's pretty pleased with herself. She sent me because she was sure I could convince you."

Alice chuckled again. "Well, this time she's going to be disappointed. Paige has a drippy nose and I think it's too cold for them to go camping."

"Bobbie planned on them sleeping with her."

"We could plan on the next time you go," Stuart interjected. "Maybe it will be warmer."

Stuart Townsend was every inch the bank employee with his dapper suits and neatly trimmed beard and mustache. He never interfered with his wife's raising of the children, so Jake was aware that Stuart's comment about the cold was a very real worry.

"That's probably a good idea. I'm sure Bobbie will feel let down, but like you said, there's always next time." Jake didn't stay much longer, but before leaving, Alice led him into the twins' room so he could see them. The light from the lantern didn't disturb them in the least, and as always, Jake's heart swelled with love at the sight of his grandchildren.

Just as Jake expected, his younger daughter and son were disappointed about the twins not going with them. Jake pointed out that it was cold and maybe it would work out for the next time.

As it was, it rained very hard at the time Jake, Troy, and Bobbie were going to leave for their trip, and it continued to rain all weekend. Maryanne, who had planned to sew all weekend, laid aside her plans and the four of them played games and talked for hours. It was a wonderful homecoming for Bobbie. The only dark spot on the weekend was how late they all stayed up on Saturday night, causing them to oversleep Sunday morning and miss church. Bobbie had been looking forward to seeing everyone, but consoled herself with the fact that she started her new job the next day.

She took herself to bed when it was still early on Sunday, and with the lantern turned high she lay in bed and wrote in her journal.

January Seven, 1872

It's lovely to be home. The clock did not stand still as I hoped it would, and nearly everything and everyone changed. My parents look older, but they are in some ways ageless. I'm going to contribute to the household whether my parents like it or not. Oh Troy, you're so much fun. And Paige and Wes— thank You, Lord!

Tomorrow is the big day. I'll see Jeff. I hope he likes me. Mr. Taylor too. I've got to get to sleep. Good night, journal, I'll write again in a few days.

Bobbie turned the lantern down then and fell asleep while praying for a calm heart to face her new job in the morning.

Nine

BOBBBIE WORE A GREEN dress for her first day of work. She spent a little extra time on her hair and was pleased with the way it curled softly around her face. Her fingernails, always long, were clean and well-shaped.

Maryanne had the day off, so Bobbie's send-off breakfast was a morning feast of omelettes stuffed with bacon and cheese, plus fresh muffins with jam, cider, and hot, strong coffee.

Bobbie left the house right after breakfast. Her coat kept her warm as she walked briskly away from home. She felt a little like a child on the first day of school as her lunch tin swung in her hand with every step. The shipping office was a welcome sight and Bobbie walked in the front door with a smile on her face.

May Taylor immediately rose from the desk in the corner and came toward her.

"Hello, Bobbie. It's good to see you." The two women embraced, and when May stepped away, Bobbie saw that there were tears in her eyes. "Don't mind me, honey. It's just that you're an answer to prayer and it's so wonderful to have you here."

"It's good to be here, Mrs. Taylor." Bobbie didn't say more and May could see she was close to tears herself. The two women had begun to talk about the workings of the office when Bill Taylor came in holding the hand of a young girl.

"Hello, Bobbie." Bill greeted his new employee warmly and shook her hand. They talked about her trip and whether or not she was settled in, and then May pulled the youngster closer to their circle of conversation.

"Bobbie, I'd like you to meet Marcail Donovan. Marcail, this is Bobbie Bradford. She's going to be working here at the office for awhile. Marcail's sister Kaitlin is married to our Rigg."

"It's nice to meet you, Marcail." Bobbie smiled kindly and held out her hand. Marcail must have instantly liked what she saw because she shook Bobbie's hand with enthusiasm.

"My sister's going to have a baby," Marcail informed Bobbie seriously.

"And you'll be Aunt Marcail," Bobbie replied with a smile. "I think that's wonderful. I have a niece and a nephew and they're so much fun. I know you'll love being an aunt." The little girl beamed at her newfound friend before May claimed Bobbie once again and began showing her the desk where she would do the majority of her work.

The shipping company was located in a spacious building on a corner lot. The office had a sectioned-off corner for a private office for Bill, whose window overlooked the side street. Bobbie's desk, formerly May's, sat in the opposite corner with a complete view of the entire room as well as the large windows that looked out over the loading area and the street.

May sensed immediately that Bobbie had a complete knowledge of the job. She knew everyone had his own way of doing things and wanted to leave Bobbie to her task as soon as possible. Ten minutes later May left so Marcail would not be late for school, telling Bobbie if she needed anything to knock on Bill's door.

May was not gone ten seconds when a woman came in wanting to send a package to San Francisco. Upon meeting Bobbie, the woman wanted complete details as to the whereabouts of May. Bobbie, with her kind attitude and ready smile, explained to her who she was and why May was not there. At the desk Bobbie recorded all the information for the package before accompanying the woman out to her buggy, where she gave Bobbie the large parcel she wanted sent.

The package wasn't so much heavy as it was awkward, and Bobbie walked back inside, peeking over the top of it as she moved. After closing the door she turned without looking and ran into someone whose arms came out and lifted the burden from her. Bobbie's head tipped back to see who was before her. Jeff Taylor stood regarding her with serious, almost hesitant eyes.

Bobbie grinned into those eyes, her own filled with friendship and something that might have been defined as tenderness. She had already given much thought as to how hard this might be for him.

"Hello, Jeff," she said softly. Jeff's relief was so great he sighed audibly.

"Hello, Bobbie." He smiled, his whole body losing its former tenseness. "I see Mom didn't waste any time in putting you to work."

Bobbie, trying not to laugh at the sigh and look of relief that had come over her co-worker's face, continued to grin at him.

"I don't mind. It's pretty routine and I have a tendency to get antsy if I don't have something to do."

They smiled at each other again, and Jeff mentally shook his head over the way he had tortured himself all through the night and that morning over how uncomfortable it was going to be working with Bobbie.

He had deliberately come into the office late, putting off what he was sure would be awkward: to find Bobbie handling a customer like a pro. He had watched her, unnoticed, from the doorway of the storeroom. Jeff was fascinated. Cheerful and efficient, she was not at all as he expected.

The only problem he could see was her obvious tendency to overdo. His mother would never have lifted a package as heavy as the one Bobbie had. May would have called to one of the men in the family for assistance. Jeff placed the package against the wall, taking note as he did that it was already wrapped for travel, and turned back to Santa Rosa's newest shipping clerk.

"Bobbie, in the future be sure to call one of us to help you with packages that heavy."

Bobbie was surprised. What was she there for if not to work? There was absolutely no way she was going to go running for help every time a large package came in. Why, the very thought of it!

Jeff was still staring at her, so Bobbie decided to reassure him. "I wouldn't lift something that I couldn't handle, Jeff."

Jeff smiled and kept still, having accurately read what was going on in her mind. He would let his father handle this one. They were discussing more aspects of the job, such as the storage room at the back of the building, the stage depot next door, and the hours both offices were open, when Gilbert came in.

"Hello, Bobbie." Bobbie could only stare at him.

"Gilbert?" She finally managed to say.

"It's me." Gilbert stated the obvious and waited for Bobbie to look her fill. He had been a boy when she left, only 13. Five years later he towered over her and was almost as filled-out as Jeff. Both men sported lean frames and broad shoulders. Their arms were corded with muscles, brought on by the daily tasks of lifting, loading, and packing every conceivable size of crate and package.

"Well, I see you're following in the same homely footsteps as your brother," Bobbie said, her voice becoming dry and giving the men a first glimpse of what working with Roberta Bradford would be like. "I suppose girls go out with you because they feel sorry for such an ugly little pup. Well, look at that smile I'm getting! And after all those insults! You're obviously very disagreeable too."

It was too much for the Taylor men; they couldn't hold their laughter. Bobbie joined them, and then a man came in with an armload of small boxes. Bobbie turned serious in the blink of an eye and the customer was explaining his need and paying his money in record time.

Gilbert was impressed with his first look at Bobbie in action. Gil wondered if his parents knew what a treasure they had found.

"Where's May?" Bill asked as he came out of his office and approached the desk where Bobbie was seated.

"She and Marcail left a little while ago."

"I'm sorry, Bobbie," Bill stated sincerely. "I had no idea you were out here trying to deal with the customers on your own." Bill stopped when his sons began to laugh. Bobbie didn't hear the explanation they gave their father because someone else had come in off the street and Bobbie moved to help them.

It was Bill's turn to watch his new employee in action, and he felt like May did—that he could cry over how good it was to have her with them.

The next hour flew by in a frenzy of activity, and no one was given any more time for socializing. At one point Jeff and Gilbert watched their father take a large box from Bobbie and tell her she was not to be lifting anything that heavy. Bill turned away as though the matter was settled, but both of the younger men could see that Bobbie had a mind of her own on this subject. It wasn't until after lunch that the situation came to a head.

"Bobbie," Bill said as he plucked, yet again, another heavy package from his newest employee's arms. "Am I or am I not your boss?"

"You're my boss," Bobbie admitted quietly.

"And as your boss, I've told you that you're not to be lifting articles that are too heavy."

"I'm not lifting too much," Bobbie stated in respectful logic.

"I think you are."

"Mr. Taylor, did you write and tell me you needed a shipping clerk, or did I misunderstand your letter?"

"Yes, I need a shipping clerk, but—"

"Then I'm only trying to do my job," the small blonde cut him off, her voice and posture a picture of respect. "I'm young, strong, and healthy, and I haven't lifted a thing today that was too much for me."

Bill could only stare at her. He had *never* had an employee stand up to him before. He was a reasonable man but his word was law. He only had to say something once to have it obeyed. And now this young woman with the beautiful green eyes and the adorable glasses perched on her nose, a woman who had to tip her head back to look up at him, was telling him she could lift and tote like his sons.

Bobbie waited a moment for her employer to say something, but when he remained silent and when someone else needed her, she went off without a word, thinking as she did that he had seen her point and the matter was settled.

Bill stood still and watched Bobbie handle one of his toughest customers. He stared in amazement when she actually wrung a smile from the old coot. A moment later he motioned Gil and Jeff, both of whom had again witnessed the entire conversation, into his office.

"Does she ever stop moving?" Bill came right to the point and his sons smiled.

"I think she took about five minutes to eat her lunch," Gil told his dad.

Bill nodded and was silent a moment. "I want you to keep an eye on her. Now, I don't mean for you to babysit her and ignore your own work, but if you see her lifting something she shouldn't, take it from her. If that's too distracting for you, then I'll talk with her again."

"Lay down the law, Dad, like you did today." There was a teasing glint in Jeff's eyes and Bill smiled.

'She's certainly a surprise,' Bill thought to himself, staying at his desk long after his sons exited. Bobbie wasn't a person that drew any attention to herself. If something needed doing, she did it in silent efficiency. Bill thought that might take a little getting used to.

He knew he had babied May over the years. When it came to some of the tougher jobs or customers, he had always dealt with them. When it came right down to it, May could have handled everything as easily as he did.

What he was feeling today might have stemmed from the fact that he kept forgetting Bobbie was there. She was so quiet and efficient that he was already taking her for granted. By enlisting the help of his sons, he hoped they would all be more aware of her.

The sight of Bobbie, looking at him through those glasses, confident and unwavering, came to mind. It would do them all a little good to have someone like her working around the office, and he would do whatever he had to do to keep her working there—that is, until she completed her plans for marriage. Bill found himself thinking that the guy who snagged Bobbie Bradford was one lucky fellow.

Ten

"ARE YOU GOING to work here all the time?" The question came from Marcail who was standing beside Bobbie's desk in the shipping office. It was near closing time and Bobbie was filling out some papers and preparing to leave for the evening.

"Well," Bobbie said slowly, "for awhile."

"I'm not going to work here when I grow up. I'm going to teach school like Katie."

"Katie is your sister?"

The little girl nodded. "Her real name is Kaitlin. She used to be Kaitlin Donovan but now she's Kaitlin Riggs because she married Rigg."

"And she's a schoolteacher?"

"Right. She's my teacher and Sean's too. He's my brother. He's 14."

Listening to all of this in thoughtful silence, Bobbie did not want Marcail to know that none of this was news to her. She had of course known Marshall Riggs, or at least *of* him, for years. And when he had married the schoolteacher, her mother had written and told her all about it.

Marcail was at Bobbie's desk because Rigg was in the office with his father. They had come in a few minutes ago, and Marcail, who had already decided that Bobbie was very nice, had come straight to her desk to talk.

"How was school today?" Bobbie asked her young companion, who was regarding Bobbie's long fingernails with dark, serious eyes.

"It was fine. Katie's pretty tired. She says it's because of the baby. Have you ever had a baby?"

"No," Bobbie answered softly.

"But you're an aunt?"

"Yes. My sister has five-year-old twins named Paige and Wesley."

"Twins!" Marcail's eyes grew very round. "Do you think Katie will have twins?"

A deep chuckle sounded behind them and both ladies turned to see Rigg listening.

"I'm not sure you should say that to your sister, Marc. She's so tired right now she can't think straight. Hello, Bobbie," Rigg continued. "You've grown up a little bit since I last saw you."

Bobbie smiled, almost mischievously. "You look the same, Rigg. A bit happier, perhaps, which I suspect has something to do with your recent marriage. Allow me to offer my congratulations on your having acquired a wonderful sister-in-law." Bobbie winked at Marcail on these words.

"Thank you," Rigg said as his own eyes began to sparkle. His father had said it was going to be fun having Bobbie around and he could already see why.

"Oh, I guess I should also offer my best wishes, since you now have a wife, and a baby on the way." Bobbie said this as though it had just come to mind.

Rigg, caught up in the spirit of Bobbie's teasing, bowed to her most formally and asked how the job was going.

"Very well, thank you. Most of it is routine, but the code system your father uses, along with all the different faces and names of the customers, is going to take awhile for me to learn."

"Something tells me you'll catch on with no trouble at all. We better go, Marc, so we can help with supper."

"Bye, Bobbie. Maybe I'll see you tomorrow."

"I'll look forward to it," Bobbie told Marcail as she walked them to the door.

The clock on the wall told her it was past closing time, so Bobbie put the sign out and shut the front door. With the sun sinking rapidly it was growing chilly outside. Bobbie thought she best get home before it grew much darker.

"Mr. Taylor," Bobbie called softly through his office door, "I'm going to go now. I'll see you in the morning."

The door opened before she could walk away and Bill stepped out. "Thanks, Bobbie, for all your work."

"It was my pleasure. Do you want me at the same time tomorrow?"

"Yes. I think you should plan on working the same hours as you did today, except for Saturdays. Some of those you'll have off and on others you'll work until noon. And of course we're closed on Sunday."

Bobbie looked a little surprised to learn she would have some Saturdays off. Bill figured she was used to working an office where there was little or no help at all and having to put in ten-hour days for at least six and possibly seven days a week.

"All right, Mr. Taylor. I'll see you in the morning. Good night."

"Good night, Bobbie."

Bobbie's step was light as she walked the distance home. It had been a long day, but she was pleased with her work and believed her employer to be also. Still praying and thanking God for the way He provides and cares, Bobbie walked up the steps of her house.

Rigg and Marcail headed right home as planned and entered the warmth of the house through the back door. This put them in the kitchen, where they hung their coats on hooks and then moved to help Kaitlin with supper.

Sean, who lived with his sister and brother-in-law, just as Marcail did, was nowhere to be seen. Marcail assumed his job and set the table. Kaitlin was stirring over a large pot and Rigg slipped his arms around her for a brief moment.

"Let me do this."

Kate surrendered the spoon easily. "Thanks, Rigg. Did you guys see Sean?"

"Isn't he here?" Rigg's face darkened with concern and some suspicion.

"No. I think he said he had to work today."

Rigg's face clouded with very real anger and his wife put her hand on his arm.

"He wasn't scheduled to work today and he didn't even come in to check. How did he think to get away with such a lie, Kate?" Rigg's voice had turned from anger to anguish over this betrayal. "He knew I would be at the store and he would be found out."

"I don't know, Rigg. There's just no figuring him out these days." Kate's voice was weary, and as always her father's face came to mind.

Sometimes it was hard to believe that just a year ago she had been living with her family in Hawaii. A wonderful, almost idyllic life. Her parents had been missionaries. Kate had lived there nearly all her life, and both Sean and Marcail had been born in Hawaii. Now things were so different.

Her parents had surprised her on her twentieth birthday by announcing they would be taking a furlough. They had sailed to California and stayed with her Aunt Maureen Kent, her father's older sister.

The trip had a wonderful beginning but it hadn't taken very long for things to turn for the worse. Almost upon arriving, her mother, Theresa Donovan, was diagnosed with tuberculosis. Mother's last weeks with them had been so brief, and then her father returned to the islands to settle affairs. That had been nearly a year ago. It seemed that every few months something arose to keep Patrick Sean Donovan II separated from his family.

At first the children stayed with their aunt in San Francisco, but that arrangement didn't work. They then headed north to Santa Rosa, where Kaitlin took a teaching position and met Marshall Riggs.

It was love at first sight for Marshall—"Rigg" to friends and family alike. But for Kate, whose world was a painful place with the loss of her mother and absence of her father, their relationship was strained.

But Rigg was not easily discouraged, and he lovingly befriended all three Donovans, eventually winning Kaitlin's heart. They had been married since October, and now Kate was due in August.

Kaitlin had kept in as close touch with her father as the mails would allow, but at times like this, when Sean was acting up, or on her wedding day, she missed his presence so much that she wanted to sit down and cry. It didn't help to be pregnant, teaching school, and in a constant state of fatigue.

"Sit down, Kate," Rigg instructed his wife, who had been standing next to him for a few minutes without saying a word.

"No, I'll get the biscuits ready."

"I've already done that." He led her to a chair and pushed a mug of coffee into her hand. For the first time Kate realized Marcail had set the table. The sisters looked at each other and Marcail smiled uncertainly.

She had never seen her big sister tired like this, and watching her brother grow daily more rebellious was really something new. It was hard to have Father gone, and the nine-year-old missed him a lot, but not like Sean did. In fact, to watch Sean, you'd think that Father was gone just like Mother and not coming back at all! Marcail took great comfort in the fact that he would return someday. If anything was bothering her right now, it was that Kaitlin was so tired and had to see a doctor because she was pregnant. Marcail didn't like doctors.

"Did you see Bobbie again?" Marcail, who had been working at not chattering when her sister was tired, simply nodded.

"You'll have to tell her sometime how much you liked her the very first time you met." Marcail nodded again. May had taken her to school and she had immediately told her sister all about Bobbie Bradford and how nice she had been.

"She wears glasses, Katie, and they make her awful cute. Do I need glasses?" Kate had told her no, even as she wondered about this woman who worked for her father-in-law. She knew that she and Jeff had been in school together and she knew the Bradfords from church, but beyond that Bobbie was a mystery.

Sensing that Marcail needed a hug, Kate reached for her. Marcail stood by her older sister's chair, secure in the embrace while Rigg continued to put supper on. They had just sat down to eat when Sean came in the back door.

$\mathscr{E}leven$

THE NIGHT WAS cold, but Jeff was in no hurry to get home. He had dropped Sylvia off at her sister's house and was taking the long way home. They had parted on good terms even though an hour ago she had been furious with him.

Conversation over supper was light and Jeff had been having a great time until Sylvia asked how work had gone that day.

"It went well. Bobbie is a hard worker and off to a great start."

"Bobbie?"

"Bobbie Bradford. She started work at the office today. I told you about it."

"No, Jeff, you didn't." Sylvia's voice had become very low and Jeff could see she was angry. It always amazed him at how quickly that could happen.

"I must have forgot. Well, anyway, she's doing great."

"I wasn't aware that your father was in the market for a new employee." She was still furious. Jeff, hoping she would calm down, answered carefully.

"He never advertised, but Mom needed a break, and when he found out that Bobbie was coming back into town and that she was experienced, he scooped her up."

"So you've known for some time that Bobbie was coming back to Santa Rosa?"

Jeff immediately saw his mistake and struggled to find words that would erase the anger from his date's face. "Sylvia, I'm sorry that I

307

never mentioned Bobbie's return. But we don't talk about my job very often and it just never came up. I wasn't trying to hide anything from you."

Sylvia saw his sincerity, and knowing that she was overreaching, she tried to calm herself. She knew that her eyes weren't as pretty when she was angry and she never wanted Jeff to find her unattractive.

With her mass of blonde hair and startling blue eyes, most men did find her attractive. But Sylvia wasn't interested in what *most* men thought, just Jeff Taylor. Jeff of course didn't know that, since she did see other men and always let him know about it. But if she stayed with it long enough, she was sure she could bring him around, was sure she would see that spark of jealousy in his eyes that told her he cared. So far it hadn't happened, but Sylvia was patient. She had let him get away once before when they were just 17. It wasn't going to happen again.

An image of Bobbie and the way she looked at the lagoon picnic sprang to mind. 'You don't suppose she'd come back beautiful, do you?' Sylvia asked herself and then had to work at not laughing at the thought; it was simply impossible. Ladies did not laugh out loud at the supper table, and besides, she didn't want to explain to Jeff what she was thinking.

Jeff was blissfully ignorant of Sylvia's thoughts as they finished their meal and then parted company an hour or so later. Jeff was tired as he climbed the stairs to bed, but a light glowing faintly from beneath Gilbert's door propelled him to his brother's room.

"Gil," Jeff opened the door a crack, "are you up?"

"Yeah." Gil answered from the bed, where he had lain down with his Bible. He rolled to his side and propped his head on his hand as he watched Jeff drop into the room's only chair.

"Out with Sylvia?"

"Yeah, we had supper at the hotel. Their meat loaf is good." Then Jeff fell silent, staring at the floor.

"How did it go with you and Bobbie today?"

Jeff stared at his younger brother. Gilbert had always been able to read his mind, and sometimes it was very disconcerting. This time he had understood, without communication, that Jeff was nervous over Bobbie's return.

"I was fine as soon as I saw her and saw that *she* was okay. Before that I was sure it was going to be awful."

"She's pretty nice, I'd say, and no one would ever call her lazy." Both men smiled. Before the day was over they had both followed their father's orders and taken large boxes from her or just plain stopped her from lifting one. They were then able to witness a stubborn look cross her face, one that was so cute and determined it made them smile.

"Definitely not lazy." Jeff agreed and once again stared at the floor, causing Gil to wonder what was on his mind.

"What's wrong, Jeff? Did she say something that's bugging you?"

"Do you ever get the feeling that something is going to happen and you're not sure you want it to, but you can't do anything about it?"

"Not really. What do you mean?"

"I'm not sure myself, but I'm really afraid I'm going to hurt Bobbie all over again."

Gilbert was silent until his eyes dropped to the open pages of his Bible. "Can I tell you about what I was just reading, Jeff?"

"Sure." Jeff seemed almost relieved by the distraction.

"I'm in the book of Job right now, and I know you're familiar with the story, but I never read this without marveling at all he went through. He loses everything! And, Jeff, he didn't have a clue. I mean, he had no idea any of this was going to happen! In a very short time, however, his wealth is wiped out, all ten of his children die, and he ends up covered with boils.

"And then to make matters worse, his own wife is angry because he's still giving his allegiance to God, and this is what he says to her in chapter 2 verse 10: 'Thou speakest as one of the foolish women speaketh. What? Shall we receive good at the hand of God, and shall we not receive evil? In all this did not Job sin with his lips.'

"Do you see what I'm trying to say, Jeff? Job made a choice, a quick decision as to how he was going to react to those trials that are far more difficult than most of us will ever have to handle. He decided *not* to sin and here you are already telling yourself that you might hurt Bobbie.

"I think you should be saying just the opposite—that no matter what anyone else says or does, you, Jeff Taylor, are going to do the right thing by Roberta Bradford."

Staring at Gil, Jeff thought, not even his pastor was able to touch him as Gil just had. Of course it would help if he spent more time reading his Bible—Jeff was well aware of that.

"Thanks, Gilbert," Jeff answered solemnly before going to his own room. He didn't immediately fall asleep. In fact, he prayed for a long time about all his brother had said.

The next morning found Bobbie and Gilbert working together in the storeroom. Unclaimed packages were stacked on shelves against one wall. Bill's policy was to go through these shelves every other month and clear them for incoming packages.

At the same time, inventory was done and the supplies were checked and reordered for the month. Gilbert went from a position on his knees to a step stool, time and again, in order to reach all the shelves and check each box. Bobbie stood beside him making a list of the nearly depleted supplies as Gil called them to her.

At one point, when Gil was high on the stool, his elbow bumped a small box off the shelf. Bobbie never saw or heard a thing and chose that moment to look up and say something. Gil was off the stool in a shot, but the damage was done; Bobbie's glasses were broken.

"Bobbie, are you all right?" Gil was nearly frantic as Bobbie kept her head down, leading him to believe she was seriously hurt.

"Be careful where you step," Bobbie said softly, and it took him a moment to see that she was looking for her glasses. Gilbert found them at her feet and picked them up in two pieces.

"Bobbie, I'm sorry." He placed them in her hands and watched as she brought them nearly to her nose for examination.

"It's just that small hinge in the middle. I'm glad it's just the frames; my dad has a little tool to fix them. Unfortunately I'll have to go home to get it."

"Okay." Gilbert shot out the door to his dad's office. He didn't notice that other than Bobbie turning to watch him go, she stood absolutely still. A few minutes went by and Bobbie prayed that Gilbert would come back soon so she could explain she needed his help. It crossed her mind that since no one seemed to understand the extent of her eye problem, she might lose her job over this.

"Bobbie?" It was Gilbert's voice.

"Oh Gilbert, I'm glad—"

"No, it's Jeff."

Bobbie hesitated. For some reason she was reluctant to bother him.

"Jeff, do you know where Gilbert went?"

"Yeah, he's in talking with my dad."

"When he's through, could you tell him I need him?"

"Sure."

Bobbie heard the front door open and then Jeff walking away. She looked around her. Everything was very blurry. Well, not the shelf beside her, but that was because her shoulder was nearly touching it. Bobbie put her hand on the shelf for balance and then slid her foot carefully along the floor. She was afraid to actually take a step because she had no depth perception and everything looked so fuzzy and distorted.

Picking her way along slowly, Bobbie knew she was running out of shelf. She was also completely unaware of the fact that Gilbert and Bill were standing in the doorway watching her. Bill was silent and thoughtful as he watched his son approach Bobbie.

"Did you need me, Bobbie?" Gilbert asked from about two feet in front of her.

"Is that you, Gilbert?"

"It's me."

"Oh, good. I'm sorry I didn't explain—"

"You need to go home?"

"Right. But I need—"

"I'll take you right now."

Bobbie's features washed relief; he understood. He had also come close enough for her to see him. After watching her search his face with anxious eyes, he finally understood that he needed to draw nearer.

"Thank you." Bobbie smiled into his face, now so near her own, thinking he was the nicest guy on earth. "If you'll take me first to your dad's office, I'll explain."

"It's all right. He knows all about it." Bobbie need not know that Bill had learned much from his vantage point in the doorway.

Once out in the front office, Gil left Bobbie standing by the desk while he collected her coat. She heard conversation behind her but was again examining her glasses and paid no attention. When Bobbie's coat was dropped onto her shoulders she slipped into it and felt her arm taken as she was guided out the door. When they had gone about ten steps on the street Bobbie came to a halt.

"I need to tell you something, Gilbert. You need to be a step in front of me and let me take your arm. That way if you move I can feel it. If you come to a step, you'll need to say something or slow way down."

"I'll do just that, and by the way, I'm Jeff."

They had maneuvered into position, and Bobbie almost tripped when she heard who was escorting her.

"Where's Gilbert?" Bobbie asked in a small voice.

"He stayed at the office. I need to pick something up at Rigg's and I told him I would take you."

For some reason this was embarrassing to Bobbie. She felt that Gil was aware and concerned about her plight. Not that Jeff was being unkind, but she wasn't sure he really understood. She didn't really care to explain all over again about needing help, but in the next few minutes she wished she had swallowed her pride and explained.

"I take it you can find your way from here, Bobbie," Jeff said as he stopped before the mercantile. The shipping office was on a busier street than the mercantile and Jeff honestly believed Bobbie would have no trouble the rest of the way. He was gone before she could say a word. Bobbie found she was more frightened than she had ever been in her life.

Five minutes passed while she tried to calm herself. She did know exactly where she was, but had never been in this situation before. Maybe she could make it home.

Bobbie tried to think of where the boardwalk ended, if it was right at the corner of the mercantile or a little before. She held the broken spectacles up before her, thankful that the glass was intact. Moving slowly, Bobbie was able to get her hand on the side of the building. Afraid she would drop her glasses and never find them, they went into the pocket of her coat.

It was a chilly day and having to move slowly did nothing to warm her. Bobbie was almost to the steps when Rigg and Jeff noticed her from inside the store. They exited the building together and Bobbie was just about to step off into midair when Rigg's hand stopped her.

"Oh, thank you. Who's there?" Bobbie looked up at the blurry features.

"It's Rigg."

"Oh." Bobbie wanted to cry with relief. "I know you're terribly busy, Rigg, but I'm in a jam. I didn't explain to Jeff that I needed help getting all the way home, and now he's left. Troy is working at the livery, so maybe you could let him know I need help. I know you're busy." She finished in quiet embarrassment and Rigg led her to the bench in front of his store.

"Just sit here a minute, Bobbie. Jeff is still here."

Rigg wondered how long Jeff would have stood staring at Bobbie if he hadn't given him a shake. He seemed to be transfixed by the sight of Bobbie struggling along. Standing about ten feet away from her, he hurried forward after Rigg touched him.

"Here, Bobbie, let me help you."

Bobbie came to her feet and moved down the street with Jeff, wishing as she went that Gilbert had simply taken her home.

Twelve

BOBBIE WAS SHIVERING uncontrollably by the time they reached the house. She stood just inside her front door and tried to calm down. Jeff had come a little farther into the living room and found himself staring at her once again.

In truth, Jeff was horrified over what he had just done. He asked himself how he could possibly have left her at the mercantile after witnessing the fact that she hadn't even recognized him in the storeroom, and again as they walked down the street she had thought he was Gilbert.

Something inside him had nearly torn in two as he had felt her arm trembling on his own on the walk home.

"I'm sorry, Bobbie. I feel ashamed I wasn't more sensitive to your needs."

"It's all right, Jeff. I should have explained. I need to talk with your father. It never occurred to me that your family didn't realize the problem I have with my vision." Bobbie's voice was soft, almost resigned.

"It's not going to change your status on the job, Bobbie. I can promise you that."

Bobbie only shrugged, clearly not believing him, and began to move across the room. That it was familiar to her was obvious, but Jeff was still pretty disturbed, and so he spoke up.

"Bobbie, if you'll just tell me what you need, I can get it."

"That's all right, Jeff. You don't need to stay. I'll come back as soon as I repair my glasses."

Jeff ignored her and deliberately moved to block her path. She stopped and stared up at him, noticing absently that she was feeling warmer.

Jeff brought his face down to what he believed to be very close. "Can you see me?"

"Pretty much."

Jeff moved again, this time until his nose was no more than an inch from hers.

"Now?"

"Yes."

"I want you to tell me what you need. I really can be of much more use than I was here in the last hour. So if you'll just tell me what you want, I'll get it."

Bobbie could see that he was determined. "I need to go into the kitchen."

Jeff turned his back to her. "Grab hold of the back of my coat." Bobbie grabbed on and was led into the kitchen.

"Now," she said, "over in the pantry there's a basket with odds and ends in it." She was quiet while Jeff retrieved it.

"What I need is a small tool that repairs the tiny hinges in these frames." Bobbie reached into her pocket for the glasses, and Jeff seated them both at the table.

Jeff nearly pressed the tool into her hand but instead picked up the glasses she had laid on the table. Bobbie didn't object, but leaned very close in an effort to see him work. He worked with careful precision, no easy task with Bobbie's nose almost touching his cheek. He noticed how nice her hair smelled and nearly told her so, but just then the back door opened and in walked Troy.

"Is that you, Dad?"

"What happened to your glasses?" Bobbie's question about who he was told him instantly, before he had even looked at her, that she couldn't see. Never was Troy more protective than when his sister couldn't see. Even as a child he could become almost violent if Bobbie were threatened when she was without her glasses.

"They broke at work."

"Are you all right?"

"Yes," Bobbie answered, but would have scowled at her brother had she seen the measured look he was giving Jeff. Although aware of Troy's scrutiny, Jeff felt it was best to ignore it.

"Got it!" Jeff said with great satisfaction. He meticulously wiped the fingerprints from the lenses before handing them back to Bobbie.

"Thanks, Jeff," Bobbie said with a relieved smile when she could see again. She then looked at her brother. "How come you're home?"

Troy shrugged. A family friend had come into the livery to say he thought he had seen Bobbie in front of the mercantile. Troy had been unable to concentrate after that so he took off to find out if it had been her. There had been no sign of her in the shipping office and Troy had nearly run home in a state of panic to find her. She had been out of their life for so long and it had scared him to think that something could happen to her when they had just gotten her back.

Troy never answered her, but for the moment Bobbie didn't seem to notice his quiet behavior.

"I need to get back to work."

"I'll go with you," Jeff said, and trailed silently after her. Troy's gaze had warmed slightly, and Jeff, not inclined to take things personally, figured Troy had been worried about his sister.

The walk back to the shipping office was equally as quiet as the exit from the house. Wasting no time once she was back inside, Bobbie went straight to Bill's office. She entered when he called "come in" and Jeff walked into the storage room to find Gil.

"I'm sorry, Mr. Taylor, I really am. It never occurred to me that you didn't know. I do have an extra pair of glasses that I'll bring in so I won't be completely out of commission if this happens again."

Bill listened in patient silence. She had apologized at least six times, and even though he had assured her that everything was fine, he could see that this had really shaken her up. She wasn't anywhere near this upset when she left, and Bill couldn't help but wonder what had happened while she had been gone with Jeff.

They continued to talk, and in time Bill could see that he was finally getting through to her, making her understand he wasn't at all upset and that she still had the job for as long as she needed.

But as they finished, Bill wondered if he should question Jeff. Maybe he could shed some light on why this very efficient young woman had been totally rattled over her glasses breaking.

"I should have explained to you," Gil said quietly.

"*I* should have seen with my own eyes that she needed help." Jeff was still reprimanding himself as he and Gilbert talked in the back room.

"Well, I'm glad you spotted her at the mercantile when you did and Rigg was able to grab her. Don't look so down, Jeff. You said you apologized."

"I know." But Jeff didn't look the least bit consoled. He left the storeroom to help two customers, and by the time Bobbie came out of Bill's office, he had formulated a plan.

"Bobbie," Jeff approached her immediately. "I was wondering if you'd let me take you to lunch today?"

"That's very nice of you, Jeff, but you don't have to do that." Bobbie was in no way fooled by this sudden invitation. Jeff was still feeling badly about the morning and Bobbie admitted to herself that it had been very upsetting, but it was nothing to feel guilty about for the remainder of the day.

"I know I don't have to. I want to."

Bobbie smiled at him, but didn't answer. He was different now than when she had known him before, very different. In fact, it was like getting to know a complete stranger. She knew his treatment of her that morning had not been out of rudeness and Bobbie wished she knew him well enough to know what was going on inside his head.

Jeff had no idea how handsome he looked to Bobbie at that moment, as he looked at her in silent entreaty. 'He really is wonderful to look at,' she told herself, still wishing she knew him better.

"I brought my lunch." Bobbie tried another tactic after a moment of silence.

"Then take it home with you." Jeff was not to be dissuaded.

Bobbie cocked her head to one side. "Has anyone ever called you pushy?"

"I think you just did," Jeff answered, and deliberately mimicked Bobbie's movement with his head.

Bobbie put her head to the other side and Jeff did the same. She told herself not to smile. After all, she reasoned, it would only encourage him.

"You're trying not to smile," Jeff said knowingly, and it was too much for Bobbie. Her grin nearly split her face.

"Will you go?"

"Yes."

Jeff's grin was triumphant and Bobbie shook her head in mock disapproval as she headed into the back room.

Thirteen

THE NEXT HOUR saw a buzz of activity in the front of the shipping office. Gil and Bobbie worked steadily in the back, with an occasional trip out front to help Jeff and Bill.

The inventory would have been done long before lunch if Bobbie hadn't needed to leave. It was nearing 1:00 when Jeff looked up to see Sylvia walking in the door.

"I figured something like this must have happened. I can see you've been very busy, so I'll forgive you if you come to lunch right now, like you were *supposed* to an hour ago."

Jeff caught himself just before he began to babble. How in the world could he have forgotten that Sylvia asked him to lunch at her sister's? Now what was he going to do?

Sylvia, who had been smiling at him and was obviously in good humor, was beginning to frown over the way Jeff stood and stared at her in mute indecision.

"I'll be right with you," Jeff finally said, then rushed into the back room, leaving Sylvia alone.

"We're almost finished. Are you ready to leave?" Bobbie spoke as Jeff approached.

"Not exactly." Jeff said the words carefully, mentally measuring how he was going to explain.

"Is there a problem?" Bobbie asked with quiet sensitivity.

"Yes, there is, and it's all my fault. You see, Sylvia is out front. She asked me to lunch last night, and—"

"You forgot." Bobbie finished for him and raised her ordering sheet to her mouth. Her eyes told Jeff she was about to laugh, but Jeff didn't find the situation at all amusing. He had thought himself quite clever in coming up with this lunch idea to make up for the awful morning. Now this had to happen.

"Jeff." Sylvia's voice sounded from out in the main room and Jeff nearly groaned. Gilbert, who was listening from his place on the ladder, went out to give Jeff and Bobbie a little more time.

"Go with Sylvia, Jeff. She's waiting for you, and as I said, I have my lunch along."

"I'm sorry, Bobbie. You must think I'm very insensitive."

"Not insensitive, just forgetful," Bobbie said with another smile, and turned away so Jeff knew he could leave. His look had been heartbreaking, and Bobbie wished there was something more she could do to reassure him. He was going to have to get to know her, to understand she wasn't that sensitive.

Bobbie and Gilbert ended up eating their lunch together and talking like old friends.

"How go your wedding plans?" Gil asked kindly.

"Well, I'm not really rushing anything," Bobbie answered carefully, and Gilbert immediately keyed in on her hesitancy.

"I believe I was out of line just then and should apologize."

"Don't apologize, Gilbert. The truth is, Cleve has asked, but I haven't answered him. Marriage is a rather big step, and I'm still praying about it. Cleve told me to take all the time I need. He said he was sure he would eventually win me with his charm," Bobbie finished with a smile.

"I'm glad you told me, Bobbie. I'll be praying with you."

"Thanks, Gilbert."

The two fell silent. Gilbert searched for a change in the subject. "Will you miss living on the ocean?"

"You know, I really will," Bobbie admitted. "The sea is always so unpredictable and I love it."

"My sister-in-law Kaitlin grew up in the middle of the Pacific and she talks the same way. I've never even seen the ocean."

"You might have a chance someday. It helps to have relatives living right on the coast, but you never know, maybe when you get married you and your wife will honeymoon at the ocean."

"Are you applying for the job?" Gilbert teased her with a tender light in his eyes and then laughed without repentance when she blushed.

Jeff walked in on this scene. He looked from Bobbie to his brother for a moment, biting his tongue to keep from asking what Gilbert had said to make Bobbie blush.

Lunch had been miserable for Jeff. Sylvia was angry for most of the meal over the way he had gone into the back room and left her alone. Jeff had been preoccupied by the way Bobbie had turned away from him before he left. He thought she had been hiding her true feelings from him, masking how upset she was, and now he came back to find her laughing with his brother and then blushing like there was something personal between them.

"How was lunch?" Gil asked.

"Are you guys done in the back?" Jeff evaded the question.

"I'm going to finish up on my own," Gil told him. "Bobbie is free to help you out here."

Jeff nodded, carefully keeping his emotions off his face. He would have been surprised to know that both Bobbie and Gil knew something was bothering him. They just didn't know what.

"I'm going to head home now, Jeff. Would you mind telling your dad?"

"I'll tell him. Maybe I should walk you home. It's getting pretty dark."

"Oh, I'll be all right, but thanks for the offer."

Jeff stepped forward when Bobbie lifted her coat from its peg on the wall. His touch was careful as he assisted Bobbie with her coat. Bobbie turned while she was buttoning to thank him. She looked up and opened her mouth to express her appreciation, but something in his face stopped her.

"You haven't had a very good afternoon, Jeff," she said instead. "Is anything bothering you?"

Jeff's heart would have been made of stone had he not responded to the tenderheartedness he saw in her eyes.

"Are you sure you're not upset about today?" Jeff finally asked the question that hadn't been off his mind for a moment.

"I was scared in front of the mercantile, Jeff, very scared, but I was over it before we ever left my house. And if you're still bothered about lunch, well, let's just say, I wish there was some way for you to know how well I understand. Everyone forgets things. And while we're on the subject of the way I'm feeling, can I say something?"

"Please do."

"I have feelings, Jeff. If you cut me I'll bleed, and if someone says something cruel to me I might cry, but I'm *not* made of crystal."

"I never said you were."

"But that's the way you're treating me. You can joke with me, Jeff, just like your father and Gilbert do, and you can even bump into me without apologizing for ten minutes. I'm not going to go to pieces like I did five years ago and run away, if that's what you're thinking. You push me and I just might push back."

Bobbie's chin had raised on these last words as did Jeff's eyebrows. 'She's right,' he said to himself. 'I've been treating her like she's a fragile piece of china, when plainly she's not.'

"All right, Bobbie Bradford," Jeff said with an air of determination. "I'll treat you with the respect you deserve and no more patronizing, *if* you'll always talk to me as bluntly and as honestly as you did just now."

Bobbie's hand came out and Jeff shook it. "It's a deal, Jeffrey Taylor, and by the way, you need a haircut."

The grin Bobbie gave Jeff on these words was nothing short of cheeky. Jeff would have smiled back and said goodnight before she sailed out the door, but he was too surprised to do anything.

"Like my dad said, she's not what we expected." He addressed the words to the quiet office and then found himself whistling as he retrieved his own coat to head home.

Fourteen

JEFF HAD SUPPER at home, but left as soon as the meal was over to go to Rigg and Kaitlin's.

"What brings you out tonight, Jeff?" Kate wanted to know.

"Your haircutting skills, if you're up to it."

"She's not," Rigg said in a firm voice, but Kate ignored him. Kaitlin had been after Rigg for a week to let her cut his hair, but he always put her off. His worry over her fatigue was beginning to show, but even though Kate was tired, she wasn't an invalid.

"I'd be glad to cut your hair, Jeff. Why don't we go into the kitchen?"

"Kaitlin," Rigg pleaded softly, his voice laced with anxiety. Kate lingered next to him on the couch a moment and spoke with her face close to his.

"I'm fine, Rigg. You and Marcail did all the work for supper, so it's certainly not going to tax my strength to cut hair. I only wish Sean were here. He looks so disheveled these days."

Husband and wife exchanged a glance. Sean had been unpredictable lately, and the strain of it was worse than anything Kate had ever experienced. He did a tremendous amount of agreeing when he was face-to-face with you, but the minute your back was turned he did as he pleased. So far the things he did were not extremely serious, but there was a pattern of rebellion developing.

Rigg had already punished him for lying and also for disappearing after school with some friends and not coming in until almost bed-

321

time. While the whole family prayed fervently for wisdom in dealing
with Sean, most of the time Kate prayed for patience.

Kate and Jeff spoke easily while she clipped his hair. While not
mentioning anything to Jeff, Kaitlin wondered if he knew how many
times he referred to Bobbie.

"Bobbie said I need a haircut."

"Bobbie broke her glasses and I fixed them."

"That Bobbie sure is a hard worker."

"I made an agreement with Bobbie."

Rigg, who was reading the newspaper at the kitchen table, exchanged more than one glance with Kate over the top of Jeff's head.
Everyone in the family assumed that Jeff and Sylvia were serious
about each other. No one had ever taken the time to *ask* Jeff; it was
just something they took for granted.

Jeff hadn't done much dating in the recent years, and it was nice to
see him doing things and going places with Sylvia. It might also take a
little adjustment if in fact they really weren't serious.

Jeff took his leave right after Kate finished with his hair, and Kaitlin and Rigg were then able to talk. They didn't come to any solid
conclusions about Jeff, but they did understand that the Lord wanted
them to pray about him, Sylvia, and Bobbie.

Bobbie sat down that night and wrote to her aunt and uncle. She
told them all about her first days of work and how it was to settle into
home again. Troy was having supper at Carla's that night and her
parents had retired early. She wrote about what happened with her
glasses that morning, and then realizing just how tired she was, went
to bed herself. Bobbie fell asleep so swiftly she didn't have time to talk
over the day with her heavenly Father.

"Thank you, Mrs. Gordon. I'm sure your package will go out this
week."

Bobbie shut the office door as the woman strode swiftly down the
street. Another day at the shipping office was complete and Bobbie
was amazed at how swiftly time flew. It had been a great day, though.
Jeff had scored a major victory by walking in with his new haircut.
Bobbie had been surprised speechless, just as he had hoped. But Bobbie was rarely at a loss for words, and before it was over she had the
Taylor men laughing the workday away.

No one was around when Bobbie was ready to leave, so she let
herself out and shut the door. Her walk home was uneventful—in
fact, it was very quiet. Entering the house, Bobbie was intent upon

asking her mother what was going on in town. She found her in the kitchen throwing provisions in a large basket.

"Oh Bobbie, I thought I was going to have to leave a note. Your dad and Troy have already left for the Micklesons'. Their barn is on fire and the wind is blowing it toward the house. Gather some quilts and get them to the wagon. Your dad hitched the horse for us and I'm almost ready to leave." All of this was said with an air of urgency, but no panic.

Bobbie reacted in kind, racing to do as she was bid but with no hysteria or confusion. Within five minutes the Bradford women were on their way. Maryanne handled the horse and wagon efficiently and they arrived on the scene minutes later, joining Mrs. Mickleson and a few other ladies from the church. May Taylor was among them.

The women embraced and then talked. "Mic always lights a lamp in the barn but he's always so careful. I can't think how this could have happened."

Information on how the fire started was going to have to wait. Right now all the men were occupied with putting the flames out, or at the very least directing them from the tall farmhouse that loomed in the sky some 50 feet away.

The women who had come on the scene offered their help in one form or another. May offered to take the Mickleson children back to her house for supper and to spend the night. Lu Mickleson accepted gratefully and Bobbie offered to help round them up.

Mrs. Mickleson pointed out ten-year-old Brian standing at the corner of the house and Bobbie headed in that direction, only to have him move before she got there.

The heat from the barn hit Bobbie full in the face as she rounded the house and her eyes squinted against flames. She prayed for safety for her family and the others working. Brian had moved close to the fire and Bobbie called to him, hesitant to go further. Her shouts went unheeded and she knew she was going to have to go and get him.

She was only a few feet away from catching him by the back of the shirt when he darted away from her to circle the burning barn. Determined now, Bobbie followed without thought.

She hadn't gone ten steps when a pair of strong arms literally lifted her off the ground and bore her toward the house. Jeff began to shout the moment he put her on her feet.

"What in the world do you think you're doing?"

"I have to get Brian. Your mother is taking him and all the kids to your house." Bobbie's voice was equally as loud.

"Stay here!" Jeff commanded and ran toward the flames. He was back in less than a minute holding Brian's arm and walking so fast that the ten-year-old had to run to stay on his feet.

"Brian," Bobbie said sharply in her anxiety, "your mother wants you! Go to her immediately!" The boy left without a word and Jeff waited only a moment before once again letting Bobbie see his anger.

"That was incredibly stupid!"

"It was not stupid. I had to get that boy and I noticed *you* didn't hesitate to run right toward the flames!"

"That's different!"

"It is not!"

"Yes, it is. You're just too mule-headed to see it."

"How dare you call me a mule—" Bobbie's furious tirade was cut short by a flash of lightning, an unusual occurrence in Santa Rosa. The crowd in the yard and around the Mickleson barn only had time to look up before the deluge began.

Cheers of "hallelujah" and "praise the Lord" were heard from every corner. Their anger forgotten, Jeff and Bobbie looked at each other and laughed. Jeff scooped the small blonde into his arms once again and swung her around. They were still laughing when he set her on her feet.

"Bobbie," Maryanne called as she approached, "are you all right?"

"We're fine. Where are Dad and Troy?"

"They came over when it started to rain and I started to worry when you didn't come back."

Maryanne had a quilt in her arms and put it around her daughter. The group stood, over 30 of them, a cold but grateful mass, until the flames were little more than smoking timbers. About half the barn would have to be rebuilt, but no animals were lost and no one had been hurt while fighting the fire.

Pastor had come on the scene to help and he led the group in a prayer of thanksgiving for God's protection and for the rain that minimized the loss and possibility of injury.

Maryanne took the food she had brought into the Mickleson home and then rejoined her family at the wagon. The rain had slackened. Both Bill and Jeff were there talking with Bobbie, who sat in the back with Troy.

"Jeff tells me you're chilled to the bone. You get right into bed when you get home."

"I always knew Jeff was a big tattletale." Bobbie tried to joke, but her shivers were nearly rattling her teeth out.

"I mean it, Bobbie. I don't want you coming down with some-thing. If you feel a cold starting just stay in bed. If I don't see you by 8:00, I'll know you needed rest."

Bobbie was too cold to argue and Bill left before she could say anything. Jeff peered a bit anxiously into the back of the wagon.

"If you don't come in tomorrow I'll come by and see you."

"Thanks, Jeff."

"Good night," Jeff said to the family in the wagon and then watched as they disappeared into the dark.

Fifteen

Bobbie FELT GREAT the next morning and was on the job at ten to eight. Bill questioned her closely until he was satisfied that she was really feeling well. Bobbie's smile was a bit indulgent as she answered his questions.

"All right, Bobbie," he said when he caught her look. "Just humor me. You're under my care now and I take my responsibility seriously."

"I know you do. That's why your sons keep taking packages from me that I'm perfectly capable of lifting."

Bill was surprised that she was aware of their watchful care, but was quick to recover. "Like I said, humor me."

They smiled at each other and then Bill told Bobbie that he would be uptown for most of the morning.

Gilbert didn't come in until close to 9:00. He arrived to find the shipping office packed with clients. Nearly 20 people sat on the benches and milled around the windows. The morning stages were late and these people were the overflow from the small stage office next door.

The stages arrived within minutes of each other and Jeff showed up to meet them. He and Gil helped unload and load both passengers and packages before heading back to the empty shipping office. Bobbie had taken a seat at the desk and was working on the never-ending stream of paperwork.

"I didn't think I was going to see you today." Jeff had taken one of the two chairs that sat opposite the desk.

"You sound like your dad," Bobbie commented as she laid her pencil down and removed her glasses. Jeff watched as she rubbed the little marks left by her spectacles on the bridge of her nose.

"Do they always leave those marks?" Jeff asked, leaning close now.

"Not always, but they do pinch some." Bobbie continued to rub her nose. When she replaced the glasses she found Jeff watching her with concern.

At some point in the last few days they had become friends. It felt wonderful, Bobbie thought, to know that Jeff was her friend. He cared about her and liked working with her, and she felt the same about him.

Bobbie smiled at Jeff's concerned look and his thoughts moved in the same direction as her own. What a good friend Bobbie was turning out to be. She was fun and kind, and he genuinely enjoyed being with her.

Jeff and Bobbie were still sitting and talking quietly with each other when the office door opened.

"Well, hello." Sylvia's voice came from just inside the door and both Jeff and Bobbie turned to greet her. Jeff, knowing her well, noticed instantly that she was upset about something.

"Sylvia, come in." Jeff smiled solicitously and offered his chair, but Sylvia's look was frosty. Jeff sighed. He wondered what he was in trouble for now. A mental rundown of the last few days told him he hadn't forgotten any more dates with her and it wasn't her birthday. He figured he'd have to wait and see. Sylvia never kept her anger to herself for very long, so he was certain to hear the cause before the day was out, and quite possibly within the hour.

"I can't stay. I just stopped in to say hello. It's good to see you, Bobbie."

"You too, Sylvia. How have you been?"

"Fine, and yourself?"

"Fine," Bobbie answered with a smile.

The question was sincere and so was Sylvia's, but that was only because seeing Bobbie was such a relief. She wasn't beautiful. In truth, she wasn't even pretty. Oh, her hair looked better and she was no longer straight-up-and-down, but the glasses were just the same and she wasn't a bit taller. She still had the soft aura of a child.

The thought made Sylvia relax. That must have been why Jeff was staring at her so intently when she came in. Jeff thought of Bobbie as a little sister.

"Well, I'm headed uptown so I can't stay." Some of Sylvia's irritation with Jeff returned when he didn't beg her to stay longer or offer to go with her.

"I'll walk you to your buggy."

"You don't have to," Sylvia assured him, but was pleased when he followed her.

" 'Bye, Sylvia," Bobbie called, and the older woman gave her a smile and a wave. Bobbie sat back down in her desk chair.

"Wow!" Was the only word that would come to mind, and she said it out loud.

"What's wow?" Gil wanted to know as he came from his father's office where he had been working.

"Sylvia," Bobbie answered. "I thought she was pretty when we were kids, but now—" Bobbie let the thought hang, and Gilbert watched her as she stared off into space. She was still just sitting when Jeff returned.

"Did you think she wouldn't be as pretty?" Gil wanted to know.

"No, but I didn't think you could improve on Sylvia. I mean she was always the most beautiful girl in school, but now she looks like an actress you'd see on the stage. Her hair and eyes are more wonderful than ever."

Both men noticed that there was a tiny note of envy in Bobbie's voice and the thought saddened them. Sylvia was attractive and they were among her admirers. But both of them found Bobbie delightful, and the idea that she would wish herself to be anything other than she was made them both regretful.

Bobbie realized just then that the Taylor brothers were staring at her. "Have I said something wrong?" she asked cautiously.

"No, no," they rushed to assure her. Neither one had any idea how to tell Bobbie how they felt about her, so she was left in some confusion over their odd behavior.

Bill came back an hour or so after lunch. No one had taken any time to eat so he sent his sons and Bobbie out of the office.

"I don't want to see you back here for at least an hour." With these words he saw them out the door and shut it behind them.

"Well, I guess he told us," Bobbie laughed. "Now, I brought my lunch today, but, Jeff, you still owe me lunch out *and*, since you have such a poor memory, I think you should treat Gilbert too."

"Is that right?" Jeff's hands had come to his hips and he stood regarding the sassy little blonde beside him.

"Yes, that's right. Don't you agree, Gilbert?"

"I'll agree to anything for a free meal."

Jeff could see that he was outnumbered and gave in gracefully. Once at the hotel, they all ordered the special of the day and the men finished their meal with pie. Sipping her coffee as they made short work of dessert, Bobbie told herself to make time for the post office before she returned to work. The rule in the Bradford family was simple: Anyone who had time to get to the post office brought home the mail.

Bobbie told her lunch companions that she would see them back at the office, but when she told them where she was going, they decided to go with her. Bobbie had two letters from Jenner, one from a girl-friend and the other from Cleve.

They were back at the office before Jeff realized she had received mail from a man. He couldn't resist teasing her, even though he was well aware of her engagement. The letter was lying unopened on her desk, and when things were quiet, Jeff spotted it.

"What's this?" Jeff said with delight. "You're not getting mail from a man, are you, Bobbie?" Jeff had picked up the letter and was examining it closely. "What's his name now? Oh, Cleveland. Hmm, what do you suppose he has to say?"

"Does the word 'busybody' mean anything to you, Jeffrey? Now give that back to me." Laughing, Bobbie had come out of her chair. She reached for the letter but Jeff sidestepped her. He held it behind his back.

Bobbie stood with her arms folded across her chest, her foot tapping the floor. "Are you going to give me that letter?"

"Just like that? Give it back when I'm having such fun teasing you?" Jeff brought the letter out and waved it in the air like a trophy. Bobbie made a grab for it and felt her fingernail scrape against his hand.

"I've scratched you!" Bobbie was aghast. She had never done such a thing before.

"It's all right."

"No it isn't. I'm going to cut these nails right now."

"No," Jeff nearly shouted as Bobbie headed for her handbag. "I'm fine, Bobbie, don't cut your nails on my account."

"Jeff, I scratched you!" Bobbie repeated herself as if that explained everything.

"It's nothing. Look." Jeff thrust his hand out and Bobbie saw that he was right. It was a tiny mark on the surface of the skin that would probably disappear if he rubbed it.

"Please don't cut your nails."

"It could have been much worse, Jeff. I really shouldn't keep them so long. And really, Jeff, I can't believe it even matters to you."

"I just think your hands are very pretty and that it'd be a shame to cut your nails."

Bobbie was not sure why, but having Jeff tell her that her hands were pretty made her inordinately happy. It also made her blush. To hide her embarrassment Bobbie turned away and sat back at her desk. But Jeff had seen the flushing of her cheeks, and as he set the letter back on the desk and stopped his teasing, he understood with sudden and complete clarity why someone would ask Bobbie Bradford to marry him.

$\mathscr{Sixteen}$

The Mickleson's barn fire was the talk around town for the next few days and on into Sunday. Pastor Keller announced that weather allowing, there would be a "barn-building day" on the following Saturday.

The Micklesons were descended upon after the service with promises of attendance and help. Bobbie was thronged also. She couldn't believe how many people came up to hug her and welcome her home. It felt wonderful. When the people surrounding her finally cleared, Bobbie looked down to see Marcail at her side.

"Hi, Bobbie."

"Hi, Marcail. How are you?"

"I'm fine. I want you to come and meet my sister."

Marcail grabbed Bobbie's hand and was led to the Riggs' wagon. Kate was already seated.

"Katie, this is Bobbie. Bobbie, this is my sister Kate."

"Hello," Bobbie greeted Kaitlin with a smile, and Kate responded to the warm friendliness she saw there.

"It's nice to finally meet you, Bobbie. Marc has been planning this meeting for two days. I'm sure she told you I was expecting."

"Yes, she did. Congratulations."

"Thank you, but I'm afraid it's been a disappointment to Marcail that I haven't come to the shipping office to meet you. The truth is, I'm tired all the time and I just wasn't up to it. She finally figured out we would see each other here."

Nathan Taylor came on the scene just as Kate finished talking, and whatever reply Bobbie was going to make was cut short.

"Hi, Nate," Bobbie greeted him cheerfully. "I forgot to tell you yesterday that a girl came in looking for you. She said she'd see you Monday, and I think she said her name was Brenda." Bobbie had given this message softly so as not to embarrass Nate, but his face flamed nonetheless.

"Now there's no reason for you to be blushing like that, Nathan." Bobbie's voice was her most sarcastic. "I know for a fact that she only came in to see if you were just as homely on Saturday as you were when you left school Friday."

The teasing did the trick. Nate instantly relaxed, and Kate, who had been listening from the wagon, fell for Bobbie just as her sister had.

"Well," Nate decided to give as good as he got, "I might be homely, but at least I'm not short." Nate took great delight in his being four years younger than Bobbie and many inches taller.

"Is that right?" Bobbie cocked her head to one side in a way that was becoming familiar to them all.

"Yes, that's right."

"What you don't know, Nathan, is that I could be taller. I just don't want to be."

"Is that right?" Nate imitated her perfectly, and before Bobbie could reply, the Riggs' wagon was converged upon by Bradfords and Taylors.

Everyone seemed to be talking at once, and after a few minutes May and Maryanne decided they should all have lunch together. A hasty potluck was planned and Maryanne and Jake headed home to collect their food. Marcail begged Bobbie to ride with them, so she found herself in the back with her new little friend and a very quiet Sean, whom she had just met.

The wagon was already moving when Jeff hopped aboard and made himself comfortable on the blankets. He tipped Sean's hat over his eyes, gave Marcail a quick hug, and smiled at Bobbie, but his thoughts seemed far away and the ride to the Taylors' was fairly quiet.

"I thought Jeff was coming to lunch," Sylvia's sister commented when she came in alone after church.

"We had a fight."

"Again?"

"Yes, again," the younger girl snapped. "He's not doing anything right. He wanted me to have lunch at his house today."

"So why didn't you? Surely you didn't come here on our account." Sandra's voice was dripping with malice.

She had thought it was going to be such fun having her sister stay with her, but Sylvia hadn't grown up at all in the years she was away from Santa Rosa. She was as self-centered and conniving as she had been when they were kids. Carl had been on her to get Sylvia to end her visit and go home, but Sandra didn't know how to tell her, so she not only had to put up with Sylvia's childish behavior but her husband's angry words to boot.

"I didn't want to have lunch there," Sylvia went on as though explaining something to a simple child. "I can't ever get Jeff alone at his house. There are people everywhere. And I'm never going to get Jeff to propose to me if I don't get him alone."

Sylvia had told herself that she was never going to tell Sandra her plans for Jeff, but she was growing desperate. And just as she suspected, this news was not well received by her sister.

"Sylvia, you can't be serious."

"I don't know what you mean," Sylvia stated, but it was a lie.

"If you're in love with Jeff, why are you seeing other men?"

The younger woman tossed her head with an indignant sniff. "I should have known you wouldn't understand. Not all men are like Carl, you know. They don't all just fall at your feet the moment they lay eyes on you. Sometimes the woman has to work a little harder to get what she wants."

Sandra's look was piteous and it made Sylvia furious. Without a word she pounded up the stairs. The slamming of her bedroom door echoed throughout the house.

Carl, who sat quietly on the sofa being ignored, watched his wife. When she finally turned to face him, he felt guilty for the anguish he saw there. Some of it was his own fault. He hadn't realized just what Sandra had to deal with when it came to Sylvia, and he had put even more pressure on her.

His compassionate look was like a lifeline to his wife, and when he held his hand out to her, she joined him. Sandra cried against her husband's chest like she had never cried before. They talked for a long time and came to some painful decisions. They wouldn't try to change things overnight, but Sylvia was not going to go on staying with them forever—this much was clear. What wasn't clear was how she would be told, by whom, and when.

Bobbie opted to sit at the "kids'" table. There wasn't enough room at the big kitchen table for everyone, so a smaller table was set up in the living room for the younger family members.

Troy and Gilbert were both younger than Bobbie, but she took a place in the living room with Sean, Marcail, and Nate. Laughter was plentiful around the small table, thanks to Bobbie. Even Sean was beginning to thaw. The small blonde had that effect on people.

"So how young were you when you learned to swim?" Bobbie was questioning the Donovan children about growing up in Hawaii.

Marcail shrugged. "We just always knew."

"Our mother always said we could swim before we could walk." This was the first time Sean had offered information without a direct question and Bobbie believed they were making progress.

"I tried swimming when I lived in Jenner," Bobbie told them with a laugh. "I thought I would die."

"You almost drowned?" Marcail asked with wide eyes.

"No, it was *freezing*. I didn't think water got that cold. Every inch of me was blue. I think I shivered for two days."

"The water was always warm in Hawaii."

"I would have loved that, Sean. Anyway, I didn't try it again for a long time, but eventually I did learn to swim in the ocean and I really enjoyed it."

The remainder of the conversation was relaxed and it wasn't long before everyone was finished eating. There were more than enough hands to help in the kitchen, so Bobbie followed Marcail outside to the swing. It was cold, but the girls bundled into their warm coats and hoped it wouldn't rain.

"I'm freezing, Marcail," Bobbie called to her after the nine-year-old had the swing high in the air. "Did you want to go in pretty soon?"

"Let's go to the barn. It'll be warmer in there."

Marcail worked the swing down to a gentle glide and jumped the few feet to the ground. She and Bobbie hurried toward the barn.

"Oh, this feels heavenly," Bobbie exclaimed as the warmth of the barn enveloped her.

"Let's go up to the loft."

"I really don't think I want to climb that ladder." Bobbie said the words apologetically and Marcail didn't press her. Instead the two flopped into a stall filled with fresh hay. Reclining like princesses, they talked like best friends. They had been in the barn for about 20 minutes when Marcail heard her name being called.

"That's Katie. I've got to see what she wants. Don't go away." Marcail was up and running in the next second, slipping quietly out the barn door that stood ajar.

Bobbie removed her glasses and rubbed her nose. She felt something poking her in the leg and stood to adjust her position. But a moment after she stood she felt her glasses slip from her cold fingers. Not wanting to step on them, Bobbie stood immobile, then knelt carefully and began to feel along the ground.

A well-known feeling of frustration rose within. To be so dependant on a pair of wire rims filled with glass was at times more frustrating than Bobbie felt she could endure. But whenever these thoughts came to mind, a Bible verse came with them.

It was 1 Corinthians 10:13, and Bobbie knew it by heart: "There hath no temptation taken you but such as is common to man; but God is faithful, who will not suffer you to be tempted above that ye are able, but will with the temptation also make a way to escape, that ye may be able to bear it."

The temptation, Bobbie knew at the moment, was the fact that she was about to blow her stack. Instead she prayed.

"I need Your help, Lord. I can't see, and that always scares me a little. Please send Marcail or someone out here to help me before I panic." Bobbie carefully sat back down in the hay. She felt around her coat and the hay surrounding her, but stayed where she was. She always caught the worst trouble when she moved.

The barn was feeling quite chilly when Bobbie finally heard someone enter.

"Who's there?"

"Where are you glasses?"

Bobbie sighed at the sound of her brother's voice. "Hi, Troy. They're in front of me somewhere. Be careful where you step."

"I'll light a lantern." It was Jeff's voice but Bobbie didn't greet him. This was the second time she'd had glasses trouble since she got back. Why did Jeff have to witness both episodes? Bobbie found it humiliating.

'That's just your pride, Bobbie, and you know it,' the stranded woman rebuked herself, and waited while the search began. They were of course in plain sight to anyone who could see, and it was only a minute before Jeff said he had found them.

"Are they broken?"

"I'm afraid so. It's the same place as before, though, and not the glass."

"Dad might have something with him, Bobbie. I'll take these to the house. Are you okay where you are?"

"Sure. Thanks, Troy."

Bobbie wasn't all right where she was. She was cold and feeling a little lost without her sight, but she didn't want Jeff to know that. After listening to footsteps exiting the barn, Bobbie brought her knees up and wrapped her arms around them. Her breath came out in a gasp when she heard feet on the floor very near her.

"I'm sorry, Bobbie," Jeff's voice was pained. "I thought you knew I was still here."

"That's okay," Bobbie's voice shook.

Jeff could see that it wasn't okay, but kept the thought to himself. He could only imagine how frightening it would be to be practically blind, albeit temporarily.

"I'll come and sit beside you so you'll know where I am." Bobbie sat very still when Jeff sat down, and neither one spoke for a moment.

"I thought we were friends."

"We are," Bobbie answered tentatively, wondering what direction the conversation would take.

"Then why are you embarrassed in front of me about losing your glasses?"

"I was hoping you wouldn't notice."

"I notice a lot of things. Now tell me why."

Bobbie spoke so softly that it was almost a whisper. "You feel unbelievably vulnerable when you can't see, Jeff. To have you come in and me not know it, then stay and not see you, just adds embarrassment to that vulnerability. I suppose it's pride, but it's hard to have you see me in this position."

"Thank you for telling me," Jeff said simply and put his arm around her. Bobbie laid her head against his shoulder and felt instantly better, but then realized she had a question of her own.

"Jeff, were you upset today when you got into the wagon?"

Jeff hesitated.

"Just tell me if I'm out of line."

"Sylvia and I had a fight, but I can't really discuss it with you."

"That's understandable. I'll be praying that you can clear the air soon."

"Thank you."

The conversation moved to other things and Bobbie was a good deal warmer by the time Troy returned. Bill had produced the needed tool to fix the glasses, and when Troy returned them, he said it was time to go. Everyone felt the afternoon was a wonderful success and most parted knowing they would see one another at the barn-building, if not before.

Seventeen

BILL GAVE JEFF a choice about where he wanted to spend Saturday—at the Micklesons' or at the office. Jeff chose to work on the barn, and since it was Bobbie's full day off, both Nate and May were in to help Bill.

All the Bradfords were at the Micklesons' and the day promised to be clear. About 20 men were on the scene to help, and half that amount of women came around 11:00 to prepare lunch. Laughter and hard work were plentiful, and at the end of the day everyone was tired but feeling the rewards of a job well done. The Micklesons were thrilled with the work and sent everyone off with their repeated thanks.

When Bobbie retired for the night she reached for Cleve's letter. She had already written back to him but was having a hard time placing her feelings. She read the letter again and again in an attempt to know her own heart.

Dear Robbie,

How is work going? It's in my heart to say, 'I hope it's going well,' but you know I wouldn't mean it. Please come back. I know you said it would be October at the earliest but I still don't understand why. Your dowry doesn't matter to me. I've said this to you in person, but you don't believe me. I'm trying to be understanding about how long you've been away from your family, but my worry that you'll find someone else when you're there and never come back to Jenner and to me, is always on my mind.

I told myself not to mention any of this, but as you can see, that's all I've done. I was in to see Jasper yesterday. He looks well, but the office wasn't the same without you. Church feels just as lonely without you at my side. Please write to me.

I've got a surprise for you—I'm coming to Santa Rosa for a visit. I'll have to let you know the date and how long my stay will be. Maybe your boss would let you have a few days off.

Please write me as soon as you receive this.

Yours alone, Cleve

Still fully dressed, Bobbie sat on the edge of her bed for a long time. She wasn't even excited about Cleve coming to see her. Why was that? They were very close and she always enjoyed his company. In fact she always felt wonderful when they were together, and Bobbie knew why: Cleve thought she was beautiful.

Bobbie knew very well she wasn't, but that was the way every girl wanted her spouse to feel. And he wanted to marry her. Bobbie had only been on one date and that had been the ill-fated one with Jeff. She had never dated in Jenner; in fact, she and Cleve never dated. At first he came to the office to see her and then he would call around in the evenings at her aunt and uncle's home. He never tried to get her alone or make any advances toward her. Bobbie had been completely nonplussed when he had proposed one night three months ago, while Jasper and Joanne had been busy in the kitchen.

"What did you say to me?" Bobbie had asked.

"I said, Robbie, will you marry me?"

"Are you serious, Cleve?"

"Never more so."

"But we've never even talked about this."

"So let's talk now," Cleve said as he took her hand, touching her for the first time. Bobbie had been too stunned to speak. It was a wonderful thing to know that someone desired her for a wife, and it was simply lovely to have Cleve holding her hand so tenderly within his own, but it certainly wasn't as simple as he made it sound.

They had talked about little else in the weeks to follow, or rather Cleve had talked and Bobbie had listened. He had every imaginable argument as to why they should be married. The only thing he never mentioned was love. Bobbie said as much one night.

"I've never tried to analyze it before, Robbie, but I do know that I feel something for you that I've never felt for anyone before. I'm not at all worried that we're not gazing into each other's eyes like lovesick teenagers. Our marriage would be built on commitment and trust. And love, if not now, would come in time."

Cleve had kissed her then, the only time. Bobbie had been a little dazed after the kiss and even more so when he told her she was beautiful. She was also more confused than ever.

Bobbie's reverie was interrupted by a knock on her bedroom door. "Come in."

"It's me, Bobbie."

"Hi, Mom."

"I saw the light under your door. Everything okay?"

"Not really, but I wouldn't know how to tell you what's wrong."

"Cleve?"

"Cleve." Bobbie answered, glad that her mother understood. "Do you know, Mom, that when he kissed me I thought I would melt? Does that make me kind of . . . promiscuous?"

"No," her mother said tenderly and felt tears sting her eyes.

"I also like it when he holds my hand."

"I'm sure you do. I would say that's pretty normal. Did Cleve kiss you often?"

"Just once."

"But wonderful kisses or not, you're not sure you want a lifetime of that?"

"Right. I mean, marriage is more than intimacy, isn't it? And I want to be sure that we can live as man and wife in every room of the house for the next 40 years. No regrets, do you know what I mean?"

"I know exactly what you mean," Maryanne answered calmly, but her heart was crying out to God. 'Oh please, Lord, give her a godly man who will cherish her as I've been cherished by Jake.'

"You better get some rest," Maryanne said after a moment of quiet.

"He's coming to visit."

"So you said. Now maybe that will settle the whole thing. He'll come and your father and I will loathe him on our first meeting and that will be the end of that."

Bobbie laughed. "I'm afraid it's not that easy. You'll probably think he's the greatest."

"Well, he does have one thing going for him—he's in love with my daughter." Maryanne stopped with her hand on the door. "Bobbie, what does that look mean?"

"Actually, I can't really say that we are in love."

"Do you mean that Cleve has never told you he loves you?"

"No, he hasn't. We've talked about it, and I'm not sure I love him either, but Cleve believes our marriage will be built on other things, and that love will come later."

Maryanne appeared pensive. *Alarmed* better described her mood, but she didn't want her daughter to know how dismayed she was.

"Bobbie, answer one question for me: Are you afraid that if you don't marry Cleve, you never will be married?"

"Not afraid, just aware. I'm not the sort of girl men notice. Since I grew up here, I doubt that there's a love match for me in this town, but the thought doesn't devastate me. I promise I will not accept Cleve because I feel he is my only hope."

Bobbie could see she had put her mother at ease. What Bobbie didn't know was that Maryanne cried herself to sleep that night. She couldn't even tell Jake what was wrong. He didn't press her, knowing that when she could talk, she would. As it turned out, they were both awake in the middle of the night and talked then.

It was wonderful for husband and wife to share how they felt. And Jake had to admit that some of his joy over knowing that his precious Bobbie had found someone special had diminished slightly. They talked until nearly dawn and once again overslept for church.

It was unusual that this should happen twice in the same month, but when it did, Maryanne always fixed a special breakfast and then the family had their own Bible reading and discussion at the kitchen table. No one was happy to miss services, but they all thoroughly enjoyed these family times in the Word.

After church Jeff commented to his father about not seeing the Bradfords. Bill seemed unconcerned and told Jeff that the Bradfords loved to go camping and possibly left after the work at the Micklesons.

Jeff had never known anyone who went camping as a recreation. He decided he would ask Bobbie about it in the morning.

Eighteen

"I CAN'T BELIEVE YOUR whole family overslept."

Bobbie laughed. "It's not the first time."

"My dad thought you might have gone camping." Jeff said this thinking Bobbie would laugh at the idea.

"I wish," she said with feeling. "We tried to go my first weekend back but it poured."

"Where do you go? I mean, where do you set up camp?"

"We head east on the Sonoma Road. My dad knows a man who owns a ranch that goes back up into the hills. We camp in a wooded area of his land, near the creek. Some parts are so dense with trees that you stay dry in the rain. But it doesn't work if we leave the house in the rain and all our gear is soaked before we arrive."

Jeff was captivated. "What do you take in the way of gear?"

"Everything you need to survive the weekend—food, a change of clothes, fishing gear—"

"Do you fish?"

"Sure."

"Does Gilbert know?"

"I do now." Gilbert spoke from the doorway. "So when do we leave?"

"Not until I find out more about this camping," Jeff told him.

Bobbie could see that their questions could go on all day, and she knew she had to get some work done. "Why don't we talk at lunch?"

"I think she's trying to tell us to get back to work," Jeff commented.

Jeff and Bobbie tried again at lunchtime to talk, but Rigg came in. The conversation turned to business at the mercantile, and again Jeff's questions to Bobbie were put off.

Bobbie thought nothing of this. In fact she had forgotten the entire discussion, so she was doubly surprised when Jeff appeared at her side to walk her home.

"You can tell me about your camping on the way."

"All right," Bobbie agreed after a surprised moment.

"What do you usually eat?"

Bobbie was having a hard time understanding why this was so interesting to Jeff, but she was a good sport and answered his queries.

"My mom packs enough food for an army, but we fish and pick berries if the season is right. My dad always makes hot coffee and flapjacks over an open fire in the mornings. In fact there's nothing quite like an outdoor breakfast with a hot cup of coffee in your hand."

Bobbie's voice was so wistful that Jeff found himself wanting to try this camping business. He wondered how Bobbie and her mother managed in their long dresses but figured that was none of his business.

"Do you sleep on the ground?"

"We might now, I don't know. But when we were little we all laid our bedrolls in the back of the wagon. Don't forget, Jeff, I haven't done this in five years." The statement was completely innocent, but Jeff felt like she had punched him in the ribs.

"I'm sorry, Bobbie."

"Oh Jeff," Bobbie said as she immediately realized her mistake. "I didn't mean it that way!" Bobbie brought them to a halt with a hand on Jeff's arm. She could see he was still hurt.

"It's time we talk, Jeff," Bobbie said quietly. "I know it's suppertime, so if you don't want it to be now, then we need to plan on another time. You need to understand why I didn't come back for all those years. Otherwise I'm going to have to weigh everything I say to you."

"I think you might be right. Why don't you plan on having supper at my house tomorrow night and we'll go for a walk afterward."

"That sounds fine, and you'd better head back now because it looks like it's going to rain."

They were almost to Bobbie's house as Jeff agreed. Bobbie entered the house to find the family just sitting down. She had forgotten that Troy was having Carla Johnson over for the evening. Stuart, Alice, and the twins would be joining them later for dessert.

"Hi, everyone. Sorry I'm late."

"That's all right, we haven't really started," Jake assured his daughter.

Bobbie, who had been feeling preoccupied with her discussion with Jeff, found her mind moving to other things during the meal, the foremost of which was Troy's demeanor toward Carla.

Across the table from Bobbie, with her parents on either end, they were giving her a perfect view of their interplay. Bobbie felt something catch in her throat time and again over the way Troy leaned to hear Carla when she spoke.

Carla was a very sweet girl; Bobbie remembered her well from school. She had beautiful brown hair and it was obvious that Troy was devoted to her. Bobbie thought, with a certain bias, that Carla wouldn't find a man more wonderful than Troy, and if the look in Carla's green eyes was any indication, she felt the same way.

The meal began to drag for Bobbie. It was becoming increasingly hard to watch her brother in the beginning stages of love. Something almost resentful rose up in her over the fact that Cleve had never been as solicitous to her as Troy was being to Carla.

Bobbie immediately confessed the thought. It was unfair of her to judge Cleve in such a way. She knew what he was and it had never bothered her in the past that he didn't make over her all the time.

Even as Bobbie told herself this, she knew it wasn't entirely true. She did want someone who would look at her with love-filled eyes and who listened when she spoke because he believed what she had to say was important. But there was something else—something that Bobbie had not wanted to face. Bobbie wanted, no *needed*, a man who would be a spiritual leader in her home the way her father was. Bobbie knew that Cleve did not fit the bill.

He had admitted to her on more than one occasion that he had a hard time reading the Bible. And one time when they had discussed memorization, he told her he thought it was a waste of time. "After all, I've got the whole book right here," had been his words, and they had bothered Bobbie immensely.

Bobbie often shared with him from the latest passage she had been reading, but Cleve never reciprocated. And another thing—she worried about his concept of prayer because of yet another conversation they had had.

"Will you be praying with me, Cleve? I've misplaced my spare set of glasses and I really want to find them."

"Honestly, Robbie, you don't actually bother God with those types of things, do you?"

"Well, yes," Bobbie had answered uncertainly. "I mean, whenever I need help of any kind, I go to God. What sort of things do you pray about, Cleve?"

"Well, not little things," he had replied almost defensively. "After all, God did give us brains and I think we need to use them."

Bobbie had thought on his words for a long time and did some studying in her Bible. If they weren't to call on God for everything, then why were the Psalms filled with pleas for help and praise to God for His every provision? Why did God state repeatedly that the very beasts of the fields were in His care if He didn't want his children to go to Him for their needs?

Bobbie ended her search with the verses in Luke 12, verses 6 and 7: "Are not five sparrows sold for two farthings, and not one of them is forgotten before God? But even the very hairs of your head are all numbered. Fear not, therefore; ye are of more value than many sparrows."

Bobbie had shared the verses with Cleve, but he had only shrugged, noticeably uncomfortable. There were times when Bobbie wondered how she could even entertain thoughts of marrying Cleve. Yet there were those occasions when he made her feel special or cared for, and she was almost sure he was the one. But the operative word was *almost*.

Bobbie knew that if she married Cleve, she was doing so with her eyes open. She didn't have doubts about his salvation, but Cleve did not seem to be growing in the Lord, and what was worse, he seemed content to stay that way.

Bobbie's beliefs were quite different. She knew the first step had to be an acceptance of the gift that God offered through His Son's death on the cross, but it didn't stop there.

The Bible said that when a person is in Christ he is brand new, and it was upon these words that Bobbie faced the fact that she couldn't go on living as she always had. God was in control now, and old things like selfishness and pride were no longer to be tolerated because they were not pleasing to her Lord.

Some people would have said that Bobbie was some sort of fanatic, but Bobbie knew better. Never had she experienced such peace. It was indeed a peace that passed all understanding, a peace in knowing that her eternity was secure and that God cared about her every moment on earth, and was there for all her needs.

Bobbie knew she had to share her feelings with Cleve in a letter. He was quite sure that she would eventually be his wife, and Bobbie was having to face facts: Unless Cleve did a tremendous amount of changing in the time they were separated, she simply could not marry him and still be in obedience to God.

Maybe she hadn't answered her mother's question honestly. Maybe she was entertaining thoughts of marriage to Cleve because she was quite certain he would be the only one who would ever ask.

$\mathscr{N}$ineteen

TUESDAY DID NOT start well for Jeff. Sylvia was at the office very early wanting to see him. They hadn't talked for over a week, specifically since the Sunday before when she had left the churchyard in a furious display of dust. Jeff's several attempts to talk with her had availed him nothing. Three times he had gone to her sister's house and tried to see her, but she refused to even come downstairs. Jeff figured she needed more time and decided to back off.

When by the next Sunday Jeff had made no effort to approach Sylvia, her fury mounted. She waited all that day and Monday for him to try again, but by Monday evening he still hadn't made an appearance. Sylvia found she couldn't take anymore. Tuesday morning she was at the shipping office just after 8:00, dressed to perfection and wearing a forgiving smile on her face.

"Have you got a minute, Jeff?" Sylvia asked in her most humble voice, and Jeff, sincerely wanting to clear the air, walked her to the buggy.

"I'm sorry I didn't see you last week," Sylvia started right in. "I'm afraid I wasn't feeling very well."

Jeff saw her excuse for the lie it was, and for the first time he wasn't sure what to say to this woman he had been seeing. He was still trying to figure out what had been so upsetting about his suggestion that they eat at his house.

"Well, I'm glad to see you're feeling better now." Jeff replied with the first thing that came to mind, but he almost felt as if he had lied himself.

"Thank you." It wasn't what Sylvia wanted to hear, and she just barely controlled another show of temper. Jeff was looking uncomfortable, and Sylvia knew then and there that her plan had backfired.

She had deliberately let Jeff think she was angrier than she was, in hopes of bringing him to his knees. But all it had accomplished was to drive him farther away. The beautiful blonde couldn't help but wonder how long it would have taken him to come to her if she hadn't made the first move. She could see she had a lot of repair work to do.

"The main reason I came today," Sylvia improvised, "was to ask you to supper tonight at the hotel." Sylvia's voice could have charmed the birds from the trees. "Just the two of us in one of those cozy little tables by the bay window. It'll be my treat." Sylvia was smiling in a loving, almost intimate way.

"Thanks, Sylvia, it sounds great, but I've made plans. Can we make it tomorrow night?" Jeff was completely sincere and he smiled at her in true kindness. He desperately wanted to clear the air and even wished he could leave work on the spot to do so. But his talk with Bobbie was equally important and he knew he must not cancel it.

Sylvia was in a near state of shock. Time and again Jeff had asked her out and she always made sure he knew her refusal stemmed from another man's invitation for the evening. But *never* had Jeff turned her down. In fact, Sylvia was tremendously prideful knowing that he dated no one else and hadn't dated anyone long before she came back to visit.

"You've made plans?" Sylvia asked uncertainly, and Jeff answered unsuspectingly.

"Right. You see, Bobbie and I need to talk, so she's coming to my house for supper tonight."

"You and Bobbie?" Sylvia's voice had gone very soft.

"Right. We should have talked when she first came back. There are some things which have waited too long to be cleared up."

It never occurred to Jeff to lie or try to cover up his evening with Bobbie. He saw the look on Sylvia's face and stood in surprise as she climbed into her buggy without a word. She ignored Jeff when he called her name and even shrugged off the hand he had laid on her arm. Jeff stood and watched her whip her poor horse into a frenzy as the buggy bolted down the street.

"What's the matter?" Bobbie inquired of Jeff, who had gone back into the shipping office and was standing by her desk like a man lost.

"I'm not sure. Sylvia wanted to go to supper tonight and I told her we'd have to make it tomorrow because you were coming over. She wouldn't even talk to me. Climbed in her buggy and rode away."

"Oh Jeff," Bobbie whispered, "how could you?"

"How could I what?" the young man asked in all honesty.

"How could you tell Sylvia that you can't see her because you're having dinner with another woman?"

"But we're not—you know." Jeff finally caught on and was looking at Bobbie incredulously.

"Well, *I* certainly know that, and so do you, but obviously Sylvia doesn't."

Bobbie watched Jeff turn from her desk and stare out the window for a long moment. When he was still quiet after a time, Bobbie spoke.

"You need to go see her and explain. In fact, I think we should cancel tonight so the two of you can go out."

Jeff turned and looked at the woman standing behind the desk. A wish rose up strongly within him that Sylvia was as understanding as Bobbie. But Jeff immediately pushed it away; it was a disloyal thought.

"Jeff." Bobbie called his name softly. He was looking at her but he didn't really seem to know she was there.

Jeff made an instantaneous decision. "Thanks for offering, Bobbie, but I'd still like you to come to supper."

"Are you sure?"

"I'm sure. I'll try to see Sylvia at lunch, but we'll keep our plans for tonight."

She only nodded, hoping that Jeff knew what he was doing.

"Hello, Sandra. Is Sylvia here?"

"Yes, Jeff, she's here. Come in." Sandra was faintly satisfied to see Jeff on her front steps. She had just told her sister the day before that she would not lie for her again. Sandra thought Sylvia was crazy to have a gorgeous man like Jeff Taylor calling on her and pretending to be sick or out.

"Have a seat. I'll tell Sylvia you're here." Sandra walked up the stairs, glad to have an opportunity to show her sister she meant business.

"Sylvia, Jeff is here." Sandra poked her head in the door of her sister's room, which always looked as though a tornado had just passed through. Sylvia answered from the unmade bed where she had been crying.

"Tell him I'm sick."

"No," the older woman answered calmly.

"What do you mean no?" Sylvia's voice was shrill with panic. Surely Sandra hadn't meant what she said; she never did.

"I mean that if you don't come down right now and see Jeff, I'll tell him he can come up."

"You wouldn't!"

Sandra's answer was to shut the door and start back down the hall. But Sylvia snatched it open before her sister could move five feet.

"All right, all right," Sylvia whispered furiously. "I need a few minutes."

"Okay, I'll wait for you."

Sylvia gave her sister a withering look before slamming the door and rushing to the mirror. She stopped just short of repairing her face, a new plan forming in her mind. 'Maybe it would be a good idea to have Jeff see me like this.' Sylvia realized that she didn't look too bad. She touched up her hair a bit, took the last lace-scented hankie from her top bureau drawer, and went into the hall, her face a picture of rejection.

Sandra's eyes rolled in her head at the obvious display, but Sylvia's mind was made up and she ignored her. Jeff stood up from his place on the sofa as soon as he spotted the women on the stairs. Sandra smiled at Jeff as she passed through the room and Sylvia sat on the sofa and waited for him to be reseated.

Jeff didn't immediately notice that Sylvia had been crying. He was too busy trying to find words to breach the awkward silence that stretched between them. Then Sylvia spoke first.

"Why are you here, Jeff?"

"I'm here to find out why you're so angry with me all the time." Jeff hadn't meant to say that, but was glad he did. He was, by nature, a noncombative person. He would usually go out of his way to avoid a fight, which included stuffing his real feelings deep inside, something that was often a mistake.

Sylvia didn't know what to say. He had never mentioned her temper before. She decided to go with that.

"You know I have a temper, Jeff. It doesn't really mean anything when I get mad." But the words didn't wash with Jeff and he again surprised himself by saying exactly what was on his mind.

"I can't agree with you, Sylvia. It does mean something. I somehow doubt that you would care to be on the receiving end as often as I am."

Jeff looked as vulnerable as he felt, and Sylvia felt ashamed. She felt instantly contrite and wanted desperately to tell him why she did the things she did, but if he knew how much she cared he would certainly use her; after all, that was the way men were.

It never once occurred to Sylvia that she herself used people constantly, with her schemes to trap Jeff into marriage, her sister and brother-in-law, and the men that she dated to make Jeff jealous. And in one sense Sylvia used herself. She knew if she ever got Jeff alone, really alone, she planned to use every wile in her power to get him to say he loved her or force him into a proposal.

"I'm sorry, Jeff." Sylvia could think of nothing else to say, and indeed the words did not come easily, but Jeff was waiting her out, Sylvia could see that.

"I'm sorry too," Jeff replied, "if I've done something to hurt you. I really would like to go out tomorrow night. Is there anything I can say to change your mind?"

Sylvia stood and walked to the front window. 'So he hasn't come to say he's broken his dinner date with Bobbie.' The thought infuriated her but she fought to regain control. She kept her back to the room until she was sure she could manage a smile.

"Of course we'll go out tomorrow night. I shouldn't have run off. What time shall I pick you up?"

Jeff smiled. "You're going to pick me up?"

"Indeed. When I ask a man to dinner, I do it up right."

Jeff laughed with relief. It was awfully nice to have Sylvia smiling at him again.

Jeff had a quick bite to eat before he went back to work, and when he left Sylvia was smiling and waving at him from the door. To have Sylvia not speaking to him had been a dark cloud hanging over his head. It felt good to know that everything was out in the open. He should have told Sylvia a long time ago that it made him uncomfortable to have her so angry with him all the time.

Bobbie could see that Jeff's mood was improved when he returned from lunch; she was happy for him. Everyone's mood was light as they worked the afternoon away, and then Bobbie found herself between Jeff and Gilbert for the ride to the Taylors.

She hadn't felt hungry until she walked in the back door and smelled May's supper on the table. Gil assisted Bobbie with her chair at the table, and as she was seated a feeling of contentment rose within her. She had prayed a long time this morning and last night in regard to her conversation with Jeff.

As Bobbie began to eat she knew that God was going to bless her and Jeff for making this effort to clear the air and settle the past once and for all.

Twenty

"THANKS, MOM."

"Yeah, thanks."

"Thank you for supper."

The words came from the men around May's kitchen table, and Bobbie was impressed. Bill had punctuated his gratitude with a kiss and Bobbie found the gesture extremely tender, but oddly enough, when the room cleared and she and Jeff were left to work on the dishes, she felt embarrassed.

It wasn't that she was unaccustomed to seeing shows of affection. Bobbie knew that she wouldn't have been embarrassed if Jeff hadn't been in the room. Why that was, she wasn't sure.

"Do you want to wash or dry?"

"I'll wash," Bobbie answered with relief, seeing a chance to hide her flaming face. Jeff had volunteered them for kitchen duty in hopes they could talk, but the piles of plates, cups, and pots were diminishing rapidly and still they had only discussed work and which kids from school were married and starting families.

"How did you meet Cleve?" Jeff asked suddenly.

"Well, he lives and works in Jenner and attends the same church as my aunt and uncle. We got to know each other when he started coming into the shipping office every day for lunch. Then he began to stop by my aunt and uncle's, and well, we just got to know each other."

"I must say, Bobbie, I'm a little disappointed."

351

Bobbie turned from the dishpan to look at him. "Disappointed? In what?"

"You." Jeff was actually teasing, but he was in for a surprise. "You don't sound at all like a woman who is head-over-heels in love."

Bobbie turned back to her washing. "Love is not the only reason to get married, Jeff." The words were said softly and sincerely. Stunned, Jeff had to tell himself to go slowly.

Jeff believed love was the *only* reason to be married, but something in Bobbie's voice told him that if he said that to her right now, it would hurt her deeply.

"I've always thought that love needed to be at the top of the list. What reasons were you thinking of?" Jeff's voice was nonchalant, not once betraying how fast his mind was working.

"Oh, things like companionship, wanting children of my own, security—those types of reasons."

"But not love?"

"I think love could come, especially if the two people care about each other."

"Does Cleve share your beliefs?" Jeff asked, still speaking with more calm than he felt. He was jumping to the same accurate conclusions as Maryanne had the night she and Bobbie talked in the bedroom.

"Actually they're more his ideas than mine, but I think they might have some validity."

"Might?" Jeff questioned her. "Then you're not entirely sure?"

"No, I guess I'm not. The truth is, Cleve has asked me to marry him, but I haven't given him an answer. He's coming for a visit sometime this summer and he thinks I'll say yes then."

"He's sure you'll say yes?"

"I think he is."

"And you?"

"I'm not sure one way or the other." They worked in silence for a few minutes as they finished the job.

"What does that look on your face mean, Jeff?" Bobbie was untying her apron and taking a seat at the kitchen table.

"I'm confused. I thought you stayed in Jenner all this time because of Cleve and here I find out you're not even in love with him." Jeff thought his words might have hurt her, but she answered as though everything was fine.

"I've only known Cleve for about a year. And one of the main reasons I've hesitated in saying yes to his proposal was because of how badly I wanted to come back to Santa Rosa."

"Then why did you stay away five years?" 'It's finally on the table,' Jeff thought. 'The question I've been wanting to ask for years.'

"You may not agree with me, Jeff, but I honestly believe I was in Jenner all those years because that was exactly where God wanted me." Jeff looked uncertain but kept silent.

"You can't believe how many times I planned to come home, but something always detained me. When I first arrived in Jenner I dreaded having to come back and face all the kids at school. My aunt was really sensitive to that and wrote, without my knowing, to ask if I could stay until Christmas. My folks said yes. Well, the studies were very different from what I'd been taught, and everyone felt it was best that I finish the year.

"By the following summer I'd made some wonderful friends and again my departure was put off. Then it was time for school to start and I was so torn I was miserable. You see, I still hadn't changed at all physically and I *so* wanted to come back—"

Bobbie stopped as all the pain she felt that summer crowded in upon her. She remembered the desperate desire to see her folks and the kids at school, but wanting also to mature and return looking like a young woman instead of a little girl.

Jeff was careful to keep his emotions off his face, but the look in Bobbie's eyes was almost more than he could handle. His hand clenched where it lay on his knee beneath the table, in an effort to keep from reaching for her.

"Anyway," Bobbie went on softly, "I told myself, one more year. But by the end of the next school year I'd begun work at the shipping office and my presence became necessary. The passage of time ceased to exist. I was needed and leaving was nearly out of the question.

"There was one time when I was ready to go. My bags were packed and I was going to catch the morning stage, but my Uncle Jasper got very sick in the night and again—" Bobbie shrugged and Jeff nodded in understanding.

"I did want to tell you, though, how much your note meant to me. When I first left I hoped you were suffering as much as I was, but I soon saw that there was no living with bitterness. It eats at you until there's nothing left of the original person and I knew that would be the worst thing I could do.

"The hardest part about being away was knowing that everyone knew. It was also hard not to hear from anyone. I realize, Jeff, that you weren't the only one involved that day, but I never heard a word from any of the other kids. Pastor and Mrs. Keller wrote, and so did you, but other than my family—"

"Not even Angie?" Jeff remembered how close the two girls were.

"She wrote but she never mentioned the lagoon. I think she felt that was best, but it's like having your mother die and everyone trying to pretend it never happened. I wish Angie hadn't moved up north so I could talk with her about it. I mean, I didn't need her or anyone else to belabor the point, but a word or two of understanding would have been welcome."

"I'm surprised no one else wrote," Jeff replied, "and now that I look back on it, I wish I'd written more than once. I thought about you an awful lot and I wished we'd kept in touch."

"Tell me something, Jeff. What's become of Richard Black? My mother kept me as up-to-date as she could, but she never mentioned Richard."

"His family moved out of the area about a year later. I don't know where they are now."

Bobbie nodded and then took Jeff completely offguard. "Okay, Jeffrey, now it's your turn. Tell me what happened with that whole outing at the lagoon."

Jeff looked shocked and then decidedly uncomfortable, but Bobbie just sat and watched him. He knew she deserved to know the truth, but he couldn't stand the thought of hurting her. He couldn't see any way out of it, so he looked her in the eye and started in.

"In those days I was seriously infatuated with Sylvia. So was Richard. I wasn't sure where I stood with her, and when Pastor Keller came to see me with the idea of the guys asking the girls to the boating, I grabbed at it with purely selfish motives. I planned on asking Sylvia.

"All six of us guys came here, and it didn't take very long for everyone to see that two of us wanted to take Sylvia. That left an extra girl, and that girl was you." Jeff stopped because he was feeling a little sick inside.

"Go on, Jeff. Remember, I did ask."

He took a deep breath and studied the face across from him. Bobbie became more attractive to him every day. But it wasn't just her looks. There was something wonderful and special about her to which Jeff was terribly drawn. Right now he could see she was trying to cover the vulnerability she was feeling inside, and once again he wanted to hold her.

"We hid in the barn to draw straws, which tells you how ashamed we felt, but we were too selfish to let that stop us." There was no reason to go over what happened at the lagoon; they both knew it well, so Jeff skipped ahead to when he dropped off Bobbie.

"I went straight home after I left your house and waited for my folks. They weren't long in coming and they knew everything. The church has matured since then, but unfortunately the gossip was pretty rampant. To say that my folks were upset would be a gross understatement. I've never seen my mother like that, but I had no one to blame but myself.

"I came the next day to see you, but you'd already gone. My dad went the next day to see Richard and Sylvia because I'd told him everything. He was very upset over the way you were treated at the lagoon. He talked with them privately and then left it up to them to tell their parents. I honestly thought they'd written you." Jeff paused for a moment in thought, remembering that at least Sylvia said she had sent a letter.

"Anyway, Pastor called all of us together to apologize too. He felt responsible. It just never occurred to him that there would be a problem; they were really trying to give us a special day."

Bobbie and Jeff stared at each other in silence. "I'm sorry, Bobbie," Jeff finally said.

"I'm sorry too, Jeffrey, for the years of hurt and scars. I don't harbor any bitterness in my heart, and I hope no one else does either, but it was time for me to hear the entire story. For that I thank you."

Bobbie slid her hand across the table and Jeff took it. There was nothing romantic about the gesture; it was a friend reaching out to another friend in comfort and caring.

Not long afterward Jeff drove Bobbie home in the wagon. Their conversation moved to Cleve again, and Bobbie said some things that disturbed Jeff tremendously, but he was in no position to offer advice to anyone on her romantic life. It seemed as though his own was in a constant state of turmoil.

Of course, he wasn't really sure that he would term his relationship with Sylvia romantic, but why it wasn't was a question that plagued Jeff until he fell asleep that night.

Twenty-One

SYLVIA WAS IN her best winter dress for her evening out with Jeff. She had worked for hours on her hair after lying down for a full two hours to rest her eyes. Her dress was a deep sapphire that highlighted her eyes to their best. The nap was to ensure that her eyes were clear and not puffy or red.

Jeff was in a suit and Sylvia was very pleased that he had dressed up for her. He was, she admitted, quite the best-looking man she had ever seen. None of the rich men back East could compare with Jeff Taylor's tall, broad-shouldered physique. And if that wasn't enough, he had the most wonderful face. Very masculine, yet boyish when he smiled or laughed. His brown hair was a bit wavy and always shining with health.

Sylvia's head was raised proudly as she slipped her arm into Jeff's for the walk across the crowded dining room. They were given a table for two by a window. It wasn't really private, but the angle at which it was set and a large potted plant made it feel a little more remote. Sylvia had stopped earlier to reserve the table she wanted, and since Jeff was unaware of this, it confused him as to why the woman taking their order kept grinning at him as though they harbored a secret.

"So tell me," Sylvia said as soon as the woman walked away, "how did your evening go last night?"

"It was fine," Jeff answered easily. "We were able to discuss everything from five years ago, and I'll tell you, Sylvia, we needed that."

"In what way?" Sylvia always felt a little tense when the summer at the lagoon was mentioned, but Jeff's comment intrigued her.

"Well, Bobbie didn't know everything and naturally she wanted to, and I needed to know why she stayed away all those years. There was no anger or bitterness in either of us, but it felt good to get everything out on the table."

"Well, I'm glad to hear that. She and I cleared things up long ago. I wrote to her when she was in Jenner."

"You did? Did you mail the letter?"

"Well, of course I mailed it." Sylvia laughed as though Jeff was trying to be funny. "Bobbie wrote back, too."

Sylvia chatted on but she had lost Jeff. Why in the world was Sylvia lying? He wasn't sure how much of the conversation he had missed when he began listening again.

"And while we're on the subject of Bobbie, there's something I think you should consider, Jeff." Sylvia's voice had dropped and her face was a picture of compassion. "You know you spend a lot of time with her, and you want to be careful that you don't lead her on in any way. I mean, you wouldn't want to hurt her like you did before and—" Again Sylvia prattled on and Jeff could only stare at her.

"I'm not saying that you can't be friends, but you are very attractive, Jeff, and let's face it, Bobbie isn't used to having men pay attention to her. You understand that it's her I'm thinking of."

Their food arrived at that moment and Jeff was spared from making a reply. He found himself praying and asking God to show him what to do. Sylvia was lying through her teeth and Jeff knew that if he called her on it they would have a huge argument right here in the hotel.

Jeff drew a sigh of relief when the topic changed to Sylvia's family. She didn't have a good thing to say about them, and for the first time Jeff wondered how much of what she was sharing was true.

Jeff didn't remember very much about the meal or even what he had eaten, but an hour later they were walking toward Sylvia's buggy. Jeff was fairly quiet until he saw that Sylvia was not headed toward his house.

"I have to work tomorrow, Sylvia."

"You have time for a little drive, Jeff. Sometimes I think you're an old man."

Jeff fell silent under the attack, but began to feel increasingly nervous when he saw where Sylvia was taking them. They headed to a very quiet area of town that he had never visited at night. It was always talked about when he was a kid because it was said to be the place where teens in town went to be alone.

Sylvia pulled the horse to a stop beneath a huge willow tree. She turned to look at Jeff but he kept his eyes forward. There was a three-quarter moon and Jeff was well aware of the way it bounced off Sylvia's hair.

"Jeff?"

"What?" Jeff almost snapped at her as he tried to gain control of his emotions.

"Why don't we get out and walk around a bit?"

"Good idea." Jeff jumped at the idea in an attempt to put some space between them. Sylvia had pressed up against him in a way that was most distracting, and he couldn't get out of the buggy fast enough. He didn't help Sylvia step down because he didn't want to get that close, and he could once again feel her eyes on him.

Jeff was just standing and looking off into the darkness when he again felt Sylvia at his side.

"Look at me, Jeff."

Jeff complied and knew instantly that it was a mistake. Sylvia's eyes were filled with entreaty, and Jeff couldn't look away. When he didn't, she moved her hand to cup the back of his neck. Not until she had brought Jeff's head down and kissed him did he react. He stepped backward so hastily that he almost pulled Sylvia over.

Her voice revealed her hurt when she called his name in the darkness, but if Jeff opened his mouth right now, he knew he would be sick to his stomach. He had thought about kissing Sylvia, after all she was beautiful, but something inside him had frozen when he felt her lips on his own.

"Jeff." Sylvia's voice was no longer hurt. She was angry—furious, to be exact. She knew very well that Jeff had been waiting years to kiss her, and now she had practically thrown herself at him and instead of the passionate embrace she had imagined, he had stepped away.

"I'm sorry, Sylvia." Jeff's voice was hoarse. "This is moving a little too fast here."

"Is that right?" Sylvia's voice betrayed her anger, and Jeff's own temper came to the fore.

"Yes, it is," Jeff snapped right back at her, the inner turmoil of emotions emerging in one livid burst; he felt like he could drive his fist into the tree behind him.

Jeff watched as Sylvia stomped her way back to the buggy and then began to follow slowly. But he was about five steps too late. Sylvia slapped the reins and the buggy began to move away.

"Hey!" Jeff shouted. "Sylvia, get back here!" But the angry blonde kept right on going. Jeff stood for just a moment before he set off for home. He took the shortest route, across open lots and behind buildings, some deserted. It wasn't the safest, but he was wearing his good shoes, and if he went the long way around he knew they would be killing him by the time he walked into his own yard.

That, along with the fact that he found he had a raging headache. The only place he wanted to be right now was in bed, and as quickly as possible.

Troy bent his head and tenderly kissed Carla. His hand came up and touched the softness of her cheek and he felt as he always did—that leaving her was torture.

"I'll come by tomorrow night."

"Can you come for supper?"

"I came for supper last night. Your folks are going to get suspicious. They might suspect that I want to marry you."

The words always made Carla smile, and that smile got her kissed again. With reluctance Troy pushed away from the porch and walked into the night.

The wind had picked up some, so Troy took a shortcut home. He was a couple of blocks away from his house, in a quiet area of town, when he heard a scuffle in the dark. The shadows were deceiving but it appeared to be three on one.

"Hey!" Troy shouted as he ran without fear toward the fighting men. His presence frightened away the attackers and Troy knelt carefully beside the man who had been left on the ground.

His face was turned away from the moonlight, but Troy could see that he was well-dressed and that the side of his head was a bloody mess. He had the shock of his life when he rolled him over and found himself looking into Jeff Taylor's face.

It was by sheer determination that Troy lifted the older man. Troy was huskier but Jeff was taller, and not a featherweight by any means.

"Come on, Jeff," Troy panted, "wake up and help me."

"I don't have anything," Jeff mumbled as Troy got him onto his feet. But the next instant he started to collapse, so Troy drove his shoulder into Jeff's middle and hefted him up onto his right shoulder. The dead weight nearly staggered him, but he pressed on. Troy laid Jeff on the Bradford front porch and threw open the door with a shout to his family.

Twenty-Two

THE NEXT HOUR at the Bradford house was like a nightmare. Troy was sent to tell the Taylors that Jeff was hurt and at their house. Jake went for the doctor.

The men had carried a semiconscious Jeff up to the first bedroom, which happened to be Bobbie's. Bobbie was by nature a pretty cool customer, but the sight of Jeff covered with blood was almost her undoing. The women stripped him down to his pants before the doctor arrived and then had only a few minutes' wait before the Taylor wagon thundered into the yard.

"The doctor is in with him now," Jake told the anxious family. While they waited Troy filled them in on what he had seen. When he was finished speaking Bill Taylor thanked him.

"We're just so glad you found him, Troy, and can't thank you enough for bringing him home. Nate, go to the Riggs' and let them know what happened."

"I'll go," Troy offered. "You need to be here, Nate."

The family thanked him again and then Bill went up the stairs to check on his son. Troy was back with Rigg just minutes before the doctor came down.

"He's got a hard head, May," Dr. Grade said from the stairway, "but someone tried to put a dent in it tonight. I stitched him up. His ribs are pretty bruised too, so I've got him wrapped. He was awake long enough to tell me that his attackers wanted money. He tried to tell them he had almost nothing on him and that's when they got rough. You can all go up but just stay a few minutes."

"Can we take him home?"

"No, don't move him. I'll come by tomorrow and check him again. He's got a concussion, so someone needs to sit with him through the night."

He gave a few more instructions and then Jeff's family mounted the stairs. He awoke when his mother took his hand. May couldn't keep the tears from her eyes when he tried to smile.

"Hi, Mom."

"Hi, honey." May's voice broke and Bill put his arm around her.

"My head hurts."

"I'm sure it does." Bill spoke quietly and just barely held his own tears. There were a million questions running through his mind, but he knew they were going to have to wait.

May was staying the night, so the men in the room told Jeff they would see him later. He was asleep by the time the door closed and wasn't even aware of the way his mother pulled the chair close and sat without taking her eyes from him, thanking God that he was still alive.

May sat almost without moving for nearly an hour before the door opened. It was Bobbie, and she whispered her apology.

"I'll just be a minute, Mrs. Taylor. I need my nightgown and robe."

"Oh, this is your room," May replied, startled. Now that she took a moment to look around she saw that everything was decidedly feminine.

"Bobbie, where will you sleep?"

"Troy has two beds in his room. We were caught offguard or we'd have put Jeff in there." Bobbie stopped and looked at the man lying in her bed.

He looked strangely out of place under the white lacy coverlet, but Bobbie didn't feel like laughing. Her eyes flooded with tears as she looked at his bandaged head and wished she could stay and hold his hand for awhile. But his mother was here and that was best. She knew if it had been her son in that bed, nothing could take her away.

The night was a long one for May. Jeff rested comfortably but May only dozed in the chair. Maryanne checked on her twice and even made coffee about 3:00 A.M.

Bill was at the house before 7:00 to check on his wife and son. He insisted that May let Gilbert take her home to sleep.

"But I want to be here when Dr. Grade comes."

"I'll stay. You're about to collapse."

Rigg knocked on the door just then and Bill was relieved. Rigg would be able to get May home better than Gilbert. But it was not to be. May was adamant and Bill knew he was going to have to see to the job himself. After a long discussion, it was decided that Gil would open the shipping office. Rigg needed to get to the mercantile and Bill would take his wife home.

Bobbie was very compassionate with Mrs. Taylor's plight but she did look utterly drained. Offering to stay with Jeff until someone came to relieve her, Bobbie found herself at Jeff's bedside a few minutes later. She carefully opened the curtains over the two windows in her room, since it was a cloudy day, and sat in the chair with her Bible.

Certain that someone was beating him in the head with a sledgehammer, Jeff's hand came up to push the pain away, but all he encountered was a cloth of some sort and more pain.

A small, warm hand grasped the hand he had put on his head and held it on the edge of the mattress. Jeff told himself to look at the owner of the hand, but his body wouldn't obey.

"Mom?"

"No, it's me, Bobbie."

Jeff didn't speak again but maneuvered his hand until his fingers were linked with those of Bobbie's. The act brought fresh tears to Bobbie's eyes and a prayer to her heart.

'This is my friend, Lord, and he's hurt. It's been so nice to have Jeff for a friend. Please take away his hurt. Please ease the pain in his head and side. Help him to know that You're right here in the room with him, and to know Your comfort. Help him to remember who did this, Lord, so they can be brought to the law.

'Please comfort his family, especially May. Help her to get some rest today. Thank You for the special family that they are, and thank You too for sending Troy home the short way so he could find Jeff.'

Bobbie felt much better after giving Jeff over to God. She was a doer, and it was hard not to be able to *do* something for Jeff's pain. And then the Lord reminded her that she *could* do something—in fact she already *had* done something: She had prayed.

Jeff wanted a drink about 20 minutes later and Bobbie found out what an inexperienced nurse she was. He did get some in his mouth but he also got some in his ear and down the side of his neck.

"I'm sorry, Jeff." Bobbie was not very happy with herself, but Jeff peeked at her from one slitted eye and managed a small smile.

"Are you trying to drown me?"

"I think so," Bobbie said as she carefully mopped his neck, ear, and then the pillow.

"Is this your room?"

Bobbie glanced up in surprise to see that Jeff's eyes were both open.

"Yes, it's mine. Is the bed all right?"

"The bed is wonderful, maybe a little short, but what can I expect when it belongs to a little person like yourself?" The words were said with a tired sort of tenderness that Bobbie found oddly touching. He had made the words "little person" sound like an endearment.

Jeff was drifting off again and wasn't aware of Rigg arriving to spell Bobbie. Bobbie took herself off to the shipping office with plans to check back at lunch. Business was quite heavy that morning so Bobbie didn't return home until almost 1:00. Her mother was sitting at Jeff's side with some mending when Bobbie appeared in the door. Maryanne set her work aside and joined her daughter in the hall.

"How are things going?"

"Good. Are you home for the day or do you need to go back to the office?"

"Bill was going to come in at 2:00 so I can stay here if I'm needed. What did Dr. Grade say?"

"He wants Jeff to keep still until he gives word otherwise. It could be a week."

"So he's pretty bad?" Bobbie's eyes showed her concern and Maryanne reached out to hug her.

"He's not in any kind of danger, but then he's not going to do any strenuous work for a few weeks either."

Maryanne went to the kitchen to prepare some soup for Jeff and Bobbie took the chair by the bed. Jeff didn't move for over an hour, so by the time he awoke Maryanne was back upstairs with a tray.

She helped him with the soup bowl and spoon and Bobbie went to answer a knock at the door. It was May, and she looked like a new woman.

"Hi, Bobbie," she said as she slipped out of her coat. "How's Jeff?"

"Mom is helping him with some soup."

"Okay, I'll head up and see if I can be of some help."

Bobbie followed May up the stairs, but only to tell her mother that she was going to go back to the office for the rest of the afternoon. Jeff was awake and grinned at her.

"You need to take some lessons from your mother, Bobbie; she hasn't spilled a drop!"

Bobbie laughed. "Actually I didn't *spill* anything. You looked a little hot and I was trying to cool you off."

Jeff chuckled and then winced.

"You better go, Bobbie," her mother told her. "You're going to hurt this poor boy if you get him to laughing."

When Bill found out from Bobbie that Jeff was awake and having something to eat, he immediately left for the Bradford home. Gil, who had been holding down the fort but was just as concerned as everyone else, questioned Bobbie about Jeff's health.

"He was pretty pale last night. How did he seem today?"

"He's still pale but he's talking and even making jokes."

"Did he say anything about how it happened?"

"No. And I have a feeling that's why your dad went to my house. It does make you wonder what Santa Rosa is coming to, doesn't it?"

"Yeah, I thought of that, but I also can't help wondering what Jeff was doing in that area of town when he was supposed to be having supper with Sylvia."

The two stared at each other, their thoughts running in speculative veins. It was almost a relief to have someone come in with a box he wanted shipped. Bobbie found her mind wandering in between customers, so she was thankful for a busy afternoon.

The lone shipping clerks walked to the Bradfords' after closing up for the night. There was quite a crowd there to greet them, but they were all family. Word had gotten out that Jeff was hurt and staying at the Bradfords, so someone from the church had brought over supper. Nate, May, Bill, Jake, and Maryanne were all sitting down to eat. Kate and Rigg bid their hellos and goodbyes, as they were just headed home. Marcail was upstairs with Jeff. Bobbie decided to eat but Gil climbed the stairs to see his brother.

"Are you thirsty, Jeff?"

"No, I'm fine, Marc."

"Will the doctor be back tonight?" the petite child asked from the edge of her seat.

"No, Marc, he won't come again until tomorrow."

Marcail was nodding with relief as Gil came in the room. Gilbert scooped the little girl up and took her chair. He resettled Marcail on his knee and then smiled at his brother, who was regarding them with half-closed lids.

"Your color is better; how do you feel?"

"Sore."

"Has Dad reported this yet?"

"Yeah. Just a little while ago."

Gil wanted to ask details but was very mindful of the little girl in his lap.

"Would you like me to read to you, Jeff?"

"Thanks, Marc, but I don't think I can stay awake."

"Did you have supper, Marcail?" Gilbert wanted to know.

"No. I told Kate I'd eat later."

"Why don't you run down now? I can stay with Jeff."

Marcail complied and Gilbert settled back in the chair. He reached for a book he spied on Bobbie's nightstand but replaced it as soon as he saw it was her journal.

Jeff had fallen back to sleep and Gil was left alone with his thoughts. He wasn't usually a nosy person, but what had happened to Jeff was really bothering him. He prayed about how to handle the idea forming in his mind.

He made his decision before his father came to give him a break. After he'd had a bite to eat he walked Marcail home and headed to see Sylvia Weber.

Twenty-Three

"SOMEONE IS HERE to see you."

"Is it Jeff?" Sylvia stood up quickly from her place on the bed.

"No, it's his brother Gilbert."

Sylvia looked at her sister to see if she was teasing, but Sandra's face was completely serious.

"Tell him I'll be right down."

Gilbert had not taken a seat and he knew that Carl Boggs was eyeing him strangely. Gil spoke the moment Sylvia came into the room.

"Is there some place I can talk to you, Sylvia?"

"Sure," she answered uncertainly. "We can go in the kitchen."

Gilbert followed her to the kitchen and spoke as they sat at the table. His voice was kind and Sylvia responded to that kindness.

"Did you and Jeff have a date last night?"

She nodded. "We went to supper at the hotel. Why, Gil, why do you ask?"

Gil explained briefly. Sylvia looked almost faint when he was done. He opened his mouth to comfort her when she burst into tears and told Gil the whole story. He knew his face showed his surprise over the way Sylvia tried to manipulate Jeff, but Sylvia was too wrapped up in her tears to notice.

"Maybe I'm out of line to say this, Sylvia, but I don't care how angry you were. You had no business leaving Jeff out there by himself."

"I know that now, but I was incensed." The tears went on and so did more confessions. Gil wondered how he had ever envied his brother the fact that Sylvia had fallen for him. The thought of being such an obsession for this woman was a little frightening.

"I must go to him right away."

"Not tonight," Gilbert spoke firmly. "He'll be sleeping now. You could go by the house tomorrow. By the way, he's at the Bradfords'."

"The Bradfords'? What's he doing there?" Sylvia looked uncertain and Gilbert rushed to assure her.

"Don't hesitate to go there, Sylvia. They've been just wonderful."

"But why is he there?"

"Because it was Troy who found him and took him home." Gilbert's explanation seemed to put her at ease and he took his leave a short while later.

Gil was seen out the door by Sandra, who upon his exit went immediately to the kitchen. Both Sandra and Carl had heard Sylvia's crying.

"What's happened, Sylvia?" Her sister asked with genuine concern.

The younger woman was quiet for a moment before bursting into tears once again. "Oh Sandra," she sobbed. "I've done something awful."

Jeff had a fairly decent night, with his mother again at his side. Gilbert was there first thing in the morning with his father. Bill again took May home and Gil stayed this time to sit with his brother. Bobbie, along with Nate, who had taken the day off from school, opened the shipping office.

Dr. Grade came by a little after 9:00 and said that Jeff no longer needed someone to sit with him around the clock. He also said he could sit up and even walk if he felt like it, but unless Santa Rosa experienced a heat wave, he was not to leave the Bradford home.

An hour later the house was empty except for Jeff and Gil, who was helping his older brother shave and clean up.

"I went to see Sylvia last night, Jeff."

"You did?" Jeff wiped the remaining soap from his face and looked at his brother in surprise. The simple act of cleaning up seemed to exhaust him, but he perked up at Gil's words.

"You might be angry with me, but I was worried about how you came to be in that part of town, so I went over to the Boggs' to get some answers." Jeff's eyebrows nearly rose to his hairline, but he kept silent.

"I couldn't figure out how you happened to be where Troy found you if you were on a date with Sylvia, so I went to see her and she told me everything."

"Everything?"

"I think so, and probably some you don't know. She said she practically threw herself at you to get you to propose."

"There was nothing *practically* about it, Gil," Jeff said softly and with regret. "She pulled my head down and kissed me." This time it was Gilbert's brows that rose as he gave a long, slow whistle.

"But you're right," Jeff continued. "I didn't know she did it to get me to propose."

"There's one more thing you should know. She's coming to see you today." As if on cue, the men heard a knock downstairs at the front door.

"If that's Sylvia she's going to want to see me alone, but I want you fairly close by because I don't think it looks right."

"Are you sure you're up to this? I can tell her you need to sleep."

"No, I'll see whoever it is."

"You're angry."

"No, Sylvia. Honestly, I'm not."

"Then I still don't understand why we can't see each other anymore."

Jeff was nearly drained, but Sylvia seemed oblivious to that fact. He took a breath and tried again.

"Sylvia, I'm not going to be seeing anyone. I think my priorities have been messed up for a long time and I want to cut back on some of my social activities and rethink my purpose on this earth."

"So all I am to you is a social activity!"

Jeff's eyes slid shut in defeat, an action that Sylvia didn't miss.

"I'm sorry, Jeff, I didn't mean that." This time she was sincerely contrite. "I told myself all the way over here that I was never going to get mad again, but it happens so easily."

Jeff nodded and managed a compassionate smile. Sylvia reached and touched his arm briefly before pulling on her gloves.

"Well, I'll see you around," Sylvia said with a false cheerfulness.

"I'm sure we'll see each other at church. Take care of yourself."

"You too. And Jeff, I'm really sorry."

"Thanks, Sylvia."

Gilbert let a very quiet Sylvia out the front door. She had smiled and thanked him for telling her about Jeff, but the usual sparkle was gone from her eyes.

Gil stepped quietly up the stairs to check on his brother, but just as he expected, Jeff was sound asleep.

Twenty-Four

J EFF WAS REMARKABLY improved by Friday morning and Dr. Grade said he could go home anytime. The problem was that only Maryanne was present and she had no way of getting him there. Jeff wasn't too concerned because he knew someone in his family would be by to see him and he would bum a ride home then.

Jeff navigated the stairs carefully and without assistance, nearly scaring a year off Maryanne's life when he walked slowly into the kitchen.

"Are you sure you should have done that?" Maryanne eyed him with concern when her heartbeat returned to normal.

"Yeah. I didn't try to gather my gear, but I figured you'd forgive me for that."

"I'll think about it." Maryanne teased him and Jeff saw instantly from whom Bobbie inherited her sense of humor.

"Speaking of forgiveness," Jeff said softly, "have you ever forgiven me for Bobbie's being away from home for five years?"

Maryanne turned slowly from the stove. She looked at the young man at her table and felt something stir inside her. When Bobbie first returned, Maryanne had known some very real fear that he would somehow hurt her again. Suddenly she knew better.

Breakfast was forgotten for the moment as Maryanne retrieved two coffee mugs and the coffeepot, and joined Jeff at the table.

"I'm glad you asked me that, Jeff," she began in quiet sincerity, "because it's obviously been on your mind. Had I known, I'd have talked to you a long time ago about it.

"Bobbie told me how well your talk went and what she said to you. And I have to tell you, Jeff, Jake and I believe as she does, that she was in Jenner because God wanted her there.

"I missed her, Jeff, more than I can say, but in some ways we were closer during those years than we might have been if she'd been living beneath this roof.

"But, Jeff—" Maryanne didn't raise her voice but her eyes grew urgent, almost pleading as she leaned forward across the table—"I need to tell you something that Bobbie didn't. She came to know Christ at Jasper and Joanne's. Now tell me, Jeff, how could I wish her back from that? When she left here she believed like my daughter Alice still does, that God would never send anyone to hell. And $5^1/_2$ years is a long time, but Bobbie came back a new creature in Christ.

"Do you understand what I'm saying, Jeff? I forgave you long ago. What happened that day at the lagoon was awful, but so was what happened to Joseph in the book of Genesis, and look at the way God used him. And look at the way He saved my Bobbie."

Maryanne Bradford's eyes filled with tears and Jeff felt a stinging sensation behind his own. He had asked and she certainly told him. It was becoming more and more clear to him all the time why Bobbie was the way she was. There was no pity in this house.

"I too wish I'd come to you a long time ago, Mrs. Bradford. You've lifted a burden from me that's been weighing me down for a long time. I should have ignored my fear and come to you years ago. Thank you."

Maryanne smiled at him—a smile so like Bobbie's that Jeff found himself grinning at her. She had already had her breakfast, so after putting a full plate in front of Jeff, she sat and visited with him. It didn't take long for the subject to come around to Bobbie.

"I know this is none of my business, but have you ever met Cleve?"

"No. Bobbie has told us about him, but the only ones who know him are Jake's brother and sister-in-law."

"Do they like him?"

"It's hard to tell in letters, and I probably shouldn't try to read between the lines, but I almost get the impression that Joanne wants Bobbie to marry Cleve so she'll make her permanent home in Jenner. Has Bobbie talked to you about Cleve?"

"A little, and I can't say as I really like the guy, which is unfair on my part, but I can't get Kaitlin's face out of my mind."

"What do you mean?"

"I mean the way she looked after she said yes to Rigg's proposal. She was radiant, but Bobbie's not. She could be talking about her dog for all the emotion she shows when discussing Cleve, and I just—"

Jeff left the sentence hang. He wasn't sure what he would wish for Bobbie, and besides, he must have upset Mrs. Bradford because her eyes were filled with tears again.

"Don't stop on my account," she said as a single tear rolled down her cheek. "It's just that I'm afraid that Bobbie is only considering Cleve because she thinks no one else will ever ask her." The words were accompanied by yet another teardrop, and Jeff, who had suspected something like this, felt he could cry himself.

"Is it true, Jeff, that no one would want my precious Bobbie? I'm sorry. That was unfair of me."

"I don't mind your asking," Jeff told her sincerely. "I understand how you feel. You want Bobbie to be loved. The more I get to know her the more I like her and want that for her too. But there's something very important missing in Bobbie's relationship with Cleve, and I can't get past that whenever I think of her married to him."

Maryanne used the corner of her apron to dab at her eyes, thanking God as she did that Bobbie had a friend who cared so much. Bobbie would be hurt if she knew she was being discussed, and Maryanne said as much to Jeff.

He told his hostess that he would be praying for all of them and the subject shifted to ways of making Jeff comfortable in the living room until his family came.

Maryanne gathered all of Jeff's belongings and was again visiting with him when May and Bill arrived. Jeff was growing tired so they bundled their son into the wagon right away and headed for home.

Maryanne changed the bedding on her daughter's bed and cleaned the room. It wasn't until she was done and on her way out the door that she realized she would miss having Jeff around.

Another thought assailed Maryanne at the same time, and she immediately wished it had never come to mind. She took herself off to her own bedroom to pray. She stayed on her knees until she had given her daughter, Cleveland Ramsey, and Jeff Taylor all to the Lord.

Twenty-Five

Jeff was out of work for two full weeks, but long before those weeks elapsed it became apparent that the forces of law in town were not going to locate Jeff's attackers. An officer had come to question Jeff the same night he went home, but other than finding evidence of a struggle and a piece of fabric from Jeff's jacket, they told Bill there was not enough evidence. With so little to go on, including no identification of the assailants, they would have to consider the case closed.

Bill stayed in Jeff's room after the officer left and Jeff shared with his father why he had been walking home alone. Bill's face showed grave concern and then relief when Jeff revealed he had told Sylvia he couldn't see her anymore.

"I've been living for myself for a long time, Dad, and I think it's time I stopped. I could have died the other night, and I think maybe God used the attack to get my attention."

Bill had held his son in a long, unembarrassed embrace. They continued to talk for the better part of an hour. Jeff, having just arrived home, was very tired when his father left the room, but was also experiencing more peace than he ever had in his life.

The doctor cleared Jeff for work one week after he arrived home, but things were going well at the office and May asked Jeff to humor her by staying home an extra week.

By the last weekend of Jeff's confinement he was like a caged animal. It was Bobbie's half-Saturday at the office, and on Bill's request she agreed to go and see Jeff as soon as she got off work.

"Your father tells me you've begun to pace." Bobbie's voice came from the edge of the room and Jeff peeked over the newspaper he had been reading.

"I can't imagine what he's talking about," Jeff commented with extreme nonchalance. "I'm finding I could enjoy the lifestyle of the idle rich."

Bobbie spoke as she turned and walked toward the door she had just entered. "Then I guess you don't need company. I'll see you tomorrow or Monday at work."

Bolting out of his chair, Jeff raced across the room and pressed the door shut when Bobbie tried to open it. She turned and leaned against the wood, and then cocked her head to one side as she looked at the man above her.

"I take it you're feeling better?"

"Much," Jeff answered with a grin, thinking she was the most adorable thing he had ever seen.

"And perhaps you would like some company?"

"Are you going to make me beg for it?"

"Oh, now that's a wonderful idea. You could get on your knees and for once I'd be taller."

Bobbie put one hand to her mouth, her eyes brimming with laughter, when Jeff dropped to one knee and took her hand.

"Will you please tarry awhile and talk with me, Miss Roberta Bradford?"

It was too much for the small blonde. She dissolved into giggles and then followed him into the living room, laying her coat across a chair on the way to the couch. After they were seated together Bobbie removed her glasses to rub her nose. This particular action always drew Jeff's attention because she never complained about wearing them or said they hurt, even though it was distinctly clear they weren't the most comfortable.

"The office was busy this morning. Half the time was spent telling people that you hadn't been hit by a runaway stage or mowed down in a gunfight. It's been like that for days." Bobbie shook her head. "It's amazing to me how the facts get tangled. It wasn't like that in Jenner."

"You mean not everyone knew everyone else's business?" Jeff was amazed.

"Of course they did, but they had their facts straight." Bobbie's dry tone made Jeff smile.

"How are you at checkers?" Jeff asked a moment later.

"Fair," Bobbie said with a mischievous grin. "It all depends on who's on the other side of the board."

"Who do you usually play?"

"My dad or Troy."

"And do you win?"

"Now that would be telling!" Bobbie said, and then accompanied Jeff to the kitchen, where he set up the game. Jeff and Bobbie found themselves evenly matched.

When Jeff took too long to make his move, Bobbie would begin drumming her fingernails on the table. The scheme worked every time. Thinking she was merely distracting him, Bobbie was unaware of how drawn Jeff was to her beautifully shaped nails and exquisite small hands.

Jeff, on the other hand, found that nothing could distract his opponent from her move. She would cock her head in the way he found so adorable and study the board as if the checkers themselves were going to talk to her.

Jeff thought that if he bent over and kissed Bobbie's exposed neck, it would definitely snag her attention! Jeff suddenly sat up a little straighter. He was so shocked by the direction his thoughts had taken that when it was finally his turn, he just sat in flabbergasted surprise.

"Jeff-rey," Bobbie called in a singsong voice for the second time.

"Oh," was all he said, and Bobbie could see he was returning from miles away.

"We can stop if you're tired." Bobbie's voice had become very soft, and she tried to read Jeff's mood from the look on his face. He was staring at her so strangely.

After a moment Bobbie's hand went to her hair in a self-conscious gesture and then traveled to her glasses to finger the frames. Her movements pulled Jeff back to the present—the movements *and* the disturbingly vulnerable look on Bobbie's face.

"Well now," Jeff said with a shake of his head, his tone light, "I was certainly out of things just then."

"We can quit, Jeff."

'There it was again,' Jeff thought, finally putting his finger on the look. How many times had he seen Bobbie look at him with that expression of tender concern? But there was also a hesitancy in that look which told Jeff she was afraid her desire to help would be rejected.

"I'd like to finish the game."

"Okay," Bobbie agreed, "it's still your move." She wasn't at all sure what had bothered him just then, but his light tone told her he was either all right or didn't want to talk about it.

"Did Sylvia come into the office this week?"

"No, I don't think so—that is, I didn't see her. Hasn't she come to visit you?"

"No, she hasn't, but that's because we're not seeing each other right now."

"Oh Jeff, I'm sorry."

"No, it's all right. I've been burdened for a good while that I need to begin focusing on things other than my social life. It seems as though that's all I've lived for lately."

His words surprised Bobbie, but she didn't show it. She had been under the impression that he and Sylvia were quite serious, and now he had just labeled her under his social life. Bobbie was learning that there was really quite a lot about Jeff that she didn't know.

"I'll be praying for you, Jeff."

"Thanks, Bobbie."

Jeff won the checkers game and then May, who had stayed in the background during their visit, fixed them something to eat. Nate came home early from the shipping office and Marcail was with him.

"My birthday is coming up in two weeks, Bobbie, and we're going to have a party. Can you come?"

"I'd love to, Marcail, but I think you should check with Kaitlin."

"I already did. It's going to be here at May and Bill's, and Katie said I could ask whoever I want."

"Are any of your friends coming?"

"You're my friend, Bobbie." Marcail stated this as though it was the most obvious thing on earth.

Bobbie hugged her. "I realize that, but I just wondered if this was a family party or a party with a bunch of giggling little girls."

"It's a family party."

"Oh," Bobbie said with a disappointed face. "I really wanted to be one of the giggling little girls."

Marcail must have thought this was wonderful, since she threw her arms around Bobbie's neck and gave her a mighty squeeze.

Only Nate noticed how quiet Jeff had been through the entire exchange and the way he watched Bobbie. Jeff's eyes studied her face when she wasn't even aware of his scrutiny.

"Here we go again," Nate mumbled so no one heard him, but he couldn't have been too upset, since it didn't keep him from reaching for another slice of gingerbread and the pitcher of cider.

Twenty-Six

BOBBIE WENT STRAIGHT to Riggs Mercantile on her next half-Saturday because the next day was Marcail's tenth birthday party. She had wandered around for a good 20 minutes when Rigg appeared at her side.

"Hi, Bobbie, how are you?"

"I'm fine, Rigg, but I'd be even better if I knew what your sister-in-law would like for her birthday."

"Ahh," Rigg said with a smile. "I honestly think you could just bring yourself. Marcail would consider you gift enough."

Bobbie smiled. "I think she's pretty special too. How is Kaitlin?"

"She's feeling better physically, but she just heard from her father and he's decided to stay in Hawaii for at least a year. It was difficult to hear, but in the long run it will be easier than getting news with every letter that he's going to be delayed."

"I think you must be right," Bobbie answered with more knowledge than Rigg realized.

She had written to Cleve and told him how she was feeling about their relationship. He seemed almost panicked because his next letter said he was coming to Santa Rosa right away. Wanting to settle things with Cleve as soon as possible, Bobbie had been relieved, but another letter came right after that to say that he wouldn't be able to get away until the spring and quite possibly the summer. It was a tremendous letdown, and Bobbie was discovering that the feeling of being in limbo was not pleasant.

"I saw Marcail looking at these last week," Rigg was saying as he pointed to some hair combs and ribbons. "And I know she likes lacy undergarments because she touches them and holds them to the front of herself every time she comes in."

Bobbie's interest was immediately piqued. "Does Kaitlin usually buy her this type of thing?" Bobbie held up a child's shift that was bordered with bright blue ribbon.

"I don't think she does. Kate's pretty drawn to that stuff too, so I think it's probably something they haven't had a lot of."

"Thanks, Rigg, I don't think you need to show me anything else," Bobbie said without looking at him, her eyes on the clothing before her. Ordinarily she might have been embarrassed to discuss intimate apparel with Rigg, but right now her mind was too busy figuring out what she could afford and exactly what Marcail might like.

Bobbie's stomach was beginning to growl from hunger before she made her final selection and started home. She was very pleased with her purchase and hoped her ten-year-old friend would be as well. She had only about 24 hours to wait before she found out because Marcail's party was right after church the next day.

Bobbie had checked with May about what she could bring for lunch but May told her that she and Kaitlin were preparing everything. The weather over the weekend would have been perfect for a camping trip but Bobbie told herself that she wouldn't miss Marcail's party for anything. She also asked the Lord to give them sunshine for the party. It was a selfish request, but Bobbie's heart was tender toward Marcail and she wanted everything to be just right.

Just right were the perfect words to describe the day of the party. Marcail waited outside the church and then asked Bobbie to sit with her during the service.

Their pew was full, with Sean on the far end and then Rigg, Kaitlin, Jeff, Bobbie, and Marcail on the outside aisle. Bobbie and Jeff only had a chance to exchange smiles before the service began, but on the first song Jeff leaned to whisper in her ear.

"Why aren't you singing?"

"I'm trying to hear Marcail's voice." Bobbie's eyes were wide with wonder.

"You need to hear her when she sings with Kate and Sean. The word beautiful doesn't do them justice."

Bobbie was awestruck. Marcail's voice was the clearest soprano she had ever heard, and as Bobbie turned to watch her she could see that it was effortless. The whole morning was special and it was with high spirits that Bobbie made her way to the Taylors'.

'You're going to have to face facts, Jeffrey,' he said to himself. 'You're finding Bobbie Bradford more and more distracting all the time.' Jeff sat in the living room of his house and couldn't believe he was having this conversation with himself.

The room was packed. Jeff's folks were there, along with all his brothers, plus Kate, Sean, and of course Marcail. Mr. Parker and Joey Parker were also present. They were friends to whom the family had a special outreach, but the only person Jeff had eyes for was a curly-headed blonde who wore glasses on her delightfully upturned nose.

Jeff couldn't believe how many times he had thought about kissing that nose over the last two weeks. Maybe it was because Sylvia had kissed him, but Jeff knew he was terribly preoccupied with hugging and kissing lately. He found himself envying Rigg, who had a wife to hold whenever he so wanted.

Jeff always assumed that he would marry someday, but lately it was becoming something of an obsession. He even found himself imagining what his and Bobbie's children would look like. He had never had such thoughts of Sylvia, and Jeff spent a lot of time asking God to show him what it all meant.

What if he *was* falling in love with Bobbie? She was committed to Cleve. Jeff found the name more distasteful all the time. And on the rare moments when he thought about Bobbie kissing Cleve, he felt something akin to grief. He had almost slipped one day at work and asked her if they had kissed much. He knew the question was none of his business, but it plagued him nonetheless. Maybe he should just ask her, get his face slapped, and have it out of his system.

The room had emptied while Jeff sat in a daze. Marcail had opened all her gifts and the family was gathered in the kitchen for cake. Bobbie noticed that Jeff wasn't present and went back to find him in a chair in the far corner of the living room.

"Jeff, are you coming to the kitchen?" Bobbie asked the question after she had stopped by his chair.

"Yes, I'll come right now," Jeff answered, glad for the diversion.

Marcail shot into the room just then and made straight for her presents. She scooped up the lovely undergarments that Bobbie had picked out for her and rushed over to Jeff.

"Jeff, did you see these? Bobbie gave them to me. Aren't they pretty?"

"Very nice," Jeff answered, thinking how grown-up Bobbie had made Marcail feel with such a gift. Marcail was holding up a cotton undershirt and bloomers; both were piped in pink braid.

"Marc!" Kate's voice called from the kitchen and the three went out together. Marcail skipped out to have her cake, thinking that this day had been almost as good as Christmas.

Twenty-Seven

"OH SEAN, NOT again." The words were uttered in agony and came from the 15-year-old's sister. Kaitlin had been sitting in the living room for hours waiting for Sean to come home. Rigg had sat with her until close to midnight, but he had to work the next day and Kate told him to go to bed. They were both too tired to give thought to the fact that Kaitlin had to work in the morning as well.

"Sit down, Sean." Kate moved toward her brother and then almost stepped back when a wave of alcohol fumes assailed her senses.

Sean mumbled something unintelligible as Kate put her arm around him, but she ignored her inebriated brother. Her pregnancy made her ungainly, and when Sean tripped on the edge of the rug, he almost took them both to the floor.

Kate wanted to rail at her brother. This was the second time he had come home drunk and she was just sick as she looked at him. It had all started around Marcail's birthday, when their Father had written to say he would be away at least a year. A few days after Marcail's party, Sean had gone out with friends on a Friday night and been gone until dawn. He had come back so drunk that his family barely recognized him. Now it was weeks later and it wasn't a Friday night, so they wouldn't have the weekend to recover.

For a long time Sean had been very sorry over what he had done and it looked to everyone like he had learned his lesson, but the boys Sean ran with were a strong lure, and in a matter of weeks he was seeing them again. He managed to keep this a secret for over a month, but now he saw them every afternoon that he wasn't working.

Rigg and Kate discussed the possibility of Sean working every day, but they knew that would be treating the symptoms and not the cause. Kate didn't like to think what was going to happen when school let out in two weeks. Unless Sean agreed to work at the mercantile, he would have hours of free time on his hands every day.

Kate was afraid to try the stairs with Sean, so she led him to the couch and helped him lie down. He fell asleep as she removed his shoes. Rigg came out to check on her just as she was covering him with a blanket.

"I could smell him from across the room." Rigg's voice was thick with pain. "How are you holding up?"

"I think I'll be okay. I came to some conclusions tonight as I was sitting here waiting, and I think I'm going to give Sean a choice; he can straighten up or I'm going to put him on the next ship for Hawaii."

"Will you be able to go through with it if he chooses to sail?"

"I don't know, Rigg, I honestly don't know." The tears that had threatened for hours finally spilled forth.

Rigg quickly checked Sean, tucking the blanket close around him, and then lifted his sobbing wife in his arms. The pregnancy made her heavier but she was still no problem for Rigg to carry.

He laid her gently in their bed and then crawled in beside her, covering them both with a light blanket. Rigg didn't try to talk to Kate as she cried against his chest because he half-expected she would cry herself to sleep. But Kate needed to talk, and after her tears were spent she spoke.

"I don't know what to do next. I love my brother, Rigg, but he's become so hard against me that I feel I barely know him. I know he's a different person when he's with his friends, and I feel that everything he says or does around here is a lie."

"It probably is. I mean, he's embracing the world with both arms right now and that means he has to weigh every word he says when he's here."

"What are we going to do, Rigg?" Kate said after a moment of silence.

"I don't know. I haven't wanted to involve my whole family even though I'm sure they've noticed Sean's behavior."

"But now you're thinking of talking to your dad?"

"Yes. He loves Sean, but he's not as emotionally involved as we are, and maybe he can shed some light on things for us. And just maybe, Kate—and this is something we'll have to face—Sean will have to make his own choice on this. He has a free will, and God wants Sean to come to Him of that free will.''

They didn't talk much after that and it wasn't long before they were both asleep. Morning was a trial with so little rest, but they were up on time anyway. Rigg moved his hung-over brother-in-law to his own bedroom upstairs, and then left him a note telling him not to leave the house before Rigg returned at lunch.

Kate and Rigg sat down with Sean that very night and talked over the options available to him. Kaitlin did not give her brother any ultimatums, but she did ask him if he wanted to sail for Hawaii. He was immediately against the idea and Kate found that she was relieved.

Rigg took over the conversation about halfway through, and most of what he told Sean echoed the advice he had received from his father that morning.

Sean was given until school let out to find a full-time job for the summer, not a job with Rigg or at the shipping office, but one where he walked in, introduced himself, and asked for full-time work for the summer.

''And what if I refuse?'' Sean asked, not belligerently, but needing to know his boundaries.

''Then you'll find yourself out on your ear, because this is what it's going to cost you to live here this summer.''

Rigg pushed a piece of paper toward the young man. On it were the weekly costs for Sean's rent and food for the entire summer. Rigg also told him he would have to buy his own clothing. Sean read the list over several times, and then looked into the eyes of Rigg and his sister. They were regretful, but serious.

Sean nodded slowly. He hated to admit it, but he knew he had no one to blame but himself. Maybe a job would help him say no to the friends who got him into the most trouble. Not that he blamed them completely; he knew the choice was his.

The next day being Friday, Sean knew he had just one more day before setting off to find a summer job. He thought he might have seen a sign at the livery. He didn't know the pay, but it had to be fairly high or else he would have to put in plenty of hours for his rent and expenses.

He also wanted to buy Katie's baby something special. She was due in about three months and he had put her through a lot. He thought if he could buy a gift for his new niece or nephew with his own money, he could prove to Kate that he did think of other people besides himself.

With this in mind Sean rose from the table to find Marcail. He had shouted at her today because he'd had a headache. Knowing he needed to make amends, he nevertheless wished his family understood him more. In fact, he wished he understood himself more.

Twenty-Eight

JEFF SMILED AT the sight of Bobbie on the step stool in the storeroom; she wasn't supposed to be up there. But then, it was only her
boss who told her that, and since Bobbie saw no reason for the rule,
she disregarded it when she felt it necessary.

"You're not to be up there, Bobbie," Jeff stated as he came to stand
below her.

"Oh, it's all right. You see, Gilbert just had to run a quick errand
and I want to get this done before lunch."

Jeff shook his head as she went back to organizing the unclaimed
packages, even as his hands lifted to grasp her around the waist.

Once on the floor Bobbie glared up at Jeff, but he smiled engag-
ingly, which only deepened her scowl. Sidestepping her, Jeff hopped
on the ladder himself.

Jeff had been working on the back-room shelves for so many years
he was sure he could do it in his sleep. As usual, his mind began to
wander and this time it wandered to Bobbie. He had never had a
friend like her, and indeed she was a *friend*.

It had seemed for awhile that working with her was going to be
very difficult because of the way his heart was changing toward her,
but he had fully surrendered his heart to God where Bobbie was concerned, and his heavenly Father sustained him in a way that Jeff
never anticipated.

Bobbie had become his friend. It was really that simple. He could
touch her arm or even give her a hug in true friendship. There wasn't

anything they couldn't talk about. They shouted at each other once in awhile, but there wasn't a week that passed when they didn't laugh themselves to tears over something.

They even had a Scripture memorization contest going. It had been Bobbie's idea, and Jeff, having been raised in the Word of God, thought himself a sure win. But as usual, Bobbie surprised him. They would stand almost nose-to-nose and recite any verse that came to mind. The last person to say a verse won.

Jeff found out in a hurry that Bobbie was as competitive as he was. They were evenly matched at the moment, and both hated to be the last one standing there searching his or her memory for a verse.

"That's the lot," Jeff told Bobbie as he came down to stand beside her.

"Thanks, Jeff." As always, she had to tip her head back to see him. "I guess Gil was delayed."

"Well, no matter. Nate will be out of school in a week, and Dad always puts him in charge of the stockroom for the summer."

"I'm glad to hear that. Nate is fun to have around."

"Speaking of being around, I understand you guys are coming to supper tonight."

"Yep. Are you going to be there?"

Jeff gave a negative shake of his head. "I have a date."

"Anyone I know?"

"Penny Larson."

"Penny Larson? I thought she lived down south."

"She does. But she's here to visit her grandmother and we're going to supper."

"Tell her I said hi."

"I'll do that. How many more days until Cleve comes?"

"He'll be here Friday."

"*This* Friday?" Jeff was surprised.

"Yes. When did you think it was?"

"I don't know, but I just didn't realize it was so soon. You don't seem very excited."

"I am," Bobbie said, but her voice held no conviction. She met Jeff's eyes for just a moment and then turned away.

They had talked all about Cleve when Bobbie was still undecided, and Jeff had finally told Bobbie outright that her marrying Cleve was a big mistake.

"You don't even know him, so how can you say that?" she had retorted in anger.

"I don't need to know him to see that you're not in love with him." Jeff's voice had been gentle, and Bobbie couldn't take it. He had watched helplessly as tears puddled in her eyes.

"I'm sure you've noticed how hard it is for you to get into the office every day, Jeff, because of all the men lined up outside waiting to see me."

"So you are marrying Cleve because you think no one else will ask you?"

"You make it sound so cynical, but you don't understand." A single tear slid down her face and Jeff felt something squeeze around his heart. "Plain girls have dreams too, you know. We want families and homes as much as beautiful girls like Sylvia."

"Oh Bob," Jeff whispered, and reached to hold her, but Bobbie stepped away from his arms.

"Don't pity me, Jeff. I don't need your pity."

But Jeff was not to be put off, and he pursued Bobbie right around her desk and then pulled her into the storeroom so they could talk.

Everything had been cleared up between them before they had gone back to work, but at the time Bobbie's future was still very unsettled.

Bobbie now knew she wasn't to marry Cleve, but she couldn't tell anyone. She felt it a serious matter to tell Cleve first *and* in person, even though she desperately wanted to discuss it with her best friend—Jeff Taylor.

For the moment Bobbie was spared having to give any more thought to the weekend and Cleve's arrival because Marcail came in.

"Hi, Bobbie."

"Well, hello, Marc. What brings you in right after school?"

"Kate's at the doctor."

Bobbie looked at her with understanding. She and Marcail had discussed this before, and Bobbie, even though she didn't share Marcail's fear of doctors, was very compassionate.

"I'm ready now," Marcail said as she took a seat by the desk.

"Ready for what?"

"To hear about the camping trips."

Bobbie smiled. She had completely forgotten that they had been talking about it on Sunday when Kaitlin told Marcail she had to get into the wagon. Bobbie had promised her they would talk the next time they saw each other.

Bobbie glanced down at the paperwork on her desk and then at the clock. If she kept it short she could still get her work done. Bobbie was just finishing her explanation when Jeff came in and took the other desk chair.

"So when can I go with you?"

"Well, we're not going again until after Cleve's visit, but if Kaitlin and Rigg say you can come, then it's fine with me."

"What about me?"

Bobbie blinked at Jeff in surprise. "Are you serious?"

"Sure. I've been waiting for you to invite me all spring, but since Marc just came out and asked, I figured I'd do the same."

Bobbie looked from one to the other. Why had she never thought to invite them?

"Of course you can come," she said simply. "I'll discuss it with my dad and let you know what to bring."

Jeff and Marcail grinned at each other, and Bobbie was amazed to see how sincere they were. She wondered what it was that they both found so intriguing about her going camping with her family.

What Bobbie was unaware of was the way her eyes lit up when she spoke of waking up in a still forest, or going to sleep with a million stars shining overhead. She made cooking over the fire and hiking through the woods sound magical, easily capturing the attention of anyone listening.

The next day their plans were made. Marcail gained permission from her sister and Jeff asked his mother to fill in for the weekend. Bobbie was glad for something to distract her thoughts until Cleve arrived in six days. Before she knew it, Friday was upon her and the stage from Jenner would be in around suppertime.

Bobbie had the next day off, but she might as well have had Friday off, since she accomplished little. Jeff noticed her restlessness but refrained from commenting.

Around 5:30 Bobbie stood at the shipping office window watching the passengers disembark in front of the stage office. Her anxiety was overwhelming as she waited for that familiar face to appear. Finally Bobbie watched Cleve jump down from the stage, the last person off.

Taking a deep breath, she wiped her damp palms together and opened the shipping office door, completely unaware of the way Jeff and Gilbert moved to watch her from the window she had just vacated.

Twenty-Nine

CLEVE SPOTTED BOBBIE the moment she emerged from the office, and he watched her approach. He searched her face, although for what he wasn't sure, and tried to smile as she came to stand before him.

At once he knew that staying away had been a mistake. He had been sure that if they were apart Bobbie would miss him. Not just miss him, but *long* for his companionship, as he had longed for hers. Her face told him that hadn't happened.

But he had a week in Santa Rosa, and he told himself that maybe it would be enough time to convince Bobbie Bradford that she needed to come back to Jenner.

"Hello, stranger," Cleve greeted her without restraint. It was so easy to talk to Bobbie.

"Hi, Cleve, how was the trip?"

"Long and dusty."

"I'm sure it was," Bobbie said with a smile. Cleve was so honest.

He didn't touch her. Even though Bobbie knew he wouldn't, she was somehow disappointed.

"Are you off work now?"

"Yes. Would you like to come in and meet my boss?"

"Sure. Do you work tomorrow?"

"No, I'm off until Monday."

"Good." Cleve looked very pleased and Bobbie wondered if maybe he cared for her more than she thought. At one time the thought would have pleased her, but now . . .

"He didn't even hug her."

"What?"

"Nothing."

Gilbert turned slightly in the wagon seat to stare at Jeff, who held the reins loosely in his hands and continued to mumble to himself.

"What Bobbie does with Cleve is none of our business, Jeff."

"I know that." Jeff answered with a long sigh and then glanced at Gilbert. "But it bothered you too, didn't it?"

Gilbert didn't answer, but then he didn't have to; Jeff could read his thoughts. Jeff told himself again that it was none of their business, but his feelings for Bobbie made him wonder anew how Cleve could have kept from hugging her, even though they were in public.

"They're coming to dinner after church Sunday."

"Yeah," Jeff commented quietly.

"You were all prepared to hate him, weren't you?"

Jeff gave a small smile. "I guess I was."

"And it wasn't that simple," Gil remarked, and once again the two fell silent for the remainder of the ride, both contemplating the scene when Bobbie brought Cleve in to be introduced.

"Mr. Taylor, this is Cleveland Ramsey. Cleve, this is my boss, Bill Taylor." The men shook hands and then Bobbie introduced Jeff and Gilbert.

Cleve conversed easily with the men, his manner quietly charming. He was knowledgeable in the shipping field because of his close contact with Jasper and Joanne, and the Taylors were impressed.

Not a big man, Cleve was a few inches taller than Bobbie, with well-built, broad shoulders and a firm handshake. He was a perfect gentleman with Bobbie, and that was a plus for a man who had points against him before the game even began.

All in all, it was a good first meeting. Jeff did some serious praying as he settled the horse and wagon in the barn for the night. He was going to be seeing Cleve with Bobbie off and on for the next week, and he might very well have to say goodbye to his friend because of Cleve.

'Please, Lord,' Jeff prayed, 'help me to trust You for Bobbie's future. And help her to make the right decision.'

"What *are* you staring at, Cleve?" Bobbie asked softly from her place on the front porch.

"You," he answered simply, and she felt her face warm.

Supper was over and the two of them were sitting on the front porch. It was a warm summer night and the song of crickets could be heard all around them. Their silence was a comfortable one, and Cleve had enjoyed just looking at the woman across from him before she became aware of his scrutiny.

"Did you want to ask me something?" Bobbie questioned him uncertainly when he continued to watch her in silence.

"I think I've already done the asking, Robbie."

Bobbie's heart began to pound. She had asked the Lord to help her bring this up at the beginning of his visit, but really hadn't had a clue as to how to go about it. Now Cleve had given her a starting place, and she wasn't at all sure if she was ready.

"Yes, you have asked, Cleve," Bobbie said softly, "and I felt it was important to answer you in person."

"I'm pretty sure I know what you're going to say."

Bobbie was quiet for a moment then. How did a woman tell a man that she was afraid she would someday regret marrying him? Bobbie was searching for the right words when Cleve spoke again.

"It's because I don't pray that much or read my Bible, isn't it?"

Bobbie thanked God for the opening. "I think," she answered carefully, "that people need to enter marriage with their eyes open. I mean, if there's something that makes a person uncomfortable, then he or she needs to understand that before the vows are spoken and not plan on changing that person once the wedding is over. Am I making any sense?"

"Yes."

"We've always been very honest with each other, Cleve, and I don't want that to change now. I'm not comfortable with the fact that you talk about love as though it's not important. I mean, getting married with the assumption that someday we'll love each other is not enough for me. But that's the way you believe, and I wouldn't try to change that.

"But the reason I can't say yes to you, Cleve, is much more serious. It's the exact reason you just mentioned." Bobbie's voice grew very tender and tears stung the back of her eyes. "God doesn't seem important enough to you, Cleve, and I just can't live with that. I know I didn't explain myself very well in the letter, but I had a reason. If you change spiritually, Cleve, it needs to be because of God, and not because you want to marry me."

Bobbie held her breath. The words were all spoken kindly and without judgment, but they were words that Bobbie was sure would make him angry. She was wrong.

"Thanks for telling me, Robbie."

Bobbie didn't know what to say. In fact, all she wanted to do was burst into tears. She had just hurt a man she cared for and also turned down the only proposal she was sure she would ever get.

"Are you okay?"

"I should be asking you that, Cleve." Tears streamed down her face as she answered. "I never meant to hurt you."

"I know you didn't, and the truth is, I haven't been completely honest with you." Bobbie looked surprised and he continued. "You see, I deliberately stayed away from Santa Rosa to see if you'd come back because you missed me. In fact, there wasn't a day that the stage came in that I wasn't there to meet it, always hoping you'd be on board." Cleve's voice was quiet, almost resigned.

Bobbie cried in earnest then. She took off her glasses and buried her face in her hands. Cleve watched helplessly.

"Robbie, please don't do this."

Bobbie tried to contain herself so she could talk with him, but the tears kept coming.

"I was really hoping you'd let me stay. I haven't had a vacation for a long time and I won't push you or anything—"

"What?" His words surprised Bobbie out of her tears.

"Well," Cleve continued, "it's just that maybe your parents would rather I didn't stay here, since we're not going to be—"

"You mean you'll stay all week, you'll really stay like you originally planned?"

"I'd like to."

"Oh Cleve, I was so hoping you would. But I was sure that as soon as we talked you'd want to leave. In fact I was afraid you'd even move to the hotel tonight and leave on the morning stage."

"I'd like to stay, and," he held up his hand as though making a solemn vow, "I promise we'll be friends. No hinting about your coming to Jenner."

"Oh Cleve," Bobbie said again, wanting to tell him she thought he was wonderful, but no words would come.

Bobbie had put her glasses back on and they smiled at each other in understanding. Cleve confessed to being very tired a little while later, and then took himself off to Troy's room, where he would sleep in the extra bed. Bobbie stayed downstairs for awhile to talk with her parents.

"He's awfully nice, Bobbie," her mother commented.

"Yes, he is," she said with soft conviction. "And he'll make some girl a good husband."

"But not you," her father interjected.

"No, not me."

The three were silent for a minute and Bobbie was glad that Troy was out with Carla.

"Are you all right?" Maryanne asked her daughter.

"I've been better. You don't mind if Cleve stays, do you? I mean, even though we're just friends?"

"You know better than to even ask, Bobbie." Her father's gentle voice was her undoing.

"I'm going to bed now." Bobbie stood and more tears fell. She was almost out of the room when Jake came up behind her.

"Oh Dad," was all Bobbie could say as she was enfolded in her father's embrace.

"You did the right thing, didn't you, Bobbie?"

"Yes."

"And you have peace."

"Yes, but I hurt."

"I know you do. God knows too."

Bobbie let herself cry against her father's shirt. When she pulled away he offered her his handkerchief. Bobbie shook her head and reached into her skirt pocket. Her own was so damp from her cry on the porch that she giggled.

Jake recognized the signs of exhaustion and turned her toward the stairs.

"Good night, honey."

"Good night, Dad."

Jake turned back to the living room, reaching as he walked to put his handkerchief into his pocket. His wife's face stayed the movement. He joined her on the couch, handed her the cloth in his hand, and pulled her against his chest.

He didn't ask Maryanne why she was crying, since he was sure she wouldn't be able to answer. But he suspected that it might have something to do with the light they saw in Troy's eyes in the last weeks and whether or not Bobbie's eyes would ever have that gleam.

Thirty

WELL-RESTED AND ready to take Santa Rosa by storm the next morning, Cleve and Bobbie borrowed one of the Taylors' wagons. Bobbie took Cleve over every square inch of her hometown. Cleve was truly impressed.

"No wonder you missed living here—it's a great city."

"I think so," Bobbie said with a smile.

"I'm going to miss that smile, Robbie."

"And I'm going to miss being called Robbie."

They looked at each other for a moment and Bobbie silently praised God with a sense of wonder in her heart. It was miraculous that they could be friends after they had talked of marriage.

Their last stop on the way home was the shipping office so they could collect Bobbie's pay for the week. Bill, Gilbert, and Cleve became involved in a discussion as soon as they walked in the door, and Jeff, offering a ridiculous excuse, nearly dragged Bobbie to the back room.

"How's it going?" he whispered close to her ear as soon as they were at the back of the room.

"How is what going?"

"You know, with Cleve."

"It's fine," Bobbie answered, a bit puzzled. "We've had a lovely day."

"So it's going all right between you two?"

"Yes."

"When do you leave for Jenner?"

In the shadowy room Bobbie didn't catch the pained look on Jeff's face, but his voice told her something was wrong. She knew it was time to explain.

"Jeff, I'm not going to Jenner."

"You're not?"

"No."

"Why not?"

Bobbie brought her hands up to frame Jeff's face. He was bent over her and Bobbie spoke while holding his face very close to her own, thinking as she did that he was such a dear friend.

"Jeffrey, Cleve and I are not going to be married. But we are still friends, and he's going to stay the week because this is a break from work for him."

Even after Bobbie dropped her hands it took a moment for Jeff to respond. "How long have you known you weren't going to marry Cleve?"

"For a while now."

"Why didn't you tell me?"

"Jeff," Bobbie's voice was kind but very logical, "if you asked a girl to marry you, wouldn't you appreciate her giving you an answer before she talked to anyone else?"

"Yeah, I guess I would."

Bobbie looked away from him then, and Jeff realized how insensitive he had been in the last few minutes.

"Are you okay?"

"Yes." Bobbie's voice was nearly inaudible.

Jeff was not convinced. His hand came up to gently grasp Bobbie's jaw. He held her lightly and looked into her eyes. He saw pain there and something he couldn't quite interpret. He pressed a soft kiss to her forehead before freeing her.

As Jeff straightened he saw that Gilbert was rushing toward them. He appeared to be very upset.

"Honestly, Jeff, Bobbie's fiancé is in the next room and you're in here kissing her!"

"It's all right, Gilbert—" Bobbie began.

"How can you say that, Bobbie?"

"Oh Gilbert," she chuckled softly, "you're so sweet. Please explain to him, Jeff. I've got to be going."

The men watched her leave, and then Jeff explained to his brother, who promptly apologized for jumping to conclusions. They talked for a few minutes longer, and Gilbert admitted that he was relieved over Bobbie's decision. Jeff agreed, but kept some of his thoughts to himself. Mainly his worry over the expression he had seen in Bobbie's eyes—the one he couldn't quite define.

"You better keep an eye on him, Mom. He'll make it so spicy that we'll all have tears in our eyes."

"Don't listen to her, Mrs. Bradford," Cleve broke in. "You'll love this chili."

Maryanne smiled to herself. She had never met a man who loved to cook. Jake and Troy were both quite capable in the kitchen, but they always preferred to have her or Bobbie do the work.

"Okay, Robbie, I'm ready for that pot."

Bobbie and Cleve worked well together in the kitchen, and Maryanne felt a twinge of regret that he wouldn't be a permanent part of the family. She quickly reminded herself that her daughter was a grown woman who had prayed long and hard about this man. She was not about to be an interfering mother!

The meal was wonderful. Cleve met Carla, who was over for the evening, and after the dishes were washed and put away, the four young people played a game.

When Troy walked Carla home, Cleve and Bobbie headed outside to sit under the tree in the front yard. It was another warm night, and the air was fresh and inviting.

"I've been thinking all day about what you said last night."

"What was that exactly?"

"That God doesn't seem that important to me."

"Cleve—"

"No, Robbie, don't say anything. I needed to hear that." He was silent for a moment, and then went on in a contemplative voice.

"You seem to have something that I don't. God seems to be very special to you, and I can't help but wonder why I don't feel the same way. In fact, I wonder if I'm even saved."

Bobbie opened her mouth to deny Cleve's words, but shut it again. She had no business telling Cleve that she was sure he was saved; that was between him and God.

"Is there a time that stands out in your mind as to when you accepted Jesus Christ?" Cleve asked the woman beside him.

"Yes, there is, a very definite time. It was after I came to live with Aunt Joanne and Uncle Jasper. Suddenly one night I was very afraid that I would die. My parents were sure of their eternity, but I wasn't and I wanted to be. Uncle Jasper talked with me for a long time. I found out later that Aunt Jo was praying her heart out in the next room.

"It was that night that I knew I needed a Savior, and I turned to Jesus Christ."

"I don't have anything like that to look back on," Cleve admitted quietly.

"It doesn't happen the same for everyone, Cleve."

"I'm sure you're right, but that's not what I mean."

He was quiet for a moment, and Bobbie wanted to ask him what he did mean, but she stayed silent and prayerful.

"I've just always gone to church," Cleve began. "I've spent time with the people who attended church and I've tried to read my Bible and pray, but I'm not sure I've ever made that step. I'm not sure that if I died right now, I would spend eternity with God."

"You can be sure, Cleve. Right now, even."

Cleve turned his head to look at her. "I think you're right, Robbie, but after all this time, thinking everything was fine, it feels awkward to try and talk to God about this."

"He's the only One you can talk to, Cleve. God alone can give you a peace about your eternity. If you're not sure, then be sure right now. Don't let pride stand in the way. Tell God you know you're a sinner, and that you believe His only Son died for those sins."

Cleve was again silent for a moment. "I think I'm going to go up to the bedroom now, Robbie. Troy isn't back yet and I need some time alone."

Bobbie watched him stand, her heart aching. "I'll be praying for you, Cleve."

"Thank you."

The moonlight allowed Bobbie to watch him walk to the house, and as soon as the door closed she prayed as she told Cleve she would.

'I never dreamed, Lord, that he might not know You. Please show him, Father. He's searching. Please let his search end in You.'

Thirty-One

JEFF RAN HIS hand over his jaw and leaned closer to the mirror. He didn't have a heavy beard, but he did have to shave every day, and as usual he missed a spot on his chin. A moment later he wiped the remaining lather from his face and went upstairs to dress for church.

He was buttoning his shirt when he thought of Sylvia again. During his quiet time that morning, when he had read his Bible, she kept coming to mind.

After Jeff was injured he had missed three Sundays in a row. When he finally returned he noticed that Sylvia was not there. He looked for her the next week, and when he didn't see her he went to the Boggs'.

Sandra told him that Sylvia had gone to Ukiah to visit an elderly aunt. She didn't know how long she would be away, but when Sandra wrote, she told Jeff, she would mention his visit.

That had been weeks ago. Jeff hadn't given much thought to Sylvia until this morning. He couldn't get the thought out of his head that she might be hurting in some way, so he prayed very specifically for her.

With all of this in mind Jeff was not at all surprised to see Sylvia in church. She was quite a way away from him, but even from a distance he could she was very thin. He determined to talk to her immediately after the service, but when Pastor Keller dismissed the congregation she was nowhere to be seen.

Jeff decided to go and see her right away, but then he remembered that the Bradfords and Cleve Ramsey were coming to lunch. He would have to wait to see Sylvia.

"Of course the Taylors won't mind, Cleve," Bobbie told the man standing before her. "And I don't mind waiting for you."

"No, Robbie, you don't need to. Just tell me how to get to the Taylors' and I'll walk over when I'm done."

"Hi," Jeff said as he approached, not realizing until he was on top of the debating couple that his timing was lousy.

"Hi, Jeff," Bobbie said quietly.

"Hello, Jeff," Cleve greeted him in relief. "I was wondering, Jeff, if your family would be upset with me if I stayed for awhile and talked with Pastor Keller. I don't want to be rude, but if you could just give me directions to your place, then I'll walk over as soon as I'm done."

"That's fine, Cleve," Jeff said, instantly sizing up the situation from the distraught looks of the people before him. "In fact, we have enough transportation to leave you a wagon." Jeff went on to explain how to get to the farm, and then Cleve said goodbye and headed back into the church. Bobbie would have followed, but Jeff caught her hand.

"I'm not sure exactly what's going on here, Bobbie, but if he doesn't want you to stay, you need to respect that."

"I know, it's just that—" Bobbie hesitated.

"Just what?" Jeff wanted to know, but Bobbie couldn't explain; she was too upset.

"Come on," Jeff said as he took her arm. He decided, for the moment, not to push her. "Let's find my dad and tell him Cleve needs a wagon."

Bobbie accompanied him reluctantly. She knew she shouldn't follow Cleve, but she felt so responsible for the devastated look on his face that she didn't want to leave him alone.

"Do you want to tell me what's going on?" Jeff's voice came through to Bobbie where they stood by the wagon waiting for their folks. She looked ready to cry, and Jeff thought he might be able to help if he knew the situation.

"Oh Jeff!" Tears filled Bobbie's eyes and she felt like all she did lately was bawl. "Cleve told me last night that he's not sure he's saved, and when Pastor Keller talked about Lazarus and the rich man this morning in Luke 16, well, I could just see that he was really shaken."

Jeff's face clouded with concern, and he put his hands on Bobbie's shoulders. "Don't you see what a good sign this is, Bobbie? You know how gentle Pastor Keller is. He'll know how to answer Cleve, and we'll pray until we see Cleve that he'll know before he leaves the church where he'll spend eternity."

"Thanks, Jeff." Bobbie's throat was again clogged with tears. Jeff gave her a hug just before they were joined by Jake Bradford, allowing Jeff to explain the situation about Cleve.

"I've kept you from your dinner."

Pastor Keller grinned at the young man across from him. "I find I'm not the least bit hungry, Cleve."

Cleve returned the smile. He wasn't buoyant and he wasn't upset; he had peace for the first time he could ever recall. He had fallen asleep the night before without really facing what Bobbie had said, only to be confronted head-on by Pastor Keller's sermon the next morning.

Pastor and Cleve talked for another 20 minutes and Cleve left with some key passages of Scripture to study in the days to come. He was partway to the Taylors' when he stopped the wagon and opened his Bible once again to John 3:16.

It had been there all the time; he could even recite it by memory. But not until this morning, when he looked into the kind eyes of Bobbie's pastor and heard him say the verse, did he really understand that it applied to him.

Sitting on the road with his foot on the horse's reins, Cleve read aloud: "For God so loved the world that he gave his only begotten Son, that whosoever believeth in him should not perish, but have everlasting life."

Cleve held the Bible against his chest. This verse was for him. He wanted everlasting life, and all he had needed to do was believe on the Lord Jesus Christ.

It had been rather simple, really. Pastor Keller had said a short prayer, something about confessing your sins to God and acknowledging that you needed His Son as Savior. Cleve had repeated the words after him, words that were from his heart.

"I always tell people," Pastor had said, "that if they *really* meant what they prayed, then they are now a child of God, but I don't think I need to say that to you, Cleve. There's something in your eyes that tells me this is genuine."

"I don't feel much different," the younger man had confided.

"Some people don't, but I assure you it's real. The Bible says to believe, and you do. Since the Bible is the Word of God, then that's all the assurance we need."

Bobbie had been watching out the window for Cleve almost from the time she had arrived at the Taylors'. She had declined dinner, telling her hostess that she would eat with Cleve when he came. So when he finally pulled into the yard Bobbie was there to meet him.

"Are you all right?" was her first question after Cleve's feet hit the ground.

"I'm fine, Robbie," Cleve told her calmly. "I'm better than I've ever been in my life."

Bobbie looked at him for a moment. "You're sure now, aren't you?"

"Yes, I'm sure," he said with quiet conviction, "quite sure."

The couple embraced, and when Bobbie stepped back she saw tears in Cleve's eyes. It had been such a painful time, one of uncertainty and hard decisions. But she would do it all over again, she told herself, if only to see Cleve Ramsey's face when he said, "Yes, I'm sure, quite sure."

Thirty-Two

SYLVIA WEBER WAS in a state of mourning. No one in the family had died, but her grief was just as great as if someone had.

After Sylvia had left Jeff at the Bradfords' those weeks ago, she had gone back to her sister's house, repeatedly telling herself she was going to control her temper for good this time. It was evident that for years all her thoughts had been of herself. What was further evident was that it had to stop.

As Sylvia rode home that day, her prayers were altered for the first time. Instead of mindlessly naming everything she wanted to, she asked God to help her change. She was certain that everything was going to be completely under control from then on, but Sandra met her at the door with a letter.

"I've heard from Aunt Velvet. Her letter says you're welcome to stay with her."

"Aunt Velvet?" Sylvia had asked in genuine confusion.

"That's right. I wrote to her and asked if you could come and see her for a few months. It's either that or back home to Mom and Dad. Carl and I need a break."

Sylvia's lovely ideals about her temper evaporated, and she exploded at her sister. Even though Sandra looked guilty, she remained steadfast.

Sylvia had cried, even pleaded, but her older sister said it was time. Sylvia had left, but not in good humor. In fact she had vowed never to speak to her sister again, and Carl and Sandra were met with a stony silence right up to the time Sylvia boarded the stage.

Sandra, terribly guilt-ridden, had written to her the very day she left and every few days in the coming weeks. Sylvia, however, didn't reply. Worried that something had happened to her spoiled sister, Sandra finally received a letter from Sylvia almost a month after her departure.

She had said little, but Sandra began to sense a change in her. What Sandra didn't know was that Sylvia had met an older version of herself: Aunt Velvet. It was enough to send Sylvia into a near state of shock.

Sylvia had never met her Aunt Velvet, and never really believed all the stories she had heard about her. But they were all too true. The older woman had never married, although she must have been a beauty in her day, and Sylvia quickly found out why: There was no living with her. Not a minute passed when she didn't insist on having something her own way.

If it wasn't a fit about Sylvia not taking the teacup with the chip in it, it was the silent treatment because her niece had dared to disagree with her over some trivial matter.

Aunt Velvet had little money, but she tried to live like a queen. She owed people all over town, and Sylvia was mortified when the shop-keepers in town would look at her lovely clothes and pull out an invoice from behind the counter. "Can you pay your aunt's bill?"

Sylvia heard the words so many times that she dreamt about them. In short, her aunt was held in contempt by the community, and to be associated with her was far and away the most humiliating thing Sylvia had ever experienced.

That Sylvia was headed in the same direction occurred to her one morning before her aunt arose. Standing in the living room of Velvet's ramshackle house, Sylvia looked at the possessions of a woman who never cared about anyone but herself.

On every wall there was a mirror, sometimes two. Keepsakes from days gone by lined the shelves, little mementos that Aunt Velvet must have received from the men who had courted and tried to woo her.

Tears streamed down Sylvia's face when she thought of her bed-room at Sandra's home. On the dresser was a dried-up flower that Jeff had given her months ago, and beside it was a torn page that had fallen from his Bible one day in church. Sylvia had taken it without telling him for a keepsake, and now felt ashamed.

That day Sylvia wrote and asked Sandra if she could come back. Sandra had not immediately acquiesced, and Sylvia had been misera-ble. Sylvia asked in every letter to Sandra when she could return.

Finally a letter arrived telling Sylvia she would be welcome. She had packed her things and left that very day.

Sylvia still had Sandra's letter that told of Jeff's visit, but she didn't hold out any hope for the future. Her return to Santa Rosa was not to see Jeff, although she would love to talk with him. No, her return to Santa Rosa was to put some space between her and Aunt Velvet so she could mourn in private—mourn for the 20-plus years spent living for herself and accomplishing nothing for God and in reality nothing for herself.

Sylvia stayed away from church the first Sunday back, feeling that she still needed some time to think. On the Sunday she did attend, it caused her almost a physical pain to see Jeff talking so easily with Bobbie Bradford, but it didn't make her angry.

Several people came right out and asked Sylvia if she had been ill, making her uncomfortably aware of how thin she had become. Her pride came to the fore over this matter, and she didn't stay after church because she didn't want Jeff to see her.

Surprisingly enough, though, she was not at all upset when Jeff came to the house that night. In fact, she was so glad to see him she had to swallow hard against the lump in her throat.

"Hello, Jeff."

"Hello, yourself. Welcome back."

"Thanks."

Sylvia motioned him to a seat in the living room and sat across from him.

"I was all ready to ask how you were doing, but I think I can see you're okay." The words were said kindly, and Sylvia realized Jeff was looking at her eyes, and not the way her dress hung on her frame.

"I am doing okay. How about yourself?"

"I'm fine. How was your visit with your aunt?"

"Interesting," Sylvia said, and then smiled. Jeff smiled back and wondered at the emotional change in her.

To look at her one would think she had been quite ill, but her eyes belied the frail look of her body. Those big sapphire-blue orbs looked out with a guileless serenity that Jeff had never seen there before.

They talked for over an hour, and as Jeff was ready to leave, something compelled him to ask Sylvia out.

"Maybe we could go to supper sometime."

"Oh, I'd like that, Jeff," Sylvia answered, her eyes shining with pleasure.

"Great! How's Thursday night?"

"Thursday is fine."

"Okay, I'll stop by about 6:30. See you then."

"Good night, Jeff." Sylvia stood at the front door and watched until he was out of sight. She begged God to help her keep her heart in check. But Jeff Taylor was a wonderful man and Sylvia had always been a little bit in love with him. She wasn't sure it was possible to see him socially and not fall for him all over again.

Sylvia recognized the fact that there weren't many men who would still be friendly with her after the way she had acted. In fact, she meant to apologize about that. Thursday night, she told herself, as she went into the kitchen to tell Sandra she had a date.

Thirty-Three

THE WEEK FLEW by and Cleve could hardly believe he was leaving town the next day. He had a wonderful time with Bobbie, and praised God for her spiritual influence and the opportunity to come and see her.

Cleve had gone every day to the shipping office to eat lunch with Bobbie and the Taylor sons, and every day he wondered the same thing: How long would it be before Jeff and Bobbie knew they were in love?

Strangely enough, he was not jealous, but to him the way they cared for each other would have been obvious to a blind man: their specific smiles for each other with which no one else was gifted. Private jokes, although shared with everyone, nevertheless singled them out as something special.

Their last lunch together was at the hotel on Thursday, before Cleve would be taking the morning stage home. Bobbie announced she would treat.

"Have you fallen into a large sum of money?" Jeff wanted to know.

"It's impolite," Bobbie informed him with her nose in the air, "to ask a lady about her age, weight, or bank account." Bobbie said this with the snootiest voice she could muster.

"Is that right?"

"Yes, that's right, and anyone who's anyone would certainly know that."

"Well, I know your age and I would guess that your weight is somewhere in the neighborhood of a hundred pounds soaking wet, but your bank account, now that's a mystery." Jeff wagged his finger under her nose and tried to look stern.

"Get that finger any closer and I'll bite it," she promised him.

Cleve could only shake his head. They played around like sweethearts. Even the fact that Jeff had a date with another woman that night couldn't change Cleve's mind. Too many times he had seen Jeff drop his arm protectively around Bobbie's shoulders, and even kiss her cheek or forehead. Brothers and sisters wouldn't have acted this way.

Cleve knew that Bobbie considered Jeff a friend, and vice versa, but Cleve believed these two were on the threshold of something far more intimate. He said as much to Mrs. Taylor the night before he left town.

"Yes, Cleve, I have noticed that they have a very close relationship. Jeff is going camping with Jake and the kids the weekend after this, and something tells me things might come to a boil," Maryanne shrugged noncommittally. "But then I've been wrong before."

"Honestly, Cleve, this has been some kind of a miracle—I mean your coming here and talking with Pastor Keller."

"Yeah," he agreed with a smile.

Every evening Bobbie and Cleve had spent time in the Word. Bible lessons that had been no more than stories to Cleve now had personal application. The look of wonder, and often conviction, that Bobbie saw on his face was at once joyful and sobering.

"I'll be praying for you, Cleveland."

"And I'll be praying for you." They hugged each other, and Cleve told her how excited he was to go home and tell Jasper and Joanne of his salvation.

"Give them my love."

Jeff and Gil came from the shipping office just as the stage arrived, and all the men shook hands. Jeff's arm dropped around Bobbie's shoulders in a familiar fashion and that was the last sight Cleve had of Bobbie as the stage pulled out of town.

"How long, Lord?" Cleve said inside the empty stage. "How long before they discover their true feelings for each other?"

Thirty-Four

THINGS DID NOT "come to a boil," as Maryanne had predicted, but Jeff did find out in a hurry that what he had always suspected was true: Going camping with the Bradfords was going to be fun!

Marcail shared his feelings and was in the shipping office every day to question Bobbie.

"Bobbie, did you get my bedroll all set?"

"I sure did. We're going to sleep in the back of the wagon and we'll share the blankets."

"How about Jeff's?"

"Good question, how about Jeff's?" Jeff asked as he joined the ladies at the desk. He was equally as excited and did nothing to hide it.

"We've got you all set too," Bobbie told him with an indulgent smile that might not have been as well-received if he hadn't been so enthusiastic about this outdoor excursion.

"Now let me get this straight," Jeff questioned her for at least the tenth time. "We leave Friday at about 5:00 and we have an hour, maybe an hour-and-a-half, before we reach the place where we camp."

"Right." Bobbie couldn't hide her smile. He was so much fun to watch. Of course she remembered acting the same way when her father had first taken her and Troy. They must have driven him nuts with their nonstop questions and chatter. Jeff and Marcail were almost as bad.

Everyone planned to meet at the Bradfords', with the exception of Sean, who usually worked until 6:00 at the livery. Joey Parker came with Kaitlin and Rigg to see Marcail off, and Bobbie thought he was the sweetest little boy she had ever encountered. But her attention didn't linger on Joey for very long as she watched Kate, thinking that she looked tired and uncomfortable.

Bobbie's eyes misted just a bit when Rigg helped her down from the wagon with extreme care, but then she felt like giggling at the way Kate waddled, her stomach going before her like the prow of a ship. Kate stopped in front of Bobbie and the younger woman couldn't hide her grin.

"I walk like a duck, don't I?"

Bobbie's hand covered her mouth, but her eyes told Kate she was about to laugh. "I'm sorry, Kaitlin."

Kate smiled. "Don't apologize. You can't do anything that Rigg hasn't done already, including quack like a duck when he walks behind me."

"He really does that?"

"Well, he did. But one day I burst into tears and he stopped." Kate gave a mighty sigh. "A man thinks he knows the woman he's married, but then she gets pregnant and cries for no reason, or craves fried chicken at three in the morning. And the heat—it's enough to drive me crazy!"

"This isn't a very hot summer."

"It is if you're pregnant," Kate assured her.

Bobbie nodded, remembering that Alice had said something about that as well.

"We're all set," Jake called from his place beside the wagon.

Bobbie watched Marcail hug her sister. "You listen and obey Marc," Kate told her. "Stay close to the others so they don't lose you."

"I will." Marcail was squirming with excitement, making Kate laugh. Rigg snatched her close for an instant when it looked like she had forgotten to hug him, and they all watched as she scrambled into the back of the wagon.

Jeff was talking with Maryanne as Bobbie climbed aboard, and she heard part of their conversation.

"I just assumed that the whole family went."

"I've never cared for camping and I'm also a person who loves solitude, so I don't mind having the house to myself for an entire weekend."

She grinned at Jeff before moving to kiss her son and daughter goodbye, and then she went to her husband. Jake wrapped her in his arms and they kissed, unembarrassed, for a long time. He whispered something in Maryanne's ear that made her smile and then took his seat and picked up the reins.

They were waved out of the yard with smiles and laughter, and when Bobbie turned back to settle in for the ride, she found both Jeff and Marcail staring at her from their places nearby in the back of the wagon.

"What?" Bobbie asked with a raised brow.

"Nothing." Jeff answered as they both kept smiling.

Bobbie shook her head and thanked the Lord for these good friends. She also prayed that this weekend would be all that they hoped it would be.

One hour and twenty minutes later Jake brought the wagon to a stop under a huge oak tree. The creek was in plain view some 30 feet away, and the sound it made as it tripped lightly over the rock-filled bed was immediately comforting to Bobbie.

Jake and Troy went to work setting up camp, and Jeff also pitched in, doing with quiet efficiency whatever he was instructed. Bobbie and Marcail had disappeared somewhere and Jeff figured they were collecting firewood.

Camp was swiftly put into shape, with bedrolls, fishing tackle, provisions box, and rain ponchos all unloaded. They were stacked neatly under the wagon or next to the huge logs that were laid out in a triangle around the spot where the fire would be built.

It was during the building of the fire that Jeff became confused. Troy appeared at his side with an armful of logs.

"Where are Bobbie and Marc?"

"Oh, they probably went to change," Troy told him nonchalantly, and even though Jeff was unsure what he meant, he didn't need to ask because the girls materialized at that moment, both wearing pants.

Troy headed back into the surrounding woods and Jeff was left staring at the girls as they put their other clothing under the wagon seat. Jake's voice came low to his ears from where he had come close with his own armload of wood.

"I've been getting jeans for Bob to wear camping since she was a little girl," Jake began, having seen the look on the younger man's face. "She's always very discreet about it and Bobbie asked Kaitlin's permission before she found some for Marcail. But, Jeff," Jake stopped until he was sure he had his attention, "if you're offended, Bobbie can go and change right now."

Jeff's gaze swung once again to the girls. Bobbie's pants were very baggy, and in fact he could only see them from the knees down because of the oversized man's shirt she was wearing. Marcail's shirt stopped just below her hips, and she would have looked like a boy standing there if it weren't for the fat black braid that hung down her back.

"No, she doesn't need to change, although I appreciate your giving me a moment to get used to the idea."

Jake's look was understanding as he asked Jeff to build the fire. Thinking he had put a strain on the evening, Jeff was grateful for something to do.

Bobbie and Marcail were as ladylike as always, and supper was a mixture of delicious food and laughter. They used the provisions from home for that meal, but Troy and Jake set out snares for the meals the following day. Bobbie planned to be up early to do some fishing. Jeff told himself he would join her, but she and Troy left camp so quietly that Jeff and Marcail slept through it.

Brother and sister sat side-by-side on the creek bank and talked in low tones.

"I thought Carla was going to come this weekend," Bobbie commented just as she felt a tug on her line. Troy didn't answer for a minute because his mind was still working on the fact that Bobbie hadn't lost her touch. She was one of the best anglers he knew.

"It's her dad's birthday and they're having a special dinner tonight."

"Why didn't you stay?"

Troy chuckled softly. "I love Carla, but I'd much rather go camping than attend a birthday party."

Tears flooded Bobbie's eyes when her brother confided that he loved his girlfriend. She turned her face quickly back to the water, but Troy noticed.

"What's the matter?"

"Nothing."

"You like Carla, don't you?"

"Oh Troy, she's wonderful! Please don't mind me."

They were quiet for a moment. Two more fish were snagged, one for each of them, and then Troy spoke quietly.

"I liked Cleve."

"I like him too, Troy, but *like* isn't enough to build a marriage on."

"No, I guess it isn't."

"Are you and Carla going to be married?"

"Yes."

"What are you waiting for?"

"I want to put a little money away."

"How does Carla feel about that?"

"She wants to be married right away. She says she can go to work if we need the money, but I don't want my wife working."

"Oh, I can see why you must feel that way. Your own mother has worked out of the house for years, and you can see how miserable she and Dad are." Bobbie's voice was sarcastic in the extreme, and Troy just stared at her.

"And of course," she went on relentlessly, "it's much easier to say goodbye to your future wife on her parents' front porch than in the privacy of your own home where you can hold her all you want."

"Well, I guess you told me," Troy muttered good-naturedly, but Bobbie could see her words had affected him. They were quiet again while Bobbie brought in three more fish in quick succession.

"How do you do that?" Troy asked in some exasperation, but she only laughed. They talked on in close companionship for another few minutes before they were joined by Jeff.

He was unshaven and a little fuzzy around the edges. Bobbie didn't think she had ever seen him look so cute.

"Good morning," Troy greeted him.

"Hi." His voice was gravelly from lack of use.

Bobbie smiled. "How did you sleep?"

"It took me awhile to fall asleep, but once I went out, it was for the night." Jeff rubbed his back and Bobbie asked what was wrong.

"I think I missed one of the rocks under my bedroll, and it left a permanent dent in my back."

Troy and Bobbie laughed without compassion. They laughed again a few minutes later when Jeff looked in the creel and told Troy he was impressed with his fishing ability.

"What did I say?" he asked after the laughter died down.

"Tell him, Bobbie," Troy prompted her.

Strangely enough, Bobbie was a little embarrassed. When she didn't say anything, Jeff sat down beside her and took the pole from her hands.

"You really should have brought Gil along. He's the best fisherman in the family. But then I'm not sure he could compete with you, Bobbie, since I'm sure you must be the one who caught most of those fish."

Thinking that Jeff never took long to catch on, Bobbie didn't look at him. She was still angry with herself for the way her face heated up, and knowing that he was staring at her profile just caused her face to flush all over again.

"I'll take these back," Troy said after a moment. "When you catch more you can string them." Bobbie and Jeff were silent as they listened to the sound of Troy's footsteps. Bobbie glanced over at Jeff to find him still staring at her. She returned the look and wondered what he was thinking. She didn't wait long to find out.

Thirty-Five

"You WERE EMBARRASSED in front of me just now. I want to know why." Jeff's voice was undemanding, but Bobbie knew he would sit right where he was until he had an answer.

"Come on, Bobbie," he coaxed after a moment. "There isn't anything you can't tell me."

"It's just my pride, Jeff," she admitted quietly.

"I don't understand."

Bobbie ran a self-conscious hand through her hair, wishing she had taken a comb to it. "It doesn't matter that our friendship isn't a romantic one, Jeff; no girl likes to be caught with her hair uncombed, wearing denim pants, and catching fish so well that she's mistaken for a man." Bobbie shrugged apologetically. "Like I said, Jeff, it's just my pride."

Jeff stared at her incredulously. *Was she serious?* It took him a moment to see that she was. "I don't think there's anything you could do, Bobbie," Jeff replied softly, "that would cause you to be mistaken for a man."

It was Bobbie's turn to stare. Jeff returned her scrutiny, their eyes meeting with questions and a hesitancy that had never been present in their relationship before.

Bobbie watched as Jeff's eyes dropped to her mouth, and her throat went dry. With his free hand he reached out to touch the corner of her mouth with a single finger, just brushing it with a single caress. He shook his head slowly as he spoke in a whisper.

"Maybe the most adorable thing in Santa Rosa, but definitely *not* a man."

Bobbie didn't know what to say. She turned her head back to the water and Jeff did the same.

"I don't seem to be doing very well with this pole. Maybe I'd better give it back to you."

Bobbie took the offer for what it was, a chance to return the conversation to comfortable ground. They fished for another 20 minutes and then headed back to camp for breakfast with three more fish.

Once again Jeff believed the rest of the weekend would be awkward, but all was fine. The day passed in friendship and laughter and both Jeff and Bobbie were relieved that the uncomfortable moment on the creek bank had passed without harm.

As the sun sank lower in the afternoon sky, Bobbie told Marcail to gather her things for their Saturday night bath. Jake accompanied the girls and sat well out of sight with his gun, but close enough to assist if they should call.

He had brought his Bible along, but the laughter and splashes he heard made him put his head back against the rock where he had sat down, and smile. Bobbie was always so much fun, he mused. Marcail must have thought so too, since her laughter seemed to be nonstop.

Not until this weekend did Jake notice the way Bobbie and Jeff treated each other. Maryanne had mentioned her observations to him, but he thought little of it. Jake had the distinct impression that something wasn't quite right when they returned from fishing, but the rest of the day went on in such a normal fashion that Jake doubted his own thoughts.

In fact, he put the whole thing out of his mind until he came back with the girls. He had never given any thought to it before, but a woman with wet hair needed to have privacy. At least Jake began to think so as he noticed Jeff watching Bobbie attentively.

Since Bobbie's hair was short and curly she didn't do much to it until it was dry, and then all she did was fluff the waves up to make them a little fuller. With her hair in close damp curls all around her head, she looked like she had just come from her bath, which she had, and that seemed very personal to Jake.

He watched his daughter and Jeff closely for a time, but there was nothing intimate about their actions. They shared light banter and their legs were nearly touching as Marcail sat in Jeff's lap so Bobbie could brush her hair.

Jake could make no sense of it. He and Maryanne hadn't acted that way until after they were married. Jake entertained thoughts of speaking to Jeff, but prayed instead. The Lord gave him an unexpected peace and he let the matter drop in his mind.

Bobbie prayed for just such a peace several hours later. Supper was over and it was quite dark. Everyone was in his bedroll. Marcail was sound asleep beside her, but slumber simply would not come for Bobbie. Replaying the scene from the creek again and again in her mind, the words of a friend from church spoken weeks before haunted her.

"Bobbie, if you're not going to marry Jeffrey Taylor, let him go so one of us can."

Bobbie had laughed and made some remark that made the whole group of girls roar, but Bobbie didn't feel like laughing now. Earlier in the afternoon Bobbie and Jeff had talked about his date with Sylvia.

"We had fun," Jeff had told her. "Sylvia has changed lately, and we talked about things we've never discussed before. We have another date Monday night."

Bobbie had been glad for him. She knew from Jeff's own admission how badly he felt about not seeing her, but they both had known it was for the best. The only person who hadn't known was Sylvia. Jeff and Bobbie had both prayed she would come to a peace about that. Now it seemed Sylvia had.

It also seemed that Jeff and Sylvia were going to be seeing each other again, and in Bobbie's mind that could only mean matrimony. But if that were the case, then why had Jeff talked to her and touched her as though she were someone special? Not just special, but *special*?

This and many other questions kept Bobbie awake far into the night. The next morning she was so sleepy that she figured it must have been the wee morning hours before sleep finally claimed her.

She was by nature a morning person, but today all she did for the first half-hour was sit and stare into her coffee cup. She heard the teasing remarks from her family and Jeff, but all she could do was smile.

"Are you all right?" The question came from her father after Troy and Jeff went to the creek to clean up.

"Just tired."

"I heard you tossing in the wagon for quite awhile."

"I hope I didn't keep you awake."

"No. You want to talk?"

Bobbie's voice dropped as she answered. "Not when we might be interrupted, but thanks."

Jake followed his daughter's gaze and they both watched Marcail approach. She was having the time of her young life.

"Do we really have to go back today, Bobbie?" were the first words from her mouth.

"I'm afraid so, Marcail." Jake answered for Bobbie, who was still pretty fuzzy around the edges.

"I take it you've had fun," Bobbie finally said.

Marcail didn't answer, but smiled at Bobbie and Jake with the shy smile which came over her face when she was at a loss for words.

Troy and Jeff made a tremendous amount of noise coming back into camp. Troy's hair was completely wet and both men were laughing. When Troy stopped chuckling he explained that Jeff had bumped him as he knelt on the bank, and he had gone face-first into the water. His hands had stopped the rest of his body from going in, but the whole incident had been such a surprise that he had been sure he was about to drown.

Jeff apologized twice during a breakfast of pancakes, but he was laughing too hard to be taken seriously. After the dishes were done the campers sat on the logs while Jake read from the Scriptures.

"This is James, chapter one, verses two through six. 'My brethren, count it all joy when ye fall into diverse temptations, knowing this, that the trying of your faith worketh patience. But let patience have her perfect work, that ye may be perfect and entire, wanting nothing. If any of you lack wisdom, let him ask of God, who giveth to all men liberally and upbraideth not, and it shall be given him. But let him ask in faith, nothing wavering. For he that wavereth is like a wave of the sea driven with the wind and tossed.' "

They had a time of prayer after the Bible was closed, with Jake opening and Troy closing. Jeff now understood what Bobbie meant when she said they had their own service when they slept too late at home, and why she said she always enjoyed it.

With plans to be back home for lunch, they began to break camp a short time later. Jeff, Bobbie, and Marcail were once again in the back, and Bobbie asked the youngest camper how she enjoyed the weekend.

"When can we come again?"

Jeff laughed. "I guess that answers your question."

"Did you have fun, Jeff?" Marcail wanted to know.

"Oh yes," Jeff said with conviction. "Everything was great. It was also enlightening, and that was something I hadn't planned on."

Jeff said these last words as if he were alone, and even though neither Bobbie nor Marcail questioned him, Bobbie thought about it all the way home.

Thirty-Six

BOBBIE WAS GETTING ready to go to lunch on Monday when Carla Johnson walked into the shipping office.

"Hi, Carla."

"Hi, Bobbie, are you by any chance free for lunch?"

"I was just getting ready to leave. Let me check with Bill to see if he's ready to let me go."

Carla waited while Bobbie knocked on Bill's door and was given permission to leave.

"Where shall we go?" Bobbie wanted to know.

"To the hotel."

"The hotel? What's the occasion?"

Carla waited until they were a few steps up the street. "The occasion is that Troy came over last night and told me he wants to be married right away. When I asked how come the change of heart, he said it was because of something you said."

Bobbie stopped in her tracks and stared at Carla. The next instant they were hugging and Bobbie was fighting tears. Once at the hotel Carla found them a table and they talked nonstop for the next hour.

"Can you please tell me what you said to Troy this weekend?"

Bobbie shrugged. "It wasn't much. I asked him if you two were going to be married and when he said yes, I asked what he was waiting for. To put it simply, I criticized him for his reasons. I could see it made him think."

Carla sighed. "Thanks, Bobbie. I've wanted to bring up the subject of my working for a long time, but I felt that might be pushing him. Until last night, I wasn't *really* sure he wanted to marry me because he always used that reason. I just never thought it had any validity."

"So what are your plans now?"

"First of all, your parents are coming to supper tomorrow night, and the six of us—that includes my folks—are going to talk. Will you feel bad, Bobbie, because you're not there?"

"Just awful," Bobbie said with a smile. "I'll pout all evening. Now tell me more!"

"We'd like to be married right away, say in a month, with just a quiet ceremony. Then, after we've been away for a few days on a honeymoon trip, we'd like to come home, get settled in our house, and have a reception with the church family."

"I think that sounds wonderful! Where will you live?"

"That's one of the items we need to discuss with our folks. With Troy working on this side of town, it would be nice to find a place close by."

Lunch had been served to the ladies, but they had barely taken notice. Bobbie commented that she better eat or she would go back to work hungry. Carla continued to tell her future sister-in-law of her plans, and long before they were done Bobbie had to go back the shipping office, wishing as she did that she had time to find Troy and hug him.

Bobbie was almost as dreamy as Carla had been at lunch when she went back to work. But preoccupied as she was, she did not fail to notice how distracted Jeff seemed. He was polite, but it was clear that something weighed on his mind.

Bobbie was not given an opportunity to question him, but when Sylvia came in at closing time Jeff instantly perked up. Bobbie was relieved to witness such a scene, since it gave her peace of mind over his odd behavior. Jeff excused himself for a moment to finish some business.

"Hello, Bobbie," Sylvia greeted her quietly from where she waited by the door. Bobbie finally recalled Jeff saying he had a date with Sylvia.

"Hi, Sylvia. Come over, sit down."

Sylvia took one of the chairs by the desk, and even though Bobbie had things to do, she set her pencil aside and smiled at the stunning blonde.

"How was your weekend?" Sylvia wanted to know.

"It was great. The weather was perfect and I know that Marcail had the time of her life. How were things here in town?"

"Pretty quiet, I think, although church was full." Sylvia hesitated a moment and then rushed on. "Bobbie, there's something I need to say to you."

Bobbie smiled expectantly and waited.

"I've never apologized to you for the way I acted at the lagoon, but I'm sorry. I'm also sorry that it's taken me this long to tell you." Sylvia's face was flushed and Bobbie realized how difficult it must have been for Sylvia to hold that in all these years.

"Thank you, Sylvia," Bobbie said simply and gave Sylvia a smile of such serenity that her fears of rejection drained away in an instant.

The women talked until Jeff returned. Sylvia told Bobbie about Pastor's sermon and Bobbie shared with Sylvia about her niece and nephew. Their chatter was random, and how they chose those subjects was not clear. What *was* clear was there was no more constraint between them. They laughed and talked in a normal way, with none of the awkwardness that had been the hallmark of their previous conversations.

When Jeff finally came from the office to claim Sylvia, Bobbie bid her goodbye, feeling like she had a new friend. On the other hand, her old friend Jeff was still perplexed about something. She had seen it in his face when he had said goodbye to her. Bobbie began praying as soon as she went back to her work that God would open a door for them to talk.

Bobbie would have been surprised to know that Sylvia was praying for that very thing as she sat with Jeff in the hotel. Jeff was absorbed in some private distraction, and Sylvia, although not angry, was quite determined to find out if she was the cause.

"How was work?"

"Fine." Jeff told her.

"And your weekend?"

"Great," Jeff said softly, and warning bells went off in Sylvia's mind.

"You didn't say that very enthusiastically."

"Didn't I?" Jeff was truly surprised. He then went on to describe every detail of the camping experience, and Sylvia couldn't help but wonder if Jeff knew how his eyes softened just a bit whenever he mentioned Bobbie's name. In fact he made it sound like an endearment.

Their supper together was relaxed, but when Jeff saw Sylvia home she was quiet. Jeff, who was equally silent, didn't seem to notice. Once at the house Jeff suddenly seemed to realize how preoccupied he had been.

"I'm sorry, Sylvia, I don't seem to be very good company tonight."

"It's not happening for you, is it, Jeff?"

It took him a moment to understand Sylvia as she gazed at him with her heart in her eyes. A look of profound remorse passed over Jeff's features and Sylvia did her best to smile.

"It's all right, Jeff. You can't force something you don't feel."

"I do care for you, Sylvia."

"I know you do," she said with soft regret. "I also know that there's someone who already holds your heart, and I wonder when you're going to open your eyes and see that."

Without giving Jeff a chance to speak, Sylvia went up on tiptoes to kiss his cheek.

"Goodbye, Jeff."

Jeff didn't move or reply even after Sylvia went into her sister's house and shut the door. He stood motionless for the space of a few heartbeats.

"My eyes are open, Sylvia." Jeff's voice was hushed as he walked away from the house. "But hers aren't, and I don't know what to do about that."

Sylvia leaned against the closed door and shut her eyes tightly. 'It's time for me to go home.'

"Sylvia, is that you already?"

"It's me."

"How was your date?" Sandra asked kindly as Sylvia joined her in the empty living room.

"It was fine." Sylvia's voice was quiet. "But I won't be seeing Jeff again."

Sandra was silent as she digested this new information. A few months ago she would have scathingly asked what Sylvia had done this time to drive Jeff away. But Sylvia's sudden maturity made this question unnecessary.

"Are you all right?" the older woman finally asked.

"I will be. I think I should tell you now that I've decided to go home in a few weeks."

"So soon?" The question alone spoke volumes as to the changes Sandra and Carl had seen in Sylvia since she returned from Aunt Velvet's.

Sylvia could only nod and the women shared an embrace. It had been a long time coming, but Sylvia Weber was finally growing up.

Thirty-Seven

THE NEXT FOUR weeks were taken up with preparations for Troy's wedding and his moving into the small house that Kaitlin and Marcail had lived in when they first arrived in Santa Rosa. Carla had been ecstatic to find that it was free to rent just two weeks before the date. The church reception was not planned until three weeks after the wedding, so Maryanne and Mrs. Johnson dug into their attics and trunks to find needed household goods.

It was a rather ragtag collection of bedding and kitchen supplies when it was put together, but Troy and Carla only had eyes for each other.

With only the Johnsons, Bradfords, and Pastor Keller in attendance, the ceremony was as simple and quiet as the young couple hoped it would be. The newlyweds were headed a few hours north for their honeymoon.

Troy's absence from the house made it feel empty. Bobbie's heart seemed a little empty too, and even though the void was not directly related to Troy, it did have something to do with seeing him and Carla stand before Pastor Keller and become husband and wife. Bobbie coveted the title of wife.

Unbidden, Jeff's face came to mind, and Bobbie shook her head to dispel the vision. Jeff belonged to Sylvia. He hadn't talked much about his dates with her lately, but Bobbie suspected they were becoming quite serious with the way Jeff seemed to be putting more and more space between himself and Bobbie.

Bobbie longed to talk with him, but knew she couldn't be close friends with a married man, and that it would be easier in the long run to start thinking of Jeff in that light right now.

What Bobbie didn't expect was that her feelings would be stronger than she was, and that the reception, held at one of the large homes where Maryanne worked, would end in humiliation for Bobbie.

"I can't believe Mrs. Walcott let us use her home and garden." It was the fifth time Maryanne had made such a statement, and as before, Jake smiled to himself and kept quiet.

"Do we have everything? Where's Bobbie? What time is it?" Jake was not given a chance to answer any of these questions, and actually he didn't even try.

Maryanne was quiet on the way to Walcotts', but as soon as they arrived she began giving orders like a woman possessed. Jake listened to her for a few minutes before stepping in.

"Mary," he said softly, "everything is going to be fine, and if you don't stop telling Bobbie to be in four places at once, she's going to run away."

Stopped short over her husband's words, Maryanne apologized to her daughter and prayed for calm. Things were a little smoother from that point on, and when the guests began to arrive, everything was in place.

The Walcott mansion was a tall, broad, two-story house with a backyard garden which was the envy of Santa Rosa residents. The kitchen and summer porch at the rear of the house made a garden reception a dream.

Tables and chairs were scattered all over the lush grass and faced the long tables set up outside the kitchen door for the finger foods, cakes, and fruit drinks. Guests could roam about at will or sit next to the flowerbeds, whose riotous colors only enhanced the occasion for which the church family was gathered.

Carla was radiant and Troy's smile nearly stretched off his face as he stood beside his wife. The Johnsons mingled with Jake and Maryanne while Bobbie ran back and forth from the kitchen to the beautiful garden all afternoon.

By the time the guests began to leave, the gift table was laden and the food tables were nearly bare. Cleanup was a momentous task and Bobbie was again involved. She had just pushed a wheeled cart into a rather secluded dining room where Mrs. Walcott kept her large platters, in the bottom drawer of a buffet, when she felt her glasses fall from her face.

Quickly reacting this time, she grasped both pieces as they slid down her front. She had been standing for at least five minutes trying to put them together on her own when she heard someone enter the room.

"Your mother told me I might find you in here."

"Oh, hi, Jeff." She now knew his voice so well. "My glasses came apart. I know how to fix them when they break like this, but I just can't get it."

"Here, let me have a go."

Bobbie surrendered the glasses to his capable hands, and as always drew very close to watch him work. Jeff was able to snap them back together, and Bobbie waited while he wiped the lenses before placing them gently back on her face.

He leaned close as he always did when helping her with her spectacles, and even after the lenses were in place he stayed bent over her, their noses nearly touching.

Jeff smiled as Bobbie's eyes focused on him. Bobbie smiled back, thinking how much she had missed being close to him. When Jeff did not immediately move away, Bobbie acted without thought. She put one hand, almost a caress, against the side of Jeff's face and pressed her lips to his.

As though completely forgetting that she had no right to do such a thing, Bobbie did not immediately check herself and step away, making the moment she *did* realize she was actually kissing Jeff the most embarrassing thing to ever happen to her.

Jeff's gaze was very tender as Bobbie broke the kiss and took a hasty step backward, but she didn't notice. With one hand to her throat, she began to stutter.

"Jeff, I'm s-sorry. I c-can't think what c-came over m-me."

"Bobbie, honey—"

"No, Jeff, don't say anything. I'm just so sorry." Bobbie turned away from him then, and when she looked back, there were tears in her eyes. "Sylvia will never forgive me," she whispered.

"Bobbie, please—"

Jeff stopped and didn't follow her when she rushed past him and out of the room. He found himself looking around and thanking God that the room had provided privacy. The last thing they had needed was witnesses. Jeff exited the room determined to find her and clear things up, but she was nowhere to be found.

He went to her house that evening just before supper, but Jake told him that Bobbie had gone to bed exhausted. Jeff determined to pin her down the next day at church, but she avoided him nicely, and when he went to her house on Sunday afternoon, Maryanne said she was at her sister's.

Feeling frustrated, Jeff left telling himself there was always tomorrow. And unless Bobbie had quit her job when he wasn't looking, she would have to face him at the office in the morning.

Thirty-Eight

BOBBIE'S SUNDAY WAS miserable as she walked over half of Santa Rosa. Never had she handled anything so badly as her mistake with Jeff. Running from him was the worst thing she could do, but the blood drained from her face every time she thought of facing him with an apology, or working with him on a daily basis.

It was her thought that life had gotten her into trouble, of that she was positive. Very recently she had imagined herself kissing Jeff on more than one occasion, and when he had bent so close, Sylvia had been the farthest person from her mind. She hadn't even tried to stop herself.

Again Bobbie found herself having to confess how much she had enjoyed it. If only he hadn't fallen for Sylvia. Jeff was sure to marry Sylvia. *If only*, Bobbie thought, and then stopped herself. She would never keep going if her life was a series of *if only's*.

There was no choice about her job—she would have to quit, of course. Fear of running into Jeff kept her from going to see Mr. Taylor that very afternoon. Bobbie tried to push away the pain that returned again and again on her walk.

Maryanne had not lied to Jeff. Before going on a long walk to think and pray, Bobbie had gone to see her sister for a brief visit. In no less pain when she finally returned home, Bobbie had at least told God all she felt, and she knew what must be done.

Her parents had questioned her about being gone so long, but in fear of starting tears that would never stop, Bobbie had not answered.

Neither Jake nor Maryanne had pushed the point, but they watched with concern as Bobbie played with her supper and ate no breakfast the following morning.

"Bobbie," Maryanne stopped her daughter as she was headed out the door for work. "If you're not feeling well, you can stay home."

"I know, Mom, and I know you're wondering what's going on, but I just can't talk about it right now. I hope when I get home tonight I'll be able to explain everything."

Maryanne, feeling she had no choice but to accept her grown daughter's answer, was very concerned. "I'll be praying for you, Bobbie."

Those words were nearly her undoing. How easy it would be to run to the protective arms of her parents! And then Bobbie stopped short. She was done running a long time ago. She squared her shoulders with renewed purpose.

"Thanks, Mom, I appreciate that." Kissing her mother's cheek, Bobbie headed toward the door and called over her shoulder, "I'll see you tonight."

Thirty-Nine

"You SURE KNOW how to avoid a man."

Bobbie started at the sound of Jeff's voice and felt her face flush. Overcome with regret, she didn't say anything for a few moments. A wonderful friendship had been ruined. They would never be comfortable with each other again, and it was all her fault.

That Jeff was extremely glad to see her was totally lost on Bobbie. Drowning in her own hurt, she failed to notice how Jeff's eyes sparkled with tenderness and warmth.

"Bobbie—"

"Please, Jeff, just let me say how—"

"Hello, Jeff; hello, Bobbie." Bobbie was interrupted by May's sudden entrance to the shipping office. She held Marcail's hand, and Bobbie, without delay, forgot her own problems at the sight of the white-faced little girl.

"It seems that Kaitlin chose today to have her baby, and I told Marcail it would be a good idea if she came here for a few hours."

"That's a great idea. Come over and have a chair, Marc." The words were spoken by Jeff, and with his hand on the little girl's shoulder, she was escorted up to Bobbie's desk.

May left quietly and a few minutes later Bill entered the office. Bobbie was speaking with Marcail and didn't hear the exchange between father and son, but when Bill went into his office Jeff suggested that Bobbie and Marcail take a ride with him.

Once in the wagon, Jeff and Bobbie's eyes met over the top of Marcail's head and it was with mutual, unspoken understanding that they decided to put their discussion off and concentrate on their young charge.

Marcail had said little, and as Jeff headed the wagon in the direction of the lagoon, Bobbie asked God to give her the words to comfort and help Marcail.

Kaitlin spat a sentence at Rigg in furious Hawaiian. It was the second time she had said it to him, and for the first time he was glad he couldn't speak the language.

"I can't push anymore, Rigg, I just can't do it," Kate panted after the last hard contraction.

Rigg mopped her brow and kissed her cheek. No one had ever told him it would be like this. No one had ever mentioned that his wife would be in agony for hours and he would be powerless to help.

Rigg had not previously known the meaning of the word "frustration" until Doctor Grade had come, checked on Kaitlin, and left, telling them it would probably be some hours yet. He had told them where he could be found and his manner had been kind, but Rigg, unsatisfied, had followed him to the door.

"Isn't there anything you can do for her?"

"I'm afraid not, Rigg. First babies take time."

Rigg found out in a hurry that those words had been an understatement. It felt to him as though Kate had been in labor for days, and he wasn't even the one in pain.

"Oh no," Kate gasped as another contraction began. Rigg looked at his mother on the other side of the bed to see if she was as worried as he was, but the smile she gave him was one of serene acceptance.

Illumination flooded Rigg's heart as he realized that his mother had gone through this exact process to have him. Kate needed him right now, so there was no time for talk, but when this was all over, and Rigg prayed it would be soon, he told himself he was going to thank Mabel Riggs Taylor for giving him life.

"You were really on a date here?" Marcail asked in childish wonder. "What did you do?"

"Well," Bobbie explained, "the other kids were here as well, and we had a picnic lunch under the trees. Then we sat around and talked. The whole church came later to go boating."

"Can we go boating?"

"Not today, but I think we might be able to arrange something later on," Jeff had answered from the place where he was sitting with his back against a tree. He was amazed at the relaxed way Bobbie talked about the day at the lagoon, without giving any hint of the disastrous events that followed.

He was also amazed how strong his feelings were for her. They were both doing a good job of pretending there was nothing they needed to discuss. Jeff was sure Marcail didn't suspect a thing. She was growing visibly more relaxed by the second, and that fact was directly related to Bobbie's sensitive care of her.

"I think it might be getting close to lunch. Shall we go back to my house to eat?"

"I don't know, Bobbie. Maybe I should go and check on Katie."

"I think it would be best if we didn't go over there right now."

"Why, Bobbie? Why did May take me away? What are they doing to Katie that they don't want me to know?"

Bobbie's arms went around the little girl. "They're not *doing* anything to her Marcail, but it's hard work having a baby, and it's not the best idea to have a lot of people around."

"But there *were* a lot of people around, even Dr. Grade."

"Marc," Bobbie said softly, "Dr. Grade is there to help Katie. He's there to take care of her."

Marcail was certain she was going to return home and have Rigg tell her that Kate was dying, but she didn't mention any of this to Bobbie.

"The people at the house are there for a reason. And even though I'm sure Katie wishes you could be nearby, she also sees that it would be easier if you were elsewhere. It would be the same as if you wanted to go to work at the livery with Sean. He'd like to have your company, but you couldn't really help him with his job, and it would be easier for him if you weren't there.

"Having a baby is work. If Kate is worried about you, then she won't be able to work as well as she needs to."

Some of the tension that had returned to Marcail's face drained away, and they got in the wagon to head for the Bradfords. Jeff was careful not to look in the direction of his brother's place as they rode through town, but he couldn't help but wonder if his sister-in-law was all right. He prayed for all concerned and tried to turn his mind back to the situation at hand.

Sean came out of his chair in the kitchen as though someone had jerked him up on a string. His sister had just let out a bloodcurdling scream, and he waited, his breath held, for some noise to issue from the bedroom.

Black spots dotted his vision a moment later when he heard a baby cry. He sat back down with a thud, hoping he wouldn't faint. A baby! His sister had had a baby!

Forty

SEAN WATCHED MAY emerge from the bedroom, wiping her eyes.

"A girl, a big beautiful girl."

Her words started the young man's own tears. Kate had confided in him one day that most men wanted boys, but that Rigg had wanted a daughter. She had said it was her deepest desire to give him that wish.

"Is Kate all right?" Sean asked hesitantly over the lump in his throat.

"She's fine. Just give them a few minutes and you can go in."

It was less than two minutes before the door was thrown open and Rigg appeared, disheveled but beaming.

"Sean! Get in here and see your niece! Where's Marc?"

"I'll go and find her," May said with more calm than she felt. It was an exhilarating experience to see your first grandchild enter the world, and she was feeling a bit light-headed about it.

Rigg gave his mother an enormous hug before reaching for his brother-in-law. Sean noticed tears in the big man's eyes and fought the return of his own as he stepped softly into the bedroom. He focused on his sister and she gave him a tired smile.

Sean felt his own fatigue when he saw that smile. He hadn't realized how tense he had been, but Kate was all right, he could see that. Everything was going to be fine because Kaitlin was all right.

"Aren't you going to look at her?"

432

"Oh, sorry, Kate," Sean nearly stuttered. He had been so worried about Kate that he forgot about the new little life his sister held in the curve of her arm.

Sean couldn't stop the frown that crossed his face at the first sight of his niece, and Kate chuckled softly.

"She's a funny-looking little thing, isn't she, Sean?"

"Well—" Sean wanted to disagree, but couldn't.

The baby was red and wrinkly and her face looked as if some fierce battle was going on inside of her. Her eyes opened as Sean watched, and she waved one tiny red fist in the air. Sean's heart melted.

"What's her name?" he asked when he could find his voice again.

"We thought we'd let Marcail decide," Rigg said from his place on the opposite side of the bed.

"That's a good idea," Sean said with conviction. He hadn't seen much of his family over the summer, but he knew that Kate's pregnancy had been very hard on his little sister. Marcail's naming the baby was probably just what she needed to help her adjust to the changes that would certainly enter their home in the next few months.

"There will be certain changes."

"What kind of changes?"

"Good ones," Bobbie answered. "You can be a tremendous help to Kaitlin with the baby. In fact the baby will probably think of you as a second mother, since you live in the same house."

Marcail was so pleased with Bobbie's words that she was actually able to eat some lunch. She was just finishing when May knocked on the door.

"I thought I might find you here," May said as she entered the room. "You have a perfect little niece." May gave Marcail a hug after making her announcement, or she might have noticed the worried look that had suddenly captured the little girl's features.

Why doesn't anyone say how Kate is doing? The question tormented Marcail all the way home, but she kept her thoughts to herself and tried not to vomit. Rigg greeted her at the door with a big smile and Marcail took heart. He wouldn't look like that if Kate was in heaven with Mother, would he?

More chance for speculation was cut short when Rigg led her quietly into the bedroom. She told herself not to be sick when she saw Kate's closed eyes, but she didn't know how long she would be able to hold herself together. Marcail stood stock-still about two feet from what she was sure was Kate's dead body and wished she hadn't eaten lunch.

Rigg watched his sister-in-law in silence. Her hands were clenched so tightly that her knuckles were white. Marcail's eyes were fixed on Kate's sleeping face and Rigg wondered if she might faint. She hadn't been anywhere near the basket that held his daughter, and he wished with all his heart he knew what she was thinking.

A few more seconds passed and Kaitlin opened her eyes. Rigg nearly reached for Marcail, since she seemed to go very limp. Kaitlin smiled at her little sister and that was Marcail's undoing. Rivers of silent tears poured down her cheeks and she choked when she tried to speak.

"I thought," Marcail coughed and then took a deep breath, "I thought you were dead."

"Oh Marcail!" Kate was equally choked up as she leaned toward her sister. Marcail was too far from the bed for Kate to reach her, and blinded by her tears, she didn't notice her sister's outstretched arm, so Rigg propelled her forward with a gentle hand. He took a chair by the bed and wiped the tears from his own eyes over Marcail's reaction.

It hadn't occurred to anyone that she might think her sister was dying. Of course it was blindness on their part, because they all knew how tense Marcail became whenever a doctor was called onto the scene. He realized now, as he took a moment to think, that she had almost been sick as she stood and watched Kate.

"Am I hurting you, Katie?"

"No."

Marcail had climbed right onto the bed with her sister and wrapped her arms around her neck. Kate held her protectively and her small body trembled from head to foot. Rigg had just placed a blanket over the top of her when she went very stiff. Marcail half-sat so she could look into her sister's face.

"You had a baby."

"That's right, I did." Kaitlin smiled. She had wondered when Marcail was going to ask.

"Where is she?"

"In the basket right over there."

Marcail left the bed gently and found Rigg smiling at her. She put her hand to her mouth and whispered. "I forgot about the baby for a minute."

"That's all right," Rigg whispered back.

Husband and wife watched as she made her way across the room. "Oh my," was all they heard for some moments.

"What's her name?" Marcail asked without ever taking her eyes from the sleeping infant.

"We were hoping *you* would tell *us*," Rigg answered softly.

Marcail finally turned and looked at Rigg and then her sister. Kate nodded encouragingly and Marcail's little mouth dropped open in surprise.

"You want *me* to name her?"

No one answered Marcail, but Rigg motioned her to the chair he had just vacated and scooped his tiny daughter into his hands. As Kate looked on, Rigg placed her in Marcail's arms.

"You did everything you could to make Kate's pregnancy easier," Rigg said as he helped Marcail hold the baby in the right position. "In fact I think you would have carried the baby yourself if you could have. So we want you to name your niece because we know how much you love her."

Marcail looked with wonder at the tiny person in her arms. She was just perfect. She held her a little closer in one arm and reached with her free hand to the silky thatch of black hair that covered the very top of the baby's head and hung in uneven wisps down her forehead. She fingered the hair for just a moment before turning a smiling face to the adults in the room.

"Gretchen." Marcail said softly. "How do you like Gretchen Riggs after Rigg's grandmother?"

"It's perfect."

"I love it."

"Why, we never would have thought of it!"

Rigg and Kate were so pleased over the name that their words stumbled over the top of one another. But the ten-year-old aunt holding the baby didn't notice. Her eyes were riveted on the tiny niece cuddled in her arms.

Rigg and Kate beamed as they watched the two in the chair. Rigg leaned and kissed Kate softly on the mouth.

"I believe she's feeling a little bit of what I felt when I first laid eyes on you," Rigg said softly to his wife.

"And what was that exactly?"

"Nothing short of love at first sight." They kissed again and neither one heard Marcail whispering to the baby.

"I love you, Gretchen Riggs. I love you like you were my very own."

Forty-One

BOBBIE WAS VERY pleased to be heading home for the day. She was emotionally and physically spent. It had seemed to take forever for Marcail to emerge from Rigg and Kaitlin's bedroom. Bobbie had stayed in the living room with May, Jeff, and Sean. She found the pretense of acting as though everything was fine more difficult every second.

It had been over a half-hour before she had been able to see the baby and excuse herself. May drove her back to the shipping office so she could tell Bill and Gilbert the news. Bobbie had worked the rest of the day as well as locked up that evening.

She had missed out on seeing Paige and Wesley when they were infants, and Bobbie's throat had been so tight at her first view of Gretchen that she could barely swallow.

Once home, she halfway hoped that Jeff would come by so she could apologize to him, but she ate her supper and went to bed without seeing him.

Two hours after Bobbie blew out her lamp she was still awake. The moon was full, so after slipping her spectacles back onto her nose, she found her robe and went to the kitchen. She had lit the lamp and was preparing a snack when her mother joined her.

"Did I wake you?"

"Yes, but that's all right."

The women worked on cups of tea and sandwiches in silence. When they did begin to speak it was about small things—dress material that Maryanne had seen, how nice the gifts at the reception had been, and how quickly the summer had gone. When Bobbie had finished her sandwich and half of her tea she confided to her mother about what happened in the dining room at the Walcotts'.

"I think I'm in love with him, Mom, but that doesn't give me the right to kiss him. I mean, he and Sylvia are seeing each other and I think they might get married. I told myself I would never run again, but I've got to tell Bill I'll be looking for work somewhere else in town."

Maryanne was quiet. She was praying for words of comfort and Bobbie began to think she was upset.

"You're disappointed in me, aren't you?"

"Oh, Bob, no! I don't know where you got such an idea. I'm sitting here praying for you. I don't think you should have kissed Jeff, but *everyone* makes mistakes."

Maryanne's voice lowered with intensity. "You do understand that, don't you, Bobbie? Just confess this and go on, even if you have to find work elsewhere. Apologize to Jeff and then to the Lord. Ask Him to take you on from here."

Bobbie nodded in agreement. She was coming to the same conclusion, but she felt so badly about everything that she wasn't even sure how to pray most of the time.

"It's too bad in some ways," Maryanne continued. "You couldn't ask for a nicer boss. After you'd gone upstairs this evening, he dropped by to tell you to take the morning off."

"You're right; Mr. Taylor is wonderful. And I'm going to need the morning off after staying up all night."

"My Bible is in the bedroom, Bobbie, and that's where I need to be. But tomorrow, before you go to work to talk to Jeff, read Romans 8:26–27. Those are verses about prayer, and I suspect you need them right now."

Maryanne hugged Bobbie and headed up the stairs. Bobbie followed soon afterward, and this time, with a prayer in her heart for the coming events of the day, she fell asleep quickly.

"I'm glad you were here, Jeff, since my decision to leave was so sudden and I thought I would have to miss you."

"I'm glad too, Sylvia, and I'll be praying that you have a safe trip."

"Thanks, Jeff."

"Well, I guess this is goodbye. I don't plan to be back in Santa Rosa anytime soon. You've been a true friend, Jeff, and I'll never forget you."

Jeff and Sylvia embraced in a final goodbye as Sandra came out of the stage office. Jeff stepped away to give the sisters some privacy. He stayed on the platform until the stage pulled away, waving when Sylvia's head appeared in the window.

Jeff returned to the office intent on asking his father when Bobbie would be in, but Bill sent him on an errand. 'It was just as well,' he thought as he left. The office was no place for the showdown he was planning.

"Likewise the Spirit also helpeth our infirmities; for we know not what we should pray for as we ought, but the Spirit itself maketh intercession for us with groanings which can not be uttered. And he that searcheth the hearts knoweth what is the mind of the Spirit, because he maketh intercession for the saints according to the will of God."

Bobbie prayed long and hard over the words she had just read. They were exactly what she needed. She felt with all her heart that God wanted her to trust Him.

'Thank You for these verses, Father, and for Your mightiness and power and for Your faithfulness. You know my heart and how much I want to make things right. Please give me the words with Jeff and Mr. Taylor today. I want to run from this, God, but I know I can't. Help me to trust You. Please give me the needed strength and wisdom.'

Bobbie did not end the prayer but continued to petition God silently all the way to work. She found Bill in his office and he greeted her warmly. Talking proudly about his new granddaughter for several minutes, he finally noticed that his employee had something on her mind.

"Did you need something, Bobbie?"

"Yes, actually I do. I've decided to take a few weeks off just as soon as you can spare me, and then I'm going to look for work someplace else in town." Bill opened his mouth to object, but Bobbie rushed on.

"It has nothing to do with you or the work here at the office, and I want to thank you for all you've done."

"Bobbie," Bill finally cut in, looking a little thunderstruck, "is there something I can do? I mean, your work here is excellent and if there's anything I can say to change your mind, just—"

"No, but thank you." Bobbie stood, telling Bill that her mind was made up.

"Is Jeff around?" Bobbie asked with her hand on the door handle.

"No, I asked him to run uptown."

Bobbie nodded. "I guess I better get to work."

Bobbie left the inner office still praying, and she congratulated herself over not bursting into tears. She had only been at her desk a few minutes when Bill came out and asked her to take something to Rigg.

Bobbie complied, but she was disappointed since she wanted to see Jeff right away. The Lord reminded her then to trust Him, and Bobbie stopped herself from scanning the street in hopes of spotting him.

"I'm telling you, Dad, she won't be quitting."

"Jeff," Bill said with extreme patience, "she was just in here and told me herself."

"You're repeating yourself, Dad. I'm telling you that as soon as she comes back, I'll talk with her and get this whole thing worked out."

"So you're the reason she wants to quit?" Gilbert commented softly.

"Not exactly, but my presence is making her uncomfortable. I'm sure she plans on apologizing to me and then walking away. What she doesn't know is that I'm not about to let her do that."

Bill and Gilbert were left staring at each other in confusion as Jeff walked out of the room.

Forty-Two

JEFF WAS NEXT door when Bobbie came back. She went straight to her desk to work, wondering yet again when she would see him. Jeff returned to the shipping office knowing that his father was in his office and that Gilbert was in the back room. Praying that no customers would come in, Jeff approached Bobbie's desk.

"My dad tells me you're quitting."

Bobbie had of course seen him come in, and had waited quietly for him to take a seat. Jeff's plans to be completely alone with Bobbie for this confrontation went up in smoke. Discovering that she was quitting had sent him into something of a panic.

"I had to, Jeff. I know you understand."

"I understand a lot of things, but I'm not sure you do." Jeff spoke softly from the chair in front of the desk.

"I don't know what you're talking about."

"Then it's time you did. I think we have a lot to say to each other—things we should have discussed a long time ago."

Thinking he wanted her to continue working, Bobbie gave him a negative shake of her head. "There's nothing to discuss, Jeff. Please just let me say what I need to say."

Jeff could see that she was not going to listen to reason until she could relate her feelings, so he folded his arms over his chest and waited.

"I know how upset you must be," Bobbie began, seeing she finally had his attention. "It was inexcusable of me to avoid you after what I did. I'm sorry, Jeff, for my behavior at the Walcotts', and I hope you'll forgive me. If you want, I can also apologize to Sylvia. If you'd rather I not mention it to her, I'll understand."

Something squeezed around Jeff's heart at the vulnerable way Bobbie sat across from him and bared her soul; her face and voice told of her misery. She was so precious to him, and she had done exactly what he feared—mentally chastised herself for days over a kiss he had thoroughly enjoyed.

Jeff was suddenly desperate to hold her hand and be near her, certain that if he did, his touch and words would put everything right. They had always touched in a special kind of way, and it never occurred to Jeff that such an action would not be welcome at the moment.

"Do you forgive me, Jeff?" His silence had brought Bobbie perilously close to tears. Jeff rose from his chair to circle the desk.

Bobbie, fearful that he would do just as he intended, and that his touch would be devastating to her emotions, sprang out of her own chair and moved around the desk to avoid him. "Jeff, please answer me."

"Just as soon as I get close enough, I'll answer you."

"Why when you're close?"

"Because I *need* to touch you, Bobbie," he answered as he followed her around the desk. "And will you *please* hold still!"

The couple came to a stop where they had started, since they had completely circled the desk. Jeff thought this could go on all day, so before Bobbie could react he reached across the desktop and plucked the glasses from her nose.

"Jeff." The name was said fearfully, a sound that tugged at Jeff's heart, but he had to get this settled.

"It's all right, Bobbie," he said tenderly as he took her arm. "We're just going to head into the back room here so I can talk to you."

Bobbie was unaware of Gilbert leaving the room and closing the door behind him. She was led to the back of the room, where a small window cast a patch of sunlight on the wood floor.

When Bobbie felt a wall behind her, she leaned against it. In order to hide their trembling, she locked her hands together behind her back. Jeff still had her glasses, so until he leaned, with his forearm on the wall above her head, his face nose-to-nose with her own, she could not see him clearly.

"Will you kiss me again, Bobbie?" The question was whisper-soft and Bobbie searched Jeff's eyes for why he would be teasing her in this way.

"Why?" It was the only word that would come.

"Don't you want to?"

"You know I do." Bobbie's heart was in her eyes, and she did nothing to hide how wonderful it was to have Jeff so near. But it wasn't right. "Please don't torment me, Jeff. It's not like you to be cruel."

"I'm not doing a very good job with this, am I?" He said the words almost to himself, and Bobbie was more confused than ever.

"May I have my glasses?"

"Are you going to run away?"

"I might."

"Then no, you may not," he stated without moving. "And by the way, Sylvia left town this morning. She's headed home to stay."

Bobbie was silent, digesting this newest information.

"Now will you kiss me?"

"You want me to kiss you because Sylvia left town?" Bobbie felt like her world was spinning.

"No," Jeff said with great patience. "I want you to kiss me because you're going to be kissing me every day for the rest of our lives and we need the practice."

Bobbie's hands came up and grabbed frantically at the front of Jeff's shirt. "Please give me my glasses, Jeff."

He complied this time, and Bobbie searched Jeff's face from behind her lenses. 'This is why God told you to trust Him,' Bobbie said to herself as she clearly saw the love in Jeff's eyes.

"Why, Bobbie—why has it taken us so long to see what everyone else has seen for weeks?"

"I don't know," Bobbie answered, and truly she didn't. "Do you still want that kiss?"

Jeff's eyes narrowed with emotional fervor, and that was enough answer for Bobbie. Her hands framed either side of his face and she kissed him tenderly on the lips. Bobbie would have broken the kiss after a brief moment, but Jeff's arms had come around her, causing her own to slide without prompting around his neck. She returned his kiss with every drop of longing she had ever felt.

Bobbie was still a little dazed when Jeff stepped away from her with his hands on her shoulders.

"Don't kiss me like that again until after we're married."

Bobbie smiled. "And when will that be?"

"How's this evening?" The look on Jeff's face was so comical that Bobbie giggled. That laugh got her kissed again, and Gilbert, in the outer room, smiled at the silence.

"Why is the storeroom door shut?" Bill wanted to know as he exited the office.

"Jeff and Bob are in there."

"Are they talking?"

"Some of the time," Gil answered with a grin.

Bill looked at the closed portal and then back at his son. The two grinned at each other and Gilbert watched his father sigh with relief.

"It's about time, isn't it, Gilbert?"

The younger man's smile widened. "Yes, Dad, you're right. More than enough time."

Forty-Three

THE HOURS AFTER lunch evaporated in a dreamy haze for Bobbie. Jeff had a few errands to run and Bobbie made an effort to keep her mind on the job, but Gilbert repeated questions twice before she heard and she forgot the names of two customers. After the second such customer went out the door, Bobbie looked up to see Bill grinning at her. He had been uptown and had just come in.

"Jeff tells me you're staying." Father and son had run into each other outside the office and Jeff told his father of his plans.

"I *did* quit," Bobbie said almost hesitantly. "Did you hire someone else?"

Bill had no chance to answer because May shot in the door as if she had been chased by hounds.

"Oh Bobbie, Bobbie! I can't believe it. I just talked to Jeff and he told me. I didn't think he'd ever come to his senses!" Bobbie was enfolded in May's loving embrace, and over her shoulder Bobbie could see that Bill was still grinning.

"Bill!" May suddenly turned on her husband. "Why haven't you given this girl the day off? Why, she hasn't even had a chance to tell her family!"

"Well, I—" Bill started, but May cut him off.

"Now you just run along home, Bobbie; I'll fill in here. I can't think how Bill could have overlooked this."

Bobbie looked hesitant again, and May rushed on to assure her. "I'll tell Jeff you've gone home and I'm sure he'll be along shortly.

We'll be fine for the rest of the day. Oh, here's Jeff now. Walk Bobbie home, dear, and then bring her to supper tonight. Ask Jake and Maryanne too.

"Can you believe this, Bill? First nothing, now two daughters-in-law and a grandchild . . ." May's words were cut off as she pushed the young couple out the front door and closed it behind them.

Bobbie and Jeff looked at each other and burst out laughing. "Your mother is wonderful."

"That she is. Did you really want to go home?"

"It wasn't my idea."

"Well, then, I'll have to thank my mother for the chance to have you all to myself."

They walked hand in hand toward the Bradfords', their conversation as relaxed as ever, but now with a certain intimacy that was both mysterious and exciting.

"The first question we're going to be asked tonight is *when*," Jeff told Bobbie.

"You mean, what date have we set?"

"That's it."

"Oh." Bobbie walked a few steps in silence. "What do we tell them?"

"Why, October fifth, of course!"

Bobbie came to a complete stop just before they walked into her yard. "You've already consulted a calendar?"

Jeff's look was adorably mischievous. "I've known for some time now that you were the one. Women aren't the only ones to plan and dream, you know. I didn't know when God would bring us together like He did today, but while I waited, I thought about our future constantly."

"I think I'm ready for you to tell me everything, like when you knew and all that."

"Well, I think I was pretty unsettled from the very beginning, since I was jealous of Gilbert when he ate lunch with you and I had to go to Sylvia's."

"Gilbert! Are you serious?"

"I'm afraid so, but that wasn't really the start. The start was when you came to the house to visit me after the accident. Remember when we played checkers?"

"I remember."

"I wanted to kiss your neck in the worst way."

"Jeff," Bobbie said softly, her cheeks heating just slightly, "that was weeks ago."

"I know, and all I can say is, God is a strong provider. You see, that was back when I still thought you might marry Cleve, and I knew I had no business feeling as I did, but God somehow moderated my feelings through that time.

"The *moderation* began to fade on the camping trip and evaporated completely when I felt your lips on mine."

Bobbie stared at him in amazement. "I knew something took place on the camping trip, but Jeff, the rest of what you said happened right after I came back to town."

"Yes, I know." Jeff smiled tenderly and bent to kiss her.

"I wondered when you two would get around to that," Troy interrupted the kissing couple. "I do hope this means you're going to marry her." Troy directed this question to Jeff, doing his best to look like an enraged father while a grin split his face.

"How does October fifth sound?"

"Great!" Troy exclaimed, and hugged his sister before shaking Jeff's hand. The three walked into the house and told Maryanne, who promptly erupted into tears. She couldn't speak for some moments.

"Oh Bobbie," she finally said, not caring that both Jeff and Troy were listening. "Please tell me it's love this time."

Bobbie looked to the tall, brown-haired man who quite literally held her heart in his grasp. Maryanne watched her daughter's eyes light with love, a love that matched the tender light in Jeff Taylor's eyes as he returned Bobbie's gaze.

"Never mind, Bobbie," she stopped her before she could speak. "You just put every fear to rest."

$\mathcal{F}$orty-$\mathcal{F}$our

October 5, 1872

BOBBIE TAYLOR WAS helpless with laughter or she would have tried to reason with her captor.

"Now, Bobbie, just come along quietly," Rigg said in a voice as smooth as honey. "Let me tell you how much better you have it than my wife did. She was stuck in a cubicle at the church."

Rigg stopped before a bedroom on the upper floor at the Walcotts' and opened the door with confidence. Bobbie was amazed to see Gilbert inside.

"All right, Gil, here she is. I'll head back down and you see that she doesn't escape."

Rigg bent low and kissed his new sister-in-law's cheek. "Welcome to the family." Bobbie watched in silence as Rigg sailed back out the door. She turned on Gil as soon as the door shut.

"Gilbert Taylor! I can't believe you're a part of this!"

"I had to, Bobbie," he told her with a helpless smile.

"Rigg said if I didn't help I would *never* find my bride on my wedding day."

Bobbie truly sympathized with him and couldn't hold her laughter. "Where are you going?" She stopped when she saw Gilbert head for the door.

"I'm supposed to stand guard in the hallway."

Bobbie looked a little uncertain, and he stopped short of leaving the room.

"It's all right, Bobbie. I'll be right outside the door. Just make yourself comfortable."

Bobbie tried to do as she was told, but all she did was pace. They had chosen the room well, since the door Gilbert guarded was the only exit—unless she wanted to escape out a second-story window. She also noticed that the windows were all closed tight. Not that she would have shouted out one of them, but if Jeff began to look for her it would have been nice to wave at him from above.

Resigning herself to the circumstances, Bobbie finally did as Gil instructed. She sat in a chair and put her feet on a low stool. Within the space of a few minutes, she was sound asleep.

"I've never seen a dress as beautiful as Bobbie's," Mrs. Walcott informed Jake. "But then I've never known a seamstress like your wife either."

"She has a real gift. And you, Mrs. Walcott, have a gift for generosity with your home. This is twice in the same year you've let us invade, and we thank you."

"Oh Jake," she said with a shake of her head, "you must know the pleasure's all mine. I'm a lonely old woman, and your Maryanne— well, let's just say this is a small thing in light of all she does for me."

They were joined by others, each complimenting Mrs. Walcott on her house and garden. Even though it was well into the fall, her yard was faithfully tended and still a showplace.

Jake listened with half an ear as Mrs. Walcott conversed. Having seen Rigg take Bobbie into the house and return without her, he had a keen premonition that Rigg was having one on the bridegroom. The thought made him smile, and at the same time he told himself he was not going to get involved, but he *was* going to keep his eyes open so not to miss any of the action.

Rigg couldn't have asked for a better lead-in if he had planned it. He was holding Gretchen, looking to all the world as innocent as could be, when he joined his parents, Jeff, Maryanne, Troy, Carla, and his brother Nate. He listened to their conversation in silence until Bill asked where Bobbie had gone.

"I haven't seen her lately," Troy answered.

"I think she might have gone inside for something. Didn't I see her with you, Rigg?" The conversation went on so swiftly that no one immediately noticed that Rigg hadn't answered Maryanne's question.

Jeff was about to turn away from the group to look for his bride when he caught the slightest of smiles in his brother's eyes. Halting abruptly, Jeff leveled him with a stare.

"Rigg?" Jeff's voice was deep and serious.

"Yes, Jeffrey?" Rigg questioned him with a raise of his brow, and in that instant Jeff's suspicions stepped from doubt onto solid ground.

"Where is she?" Jeff asked, and tried not to smile. He noticed that Jake had suddenly joined the group, and his gaze swung to his new father-in-law, but Jake's look told Jeff he was not an accomplice.

"Where is Bobbie? You're not having trouble keeping track of your wife already, are you, Jeff?" Rigg was shocked. "Married these few hours and already apart? That's not a good start, Jeff old man, not good at all."

Rigg's words so closely echoed those of Jeff's at Rigg's wedding that the groom shouted with laughter.

"There's just one difference, Rigg," Jeff said through his chuckles. "If I know you, Bobbie is not going to escape from wherever you put her, as Kate did."

Rigg's grin was unrepentant, and Jeff had to do a good deal of negotiating, as well as put up with plenty of laughter and leg-pulling, to get Rigg to tell. When he finally had his answer, he started toward the house.

Rigg called after him, "Don't blame Gil; I threatened him into helping."

Rigg's words made complete sense to Jeff as soon as he hit the upstairs hallway. Gilbert was leaning calmly against the wall as though he was expecting Jeff, and he smiled as he approached. No words were exchanged as Gilbert took himself off to the party and Jeff let himself quietly into the bedroom.

Bobbie awoke when Jeff's lips touched her own. "Is that how boring you find our wedding day?"

Bobbie smiled drowsily, and Jeff scooped her into his arms, took her chair, and settled his new wife in his lap. Bobbie cuddled against him and Jeff stole another kiss.

"Do you know how long I've wanted to hold you like this?"

"I think so," Bobbie answered, and rested her head on Jeff's shoulder before she spoke again in a whisper.

"Have I been worth the wait?"

Jeff kissed her long and hard. "Does that answer your question?"

"Will you do that again?"

The groom smiled. "Well, I guess that answers *mine.*"

Gilbert, who had come back upstairs to tell the newlyweds they were wanted in the garden, hesitated before knocking on the door of the silent room. A space of a few heartbeats passed and Gil shook his head in the empty corridor and started back downstairs. Bill met him on the landing.

"Did you talk to Jeff?"

"No, the door is shut and things are pretty quiet."

Bill remembered in a moment how much he had wanted to be alone with his wife after their wedding.

"I'm sure they'll come down soon. If not, Rigg can go up, since it's his fault Bobbie's up there in the first place."

Gilbert had no arguments with that line of reasoning and made a beeline for the food table. Bill, on the other hand, joined his wife, who asked where Jeff and Bobbie were.

"Newlyweds," was all Bill had to say as they walked arm in arm back to the party.

Epilogue

Christmas Day, 1872

THE TAYLOR HOUSE was filled to the brim with family and friends. Bill, May, and sons were joined by Jake and Maryanne Bradford, Mr. Parker and Joey, the Marshall Riggs family, including Sean and Marcail Donovan, the Stuart Townsend family, Jeff and Bobbie Taylor, and Troy and Carla Bradford.

Bobbie was settled on the sofa with her niece Gretchen on her lap and her niece Paige at her side. When Marcail joined them, Bobbie laughed in delight at the smile that broke over Gretchen's face upon spotting her Aunt Marcail.

"Did you want to take her?"

"No, you can keep her. I get to hold her all the time. Will you have your own baby someday, Bobbie?"

"I hope so," Bobbie said with a smile that widened when her sister-in-law Carla stepped into the room. Bobbie simply could not picture her brother as a father, but it was going to happen in early spring.

Gretchen fussed a little and Bobbie transferred her onto her shoulder. With her tiny face cuddled into her aunt's neck, she soon fell asleep. The girls deserted Bobbie a few minutes later, and when Jeff saw the couch open next to his wife, he claimed the spot.

After quickly ducking his head so he could look beneath Bobbie's chin at his niece, Jeff kissed his wife's cheek.

"What was that for?"

"Do I need a reason to kiss my wife?"

"Definitely not," Bobbie answered, and this time offered her lips for his attention. They talked a few minutes before Sean joined them.

Bobbie smiled at the sight of him, since he was wearing the shirt that she and Jeff had given him for his sixteenth birthday, just a few weeks past.

"Are you up for a game of checkers, Jeff?" Sean looked desperate for a distraction of some type, and Jeff was compassionate.

"Sure," he answered easily. "Let's go into the kitchen." Sean kissed his niece's tiny head as he left the sofa. Watching them leave, Bobbie thought that Gretchen was probably the only person Sean Donovan was tender with at this time in his life. This was Sean's second Christmas without his father, and from the little Jeff had told her, she knew that he missed him desperately.

Bobbie had never experienced the troubled teen years that Sean was in the midst of, but also realized she had made the right choices. She prayed right on the spot that Sean would make wise choices, choices based on the good advice she knew he was getting from Rigg and Kaitlin.

He had worked all summer at the livery and that had basically kept him out of trouble, but he was running with a bad crowd again and wanted to quit school. Rigg had put his foot down, but Bobbie wondered when the top would blow sky-high.

Her thoughts were interrupted when Joey joined her and wanted to hold Gretchen. The transition woke her, but she didn't seem to mind. Bobbie and Joey both watched in fascination as she stretched and yawned, tiny fingers grasping in midair as her arms reached over her head.

"Isn't she cute?"

"She certainly is, Joey."

"Are you going to have a baby?"

'Twice in one hour,' Bobbie thought wryly, but answered nonetheless, "I'd like to."

"You'll have one if God wants you to, right?"

"Right." Bobbie answered with pleasure over Joey's insight. The time this young boy took each day to pray for his father's salvation was giving him a new perspective as to the way God deals with His children.

It wasn't long before Gretchen needed her mother and Joey ran off to find Wesley, Paige, and Marcail. Bobbie reached for a section of newspaper. The checkers game in the kitchen did not last long, and before Bobbie expected, Jeff was back at her side.

"That was fast."

"Sean was preoccupied."

Bobbie nodded and was silent. She glanced up to see Jeff watching Carla. "I could look like that one of these days."

"That's quite true."

"Will you still want to hold me?"

"Definitely," he said as his arm went around her. Bobbie liked the way he said that, without a moment's hesitation.

"Dinner is served," May called from the doorway a moment later. "Everyone find a seat."

There was general pandemonium while everyone was seated either in the kitchen or living room. When all was quiet, Bill stood in the doorway between the two rooms and returned thanks for the food.

"Our Father in heaven, we thank You for the food on these tables and the hands that worked to provide and prepare it. We also thank You for the miracle of grandchildren and their presence with us today. We praise You for Bobbie, as well as the extended family she brings along, and for friends that You bring us in Your time.

"And lastly we thank You for this season and the birth of Your Son. May we be mindful of Your love, a love so great that You gave Your only Son to us. May we remember to keep You before us, today and all days. Amen."

Bill's gaze slowly encompassed the two rooms. He was met with smiles and some tears as he beamed in love at all beneath his roof.